Cognitive and Language Development in Children

John Oates and Andrew Grayson

 The Open University

 **Blackwell** Publishing

Copyright © 2004 The Open University

First published 2004 by Blackwell Publishing Ltd in association with The Open University

The Open University
Walton Hall, Milton Keynes
MK7 6AA

Blackwell Publishing Ltd
108 Cowley Road
Oxford
OX4 1JF, UK

Other Blackwell Publishing editorial offices: 350 Main Street, Malden, MA 02148-5020, USA
and 550 Swanston Street, Carlton, Victoria 3053, Australia

For further information on Blackwell Publishing visit out website:
http://www.blackwellpublishing.com

Library of Congress Cataloguing-in-Publication Data has been applied for.

A catalogue record for this title is available from the British Library.

Edited, designed and typeset by The Open University.

Printed and bound in the United Kingdom by The Alden Group, Oxford.

ISBN 1 4051 1045 7

32444B/ED209book3i1.1

This publication forms part of an Open University course ED209 *Child Development*. Details of this and other Open University courses can be obtained from the Course Information and Advice Centre, PO Box 724, The Open University, Milton Keynes MK7 6ZS, United Kingdom: tel. +44 (0)1908 653231, e-mail general-enquiries@open.ac.uk

Alternatively, you may visit the Open University website at http://www.open.ac.uk where you can learn more about the wide range of courses and packs offered at all levels by The Open University.

To purchase a selection of Open University course materials visit the webshop at www.ouw.co.uk, or contact Open University Worldwide, Michael Young Building, Walton Hall, Milton Keynes MK7 6AA, United Kingdom for a brochure. tel. +44 (0)1908 858785; fax +44 (0)1908 858787; e-mail ouwenq@open.ac.uk

Contents

Foreword

We would very much like to acknowledge the valuable contributions that were made by the many people who made this book possible. First, we would like to thank our team of editors; Julia Brennan, Helen Lanz and Bridgette Jones. Their careful and insightful reading of the chapters and the many changes that they suggested have contributed immensely to the readability and clarity of the book. We feel greatly privileged to have had the opportunity to work with all of our consultant authors and we have welcomed their flexibility in working with us to produce what we hope will prove to be interesting and effective learning material. We would also like to thank the critical readers Rachel George, Marianne Puxley and Joanne Kelly for their encouragement and constructive criticism of the drafts. Our academic colleagues Peter Barnes, Sharon Ding, Karen Littleton and Clare Wood deserve thanks for their contributions to the book and for diligently commenting on what must have seemed like an endless series of revisions. We thank Iris Rowbotham for her supportive help with managing this project. Last, but not least, we wish to thank Stephanie Withers for her patient and careful secretarial help with typing and formatting, Jonathan Davies, the book designer, Jon Owen, our illustrator, and Nikki Tolcher, our compositor.

John Oates

Andrew Grayson

Introduction: perspectives on cognitive and language development

John Oates and Andrew Grayson

Contents

1 Cognition in everyday life

Two 3-year-old children, Tom and Amy, are in the living room, playing together with some small toy figures and a toy horse and cart. The television is on in the corner of the room and someone is clattering about in the kitchen cooking a meal. Amy puts a figure into the cart and says, 'Off to market!' Tom says, 'And Daddy comes too', putting another figure into the cart. Amy then makes the horse trot along, pulling the cart, while making 'clip-clop' noises. Tom says, 'No, don't, they're not ready. They've lefted the children behind. Oh! They're crying' and he puts two child figures into the cart. Amy puts a small plastic brick in the cart and says, 'That's their food'. Then Tom makes the horse trot along pulling the cart, saying 'Off to market!' and makes trotting sounds, as Amy had done earlier.

Cognitive
Pertaining to the gaining, storage and use of knowledge.

This is a simple, everyday scene, but one that contains a wealth of cognitive activity. What knowledge have these two children gained and stored? How are they using it? This scenario can be analysed at a number of levels and illustrates many of the aspects of children's cognitive development dealt with in this book.

First, we can note that these two children know a lot about people, and horses and carts, and what they can do. This is shown in the way that they use this knowledge to make the toy horse and cart do appropriate things like carrying people to market. But this is an interesting sort of knowledge, since it is unlikely that they have actually seen a horse and cart taking people to market. What they may have done is to put together some pieces of knowledge gained from books or other media, or from other children and adults, and used them in their play.

We can note also that Tom knows that the children will be upset at being left alone. He appears to be able to understand the workings of other people's minds – knowledge of a somewhat different kind.

In addition we can see that Tom and Amy both know how to organize their behaviour into structured sequences; to have a plan and to put it into action. They know how to work together on this, taking account of and adapting to each other. This collaboration is demonstrated through, and dependent on, the language that they both use in order to communicate with each other.

Furthermore, it seems likely that a certain amount of knowledge is being gained in this brief episode. Perhaps Tom is acquiring something from observing Amy's way of playing, and maybe Amy becomes more aware of the emotional consequences for children of being left behind.

But a most significant aspect of this scene is the way that Tom and Amy are knowingly using the toy objects to stand for equivalent objects in the real world and the way in which they play with them *as if* they were real. This capacity to *symbolize*, to use one thing to represent another, is a uniquely human capacity.

Amy's and Tom's interactions and play raise a number of important questions relating to cognitive development:

- How did they come to know about the characteristics of things such as horses, carts, markets and people? At what point in their development were they able to categorize 'Daddy' and 'the children' together in a way that differentiated people from horses and vehicles?

- At what stage did the two children learn the names of the objects that they use? Did they have an understanding of the characteristics of these objects before the names emerged, or were the names acquired before any real understanding?
- Are Amy and Tom's brains pre-programmed to acquire the language that they now use so easily and flexibly, or have they had to learn it all from others?
- How have these children developed the ability to construct sentences out of the words that they have acquired that enable them to communicate apparently so effortlessly with each other? What about the sentence 'They've lefted the children behind'? Has Tom copied that from someone else, or did he make it up himself?
- What processes lie behind Amy and Tom being able to plan a trip to market, and to organize their behaviour and language into sequences that make their plans happen?
- At what age did Amy and Tom become capable of understanding the thoughts and feelings of other people? How significant for their cognitive development are their interactions with each other and with other people?

2 The structure of this book

This book addresses all of these questions about cognition and its development, though it does not pretend to supply straightforward answers. Since language is such a central part of human development, it appears centre stage, and is interwoven with chapters on other topics in cognitive development. The book is developmental in its structure: it starts with chapters on cognition and language in the first years of life and then extends the treatment throughout the period of childhood as the book progresses. The remainder of this section outlines the contents of each chapter.

2.1 Chapter 1: Early category representations and concepts

The book starts by examining how infants begin to structure the world that they perceive around them. In the first chapter, we see how a great deal of knowledge building goes on even before children are able to speak and to exploit language. Until very recently, it was impossible to have much certainty about how infants think. But infancy researchers have developed some powerful techniques that can reveal more clearly the cognitive processes that infants possess. One insight that this research has given is that infants seem to be able to differentiate between different types of things (for example, different types of objects) much earlier than previously thought. Indeed, the ability to organize the world around them into different categories can be regarded as one of the basic building blocks of cognitive development.

This first chapter introduces a theme that runs through much of the book; that as development proceeds, mental representations become progressively more abstract and freed from the specific contexts and concrete experiences from which they spring. In this chapter the mental representations in question are infants' representations of categories. Also, the chapter shows that even the very early categories formed by infants can be flexible and adaptable. The picture that begins to emerge is that of development as an active, constructive process, and that this can be seen from one of the earliest cognitive, meaning-making activities of young infants – namely, category formation.

2.2 Chapter 2: First words

The research covered in Chapter 1 shows that infants arrive at the point of uttering the first words of their language with a rich knowledge base and with competent cognitive abilities. For example, by the time Amy starts to use words like 'food', she may already have a relatively sophisticated understanding of what sorts of things can be described in this way – what sorts of things fit into the category 'food'. Chapter 2 shows how children make use of these and other abilities to produce their first words, out of the rich, social context in which they hear language being used by their caregivers and others around them. A key finding here is that infants are active and creative in making sense of language and its embedding in social routines. They are not just passive learners.

In this respect, we see another example of remarkable flexibility in infants' mental processes, in the way that they can 'tune in' to the particular sets of distinctions that are meaningful in their language community, and then use these in their developing understanding and production of speech. This second chapter also introduces the perspective on cognitive development that becomes increasingly significant as the topics of this book progress – the *social* nature of mental growth. Although there is still an important debate around the extent to which children have specialized mechanisms for acquiring language, it is becoming increasingly clear that language grows out of a fertile bed of interpersonal activity. Language does not happen in a vacuum; its acquisition is deeply contextualized in the everyday routines of social life between infant and caregiver.

2.3 Chapter 3: Brain and cognitive development

These recent findings of relatively mature cognitive abilities in young children might be taken to suggest that these abilities are genetic in origin; that children's brains are somehow pre-programmed to form categories, learn a language and so forth. However, as Chapter 3 shows, we do not necessarily need to invoke such explanations. Indeed, there is no way that our genes could possibly contain enough information to bring us into the world cognitively equipped to do all these challenging human tasks. It is now apparent that the brain may actually structure itself and develop particular kinds of neural connections as a result of the child's interactions with their environment. This is known as *self-organization*.

In adulthood there is undoubtedly some specialization of function within different areas of the brain. For example, in most people there are specific areas in the left side of the brain where language-related processing goes on. Furthermore, it seems that adult cognition is to a greater or lesser degree 'modular'. That is, different cognitive modules perform different functions, such as processing auditory information, dealing with language inputs, forming representations from visual stimuli and so forth. Chapter 3 discusses the development of such cognitive 'modules', and shows how increasingly sophisticated research methods are making it possible to link cognitive functions with aspects of brain structure. It also takes a detailed look at whether or not it is sensible to think of human brains as genetically pre-programmed to wire themselves for language, or whether a more *epigenetic* approach to understanding language development is required.

2.4 Chapter 4: The development of children's understanding of grammar

One of the major cognitive achievements of early childhood is the ability to learn and use a native language in order to communicate with others. Amy and Tom are able to combine the words that they know into well-formed sentences in order to convey sophisticated meanings to each other (despite the odd familiar mistake, such as using the wrong past tense form for the verb 'to leave'). Language acquisition is rapid and appears effortless despite the fact that its grammatical structures are complex.

The apparent ease and speed with which children move from early single word utterances (examined in Chapter 2) to being able to converse with others has led some theorists to suggest that we must be born with some kind of biological predisposition to acquire its rules. Noam Chomsky, for example, argued for an innate, language-specific capacity, unique to humans (Chomsky, 1965). This is not to suggest that all aspects of language are innate, since it is patently not the case that all the words and usages in all languages could be coded for in our genes. Rather, Chomsky was arguing for a specific potential to learn some universal features of language, especially syntax (rules for combining words and parts of words to compose sentences), being 'hard-wired' into the human brain at birth. The idea of a 'Universal Grammar', some kind of innate knowledge of how languages are constructed, is introduced and discussed in Chapter 4. This chapter shows how both nativist and empiricist accounts of grammar acquisition have been proposed and how these are being addressed and reconciled by research evidence.

2.5 Chapter 5: Executive functions in childhood

In Chapter 5, attention is turned to higher level, more abstract aspects of cognition. When Amy and Tom put together a sequence of behaviours that fit together, that flexibly adapt to each other's behaviour, and that enable them to achieve some sort of goal (such as acting out a pretend trip to market) they are making use of what developmental psychologists call 'executive function'.

Executive function is an umbrella term that is used to refer to the high-level processes that govern flexible, goal-directed behaviour. It is a complex, multifaceted concept that can be used to understand many aspects of human development. The focus of this chapter is on one aspect of executive function: 'inhibitory control'. This is the ability *not* to respond to the many and various things that can distract people from what they are currently trying to do. Typically developing children get increasingly good at inhibitory control as they get older. In the sequence described above, Amy and Tom are clearly able to focus on the key aspects of their play, shutting out sights and sounds (from the television, for example) that do not relate to getting their toys off to market. Children who have difficulties in inhibiting responses to irrelevant things can experience a range of associated difficulties. The chapter examines the proposal that children with attention deficit hyperactivity disorder (ADHD) have particular difficulties with inhibitory control.

2.6 Chapter 6: Understanding minds

One significant aspect of Amy and Tom's play is the way in which they are able to attribute thoughts and feelings to others – notably to the toy figures that represent the children in the pretend story that they are acting out. Tom recognizes that being left behind is a scary and upsetting thing to happen to a child, and so he pretends that they are crying. As children develop they become increasingly good at understanding the thoughts and feelings of others, and become able to appreciate that other people have their own minds; minds that can contain feelings, desires, and beliefs about the world that differ from one's own. The ability to understand the independence of other minds from one's own is referred to as having a 'theory of mind'.

Theory of mind underpins a considerable amount of work in developmental psychology. For example, the social context of learning, as well as the topics within which such learning is located, are increasingly being seen as central to development. Communicating with others and working with them in a truly collaborative way involves, among other things, the ability to understand their perspectives; to understand the way that they think and feel about the world. Chapter 6 presents research and theory in this area, showing how this capacity lies at the heart of social relations and cognitive development.

2.7 Chapter 7: Mathematical and scientific thinking

One of the challenges that children face in later development is coming to terms with, and making effective use of, the techniques and knowledge of mathematics and science. Not only do these involve learning facts and figures, they also demand a particular form of thinking that is quite late to emerge compared to some other areas of cognitive development. Chapter 7, dealing with the development of mathematical and scientific thinking, shows how important it is to broaden out from a consideration of the child's developing capacities (as documented in Chapters 1–6) to consider also the *context* in which these capacities are exercised. It is only towards the later stages of cognitive development that reasoning in these domains can become 'disembedded' from the particular problems in which it is used. This is yet another example of the increasing trajectory towards abstraction in cognitive development.

In some ways, learning about maths and science in formal educational settings is a source of socio-cognitive conflict for children, since they come to these settings with their own informal understandings that often follow different patterns and rules to those used in schooling. But modern perspectives on cognitive growth see these sorts of conflicts as potential motivators for change, providing they are harnessed to good effect. At one time it was thought, following Jean Piaget's theories, that children were 'solitary scientists' and that, given the right sort of learning environment, they would progress on their own. More recent theories, following those of Lev Vygotsky, accord a more significant role to working together with others as a motivator of cognitive change and development.

2.8 Chapter 8: A socio-cognitive perspective on learning and cognitive development

The book concludes by developing further the arguments set out in Chapter 7 relating to the social nature of cognitive development. It provides an analysis of situations in which children are taught and tested; common situations in both schooling and research, upon which a considerable amount of psychological and educational knowledge rests. Chapter 8 builds on ideas from Vygotsky's theory, recognizing the significance of the social context within which learning is located. The chapter argues that it is too limited to see a child as being faced only with the explicit task set by an adult in a situation in which the adult is expecting learning or performance at a representative level. There is also a more implicit, but equally challenging, problem for the child of understanding and negotiating the adult's motives and position in the relationship. Thus, a child may believe that the social situation demands failure, so as not to show superiority over the adult, while the explicit task demands otherwise. This is a much broader view than is traditionally taken, and it is capable of generating exciting research, using novel approaches and producing challenging and illuminating findings.

3 Themes and theories

Psychologists' understandings of the development of cognition and language have a long history, but a scientific approach to the study of such issues could be said to have started only within the last two centuries. In the following section we offer an overview of the way that theories of cognitive and language development have progressed, to give an historical context to the chapters in this book.

3.1 Beyond the nature versus nurture debate

Theories about aspects of child development differ in the relative importance that they give to maturation and innate factors, on the one hand, and to experience and learning, on the other. Some theories, such as Fodor's theory of innate cognitive processing modules, or Chomsky's theory about language-specific mechanisms, take a nativist stance. These theories stress innate, genetic aspects of development. Others, such as Skinner's behaviourism, adopt a more empiricist perspective. Skinner argued that much, if not all, development is an outcome of learning; that the newborn child is a 'blank slate' waiting to be written on by their environment.

Each of these positions has a history, and the field of developmental theory, stretching right back to early Greek philosophy, has tended to be dominated until relatively recently by a polarized debate as to whether 'nature' or 'nurture' is the primary driving force in child development.

However, understandings of these matters have moved forward, and a more eclectic perspective has developed. This holds that genetic and environmental contributions to development are intimately bound up with each other from the moment of conception. This is true even at a molecular level. It is now recognized, for example, that the specialization of cells into different parts of the body is a function of their position in their surrounding environment. Because of where they are, some cells become retinal receptors in the eye, some become nerve fibres in the spinal cord and others become neurons in the brain, even though all of them contain the same genetic information. We also know that the specialization of the brain is in large part a function of its own activity. Brains are designed to build themselves, not according to some 'blueprint' coded in the genes, but rather in an intimate relation to the sorts of environments in which they develop.

Similarly, taking the case of language as one example of a psychological developmental process, it is clear that although children may have brain architecture and mental processes that are well suited for language learning, the development of language abilities critically depends on the child growing up in a rich social environment, in which language is bound up with interaction and communication.

3.2 Constructivism

The work of Jean Piaget (1896–1980) made a key contribution to the field of developmental psychology, especially in the area of cognitive development. It set the scene for a much more scientific approach to understanding this area than had ever been attempted before. Piaget's theory was based firmly on the observation of children's behaviour. He found that there are many problem-solving tasks in which children behave quite differently from adults. Furthermore, he believed that children's mental abilities pass through a regular series of stages as development progresses.

Piaget's model of development (Piaget, 1955, 1959 and 1973) involves the child becoming increasingly freed up from the constraints of their own perspective and the concrete objects around them, as their mental operations become more abstract. In Piaget's theory, children are at first egocentric, dominated by, or 'centred' on, their own perceptions, because they are still very much tied to the concrete world and their actions within it. Similarly, Piaget held that the young child is unable to comprehend points of view different from his or her own. A classic example of this particular difficulty is provided by children's responses to the 'three mountains' task.

As used by Piaget, this task involves sitting a child beside a three-dimensional model of three mountains (see Figure 1). A doll is placed at the edge of the model, with a different view to that of the child, and the child's task is to show the experimenter what the doll's view is. Piaget used various ways of doing this so that the child would not have to describe it verbally. For example, the child has to arrange three cardboard mountains (like the model ones), or choose one of a set of drawings of the mountains model, drawn from different viewpoints, to indicate what view of the mountains the doll has.

BOX I

The 'three mountains' task

The mountains were made of *papier mâché* and were placed on a one metre square base. (Figure 1a shows the overall layout of the mountains and the viewing points A, B, C and D.) As seen from position A [the view shown in Figure 1b] the largest mountain was at the back of the display; it was grey with a snow-cap. A brown mountain was to the left, displaying a red cross on its summit. In the right-foreground was a green mountain surmounted by a small house [the layout is shown in Figure 1b]. There was a zigzag path down the side of the green mountain when viewed from position C and a rivulet descending the brown mountain when viewed from B. The only information given about exact sizes is that the heights of the mountains varied from 12 to 30 cm.

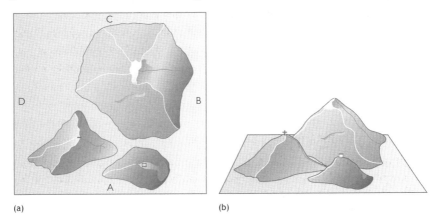

(a)   (b)

Figure I   (a) Plan of the three mountains task; (b) view of the three mountains from position A (Source: Cox, 1980).

The child was asked to represent the view of the mountains from his own position at A. Then a wooden doll (about two to three cm high) was put at position C and the child was asked to represent the view that could be seen from there. This procedure was repeated for positions B and D. The child was then asked to move to position B (or C or D) and to represent the view from there; in addition he was asked to represent the view from A or other positions he had already occupied.

Piaget and Inhelder elicited three different modes of response. First, the child was asked to reproduce the doll's view by arranging three pieces of cardboard shaped like the mountains. Second, the child was asked to select the doll's view from a set of ten pictures (each measuring 20 by 28 cm). In the third task, the child was asked to choose one picture and then decide which position the doll must occupy to have that particular view of the mountains.

Source: adapted from Roth, 1990, p. 99.

Presented in this way, the problem is usually difficult for a child of up to about 7 years old to solve correctly. A common response is for children to indicate that the view that they themselves have is also the one that the doll has. Piaget saw this as reflecting the inability of younger children to decentre from their own position. His explanation was that children in this 'pre-operational' stage have not developed the ability to recognize that there can be many different viewpoints on a scene like the three mountains, their own being just one of these. Nor are they able to hold in mind the idea that the viewpoint changes as the viewing position changes. This process reaches its end-point in the final stage of Piaget's developmental model, when mental operations become 'formal' – when wholly abstract thinking can be achieved and the child becomes able to reason hypothetically and systematically. Although this book does not cover the details of Piaget's work, the developmental journey that he describes, from concrete to progressively more abstract ways of thinking, is an important theme in the account of cognitive and language development that we give.

A classic Piagetian task, the pendulum test, which is widely used in physics teaching in many schools, is a good illustration of these points. The child's task is to find out what factor(s) affect the rate at which a pendulum swings to and fro. There are several factors that could affect the rate, for example the weight of the pendulum, the distance through which it swings, the length of the string, the force of the initial push, the thickness of the string and so on. A child whose reasoning capacities are still developing may vary these factors without a systematic approach, perhaps trying various ideas more than once as a result, whereas a child who can reason more formally can work out that varying each factor independently to isolate the important one(s) is the most effective approach.

Piaget's theory describes a child who is progressively elaborating a more abstract and general capacity to tackle problems in the world, but in an essentially solitary, independent way. This view of development was used in the second half of the twentieth century to support the pedagogic principles of discovery learning, which hold that it is a rich learning environment, rather than direct teaching, that is essential for cognitive development.

3.3 Social constructivism

Piaget's lack of emphasis on the social dimension of learning and development served as a growth point for post-Piagetian research and theory, represented well in this book in Chapters 2, 6, 7 and 8. There are three main strands to this growth, summed up in the concepts of 'human sense and situated cognition', 'socio-cognitive conflict', and 'social cognition'. A key figure in all of these areas is Lev Vygotsky (1896–1934) and his theoretical ideas are a central reference point for all of the approaches that go under the umbrella of 'social constructivism'.

Working in Byelorussia with two colleagues who also made important theoretical contributions, Aleksandre Luria and Alexei Leont'ev, Vygotsky wrote two important books which only became available after his early death (see for example Vygotsky, 1962). These books challenged some of the orthodox beliefs of the twentieth century Soviet regime and because of state suppression during and after his lifetime they took some time to come to wider attention. Vygotsky came, independently, to much the same conclusions as Piaget about the constructive nature of development.

Where he differed most substantially, though, was in the role that he ascribed to the socio-cultural world surrounding the child. Vygotsky's perspective was that human history is made up of the construction of *cultural tools*. These are things that are shared by members of a culture, such as writing and number systems, language, technology, social rules and traditions and so forth; all of which are ways of achieving things in the world. They have to be acquired in the course of an individual's development so that they can be used and passed on to subsequent generations. Importantly, these cultural tools include ways of thinking as well as ways of doing. According to Vygotsky, it is in social interactions that these are taken in by children, not, as Piaget thought, by children constructing them on their own. This progression is often summed up in the phrase 'inter-mental to intra-mental', meaning that what happens first *between* (inter) minds then happens *inside* (intra) minds.

A good example of how Vygotsky's views differ from Piaget's is seen in their respective approaches to language development. Piaget thought that language could only come about if the child had developed what he called symbolic function – an inner, constructed capacity – and that this becomes evident as children talk to themselves about what they are doing. Piaget termed this 'egocentric speech'. For Vygotsky, on the other hand, this phenomenon represents a critical stage in the child's *internalization* of speech that happens first as a social process between two people; for him, children talking to themselves is one step towards 'inner speech' and then to thinking. Thus, the role of social interaction is highlighted in Vygotsky's work, along with the embedding of language in socially meaningful activities.

The social constructivist position was also given a theoretical boost in the 1970s by the work of Margaret Donaldson and her colleagues (Donaldson, 1978). She found that modifying Piagetian tasks so that they were set in situations that made 'human sense' to children resulted in them showing much higher levels of competence than when the tasks were disembedded from a meaningful framework. So, for example, when Piaget's three mountains task was changed so that the question asked was whether a policeman could see a robber who was trying to hide from them (see Figure 2), children aged around 4 years who failed the classic Piagetian task showed that, in this new situation, they could decenter and see things from the perspective of another person. A policeman looking for a robber made greater sense to children of this age than the more abstract notion of another character's view of a set of mountains. Several other experiments in the same vein carried out around this time confirmed that children's cognition shows itself to be more advanced when the tasks that they tackle are situated in a meaningful context.

Hiding from policemen

In this study, children between 3 and 5 years of age were tested individually using an apparatus consisting of two 'walls' which intersected to form a cross. In the first stage the child was asked to judge whether a policeman doll could see a boy doll from various positions. Then the child was asked to 'hide the doll so the policeman can't see him', with the policeman at a given position. Then a second policeman was introduced, as illustrated in Figure 2, and the child was asked to hide the doll from both policemen. This required the child to consider and co-ordinate *two* points of view. Look at Figure 2 and work out where the doll should be placed (in this case the only effective hiding place is at C). This was repeated three times so that each time a different section was left as the only hiding place. The results were clear: 90 per cent of the responses given by the children were correct.

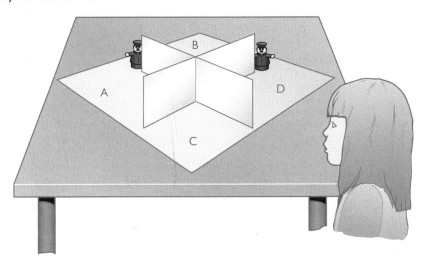

Figure 2   Plan of the experimental layout in the hiding game (Source: adapted from Donaldson, 1978).

Source: adapted from Roth, 1990, p. 115.

In Piagetian theory, conflict is a driving force for development. Cognitive conflict occurs when a task demands more of a child than can be achieved by using familiar strategies and they have to extend their competence. Conflict also plays a role in the social constructivist view of development, but here the arena is conflict between people, where, in a task situation, one person's approach to a task is different to another's. Vygotsky proposed that in this sort of situation there is the opportunity for a child to develop new ways of thinking. The interaction between less able and more able partners, working on a joint activity, can create what Vygotsky termed a 'zone of proximal development' (ZPD). This represents the next (proximal) abilities that the less able partner will be acquiring, and recognizes that the help of someone who is more competent allows the less able partner to experience new ways of tackling the task. Research by people such as Willem Doise and Gabriel Mugny (1981) has shown how peer collaboration is most effective when there is an element of socio-cognitive conflict involved. Also relevant here is the concept of 'scaffolding', developed by David Wood (1988) to describe the way in which adults or more able peers can provide structured support to a learner to help them to operate in their ZPD. The metaphor of a scaffold, which is gradually withdrawn as the learner gains the ability to work with less support, stresses the significance of the social support of learning and development.

The eight chapters that follow seek to address the sorts of questions that are posed in the first section of this introductory chapter. In doing so the chapters pick up on, illustrate and develop the themes outlined above. Although there is little explicit treatment of Piaget and Vygotsky in this book (until Chapter 8), it is important to recognize that their work underpins substantial areas of developmental psychology, and that it is difficult to understand the discipline fully without a clear understanding of their respective contributions to it. While the study of cognitive and language development in children has progressed a long way since these two theorists were working, their influence within this complex and fascinating field remains strong.

References

Chomsky, N. (1965) *Aspects of the Theory of Syntax*, Cambridge, MIT Press.

Doise, W. and Mugny, G. (1981) *Le Développement Social de l'Intelligence*, Paris, Interedition.

Donaldson, M. (1978) *Children's Minds*, London, Fontana.

Piaget, J. (1955) *The Child's Construction of Reality*, trans. by M. Cook, London, Routledge and Kegan Paul (first published 1936).

Piaget, J. (1959) *The Language and Thought of the Child*, translated by M. Gabain and R. Gabain, London, Routledge and Kegan Paul (first published 1923).

Piaget, J. (1973) *The Child's Conception of the World*, trans. by J. Tomlinson and A. Tomlinson, London, Paladin.

Roth, I. (1990) *Introduction to Psychology*, London, Erlbaum Associates/The Open University.

Vygotsky, L.S. (1962, 2nd edn) *Thought and Language*, Cambridge, MA, MIT Press (first published 1934).

Wood, D. (1988) *How Children Think and Learn*, Oxford, Blackwell.

Chapter 1
Early category representations and concepts

Paul C. Quinn and John Oates

Contents

Learning outcomes

After you have studied this chapter you should be able to:

1 define 'categories' and 'concepts' and discuss the differences between them;
2 explain how category formation in infants can be studied experimentally;
3 describe and discuss the evidence that infants can form categories before they can speak;
4 understand that infants may use certain cues to aid categorization;
5 explain what is meant by single-process and dual-process models of categorization;
6 evaluate these models in relation to evidence from infants' categorization of human and non-human animals, and developmental trends;
7 consider possible links between categorizing and naming.

1 Introduction

In this first chapter we look at how very young infants begin to make sense of the world in which they find themselves. We start by considering how important it is in everyday life to be able to see the links between similar experiences and to group them together. It is through this grouping that our mental world becomes structured and that we form concepts.

When you, as an adult, see an unfamiliar thing, it is a basic reaction to try to fit it into a category, to recognize what sort of thing it is. And much of the time this is not really a conscious process; it is only if we come across something that is really unfamiliar, such as a strange organism in an aquarium, that we are aware of our categorizing. We might for example see an odd thing in a tank that might be a seaweed, might be a worm, or might be some other sort of living being. A lot of categorizing is tied up with language; if there is someone with us at the aquarium, we are very likely to say 'What is that?' to our companion, when we see the strange creature, to try to fit it into a category that has a name.

These observations point to the idea that much of our making sense of the world is to do with the very rich and extensive system of categories that we all have. These have been acquired from all sorts of different sources, from books and other media, from schooling and from talking with other people, as well as our own direct experience.

But what about very young babies, who cannot ask what things are, who do not have 'words for things'? What sense do they make of the sights and sounds that confront them in the first weeks and months after their births? Is each successive experience totally new, or do they begin to register the similarities among repeated experiences of the same kinds of things?

Clearly, in time, young children do come to have an immense number of categories and a great many concepts in their mental repertoire, but how do they build up this knowledge base? Are all their learning capacities present and fully functioning at the time of birth? Do they categorize and conceptualize the world in the same ways as adults? Or, is it only when they learn to speak, and understand other people talking about things in the world, that they can begin to structure the world in any meaningful way? For a long time, these have been enigmatic questions, because to answer them means that it is necessary to have some way of examining the contents and workings of an infant's mind. In recent years, psychologists have begun to be able to do just this, to start to form a picture of how infants' minds operate, even though infants cannot tell us directly.

In this chapter we look at several pieces of evidence, gathered using specially designed experimental techniques, that show how even very young infants can indeed group things together and form mental representations of categories. Initially, at least, infants seem to do this mainly on the basis of the perceptual features of objects. We then see how older infants come increasingly to use less obvious features of things in order to group them together. This trend towards increasingly abstract forms of categorization is also seen in how infants develop their categorization of spatial relations like 'above' and 'below'.

We then go on to examine whether infants' categories are flexible and open to change as a result of experience. By comparing how infants categorize humans, other animals and objects, we see that even young infants seem to have some impressive general capacities to form categories and then concepts, and that they can use these in flexible ways. The conclusion we reach is that some of the developmental changes that are seen in infants' categorizing and concept formation may be a consequence of their accumulating experience and knowledge, and increasing levels of abstraction in the structures that organize these.

Clearly, cognition and its development are very broad areas and categories and concepts are only one part. They do, however, represent the basic 'building blocks' of knowledge and hence they are a central part of cognition. Without having some way of building up ideas of 'things', we can have no way of 'knowing about' those things.

1.1 Cognitive structure

In this section we first examine what it means to recognize and categorize things in the world. We then go on to discuss some of the different terms that are used to describe categorization and we consider the psychological processes involved. Finally, we discuss the importance of categories as a foundation for cognitive development.

Activity 1

Allow about
5 minutes

Recognizing and categorizing

This activity will help you to think about the ways in which people form and use categories.

Figure 1   Tropical fruits.

Look at the pictures in Figure 1 and see whether there are any fruits that you recognize. Think about what types of information you used from the pictures and from your own past experience to make this judgement. Next, decide which picture is the odd one out and again think about what information you used to make that judgement.

Comment

Before we turn to the questions about the information you used to make these judgements, let us first consider what was going on in this activity. These are all pictures of tropical fruit. They are all members of a category; in fact a subcategory, 'tropical fruit', nested in the broader category 'fruit'.

In the first sentence of the activity, the word 'recognize' was used. 'Recognize' is made up of two parts, 'cognize' (a word rarely used by itself), which refers to forming knowledge and 're', which suggests a repetition. If you have seen all these fruits before, if you have 're-cognized' them, you have made use of your previous experience and knowledge and probably found it quite easy to separate one from another. But to achieve that category distinction you made use of some features of the fruits to do so: What were they? Probably they were a mixture of visible attributes like the shape of the fruit, its inside structure and the texture of the surface, along with characteristics like taste and smell, which you might know about.

But if you are unfamiliar with some or all of these fruits, you might still have grouped two together and separated one out using visual features only. You might have focused on the fact that the inside of the durian fruit (Figure 1, right) is different from the other two fruits that have similar insides. Thus you were categorizing the longan (Figure 1, middle) and the rambutan (Figure 1, left) as members of one category, and the durian as a member of another category, (although they are all members of the category, 'tropical fruit').

Activity 1 should have helped to give you an awareness of the mental processes behind 're-cognition'. To break this process down further, you could say that to recognize something as a 'thing' that has been experienced before, as a member of a category or class, involves two basic cognitive processes. First, the storing of some sort of memory of an experience and, second, the comparing of a later experience with the memory trace and registering that there is a similarity. Human cognition thus involves the building up of an internal, mental structure that has a relation to corresponding structure in the outside world. These mental structures lie at the core of our psychological functioning, since life without any of the regularity and predictability that they provide would be chaotic and highly inefficient. Life would hardly be possible if each new encounter with the world involved working out anew, from scratch, appropriate ways of responding and behaving. Instead, it is a central, almost a defining feature of mental and behavioural function that objects and events in the world are encountered in terms of their similarities and differences; that the elements of our world are seen as falling into many classes and subclasses. The ability to recognize new things as being members of classes that we have experienced before gives humans a real advantage in responding to situations rapidly, appropriately and effectively.

Across the animal kingdom there are numerous ways that categorical forms of mental structure can be genetically programmed, as, for example, in many animals' reactions to potential predator-like entities. This is one of the most effective ways in which evolution provides animals with survival mechanisms. It is obviously a great advantage to be able to rapidly identify something as belonging to the class 'potential predator' and to behave accordingly. For some organisms, usually those that inhabit highly predictable niches, this sort of 'cognition' is all that is necessary. For example, a shrimp shoots backwards if anything large looms nearby. However, other organisms need to be able to adapt their behaviour to more varied environments, and for them it is also important to be able to generate new classes and forms of corresponding behaviours. For humans, this is the predominant way of classifying the world, through learning about things and building new mental structures that aid recognition. Thus, a central question for developmental psychologists is 'How is mental structure formed and elaborated?'

Clearly, once a child has acquired language, this provides them with a powerful tool for learning about new classes. Indeed, language is in itself a vast repository of classes. Nouns represent a multitude of objects and events, and verbs represent a vast number of actions. The natural reaction to a child's question 'What is that?' is simply to give the 'class name' of whatever it is that the child is asking about. Chapter 2 focuses on the first stages of language acquisition and considers how a child comes to understand the referential function of language and that words may represent 'invitations' to form categories (Waxman and Markow, 1995). But before infants have access to the use of language in this way, do they lack the structures that enable them to represent objects? Clearly not, because very young infants can quickly come to group objects based on their similarity, which is at least an initial form of classification.

Finding out more about infants' abilities to classify entities in the world, before they start to use language as an aid, offers an opportunity to uncover the basic cognitive processes that language builds on and to gain a better understanding of human cognition and its development. New experimental methods, which get around the problem that we cannot ask infants directly, have begun to uncover some basic features of this foundational period of development.

1.2 Classes, categories and concepts

'Classes', 'categories' and 'concepts' describe, in slightly different ways, the 'grouping together' process that underlies cognition that we examined in Section 1.1. The fact that we have these several different words for a set of overlapping ideas is one of the reasons for a certain amount of confusion in the psychological literature in the field of infant cognition.

Mandler (1997) has suggested that the word 'category' actually covers two different and important ideas. At first, she argues, infants begin to group things together on the basis of perceptual features. In the case of objects around in the home, these features might include colour, shape, texture and so on. Based on experience, then, initial perceptual categories might be formed by infants through the co-occurrence of certain visible features. Thus, a perceptual category similar to 'door' might be formed because of the visible similarity of flat, rectangular things that are upright.

This form of grouping, based on what objects look like, is what Mandler calls *perceptual* categorization. She points out that a lot of this knowledge, although based on quite complex perceptual processing, is not easily accessible to conscious reflection. In contrast, what she prefers to call *conceptual* categorization is a process that results in categories that are richer, more imbued with meaning and more open to reflection. Thus the *concept* of a door also comes to have associated with it a much broader amount of information, for example that a door swings open and shut, allows access to things, can keep out draughts and keep things safe and so forth. These features are not directly perceptual, but are much more to do with what a door 'is'. It is worth noting, since we will return to this in Section 4, that this richer form of categorization is also very much bound up with the functions that things serve. These are human uses and hence part of our cultural heritage. Thus, the feature 'handle' can be described as a bar of some sort, about 50 to 100 mm wide, with more or less of a curve, that extends from a surface, leaving a space of 2 to 5 cm between it and the surface. That is a perceptual description. But the *concept* of a handle is more abstract: it includes its human uses; to pull something open or to lift something up. Here, the 'look' of the object is rather less important. For example, you would have little difficulty in identifying a handle that is made of rope, and that does not easily fit the perceptual description.

This distinction raises further interesting questions about the development of categories in infants. Do perceptual categories appear before conceptual ones? Do perceptual categories form the basis for concepts? Are different processes involved in each? And are there changes in how infants' categories develop between the time that they are born and the emergence of language? Before we can begin to answer these questions, however, it is necessary to investigate how and to what extent infants are able to identify, form and store categories. This is the subject of Sections 2 and 3.

Summary of Section 1

- Categories and concepts are the basic building blocks of cognition.
- Perceptual categories are based on visible features of objects.
- Conceptual categories make use of a broader range of features, including, for example, the function of objects and other, more abstract features.
- Conceptual categories can also incorporate information that comes from other people, such as names and descriptions for things.

2 Do 3- and 4-month-old infants categorize?

2.1 Measuring categorization in infants

To find out if and how very young infants can form categories, some specialized techniques have been developed. These have proved to be highly effective in revealing how infants' thought processes operate. Experiments using these techniques reduce the complexities of real life situations by using simple stimuli such as dot patterns and black and white photographs. Using simple stimuli makes it easier to study infants' mental processes and means that the presentation of stimuli can be standardized, so that responses from more than one infant can be grouped together.

Using an experimental method called *familiarization/novelty-preference* (see Box 1), many studies have shown that infants aged 3–4 months can indeed form categories and furthermore, that they can do so in remarkably similar ways to adults. This result has been confirmed for several different types of stimuli.

BOX 1

The familiarization/novelty-preference method

This method relies on the strong tendency that infants have to prefer to look at new (novel) things (Fantz, 1963). For example, if a particular picture is shown to an infant for a while, eventually the infant looks away for longer and longer as they get used to (or 'habituate to') it. In a test situation, this is called 'familiarization'. If that same picture is then shown to the infant alongside a novel picture that they have not seen before, it is most likely that the infant's attention will be given more to the novel one in preference to the now familiar one. This is called a 'novelty preference'.

The familiarization/novelty-preference procedure has two stages, as you can see in Figure 2. In Stage 1, 'Familiarization', the infants are shown a number of different exemplars (members) of a single category one after another. In Figure 2, the category chosen was 'cats' and so the infants are shown four different cat pictures. In Stage 2, 'Novelty-preference', the infants are given a preference test. In the test, a novel member of the familiar category (in Figure 2, a cat) is shown alongside a novel member of a novel category (in Figure 2, a dog). The results from the preference test are then observed and interpreted. If infants look longer at the novel member of the novel category, this is a good indicator that they have formed a representation in their memories of the familiar category – 'a category representation'. So what these experiments do is play off the novelty value of a previously unseen exemplar from within a *familiar* category (of which infants have just seen several exemplars) against the novelty value of a previously unseen exemplar from a *novel* category. If infants give more attention to the latter, then we can assume that they are seeing the novel exemplar from the familiar category as 'just another one of those', whereas the response to the novel category exemplar is more like 'Aha! Here's a new sort of thing!'

Stage 1.
Familiarization set of stimuli.

First, these are shown to the infant, *one after another.*

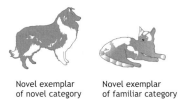

Category   Category   Category   Category
exemplar 1   exemplar 2   exemplar 3   exemplar 4

Stage 2.
Test pair of stimuli.

Next, these are shown to the infant, *both at the same time*, to see which attracts more attention. If the infant looks longer at the dog (the novel exemplar of the novel category) then we could infer that the infant is applying a category something like 'cat', based on the familiarization set and possibly also on previous knowledge.

Novel exemplar   Novel exemplar
of novel category   of familiar category

Figure 2 The structure of a typical infant categorization experiment based on the familiarization/novelty-preference method.

These experiments are usually carried out in a laboratory so that the conditions can be well controlled. Stimuli are often shown to infants on computer screens and are computer-controlled, so that the presentations of the images can be accurately timed. Infants are sat at a fixed distance from the stimulus display, close enough so that their limited ability to focus does not affect their perception.

Activity 2   *Evaluating the familiarization/novelty-preference test*

Allow about
5 minutes

This activity will raise your awareness of possible flaws or limitations in the familiarization/novelty-preference method.

When analysing scientific studies, it is always important to look for alternative, perhaps simpler, explanations of observations. With this in mind, think about the following question.

If infants generally look for longer at the dog in the experiment illustrated in Figure 2, are there other possible explanations for this result, other than the one offered in Box 1? Try to come up with two others, and make a note of your answers.

Comment

One possibility is that infants might generally prefer to look at the picture of the dog, perhaps because it is more colourful or has a more interesting shape. A way of avoiding this sort of problem is to take another group of infants who have not seen the familiarization stimuli, and test them on a number of different dogs paired with different cats. If there is no prior preference, we can be reasonably confident that any preferences found are due to the effect of the set of images shown during the familiarization phase.

Another possibility is that young infants might not be as good as adults at distinguishing between different cats; one might look much the same as another to the infant, but that does not mean that they are seeing them both as members of a single category, i.e. cats. A way of checking this out would be to show another group of infants the picture of one cat followed by just a picture of another cat. If the infants' attention declines as they looked at the first picture and then increases for the next, this would be good evidence that they can discriminate between the two within-category exemplars. These are the kinds of controls used in well-designed experiments on infant categorization that can be used to guard against misleading results.

It is worth noting that the results from the sorts of studies that we will be considering in this chapter come from analysing responses made by a number of infants. There is, typically, a lot of variation in how infants behave. Some fail to engage properly with the task and hence do not provide data. The findings reported are based on significant trends observed across whole groups of infant participants.

2.2 How do infants form categories?

Some of the first studies of infant categorization used stimuli that had previously been used to study category formation by adults. For example, one set of three experiments examined whether infants could form categories as a result of looking at a series of dot patterns that were distorted versions of simple prototype shapes such as squares, triangles and crosses (Bomba and Siqueland, 1983; Quinn, 1987; Younger and Gotlieb, 1988). In this set of experiments, young infants were familiarized with six to twelve different distorted exemplars from one category, e.g. a square, and they were then preference-tested with the prototype of this familiar category (a non-distorted square) paired with the prototype from a novel category, e.g. a triangle. This method works on the following rationale: if infants form a category representation that recognizes similarities among the distorted versions of the shape, then we can expect the representation to be close to the undistorted 'prototype' shape (e.g. a square).

Comment

If infants had established the category 'square' from the set of distorted exemplars during familiarization, which of the two test stimuli (a prototype square or a prototype triangle) do you think they would find more interesting? (Clue: remember that infants generally prefer looking at novel, unfamiliar things.)

Research summary 1 gives details of one of these studies, so that you can see how the data from such research are used to find out more about infant categorization.

RESEARCH SUMMARY I

Categorization of dot patterns by infants of 3, 5 and 7 months of age

Younger and Gotlieb (1988) carried out a dot pattern categorization experiment with 108 infants aged 3, 5 and 7 months. The infants were sorted by age into three groups, each containing 36. The infants were first familiarized with a series of six pairs of distorted dot patterns, each derived from a 'good', an 'intermediate' or a 'poor' form, as shown in Figure 3.

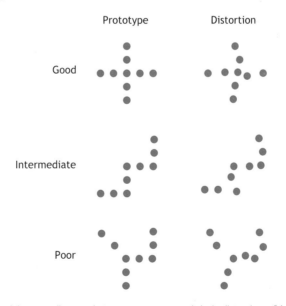

Figure 3   Good, intermediate and poor prototypes and their distortions (Younger and Gotlieb, 1988).

Next, the infants were shown a test pair that included a prototype (i.e. an undistorted shape) of the distorted forms that they had just seen, alongside a prototype of another form. This was carried out in order to test whether the infants were treating the prototype of the distorted forms as more familiar than a different form. (Bear in mind that they had not actually seen this prototype before; they had only seen a series of distorted versions of it.) The percentage of time that infants spent looking at the novel prototype was then observed and analysed as shown in Table 1.

Table 1   Preferential looking times for novel prototype at different distortion levels of familiarization stimuli

Form	Between-category comparison percentage of time spent looking at novel prototype		
	3-month-old infants	5-month-old infants	7-month-old infants
Good			
M	71.41%**	61.83%**	59.13%*
SD	9.12	15.54	14.63
Intermediate			
M	47.05%	64.92%**	62.38%**
SD	13.84	23.23	20.14
Poor			
M	53.87%	53.57%	59.66%*
SD	20.78	19.95	12.60

N =12 per cell. *$p < .05$; **$p <.01$ (two-tailed t-tests)

Source: Younger and Gotlieb (1988)

The first thing to note about these results is that in all conditions, except for the intermediate form for 3 month olds, infants were tending to look for longer at the novel prototype, which belonged to a class from which they had *not* previously seen distorted exemplars. This is indicated by the fact that all the percentage looking times (except one) are greater than 50 per cent. This shows that the novel prototype was attracting more attention than the prototype of the exemplars that they had seen before. This means that they were behaving as if the prototype of the distorted forms that they had seen was more familiar to them (even though they had not actually seen this undistorted prototype before). However, this preference was only reliably greater than chance variations (shown by the asterisks) for the good form for 3 month olds, for the good and intermediate forms for the 5 month olds and for all forms for the 7 month olds. Clearly, the older the infants, the better they were at extracting the prototype as a category from the distorted exemplars.

In the experiment described in Research summary 1 the novel prototype from the novel category was preferred by most infants, indicating that they had formed a category representation as a result of looking at the familiarization set of distorted exemplars. Even though they had never actually seen the prototype of the familiar category, they were, nevertheless, treating it as familiar. Their representation of the category was sufficiently structured so as to include novel exemplars from the same, familiar category and exclude novel exemplars from novel categories.

2.3 How do infants store categories in memory?

In Section 2.2 we examined the process that infants use to *form* categories. But, how do infants *store* these categories in their memories? One possibility is that they store a memory of *every single exemplar*, and compare new exemplars with each of these – a process called 'exemplar memory'. If infants use this process, this means that they recognize a prototype as familiar because it will closely match many of the previously seen exemplars.

However, using exemplar memory would not be a very efficient method of storing categories, because as the infants encountered new exemplars and learned new categories, it would get to be an increasingly time-consuming process. A more efficient process would be 'prototype abstraction', in other words, the storing of some sort of *average of all the exemplars* of a particular category, as a prototype of the category. (In Research summary 1, the undistorted square was described as the 'prototype' of the distorted exemplars.) If this 'averaging' process accurately describes how infants store categories, then we might expect that the prototype, once formed, would have a stronger memory trace than the individual exemplars from which it was extracted. Thus the prototype would be seen as more familiar than an exemplar that had previously been seen. For example, if the category being tested for were 'square', the distorted form of the square would be treated as less familiar than the 'perfect' form or prototype of the square.

The question of whether infants use exemplar memory or prototype abstraction to store their category representations was also examined in a study by Younger and Gotlieb (1988). In this experiment infants were familiarized with the same set of distorted exemplars as you read about in Research summary 1. However, this time, during the preference test, a previously seen (and hence familiar) distorted exemplar from the familiar category was presented alongside the prototype (undistorted shape) of the familiar category. This prototype was novel to the infants as they had not seen it during familiarization.

The rationale of this experiment is that if infants are storing a category representation of the shape by averaging the features of the distorted exemplars (a process of prototype abstraction) then that average will be most like the prototype of the category. It will also be represented strongly in their memories. Consequently, in the preference test the infants should look at the prototype less, and the exemplar will be perceived as less familiar, and thus looked at more. However, if the infants are not representing the category as a summary but simply remembering each individual exemplar from the familiarization, then they are using 'exemplar memory'. In other words, their category representation in memory is made up of multiple, weaker memory traces – one for each exemplar – rather than a single, strong memory representation which is an averaged prototype of them all. So, if the infants were using exemplar memory in the experiment, the exemplar they have already seen would be perceived as familiar (and hence looked at less) and the novel prototype would be perceived as less familiar, and would therefore be looked at more.

In fact, infants seem to be able to use *both* of these processes and researchers have found that which type of memory system they use depends on the conditions of the experiment. In conditions that are known to favour exemplar memory in adults (i.e. a small number of exemplars presented from a single category and no delay between familiarization and test), the prototype received more attention from infants than the previously seen exemplar. However, under conditions known to facilitate prototype abstraction in adults (i.e. a large number of exemplars presented from more than one category and several minutes of delay between familiarization and test), infants tended to prefer the familiar exemplar. This latter result shows that infants can, in the right circumstances, represent multiple exemplars from a category in terms of a summary structure. It is important to note that infants in these experiments were behaving in very similar ways to adults who are given similar tests. This suggests that quite sophisticated categorization abilities are operating effectively, even in young infants.

SG

Although the use of dot pattern stimuli provides the advantage of tight stimulus control and therefore allows for precise examination of how categories are represented in memory (i.e. as a single prototype or as a series of exemplars), there is also the disadvantage that the dot patterns lack the richness, multidimensional nature and complexity of the many different classes that infants experience in their everyday worlds. So it might be the case that infants do not categorize more realistic, life-like entities in the same way as they categorize the dot patterns. More recent research has addressed this issue and many studies have used classes of stimuli that commonly occur in infants' everyday lives.

Using the familiarization/novelty-preference procedure (see Box 1), it has been shown that young infants can indeed form category representations for things that they encounter on a day-to-day basis, such as animal species and types of furniture (Quinn and Eimas, 1996a). For example, in a series of experiments investigating whether young infants can categorize different species of animals, 3 and 4 month olds were familiarized with realistic, coloured photographs of twelve domestic cats, representing different breeds and depicted in a variety of positions. These infants treated novel instances of domestic cats as familiar, giving them less attention, but showed a novel category preference for birds, dogs, horses, and tigers by looking at them for longer (Quinn *et al.*, 1993; Eimas and Quinn, 1994). This showed that they had formed a category representation equivalent to 'cat', rather than just remembering the individual exemplars that they had been shown. Examples of the actual cat and dog stimuli that were used in the experiment are shown in Figure 4.

Figure 4 Cat and dog stimuli (Quinn *et al.*, 1993; Eimas and Quinn, 1994).

In addition, infants of this age range who were familiarized with horses treated novel horses as familiar, but showed greater interest in cats, giraffes, and zebras (Eimas and Quinn, 1994). These findings indicate that young infants can form separate representations for cats and horses each of which excludes instances of the other category, as well as excluding exemplars of other related animal species.

2.4 How do infants organize their categories?

The persuasive results reported in Section 2.3 have been repeated in enough studies to be taken as strong evidence that infants can form mental representations that group together similar things. Even though they do not have the use of language to help them form representations of classes of things like animals and furniture, infants are still able to recognize the similarities between things and form categories that are much like those of older children and adults. But an important feature of category knowledge in adults is that many categories are further organized into hierarchical structures. In these structures, lower-level categories (specific or subordinate categories) are nested within higher-level ones (global or superordinate categories). For example, we represent 'animal' at a global level, 'cat' at a basic level, and 'Siamese cat' at a specific level. Likewise, in the domain of furniture, 'furniture' is global, 'chair' is basic and 'garden chair' is specific (see Table 2).

Table 2 Levels of categorization

Level	Furniture domain	Animal domain
Global/superordinate	Furniture	Animal
Basic/intermediate	Chair	Cat
Specific/subordinate	Garden chair	Siamese cat

Although, as we have seen, infants can group objects into categories, perhaps they do not at first form these sorts of nested sets of categories? It is possible that at first young infants simply recognize different classes of things. For example, they might group cats into one category and dogs into another, but not recognize that at a higher level, both of these categories fall within the category of 'domestic pets' or the broader category of 'animals'.

Behl-Chadha (1996) wanted to find out whether infants are able to form the sorts of 'categories within categories' outlined in Table 2. To do this, she extended the findings of studies looking at early categorization differentiation among animal species and designed an experiment to discover whether infants could form separate categories for particular types of furniture. Furniture was chosen as a stimulus class because infants have a lot of exposure to furniture from birth onwards.

In the experiment, infants of 3 and 4 months of age were first familiarized with twelve realistic photographs of chairs (including examples of the subordinate categories: armchairs, desk chairs, kitchen chairs, rocking chairs and stuffed chairs). Then, they were shown novel chairs, along with non-chair furniture (either couches, beds or tables). The infants gave more attention to these non-chair pictures than to the novel chairs. This indicates that they had formed a category equivalent to 'chair' that did not include other types of furniture. When they were familiarized with a set of photographs of couches, they treated novel couches as familiar, but showed novel category preferences for chairs, beds and tables by looking at these for longer, showing that in this case they had formed category representations for 'couch'. This is good evidence that 3 and 4 month olds can form individuated representations for chairs and couches as separate categories, separate also from the categories of beds and tables. In other words, nested within the infants' category 'furniture' were further, 'basic' or 'intermediate' categories for chairs, couches, beds and tables.

Behl-Chadha (1996) also found that infants could form more global (inclusive) category representations for broader classes of stimuli. In one experiment, 3 and 4 month olds were familiarized with photographs of mammals (deer, domestic cats, elephants, horses, rabbits, squirrels, tigers and zebras). Then, photographs of an animal from a novel mammal category were paired with either (1) a novel example of a familiar mammal category (2) a non-mammalian animal (bird or fish) or (3) an item of furniture. The infants preferred birds, fish and furniture to instances from the novel mammal categories, but they did not prefer members of novel mammal categories to novel members of familiar mammal categories. These findings indicate that young infants can form a broad category representation for mammals that includes examples from novel mammal categories that they had not seen during familiarization, and excludes some non-mammals (birds and fish) as well as furniture. However, what is even more interesting is that within the broad category representation 'animal', they can use nesting categorization skills. In other words, within the animal category, they can form basic category representations for mammals.

Results from the same series of experiments backed up these findings, showing that 3–4 month olds can make the same kinds of 'nested' distinctions the other way round – i.e. for furniture versus animals. The results showed that infants could form a category representation for furniture that includes beds, chairs, couches, cabinets, dressers and tables, but excludes mammals. This evidence suggests that young infants can form global category representations for at least some natural (mammal) and artefact (furniture) categories and this is strong evidence that infants can, indeed, form nested category representations. These experimental outcomes are highly significant because they indicate quite clearly that young infants have the cognitive abilities to group stimuli into categories that are similar to many of the cognitive groupings that older children and adults use. This is also strong evidence that infants are forming categories on the basis of their experience, because evolution could hardly have provided us with innate templates for types of furniture!

2.5 Can infants categorize spatial relations?

Although so far we have looked at young infants categorizing objects, an interesting question is whether they can also form other types of category representations such as categories for the ways that objects can be related relative to each other. Ideas such as 'above', 'beside' and 'behind' are not marked by the same sorts of perceptual features as ideas like 'chair' or 'giraffe'. Thus psychologists are interested in whether infants can form categories for spatial relations such as 'above' versus 'below' and 'between' versus 'outside'.

RESEARCH SUMMARY 2

Infant categorization of spatial relations

The familiarization/novelty-preference procedure was used to examine whether 3 month olds could categorize the spatial relations 'above' and 'below' between a dot and a horizontal bar (Quinn, 1994). Figure 5 illustrates the design of the experiment. Infants in an 'above' familiarization group were presented with four exemplars, each depicting a single dot in a different position but always above a horizontal bar (see Figure 5a, 'Familiarization set of stimuli'). The infants were then given a preference test that showed two novel exemplars side by side, one in which the dot was located in a position *above* the bar; the other in which the dot was in a novel spatial position i.e. *below* the bar (see Figure 5a 'Test pair of stimuli').

The rationale of this test is as follows: if infants form a category representation of 'above', then the novel 'above' exemplar should be seen as familiar and not be looked at for very long, whereas the novel 'below' exemplar should be perceived as novel and therefore be preferred and looked at for longer. If, however, infants do not form a category representation of 'above', and represent only information about either the dot or the bar, or represent information about the dot and the bar independently of each other, then neither test exemplar should be preferred. Figure 5b shows how the same procedure was used to test whether infants could also form a category representation of 'below'.

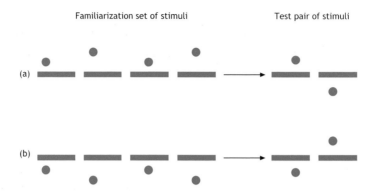

Figure 5   Spatial relations stimuli (based on Quinn, 1994).

The results were that both groups of infants showed a preference for the novel spatial category, consistent with the idea that they had formed category representations for the 'above' and 'below' relations between the dot and the horizontal bar. More recent research using the same method indicates that by 6 or 7 months of age, infants can form category representations for 'between' and 'outside' (Quinn *et al.*, 2003).

Given that infants can categorize objects in quite sophisticated ways, the finding that they can also categorize the ways in which objects are spatially located shows that they have the basic cognitive building blocks ('primitives', as they are often called) to form quite complex representations of the physical world. These representations also provide infants with a foundation for learning to communicate about different types of information: to learn the words 'dog', 'table' and 'under', and then say things like 'dog under table' if a dog is below a table. So, clearly, before they can speak, infants have the necessary mental abilities to construct category representations that will be useful in later development to support their use of language (see Chapter 2).

Summary of Section 2

- On the basis of perceptual similarities, infants of 3–4 months of age can recognize that certain sets of entities can be grouped into categories.
- Infants in this age range can form mental representations of a 'prototype' of such categories.
- Infants can use processes of exemplar memory and prototype abstraction to store their category representations. Which method they use depends on the experimental conditions.
- Young infants' category structures can also reflect nested categories such as mammal/dog.
- Young infants can also represent more location-based ideas such as the spatial relations 'above' versus 'below' and 'between' versus 'outside'.

3 What information do infants use to form category representations?

3.1 Use of cues

In Section 2 you learned that infants have a variety of quite sophisticated categorization skills. However, we have not yet considered how infants select the information that they use to categorize. Because of their limited experience, very young infants are unlikely to have acquired much abstract conceptual knowledge on which to base their category distinctions, so they are more likely to use a variety of perceptual attributes (this is discussed in Section 4). Since this may be infants' main way of identifying categories, psychologists are interested in how infants do this. Do they use all the perceptual information that is available to form categories or do they tend to pick out certain types of perceptual features as being more important than others?

What is a 'cue'?

In its everyday sense, a 'cue' is some sort of signal that launches a sequence of behaviour or some other response. For example, a green traffic light is a cue to the behaviour of moving forward across a road junction. The word 'cue' is used in a similar way in psychology, to refer to something that indicates or triggers something else, such as behaviour or recognition. A cue could be in any sensory modality; it could be a visual signal, a sound, a touch or a taste. If you were meeting someone at a railway station, for example, spotting their hat might serve as a visual cue to trigger your recognition of them. Or, if you were waiting for a particular programme on the radio, the signature tune would give you an auditory cue that the programme is about to start. In categorization, then, we often use specific cues as indicators of which category something belongs to. Specific cues might include the values of attributes such as colour or shape.

One strategy that has been used to identify the cue (or cues) that infants use to form a particular category representation is to show that they form the category representation when a particular cue is present, but not when the cue is absent. Such a strategy has been used to find out, for example, how infants form distinct category representations for dogs versus cats. Because the two species have considerable perceptual overlap (both have facial features, a torso, four legs, fur and tails) it is not immediately obvious what information infants might be using to form and differentiate the categories.

Activity 3

Allow about
5 minutes

What are the differences between dogs and cats?

This activity will help you to identify the possible cues that might be used to differentiate the category 'dog' from the category 'cat'.

What visual features mark the difference between dogs and cats for you? In other words, what would you look for to decide whether an animal that you saw for the first time is a dog or a cat? You might like to try visualizing (or drawing) a 'prototypical' dog and cat, and see what are the main features of your visual images and how the dog and cat differ.

Comment

For many people, this is not a very easy activity. Although they assert that they have little difficulty in distinguishing a cat from a dog, they have a lot more difficulty in saying how they do so. This activity serves to remind us that our categorization processes are not always fully accessible to consciousness.

It is possible that infants are able to make categorical distinctions on the basis of differences in single attributes, in the pattern of correlations among attributes or in the overall combination of attributes. For example, in the case of the visible features of birds, beaks and feathers are reliably correlated; they almost always co-occur. Hence, this correlation between attributes might feasibly form a basis for categorical distinctions. Or, in the case of the 'snake' category, a long, cylindrical body is a reasonable basis, although using this cue alone would include worms, slugs and legless lizards in the category. One way of finding out how infants select from the range of visible information is to vary systematically the attributes shown by a category exemplar.

Whether infants use a subset of cues in order to categorize was the subject of a series of studies by Quinn and Eimas (1996b), Spencer *et al.* (1997) and Quinn *et al.* (2001a). These studies found that infants categorized animals when the exemplars presented during familiarization and test trials showed only the head region of the animal, but they failed to show the categorical distinction when only the body region was displayed (Quinn and Eimas, 1996b; Quinn *et al.*, 2001a). Infants also formed category representations based on the head (and not the body) when they were familiarized with whole cats or dogs and were then preference-tested with a pair of hybrid stimuli: a novel cat head on a novel dog body versus a novel dog head on a novel cat body (Spencer *et al.*, 1997). Examples of hybrid stimuli used in an experiment by Quinn and Eimas (1996b) are shown in Figure 6.

Figure 6   Hybrid cats and dogs (Spencer *et al.*, 1997).

So it seems that, at least in the case of dogs and cats, infants do not make use of all the available cues for categorization, but they do tend to focus on a specific subset. These results suggest that infants make the most use of perceptual cues in the head region to distinguish cats from dogs and that cues from the rest of these animals' bodies are less important. From this set of experiments at least, we can say that infants may select certain attributes as a basis for categorization.

3.2 Cues in the natural environment

The experiments described in Section 3.1 showed that it is likely that infants tend to prefer to use information from the head area of cats and dogs in order to distinguish between them. However, these experiments were undertaken in somewhat artificial situations. This means that they have certain limitations because they do not reflect the complexity of the infant's experience in the natural environment. In this section you will learn about procedures used with older infants that attempt to overcome such limitations.

Cues and the sequential touching procedure

Given the silent, static and two-dimensional nature of the stimuli that were used in the experiments in Section 3.1, it is not possible to say how far this reliance on head information is still present when infants categorize cats and dogs that they come across in their everyday life. Real cats and dogs have different, distinctive patterns of movement and they make different sounds, so it is possible that such movement and sound information might also be used by infants. Another limitation is that we do not know whether infants would rely on head information if other category contrasts are involved. When cats or dogs are contrasted with birds, horses, or humans, for example, other cues such as size, the number of legs, the shape of the body or the typical posture, might become more important. Procedures such as the sequential touching procedure (see Box 2) have been used to explore such possibilities.

BOX 2

The sequential touching procedure

A procedure that has been used to measure categorization in older infants is sequential touching (Mandler *et al.*, 1991). This procedure has generally been used with infants who are 14 months of age and older. Infants are presented with a category contrast that consists of a series of toy objects (e.g. four from one category and four from another) arranged randomly on a surface. The serial order in which infants touch the objects from the two categories is recorded, and categorization is inferred if the infants touch a majority of objects from one category before touching the objects of the other category. If psychologists carefully select the toy objects – so that differences *between the exemplars* of each category and *between the categories* involve specific features – this method can be used to find out which features affect infants' categorization.

There is evidence that salient part differences (e.g. legs versus wheels) can play a role in signalling broader (global) category contrasts in older infants. Rakison and Butterworth (1998) examined categorization of toy objects by 14–22-month-old infants, using the sequential touching procedure, and found that the infants would categorically differentiate between animals and vehicles. However, in a subsequent experiment, when the legs were removed from the animals and the wheels from the vehicles, the infants no longer showed the category differentiation. This supports the idea that older infants use specific, salient attributes to make broad contrasts between global categories of objects, for example, using legs versus wheels to distinguish animals from vehicles.

Dynamic movement cues

In constructing global category representations, infants may also make use of cues based on how things move, known as *dynamic movement cues*. For example, Arterberry and Bornstein (2002) reported that 3, 6, and 9 month olds could categorize animals and vehicles when they were shown dynamic point light displays of the exemplars. It was also found that the 9 month olds were able to transfer their category-based responses to non-mobile examples of the categories seen in full light. Since point-light displays show only movement information, it is clear that dynamic motion can be a strong cue for category formation and that infants are quite likely to be using this in the real world to distinguish animals from other objects, for example.

The examples of research findings given in this section suggest that category representations may be constructed on the basis of a variety of static and dynamic features. They also suggest that in a particular context, infants may use any one or a subset of these. Research is beginning to determine the attributes that are used in this way and to identify the conditions in which they are used in categorizing. It is likely that this area of research will continue for some time, given the cognitive complexity involved in the vast number of categories that infants must be forming, each of which must be differentiated from a large number of contrasting categories. Imagine a 6-month-old infant being pushed around a shopping centre in a pushchair and think about all the different categories of objects that the infant will be likely to see, and the different attributes that they might use to differentiate them.

The next section goes on to look at how infants build on these perception-based categories to build up concepts, and considers two models that may underpin the development of children's categorization skills.

Dynamic point light displays
A display produced by putting several small light sources ('point lights') on different parts of a moving object. When the object is then filmed moving in darkness, all that can be seen is a series of lights moving around. This often gives a strong impression of the form of the object.

Summary of Section 3

- Infants are good at selecting certain cues, out of all those that are available, to categorize things.
- Infants use visual cues from cats' and dogs' heads to categorize these kinds of animals.
- Older children can also categorize by using parts of objects, like wheels or legs, to distinguish between the 'vehicle' and 'animal' categories.
- It is not just static visual cues that infants use to categorize things: sounds and movement may also be used.

4 How do infants' categories develop into mature concepts?

As you have seen from the research findings given in this chapter so far, the evidence is now clear that infants do indeed have remarkable abilities to group things into categories. Given this important finding, psychologists are interested to know how these initial categories develop into the more mature structures that we described in Section 1 as 'concepts'. This has been a matter of some debate among developmental psychologists (Mandler, 2000; Quinn and Johnson, 2000) and two competing theories have been put forward. One view proposes that a single process is operating, while the opposing view is that a second process comes into play, working along with the perceptually-based process.

4.1 A single-process model

The single-process model holds that infants' category representations develop gradually through the inclusion of more information, a process that we can call 'quantitative enrichment' (Eimas and Quinn, 1994; Madole and Oakes, 1999; Quinn and Eimas, 1996a; Quinn and Eimas, 1997; Rakison and Poulin-Dubois, 2001). According to this model, the global category 'animal' develops as infants encounter a succession of different animals as time goes by. As a result of these various encounters, the category comes to encompass an increasing number of features such as body shape, limbs, a 'face' in a head shape and dynamic features such as biological motion patterns and particular sorts of sounds. These are characteristics of animals that can be directly perceived and they can also be supplemented by other characteristics that become associated with them, such as the fact that other people consistently give them a category name (Waxman and Markow, 1995). Other less apparent defining attributes, such as 'has a heart' and 'can reproduce' can also join the category representation, for example, through caregivers talking about animals and their features (Millikan, 1998). Thus, in the case of a basic level category 'horse', psychologists supporting the single-process model would argue that infants at first build a perceptual category representation based on specific values of 'animal' features such as body shape and parts, and head and 'face' shapes, as described above. The category will include novel horses, but other types of animal and non-animal will be excluded. More abstract information, for example that horses eat hay, carry heavy loads, possess horse DNA and give birth to foals, can then be added to the representation and hence build a concept of 'horse'.

According to the single-process model, language serves as an additional perceptual input system for information that further defines representations already established through vision and other senses. For example, infants can enrich their category representations through looking at and naming objects in the world with their caregivers and when they look at picture books together. In addition, as the child gets older, parents and other people will use language to describe defining features of categories such as 'all birds hatch from eggs'. As Quinn and Eimas say in their summary of the single-process model, 'a representation like animal that may begin by picking out relatively simple features from seeing and other sensory modalities comes over time to have sufficient knowledge to permit specifying the kind of thing something is through a single continuous and integrative process of enrichment' (Quinn and Eimas, 2000, p. 57). We can call this a perceptual learning model. Computer simulations (connectionist models) of learning networks have supported the validity of the single-process framework to some extent. It has also been found that the same computer model could form category representations based only on perceptual features or on arbitrary labels that classify exemplars (Quinn and Johnson, 1997).

SG

4.2 A dual-process model

Do you think the single-process model accounts for the way in which infants form categories? Or do you think that at some point in development there might be a change? Mandler has argued that, early in development, infants start to use a different approach, based on more abstract attributes – a view closer to the idea that you came across in Section 1 that 'seeing is not the same as thinking' (Mandler, 1992, 2000). Mandler argues that category representations based on perceptual features are at first simply *perceptual schemas* that define what a group of things looks like, but they do not really define the *meaning* of something. Mandler's argument has been described as a dual-process model. She describes the dual-process model as involving a second process that works separately from the formation of perceptual schemas, that carries out more analysis of the perceptual features and also links them with dynamic information such as motion, sound and function. She proposes that this second process leads to the formation of *image schemas* (Mandler, 1992, 2000). Image schemas are the forerunners of mature concepts and can, for example, separate animals from non-animals by what have been called 'conceptual primitives'. These are more abstract attributes, such as whether the members of the concept are self-starters (i.e. they move by themselves without a visible external force acting on them). These attributes are more abstract because they cannot be actually seen (or heard or felt) but instead have to be inferred in some way. This is a very different sort of process from straightforward perception. This 'dual-process' model proposes that both perceptual schemas and image schemas (which are different systems of representation for perception and the formation of concepts respectively) operate in parallel. This dual process then leads to the formation of true concepts that are much more suffused with meaning than perceptual schemas.

The concept of 'representational re-description' of Karmiloff-Smith (1986) outlined in Box 3, describes a similar, related developmental process whereby children's knowledge moves from being implicit and procedural to being explicit and potentially 'thought about' and 'talked about'. Karmiloff-Smith's theory holds that a new ability is at first something that children can just do, without being able to reflect on it, so it is at this point represented at a procedural level. Then, once it has been practised enough and applied to a range of different problems, it becomes redescribed and becomes an 'object of thought'; a different form of

Perceptual schema

A simple form of category based only on superficial, perceptual features.

Image schema
A form of category that incorporates multiple characteristics of its exemplars, including less immediately obvious, more abstract features such as how the exemplars behave.

Procedural knowledge
Knowing how to do something, but not necessarily being able to describe it.

mental representation, at a declarative level. Another way of describing this is to consider it as a process of moving from 'knowing how' to 'understanding'. This perspective fits well with a dual-process model.

BOX 3

Concept formation by perceptual analysis

Perceptual analysis is a process in which a given perceptual array is attentively analysed and a new kind of information abstracted. The information is new in the sense that a piece of perceptual information is recoded into a nonperceptual form that represents a meaning. The process is different from the usual perceptual processing, which occurs automatically and is typically not under the attentive control of the perceiver. Most of the perceptual information normally encoded is neither consciously noticed nor accessible at a later time for purposes of thought. Perceptual analysis, on the other hand, involves the active recoding of a subset of incoming perceptual information into meanings that form the basis of accessible concepts.

Perceptual analysis is a version of what Karmiloff-Smith (1986) calls redescription of procedural information. Information gets recoded into a different format, and in the process some of the original information is lost. What we consciously attend to and store in a form that we can potentially think about involves a reduction and redescription of the huge amount of information provided by our sensory receptors and that is used to form perceptual categories. A great deal of the perceptual information that we process, from faces for example, is stored in procedural form, as illustrated by the fact that we readily learn such complex perceptual categories, but cannot state what the information is that we use. To form an explicit knowledge system requires a different format – what we might call a vocabulary of meanings. The process of redescribing perceptual information forms such a vocabulary. These meanings are not themselves accessible, but they form the basis of concepts that *are* accessible.

Source: Mandler (1997)

Activity 4   Are the single- and dual-process models competing or complementary?

Allow about 10 minutes

This activity will help you to understand the differences and possible similarities between these two models of categorization processes.

Consider these two models of category formation. Do you think that they really are alternative, competing explanations, or might they both have some validity? One way of approaching this activity could be to list the features of each model in a table, to help you to see points of similarity and divergence between the two models.

Comment

You might feel that perhaps the dual-process model is not so very different from the single-process model, in that a single-process model could incorporate functions and names, which are clearly not just straightforward perceptual features. As well, the idea of 'function' might itself be seen as a form of redescription of perceptual schemas, in other words, based on things that are visible. Similarly, we might question whether an attribute like 'has legs', which at first sight seems an obvious perceptual feature might also be tied up with the use of 'legs' for locomotion, a functional aspect: in other words, is the notion of 'legs' also tied up with these limbs being used for walking?

Experiments have not yet been able to determine conclusively whether a single- or dual-process model best describes how infants' categories develop; the question is still an open one. Although this specific issue has yet to be resolved, researchers have clarified some other aspects of infants' categorization abilities. One of these aspects is the way in which infants' categories are organized into larger structures of knowledge about the world, a topic which we turn to in the next section.

Summary of Section 4

- A 'single-process' model of categorization sees infants as starting to categorize using simple perceptual features of objects and proposes that categories develop as infants gradually make use of less obvious features.
- Studies using connectionist models have shown some support for the single-process model.
- An alternative 'dual-process' model proposes that early categories are 'perceptual schemas' and a later development involves an additional process that forms 'image schemas' that go beyond perceptual input and incorporate more abstract features.

5 How do different levels of categories emerge?

5.1 Levels of representation

As you saw in Section 2, categories can be formed at different levels of inclusiveness and they form organized systems of knowledge representation with multiple levels. Table 2 is repeated below as a reminder of the levels of categories that psychologists refer to in categorization experiments.

Table 2 Levels of categorization

Level	Furniture domain	Animal domain
Global/superordinate	Furniture	Animal
Basic/intermediate	Chair	Cat
Specific/subordinate	Garden chair	Siamese cat

To understand better how infants' categories develop, a central question is whether there is some sort of common order in which categories at these levels emerge. Does this development consist primarily of infants first forming global categories and then progressively differentiating the basic and specific levels from the global level? Or, does it reflect infants actively constructing groupings of specific representations into basic, and eventually, global levels?

By using techniques such as sequential touching and object examination (see Boxes 2 and 4), several studies of infants of different ages have attempted to answer this question. Although the findings are not entirely clear and there is debate around their interpretation, most have provided evidence that, on balance, global category representations seem to be formed earlier and more readily than basic-level representations (Mandler *et al.*, 1991; Mandler and McDonough, 1993; Poulin-Dubois and Graham, 1994; Mandler and McDonough, 1996; Younger and Fearing, 1999; Quinn and Johnson, 2000; Quinn *et al.*, 2001b).

BOX 4

Object examination

Object examination is a method that has been used for studying category representation in older infants from about 6 months of age upwards (Oakes *et al.*, 1991). This procedure, like the familiarization/novelty-preference method, depends on infants gradually losing interest in successive new members of a single category and then regaining interest in a member from a novel category.

For example, if a vehicle versus animal category contrast were being studied, infants would be given toy vehicles (e.g. a tractor, a car, a lorry, a bus, a quad-bike and a motorcycle) one after the other, each for a fixed number of seconds (typically 20–30). Infants are allowed to look at and manipulate the toys. They are then given a toy animal, for example, a horse (novel exemplar from a novel category), for the same number of seconds. A measure of active examination (that combines the amounts of handling and looking at each toy) is then used to see whether infants examine the novel exemplar from the novel category significantly more than the previous one or two vehicle toys. If we know that the infants can discriminate among the instances from the familiar category and that they do not have a pre-existing preference for the novel category exemplar (remember the precautions that are taken to rule out these possibilities) then one can conclude that categorization is taking place.

A perceptual learning account (i.e. single-process model) has been put forward to describe this differentiation-based pattern of findings on the early development of object categorization (Quinn and Eimas, 1997, 2000; Quinn and Johnson, 1997, 2000; Quinn, 2002). At first, infants seem to learn global categories like mammals and furniture based on the presence or absence of salient features. Then they go on to differentiate these into basic-level categories like cats and dogs based on specific values of shared features. This observation is supported by the fact that simple connectionist networks also learn category representations in a global-to-basic order when provided only with input features (e.g. leg length, body length) that are measured directly from the stimuli shown to the infants (in other words, they are basic perceptual attributes). This again lends some support to the single-process model of category development.

5.2 Spatial relations

As shown earlier in Section 2.5, infants can form categories for spatial relations such as 'above' and 'below', which are more abstract than categories for things like furniture and mammals. It was also argued earlier that on the whole, as infants get older, they tend to make use of less obvious, more abstract features in their categorization for things like furniture and mammals. If there is a single developmental process underlying the development of categorization in all domains, including concrete and more abstract things, then we might expect to find a similar progression towards more abstract categorization in other domains, such as spatial relations. It is known that under some circumstances children (at least from the age of 2 years and 6 months) as well as adults are able mentally to separate spatial concepts such as 'above' and 'below' from changes in the entities showing these relations (Deloache et al., 1991). However, can very young infants do this as well? Or is this an ability that develops during childhood?

To investigate this issue, Quinn et al. (1996) repeated the original 'above' versus 'below' experiment, that we described in Section 2, but with four distinct shapes appearing above or below the bar (e.g. arrow, diamond, dollar sign, or dot). Four different shapes were used so that *novel shapes* could be shown to the infants as well as *novel spatial relations*, to find out whether the infants would respond to novel positions as well as novel shapes. Three- and 4-month-old infants were then familiarized as they were in the first experiment, but with the change that, for the test, a novel shape in the familiar spatial relation was paired with the same novel shape in a novel spatial relation, as shown in Figure 7.

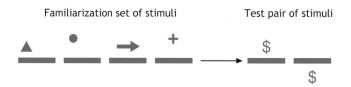

Figure 7   Example of spatial relations test stimuli (based on Quinn et al., 1996).

▼

Activity 5   *Separating location and object*

Allow about   *This activity will help you to understand how the familiarization/novelty-preference method can be*
5 minutes   *used to address a new research question about infants' capacities to categorize locations separately*
                   from the objects found in those locations.

If infants are able mentally to separate an object's position (above/below) from the shape of
the object that is in that position, which of the test stimuli shown in Figure 7 will they look at
for longer? Make a note of your answers. (Remember that infants tend to prefer novelty:
think about which of the two test stimuli would seem more novel.)

Comment

In the familiarization phase, infants became familiar with a particular shape (e.g. a dot) and a
particular location (e.g. 'above'). If they can separate out object and position information, then,
because they have been familiarized to 'above', they should see the *right-hand test stimulus* as
novel because it shows the spatial relation 'below' and they will look at it for longer.

▲

In contrast to the infants tested in the original 'above' versus 'below' experiment
described in Section 2, the infants tested in this new version of the categorization
task did not show a preference for the novel spatial category test stimulus, instead
they divided their attention equally across both test stimuli. This result suggests
that infants of this age do not form the abstract category representations for
'above' and 'below' separately from the particular objects showing the relation.

A follow-up experiment (Quinn *et al.*, 1996) found that older infants, aged 6–7
months, *did* prefer the novel spatial relation in the test phase. This result shows that
by this age they were now able to separate their more abstract categories of spatial
location from the changes in the identity of the objects. A similar concrete-to-
abstract developmental pathway has been reported for the spatial relation
'between' in the age range from 6–7 months to 9–10 months (Quinn *et al.*, 2003).
These results, taken together, support the idea that category representations of
spatial relations may be initially tied up with the objects depicting the relations, but
later become independent of the objects.

5.3 Is there a developmental trend towards abstraction?

A developmental trend that seems to be happening in both the object and spatial
categorization systems is towards increasing abstraction. With objects, the early
category representations, which are primarily based on perceptual features, may
serve as a basis onto which more abstract knowledge is built after infancy.
Similarly, representations for spatial relations appear at first to be tied to the visible
features of the objects depicting these relations, but become more abstract as the
infant's mental representations become able to incorporate a variety of objects that
show the relation. So, infants' categories for objects and spatial relations can be
seen as developmentally very useful: they organize experience in ways that
provide a foundation for the further growth of cognitive structure and content.

Summary of Section 5

- Things can be categorized at different levels, at a specific 'subordinate' level (e.g. a garden chair), an intermediate 'basic' level (e.g. chair), and at a 'global' superordinate level (e.g. furniture).
- Global level categories tend to be formed first in development.
- In the realm of spatial relations, infants' categorizing of 'above', 'below' and 'between' is at first tied to specific contexts but later becomes more context-free.
- In general, infants' categories move from the concrete to the abstract.

6   Category possession versus category formation

6.1 Categorizing non-human animals

In Sections 4 and 5 we considered different models and theories about how infants' categorizing develops. However we have not yet considered the nature of these categories, and this leads to a series of further important developmental questions. Are the categories that infants form rigid and permanent, or do they show flexibility and adaptability? Are the early categories that infants create on the basis of perceptual features a fixed foundation that is then elaborated and extended? Or is an infant's mental structure more fluid and adaptable?

In experiments of the kind that we have been describing, infants may be forming categories as the experiment progresses (bottom-up processing) or they may be using categories that they already had before the experiment starts (top-down processing). In familiarization experiments, it might be thought that the first process dominates (because of the 'learning' period at the start of the experiment) while in sequential touching experiments it might seem more likely that infants access pre-existing knowledge (because there is no familiarization or 'learning' period). However, the age of the infants is also likely to be relevant. For example, older infants, because of the greater experience that they have had, can be assumed to have a broader knowledge base that they are then more likely to draw on.

SG

Several studies have been carried out that shed some light on the relative contribution of top-down and bottom-up processing to infant categorization and its development. Since infants tend to have a lot of contact with humans, in particular during the first months after their birth, you might expect that they would be more likely to use their knowledge about humans in categorization than the more limited knowledge that they have about non-human animals. So, we might expect their 'human' category to be somewhat more fixed in its nature than their categories for other animals.

If this is true, then it should be relatively easy to modify the way that young infants categorize non-human animals. One study found that infants who were familiarized with a series of cats, then showed a novelty preference for a dog over a novel cat, suggesting that in this condition they were indeed using a 'cat' category that excluded dogs (Quinn *et al.*, 1993). However, in a second condition, another group of infants who were shown a series of dogs did not then show a novelty preference for a cat over a novel dog. This suggests that the 'dog' category formed in this second condition was an inclusive category – it was broad enough to encompass cats as well. So in some conditions infants can form narrow categories (e.g. a category of cats that excludes dogs) and in other conditions they can form broad categories (e.g. a category of dogs that includes cats). This suggests that infants do not have rigid categories for 'cats' and 'dogs' that they apply in all conditions.

Two further experiments support the idea that these are flexible categories and that the dog versus cat asymmetry only arose because of the particular sets of stimuli that were used (Quinn *et al.*, 1993; French *et al.*, 2001). In one of these experiments (Quinn *et al.*, 1993), the variability of the dog stimuli was reduced (the stimuli were chosen to be more similar to each other). In this case, 3–4-month old infants did not include cats in the 'dog' category that they found. In another experiment with infants of the same age, new sets of dog and cat pictures resulted in the 'cat' category this time including 'dogs' (French *et al.*, 2001). Thus, when familiarized with exemplars that show a lot of variation in their features and overlap between categories, infants tend to form broad, inclusive categories. But if they are familiarized with very similar exemplars within a category and no overlap between categories, their category representation tends to be much narrower. These findings, taken together, indicate that these non-human animal categories were quite fluid and determined more by the experimental condition than any prior experience.

The studies of the categorization of cat and dog images by young infants makes the important point that the infants seem to be forming their category representations for non-human animals *over the course of the familiarization trials* (i.e. bottom up), rather than tapping into pre-existing concepts that had been formed prior to arriving at the laboratory (i.e. top down). If infants in the cat versus dog categorization studies had simply been tapping into category representations established before the experiments, then the experimental changes should have had no effects. The fact that infant responsiveness *did* vary across experiments suggests that the categories were being formed during the familiarization experience and that the boundaries of categories can be relatively easily affected by modifying the familiarization stimuli. Thus we can see that infants can not only form complex category representations, but also that these are open to change in the light of new experiences.

6.2 Categorizing humans

Since it is known that infants can readily form categories based on perceptual features (see Section 2), it might seem self-evident that infants can form a category of 'human' that excludes other species of animals. In addition, infants have extensive experience of humans, and humans have many unique attributes and values of attributes (e.g. clothing, and types of clothing, upright stance and different gaits, hair colours and different styles, speech, etc.).

A study by Quinn and Eimas (1998) familiarized 3- and 4-month-old infants with photographs of twelve humans (male and female) in a variety of standing, walking and running poses. Examples of the human stimuli used in the experiment are shown in Figure 8. The infants were then preference-tested with a novel human paired with a cat and a different novel human paired with a horse. Most surprisingly, no novel category preferences for either the cats or horses were observed. (There was no spontaneous preference among the infants for humans over non-human animals, which might have mistakenly led us to believe that infants categorized humans as different from horses and cats.) It seems unlikely that infants cannot tell the difference between humans, and cats and horses, so something rather odd seems to be going on.

Figure 8   Human stimuli (Quinn and Eimas, 1998).

6.3 Human and non-human animals

One interpretation of the surprising results of the Quinn and Eimas (1998) experiment could be that the infants in this study simply did not categorize the humans as a class. However, a subsequent study reported in the same research paper (Quinn and Eimas, 1998) showed that infants did categorize humans, although their category seems to be quite broad and can include novel humans, cats, horses, and even fish; however, it did exclude cars! This very broad, global-level representation for humans seems quite different from the narrower basic-level representations that infants construct for non-human animal species (i.e. cats, horses), that were found to exclude humans, exemplars from other non-human animal species and cars, as we discussed in Section 6.1. So there seems to be a very significant difference between the way in which infants form categories for humans on the one hand and for other animal species on the other.

This striking difference suggests that humans are represented in infants' minds differently from other animals. Most 3–4-month-old infants have had extensive experience with humans relative to other animal species, even if this is limited to repeated presentations of just a few humans, for example parents, older siblings and caregivers. It is possible that humans are represented by infants as *individual exemplars* belonging to the same category in addition to these individuals being averaged in some way to form a prototypic representation (Quinn and Eimas, 1998). The less frequently experienced non-human animal species might, in contrast, be organized by *category-level information*, as a summary prototype representing an average of the exemplars experienced, rather than exemplar-specific details, i.e. details about each individual instance or member of a category (Bomba and Siqueland, 1983). This distinction between exemplar-based and prototype-based categories was discussed in Section 2.3. Infants seem to form categories for non-human things that allow them to recognize them as *members of categories*, but not as *individual things*. In effect, over the course of a time span as short as 3 to 4 months of life, the different experiences that infants have with humans versus non-human animal species may encourage them to become human 'experts'.

To examine the nature of the representations that infants form for humans versus non-human animal species, Quinn and Eimas (1998) presented one group of 3–4-month olds with twelve pictures of humans and another group with twelve pictures of cats. Both groups were administered two preference tests: in one, a novel cat was paired with a novel human (the test of categorization); in the other, a novel member of the familiar category was paired with a familiar member of the familiar category (the test of exemplar memory). The latter pairing is based on the assumption that if individual exemplars are represented, then the novel member of the familiar category should be preferred. If individual exemplars are not represented, the looking times to both stimuli should be approximately equal. It was found that infants familiarized with cats preferred a novel human to a novel cat, but not a novel cat over a familiar one. However, infants familiarized with humans did not prefer a novel cat over a novel human, but they did prefer a novel human over a familiar human. This supports the claim that young infants' representations for humans includes many other animals (at least cats, horses, and fish), whereas the category representations for non-human animals (cats, horses) exclude humans as well as other animal species (Quinn *et al.*, 1993; Eimas and Quinn, 1994). The data also support the suggestion that the category representation of humans is exemplar-based, whereas the category representation of non-human animal species is based on summary information in the form of a prototype that represents an averaging of the familiar exemplars.

Summary of Section 6

- Infants seem to categorize human beings in a different way from other animals.
- Humans appear to be categorized using exemplar-based processes, producing a broad category definition.
- Other animals appear to be categorized using narrower, prototype-based processes.

7 Categorizing and early language development

7.1 Categorizing and the vocabulary spurt

As we have seen, infants build a rich knowledge structure of categories before they begin to speak, and develop increasingly abstract types of knowledge that form the basis of conceptual understandings. The emergence of language, in the form of words for things, might seem to depend on infants having the sort of knowledge structure that is constructed by categories and early concepts. It is hard to see, for example, how children might be able to use a word like 'cat' appropriately unless they have some sort of mental structure already available for organizing the objects that the word labels. In addition, some of the ways in which young children start to use language also suggest links with categories and concepts. Often children 'over-generalize' words, for example, by calling all large four-legged farm animals 'horse' and this suggests that their word use might be based on the presence of four legs as a categorical cue.

If there are links between categorization and language use, then one might expect to find development in the categorization domain occurring at the same time as development in the domain of language. A study by Gopnik and Meltzoff (1987) set out to examine whether a link of this kind exists. This study followed the behaviour of a group of twelve children who were tested every 3 weeks from the age of 15–20 months by being given sets of objects (dolls, cars, plastic shapes and boxes) from two different categories (e.g. a set of cars and a set of boxes). In this age range, without being given any instructions to do so, infants commonly do various things with objects that suggest they are categorizing them. At the youngest ages the children in this study formed a group of objects from one category, and when a little older, they touched all the members of one set before examining the other category. When they were close to 20 months in age, they went on to move into groups the remaining objects in the other category as well, so that all the objects were grouped. For all but one of the children, this developmental sequence did not change, as is shown in Table 3.

Table 3 **Developmental changes in sorting behaviour**

Developmental sequence of behaviour	Infants' categorizing behaviour	Name
First	Infants systematically move four objects of one kind and place them together	Single-category grouping
Second	Infants sequentially touch or manipulate four objects from one group and then the four from the other group	Serial-touching of two kinds of objects
Third	Infants move all eight objects from original locations into two clear groups or piles	Two-category grouping

Source: adapted from Gopnik and Meltzoff, 1987.

Object permanence test
A test of whether infants believe that an object continues to exist after it has been hidden from view.

Means–end test
A test that involves carrying out one (or more) actions to achieve some other result. For example, pulling a cloth on which a toy is placed in order to get the toy.

As well as the categorization task, three other assessments of children's cognitive development were carried out each time that the children were observed: a measure of language use, a test of means–end behaviour and a test of object permanence. The language assessment comprised a combination of a diary and a questionnaire which the children's mothers used to give data about how many words the children were using. This measure was employed to identify the point at which children showed a sudden increase in the number of names that they used for things, the so-called 'vocabulary spurt', which is also called the 'naming explosion'. This phenomenon, which is seen to happen in many children's development, is discussed further in Chapter 2.

The means–end test assessed how well children could solve problems that involved some planning, such as using a stick to obtain an object. The test of object permanence assessed how aware children were of the continued existence and location of objects when they were not visible. The reason why these other assessments were carried out was to find out whether language use and categorization were truly closely linked, or whether they might simply be developing together as part of a more general improvement in cognitive abilities.

The findings of the experiment are shown in Table 4. The table shows the levels of correlation between the ages at which the highest levels of categorization, 'vocabulary spurt', means–ends and object permanence were achieved. It can be seen that of the only two significant correlations, the strongest was between categorization and naming, with a significant but weaker correlation between object permanence and vocabulary. This pattern of observations suggests that there is a specific link between categorization and the vocabulary spurt, and that a developmental change in categorization-related behaviour goes along with a related change in naming. The association with the development of object permanence suggests that other processes may also be operating, not just the link between categorizing and the vocabulary spurt. These children became much more interested in learning and using the names for things at the same time as they showed a development in how they categorized objects.

Table 4 Relations among means–ends, categorization, vocabulary and object permanence

	Means–ends	Categorization	Vocabulary spurt
Object permanence	0.36	0.48	0.70*
Means–ends	–	0.19	–0.017
Categorization	–	–	0.78**

*$p < .01$; **$p < .005$

Source: adapted from Gopnik and Meltzoff, 1987.

It is important to note that categorization was not strongly linked with the other cognitive measures, nor were these other measures strongly linked with each other. This helps to rule out the possibility that what was being observed was just a general improvement in cognitive ability in the children, but that something more specific, linking categorization and vocabulary, was going on.

7.2 Why might categorizing and the vocabulary spurt be related?

In the study described in Section 7.1, all the objects within a single category were identical, and it could be argued that this was a poor test of category knowledge. Gopnik and Meltzoff (1992) carried out a further study in which the objects in each category varied in their features and attributes (different shapes, models and colours of toy cars, for example). Just as in the previous study, the children who categorized well in this task were also children who were using more names for things in their everyday speech. This result was not just because the children knew the names for the objects; in fact, whether or not they knew the specific names was not related to their success. Instead, it seems that there is some deeper connection between a step forward in categorizing and the spurt in naming. Clearly, these studies cannot tell us whether the vocabulary spurt causes the improvement in categorization, or whether the improvement in categorization is the foundation for the vocabulary spurt. Indeed, it is quite likely that both of these abilities are linked in complex ways and that different domains of knowledge follow different developmental pathways. Perhaps a sudden increase in naming things marks the emergence of a cognitive ability that allows the early categories that infants form to be brought together with other aspects of knowledge to permit the formation of true conceptual knowledge.

Summary of Section 7

- When children are given a set of objects they spontaneously sort them; this gives an indication as to how they categorize the objects.
- The development of children's spontaneous sorting seems usually to follow a fixed sequence.
- Most children show a sudden 'spurt' in the growth of their vocabulary some time between the ages of 1 and 2 years.
- There is evidence that this spurt is linked to a particular stage in the development of categorizing, suggesting that there is some connection between language development and categorization.

8   Conclusion

In this chapter we have shown that new experimental techniques have provided very productive ways of gaining a window into infants' minds and how they operate. We have seen how infants are able to group things into categories in remarkably flexible and sensitive ways. They are selective in the cues that they use to categorize different sorts of things and they can, very early in their lives, build the beginnings of complex, multi-levelled meaning structures. Having the abilities to form these rich structures from the earliest months of life gives infants a powerful tool to help them in making sense of the world of people and things that surround them and provides an essential foundation for almost all aspects of human experience.

This chapter has also explored the developmental pathway of infants' categorization abilities and looked at how this fits in with language development. We found that infants' initial categories seem very much based on what things look like and that more abstract, less immediately obvious features are only used in categorization later on in the period of infancy. It is only towards the end of this period, as infants begin to use their first words, that their categorizing becomes better at handling more abstract ideas separately from the visible objects to which they relate. And when their language vocabulary suddenly begins to race ahead, this appears to have a basis in a further development in categorization, which may be the point at which categories make the transition to becoming true concepts that are richly imbued with meanings. This is the exciting time when children are learning to communicate effectively with language and enter more fully into their social worlds. But that is a topic for the next chapter.

Acknowledgements

The preparation of this chapter was supported by NSF Grant BCS-0096300 and NIH Grant HD-42451.

References

Arterberry, M. E. and Bornstein, M. H. (2001) 'Three-month-old infants' categorization of animals and vehicles based on static and dynamic attributes', *Journal of Experimental Child Psychology*, vol. 80, pp. 333–46.

Arterberry, M. E. and Bornstein, M. H. (2002) 'Infant perceptual and conceptual categorization: the roles of static and dynamic stimulus attributes', *Cognition*, vol. 86, pp. 1–2.

Behl-Chadha, G. (1996) 'Basic-level and superordinate-like categorical representations in early infancy', *Cognition*, vol. 60, pp. 105–41.

Bomba, P. C. and Siqueland, E. R. (1983) 'The nature and structure of infant form categories', *Journal of Experimental Child Psychology*, vol. 35, pp. 294–328.

Deloache, J. S., Kolstad, V. and Anderson, K. (1991) 'Physical similarity and young children's understanding of scale models', *Child Development*, vol. 62, pp. 111–26.

Eimas, P. D. and Quinn, P. C. (1994) 'Studies on the formation of perceptually based basic-level categories in young infants', *Child Development*, vol. 65, pp. 903–17.

Fantz, R. L. (1963) 'Pattern vision in newborn infants', *Science*, vol. 140, pp. 296–7.

French, R. M., Mermillod, M., Quinn, P. C. and Mareschal, D. (2001) 'Reversing category exclusivities in infant perceptual categorization: simulations and data', in Stenning, K. and Moore, J. (eds) *Proceedings of the 23rd Annual Conference of the Cognitive Science Society*, pp. 307–12, Mahwah, NJ, Erlbaum.

Gopnik, A. and Meltzoff, A. N. (1987) 'The development of categorization in the second year and its relation to other cognitive and linguistic developments', *Child Development*, vol. 58, pp. 1523–31.

Gopnik, A. and Meltzoff, A. N. (1992) 'Categorization and naming: basic-level sorting in eighteen-month-olds and its relation to language', *Child Development*, vol. 63, pp. 1091–103.

Karmiloff-Smith, A. (1986) 'From meta-processes to conscious access: evidence from children's metalinguistic and repair data', *Cognition*, vol. 23, pp. 95–147.

Madole, K. L. and Oakes, L. M. (1999) 'Making sense of infant categorization: stable processes and changing representations', *Developmental Review*, vol. 19, pp. 263–96.

Mandler, J. M. (1992) 'How to build a baby: II. Conceptual primitives', *Psychological Review*, vol. 99, pp. 587–604.

Mandler, J. M. (1997) 'Development of categorization: perceptual and conceptual categories', in Bremner, G., Slater, A. and Butterworth, G. (eds) *Infant Development: recent advances*, pp. 163–90, Hove, Psychology Press.

Mandler, J. M. (2000) 'Perceptual and conceptual processes', *Journal of Cognition and Development*, vol. 1, pp. 3–36.

Mandler, J. M. and McDonough, L. (1993) 'Concept formation in infancy', *Cognitive Development*, vol. 8, pp. 291–318.

Mandler, J. M. and McDonough, L. (1996) 'Drinking and driving don't mix: inductive generalization in infancy', *Cognition*, vol. 59, pp. 307–35.

Mandler, J. M., Bauer, P. J. and McDonough, L. (1991) 'Separating the sheep from the goats: differentiating global categories', *Cognitive Psychology*, vol. 23, pp. 263–98.

Millikan, R. G. (1998) 'A common structure for concepts of individuals, stuffs, and real kinds: more mama, more milk, and more mouse', *Behavioural and Brain Sciences*, vol. 21, pp. 55–100.

Oakes, L. M., Madole, K. L. and Cohen, L. B. (1991) 'Infants' object examining: habituation and categorization', *Cognitive Development*, vol. 6, pp. 377–92.

Poulin-Dubois, D. and Graham, S. (1994) Infant categorization and early object-word meaning', in Vyt, A., Bloch, H. and Bornstein, M. H. (eds) *Early Child Development in the French Tradition: contributions from current research*, pp. 207–25, Hillsdale, NJ, Lawrence Erlbaum Associates.

Quinn, P. C. (1987) 'The categorical representation of visual pattern information by young infants', *Cognition*, vol. 27, pp. 145–79.

Quinn, P. C. (1994) 'The categorization of above and below spatial relations by young infants', *Child Development*, vol. 65, pp. 58–69.

Quinn, P. C. (2002) 'Early categorization: a new synthesis', in Goswami, U. (ed.) *Blackwell Handbook of Childhood Cognitive Development*, pp. 84–101, Oxford, Blackwell.

Quinn, P. C. and Eimas, P. D. (1996a) 'Perceptual organization and categorization in young infants', *Advances in Infancy Research*, vol. 10, pp. 1–36.

Quinn, P. C. and Eimas, P. D. (1996b) 'Perceptual cues that permit categorical differentiation of animal species by infants', *Journal of Experimental Child Psychology*, vol. 63, pp. 189–211.

Quinn, P. C. and Eimas, P. D. (1997) 'A re-examination of the perceptual-to-conceptual shift in mental representations', *Review of General Psychology*, vol. 1, pp. 271–87.

Quinn, P. C. and Eimas, P. D. (1998) 'Evidence for a global categorical representation of humans by young infants', *Journal of Experimental Child Psychology*, vol. 69, pp. 151–74.

Quinn, P. C. and Eimas, P. D. (2000) 'The emergence of category representations during infancy: are separate perceptual and conceptual processes required?' *Journal of Cognition and Development*, vol. 1, pp. 55–61.

Quinn, P. C. and Johnson, M. H. (1997) 'The emergence of perceptual category representations in young infants: a connectionist analysis', *Journal of Experimental Child Psychology*, vol. 66, pp. 236–63.

Quinn, P. C. and Johnson, M. H. (2000) 'Global-before-basic object categorization in connectionist networks and 2-month-old infants', *Infancy*, vol. 1, pp. 31–46.

Quinn, P. C., Eimas, P. D. and Rosenkrantz, S. L. (1993) 'Evidence for representations of perceptually similar natural categories by 3-month-old and 4-month-old infants', *Perception*, vol. 22, pp. 463–75.

Quinn, P. C., Eimas, P. D. and Tarr, M. J. (2001a) 'Perceptual categorization of cat and dog silhouettes by 3- to 4-month-old infants', *Journal of Experimental Child Psychology*, vol. 79, pp. 78–94.

Quinn, P. C., Adams, A., Kennedy, E. *et al.* (2003) 'Development of an abstract category representation for the spatial relation "between" in 6- to 10-month-old infants', *Developmental Psychology*, vol. 39, pp. 151–63.

Quinn, P. C., Cummins, M., Kase, J. *et al.* (1996) 'Development of categorical representations for above and below spatial relations in 3- to 7-month-old infants', *Developmental Psychology*, vol. 32, pp. 942–50.

Quinn, P. C., Slater, A. M., Brown, E. *et al.* (2001b) 'Developmental change in form categorization in early infancy', *British Journal of Developmental Psychology*, vol. 19, pp. 207–18.

Rakison, D. and Butterworth, G. (1998) 'Infants' use of object parts in early categorization', *Developmental Psychology*, vol. 34, pp. 49–62.

Rakison, D. and Poulin-Dubois, D. (2001) 'Developmental origin of the animate–inanimate distinction', *Psychological Bulletin*, vol. 127, pp. 209–28.

Spencer, J., Quinn, P. C., Johnson, M. H. *et al.* (1997) 'Heads you win, tails you lose: evidence for young infants categorizing mammals by head and facial attributes', *Early Development and Parenting*, vol. 6, pp. 113–26.

Waxman, S. R. and Markow, D. B. (1995) 'Words as invitations to form categories: evidence from 12- to 13-month-old infants', *Cognitive Psychology*, vol. 29, pp. 257–302.

Younger, B. A. and Gotlieb, S. (1988) 'Development of categorization skills: changes in the nature or structure of infant form categories?', *Developmental Psychology*, vol. 24, pp. 611–19.

Younger, B. A. and Fearing, D. D. (1999) 'Parsing items into separate categories: developmental change in infant categorization', *Child Development*, vol. 70, pp. 291–303.

Chapter 2
First words

Margaret Harris

Contents

Learning outcomes

After you have studied this chapter you should be able to:

1 describe the task that confronts the young child in learning first words and explain how this compares with the adult experience of acquiring vocabulary in an unfamiliar language;
2 describe how infants can use cues to identify word boundaries in a stream of continuous speech;
3 outline Bruner's arguments about the importance of the social context for early word learning;
4 discuss ways in which reliable data can be collected on children's early comprehension and production of words using a variety of methods;
5 describe the typical time course of the development of children's comprehension and production vocabulary while being aware of individual differences in development;
6 describe the stages in babbling;
7 understand the range of meanings that is found in early words.

1   Introduction

In the previous chapter you learned that very young babies are able to construct and represent categories that group together similar objects. In this chapter you will discover how young children learn about the names for objects in these categories as well as the words used to describe actions and personal names. I will be focusing on the first words that children say but I will also be considering the fundamental processes and developments that lay the foundations for the emergence of first word use.

Parents usually regard the moment when children begin to say words as very significant but, by the time this happens, children already know a great deal both about the way that words sound and about the way in which language is used in familiar situations. As you have seen, they also know about object categories. All of this knowledge is crucial as children search for the meaning of words.

1.1   Understanding and producing words

In considering first words, it is useful to draw a distinction between children's understanding of words (comprehension) and their use of them in speech (production). As you will see later in the chapter, at the beginning of language development most young children comprehend many more words than they can produce, and in most cases comprehension begins some months before production. In order to begin to understand how children produce their first words it is therefore essential to start by considering early word comprehension.

Activity I   *Early word comprehension*

Allow about
10 minutes

This activity asks you to reflect on the strategies you use when learning new words and to compare your experience of word learning to that of a young child at the beginning of language development.

Imagine that you are listening to someone talking and you hear a word that you do not recognize. Note down how you could discover what the new word meant if you could not look it up in a dictionary or ask someone else about the word's meaning. What difficulties would you face?

Next, note down the difference between your experience of hearing an unfamiliar language and what you imagine the experience of a young child to be. Remember, you already know a lot about at least one language – your own native tongue. Think about the advantage this gives you when you hear a new language for the first time. Then try to imagine what it would be like if you did not know any words in any language.

Comment

At the very beginning of language development, young children do not know about the meaning of *any* words so they are rather in the position that you would be in if you heard a new language for the first time. However, you have an advantage over the young child – you already know a lot about language from speaking your own native tongue. Young children do not know any words in any language.

Speech stream
The flow of sound produced when people speak, made up of different frequencies. If a graphical plot of this stream is examined, it is often unclear where words begin and end.

The chart below summarizes the different stages that young children must go through in learning about first words. You will see that there are more requirements for the production of words than for comprehension. At the end of the chapter you will look at this chart again so that you can see the various aspects of early word learning that you have covered.

Learning first words: stages in learning

Identify a word from the speech stream	
Remember what the word sounds like so that you can recognize it when you hear it again	WORD COMPREHENSION
Link the word with some consistent event e. g. an object or action	
Repeat the sound of the word	WORD PRODUCTION
Say the word in an appropriate context	

SG

Nativism
A theoretical position in which structures of thought are held to be innate, development being relatively unaffected by experience.

So far I have been talking about the skills that are involved when children *learn* their first words, and learning tends to imply a non-nativist view. You might ask whether there are nativist theories of word learning. Several theorists, most notably Noam Chomsky, have taken a nativist view of language development, arguing that the human capacity to learn language arises from an innate mechanism.

Phonology
The set of sounds that make up the basic building blocks of speech, which vary from one language to another and even within languages to some extent.

Interestingly, nativist theories of language development have little, if anything, to say about early word learning (although they have made some claims about phonology that do not concern us here). Traditional nativist theories have been mainly concerned with children's mastery of morphology and syntax, that is, the grammatical rules for combining words into phrases. You will be reading about these aspects of language development in Chapters 3 and 4.

Summary of Section 1

- Most infants comprehend many more words than they can produce. It is therefore essential to consider early word comprehension before early word production.
- Babies need to draw on more skills for word production than for word comprehension.
- Babies do not know the meaning of any words, so their experience of word learning differs greatly from the adult experience of learning another language.

2 Recognizing speech

2.1 Identifying speech sounds

The first two skills that young children need in order to develop an understanding of what words mean are the ability to recognize and remember speech sounds, and the ability to segment words from the speech stream – in other words, to identify where words begin and end from the flow of sounds people make when they speak. These are the same abilities that you would use when listening to an unfamiliar language. At first you would find it difficult to tell where one word ends and the next begins, and if the phonology of the language is very different from English, you may well also have problems in recognizing and remembering the individual sounds that you hear.

SG

Recent research has shown that babies begin learning about the language around them even before they are born. They can hear their mother's voice quite clearly while still inside the womb and will respond to it (Richards *et al.*, 1992). Babies' responses to speech before and just after birth have now been investigated in a series of extraordinary experiments. These have shown that unborn babies can actually remember and recognize some aspects of the speech they hear.

RESEARCH SUMMARY

Prenatal speech learning

DeCasper and Spence (1986) asked a group of pregnant women to read aloud one particular passage from a Dr Seuss story, *The Cat in the Hat,* twice a day for the last 6 weeks before their babies were due to be born. *The Cat in the Hat* was chosen for the experiment because it has a very regular rhyme. Two or 3 days after their birth, the babies were tested with a special pressure-sensing dummy that was wired up to record how hard and how fast they were sucking. The babies initially sucked on the dummy for 2 minutes so that the researchers could get a base-line measure for each baby. Then the dummy was connected to a tape recorder that was controlled by the babies' sucking. The babies were divided into two groups.

When one group of the babies sucked, their sucking triggered a recording of *The Cat in the Hat.* For the other group, sucking on the dummy played a recording of a different story. DeCasper and Spence found that the group of babies who listened to the recording of the story that they had heard before birth increased their rate of sucking, but the other group of babies did not. Furthermore, they found that the babies responded in this way even if they heard the same story but read by another person. DeCasper and Spence concluded from this that the babies recognized *The Cat in the Hat* story that they had heard before birth, and that it was the story itself that they were recognizing, not simply the sound of their own mother's voice reading the story.

In the DeCasper and Spence (1986) study the babies were tested after birth for their recognition of a story they had heard before birth. In a later study, DeCasper *et al.* (1994) took the research one stage further and tested the response of babies *before* they were born. In this later study, a group of French-speaking women, who were in the 35th week of pregnancy, recited a rhyme to their babies three times every day for 4 weeks. This time there were two different rhymes and half the mothers recited one rhyme to their babies while the other half recited the other. (This was an improvement on the previous study in 1986 when only one rhyme was used for all the babies. In this earlier study this meant that there was no way of testing whether the familiar and unfamiliar rhymes were inherently equally interesting for the babies.)

At the end of the 4 weeks, the researchers placed a speaker 20 cm above each mother's abdomen so that it was level with her baby's head. They then played both rhymes to the babies while monitoring their heart rates with a foetal heart rate monitor. In order to make sure that the babies' responses to the rhymes were not affected by their mothers' response, the researchers asked the mothers to listen to music through headphones so that their level of arousal stayed constant during testing.

DeCasper *et al.* found that there was a clear difference in the heart rates of the babies when they heard the familiar and unfamiliar rhymes. When the babies heard the unfamiliar rhyme there was no significant change in heart rate from a base-line measure taken at the start of the study. However, when the babies heard the familiar rhyme – even when someone other than their mother was reciting it – they showed a significant decrease in heart rate. This difference in response to the familiar and unfamiliar rhymes showed that the babies were able to recognize the rhyme that their mothers had recited to them before birth.

Recognizing voices

These dramatic findings about babies' ability to recognize speech sounds before birth can help to explain why they soon develop preferences for familiar speech sounds after they are born. Babies prefer the human voice to other sounds and, a few days after birth, according to an earlier study by DeCasper and Fifer (1980) using the pressure-sensing dummy technique, they will increase their rate of sucking in order to hear a recorded human voice but not to hear recorded music or a rhythmical non-speech sound. Over the first weeks of life, this general preference for voices over other sounds becomes more specific, and by 4 weeks of age, infants prefer their own mother's voice to other female voices (Mehler and Dupoux, 1994).

Telling languages apart

As well as preferring familiar voices, babies also rapidly develop a preference for familiar languages. The language that is familiar to a baby will typically be the one they heard before they were born and it is also the one that they hear other people speaking after they are born. Mehler *et al.* (1994) gave 4-day-old French babies (who had heard French being spoken before and since birth) the opportunity to hear both French and Russian – a language that they had not heard before. As you can predict from reading about the DeCasper and Spence experiments, the babies preferred French.

Prosody
The 'music' of speech; aspects such as intonation, stress, rhythm and rising and falling patterns.

How is it that such young babies can tell the difference between two languages and between two voices? A study by Christophe and Morton (1998) goes some way towards answering this question. Following on from the study by Mehler *et al.* (1994) that compared babies' ability to differentiate between French and Russian, Christophe and Morton presented 2-month-old English babies with two different language comparisons. The first was between English and Japanese. These two languages were compared because they have a very different rhythmical (or prosodic) pattern. The other comparison was between English and Dutch. These languages are more similar to each other in prosody.

Christophe and Morton predicted that, if babies use prosody to distinguish one language from another, then they would be able to tell the difference between English and Japanese but not the difference between English and Dutch.

Reading

SG

At this point you should turn to the end of this chapter and read Reading A 'Is Dutch native English? Linguistic analysis by 2-month-olds' which is the paper written by Christophe and Morton (1998). While reading, think about the method that was used to assess the babies' perception of the two languages. Make notes on the authors' conclusions about the cues that the babies were using to tell the difference between the two languages.

Cue
A specific feature or marker that is used to identify an object or event, or distinguish one object or event from another.

2.2 Cues to word boundaries

So why are babies so good at recognizing prosodic patterns in language? Researchers have found that this is because infants use prosodic cues to segment speech in order to find out where individual words begin and end, as well as using these cues to recognize voices and tell languages apart.

As you have read, the speech stream is a continuous flow of sound made when people speak. When adults are talking normally there are few breaks in this speech stream because there are few pauses between adjacent words. This does not present a problem when we know a language fluently since we automatically divide speech into words. However, when a language is unfamiliar, the lack of pauses means that this is very difficult to do. The sound spectrogram in Figure 1 shows graphically how our speech is one continuous stream. A spectrogram works by showing the intensity of the different frequencies found in speech and how they change over time. Higher frequencies are shown towards the top of the chart and louder sounds are shown by the darker regions. The spectrogram clearly shows that there are no obvious boundaries between the three words in the phrase shown ('How are you?').

In these circumstances, the listener must use other cues to detect word boundaries. I will now go on to consider what other cues to word boundaries are available and what evidence there is that babies can make use of them.

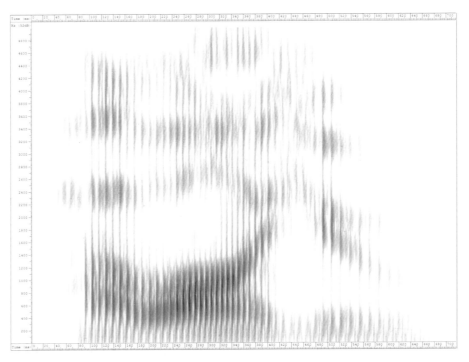

Figure 1   Sound spectrogram of the phrase 'How are you?'. Reproduced from an original recording provided by Mark Tatham (University of Essex).

Syllable stress

There are several possible prosodic cues to word boundaries. One is syllable stress. Many languages, such as Italian or Greek, have a very regular pattern of stress within words. In English, however, stress is variable as you will see in the next activity.

Activity 2

Allow about
10 minutes

Stress patterns in spoken English

This activity will help you to identify stress patterns in spoken English.

Say the following words aloud to yourself and underline the syllable that is stressed. For example, telephone is stressed on the first syllable since we normally say **tele**phone rather than tele**phone**. If you are not sure where the stress falls, it may help to think of stress in terms of emphasis. You could also try saying the word in different ways, varying the stress, and see which one sounds natural.

telephone	caterpillar	pencil	belong
accident	cricket	under	apple
ambulance	basket	across	cushion
tortoise	zebra	tickle	arctic
football	panda	guitar	ointment

Comment

In typical, conversational English, around 90 per cent of content words (i.e. nouns, verbs, adjectives, adverbs and personal names) have stress on the first syllable. You should have found that only *belong*, *across* and *guitar* were exceptions to this rule. So if babies could use the presence of a stressed syllable as a guide to the beginning of a word, they would be correct most of the time.

Stress patterns vary from language to language and they make up an important part of a language's prosodic structure. As you read in the Christophe and Morton (1998) study, babies can tell one language from another on the basis of prosody so it is perhaps not surprising to find that they are very sensitive to stress patterns.

Transitional probabilities

Although syllable stress is a good cue to the beginning of a new word, it is not always reliable. However, there are other cues available for babies to identify word boundaries which are not based on prosody. One further example of a cue is the probability of certain syllables appearing together. This is known as *transitional probability.*

Transitional probabilities about syllables provide more complex information than stress patterns. The idea is that certain pairs of syllables are much more likely to occur together than other pairs. Consider the two-word sequence *pretty baby* which Johnson and Jusczyk (2001) discuss in a study that you will be reading about shortly. *Pretty baby* contains four syllables: *pre, ty, bay* and *by*. In English, the two syllables *ty* and *bay* do not occur one after the other very often. However, *pre* and *ty* often occur together and so do *bay* and *by* because they form words. Syllables within a word are much more likely to follow one another in fixed sequences than are adjacent syllables that cross a word boundary. This is because – as in the *pretty baby* example – the syllable *ty* could be followed by any number of different syllables depending on the next word that a speaker used. For example, *ty* could be followed by *fl* (as in pret*ty fl*owers) or by *pi* (as in pret*ty pi*cture) or even by *un* (as in 'that is pret*ty un*likely').

I now want to look at two experiments that Johnson and Jusczyk (2001) carried out to investigate the use of transitional probabilities and syllable stress in the detection of word boundaries by 8-month-old infants.

■ Johnson and Jusczyk's first study

In their first study, Johnson and Jusczyk looked at the effect of transitional probabilities on 8 month olds. In order to consider transitional probabilities, they had to control the infants' prior experience of syllable sequences. To do this, Johnson and Jusczyk invented 'words' by taking twelve syllables and combining them into four sequences to make *pakibu, tibodu, golatu* and *daropi*.

There were two phases in the experiment. During the first phase – called the *familiarization phase* – the infants listened to the 'words' repeated over and over in random order for 3 minutes, with no pauses between them. Because there were no pauses, what the infants heard was a long, uninterrupted string of syllables. Furthermore, because the order of the 'words' was randomized, the sequences of syllables that resulted from two words being next to each other (for example, *bu-go-la*, heard only on those occasions when *pakibu* was followed by *golatu*) were heard less frequently than the sequences of syllables that formed the 'words' (*pa-ki-bu*).

Because the sequences of syllables that formed 'words' occurred more often than those that occurred as a result of one word following another, transitional probabilities could be used to distinguish the 'words' from other syllable sequences. To get some idea of what the babies were listening to, try saying this sequence out loud, making sure that you keep the interval between each syllable the same: *pa/ki/bu/ti/bo/du/go/la/tu/da/ro/pi/go/la/tu/pa/ki/bu*.

The second phase of the experiment was the *test phase*. In the test phase, having listened to the syllables during the familiarization phase, the babies were presented with all the words that they had heard and also with part-words where syllables from two words were recombined. For example the part-word, *tudaro*, was formed from the last syllable of *golatu* and the first two syllables of *daropi*.

Johnson and Jusczyk compared the infants' responses to words and part-words by measuring for how long they turned their heads towards a loudspeaker when a syllable sequence was being played. This is recorded in Figure 2 as the 'mean orientation time'.

The results that Johnson and Jusczyk obtained from their first study are shown in Figure 2. You will notice that the infants responded differently to 'words' and 'part-words' showing that they could tell the difference between them. You will see that infants turned their heads for *longer* to part-words, that is, they spent longer listening to the less familiar items. This preference for a less familiar 'novel' item is very typical of infant studies; babies tend to be interested in new things, things that they have not experienced before.

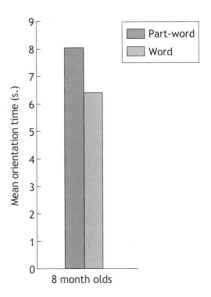

Figure 2 Mean orientation times (in seconds) for words and part-words in the Johnson and Jusczyk transitional probability study (Johnson and Jusczyk, 2001, p. 555).

■ Johnson and Jusczyk's second study

Having shown that infants could detect and remember transitional probabilities in their first study, Johnson and Jusczyk went on to investigate the role of syllable stress in word boundary detection. Using a similar experimental paradigm, with a familiarization phase followed by a test phase, they manipulated stress so that every time a part-word appeared during the familiarization phase it was stressed on the first syllable. There were three possible outcomes for the second test phase.

- The infants might still spend longer listening to the part-words, as in the first experiment. This would indicate that stress was not a strong cue; that the infants had not made use of the stress to highlight part-words.
- The infants might listen equally to words and part-words. This would imply that both cues were equally strong.
- The infants might spend longer listening to the words than the part-words, that is, they would show the opposite response to the one observed in the first experiment. This would suggest that the stress cues were very strong and had overwhelmed the transitional probabilities, that the stress on the first syllables had effectively labelled these as 'words' too.

Activity 3   *Studies of word boundary detection in babies*

Allow about
10 minutes

This activity will help you to compare the results of Johnson and Jusczyk's two studies and think about the implications for babies' detection of word boundaries.

Figure 3 shows the results that Johnson and Jusczyk obtained in their second experiment. Compare these results with those from their first experiment shown in Figure 2 which you looked at earlier.

- How have the infants responded to the words and part-words in the second experiment?

- How does this compare with their responses in the first experiment?

- What effect has the inclusion of stress had on the infants' responses?

Comment

The addition of stress as a variable brought about a significant change in the infants' behaviour. During the second test phase they now listened longer to words than to part-words. This is the opposite of the response found in the first study. Remember that infants listen more to *unfamiliar* stimuli so this indicates that they were now perceiving the part-words as more familiar than the words.

In addition, it is important to note that when stress was added as an additional cue, infants paid more attention during the familiarization

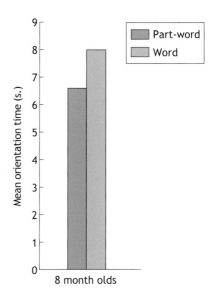

Figure 3   Mean orientation times for words and part-words in the Johnson and Jusczyk syllable stress study (Johnson and Jusczyk, 2001, p. 557).

phase to the syllable sequences that were separated by stress than to the syllable sequences that were marked out by their transitional probabilities. Also, during the test phase, the stress-marked part-words were perceived as more familiar and hence responded to less.

Johnson and Jusczyk concluded that prosodic speech cues such as stress are more important than transitional probabilities in the detection of word boundaries. In fact, adults and older children can take account of transitional probabilities even when these are in conflict with stress. In everyday speech you often hear words spoken with atypical stress patterns but you will have no difficulty in recognizing them. For example, in Activity 2 there are the examples of 'guitar' and 'across'.

Summary of Section 2

- The first essential in understanding words is to segment them from the speech stream. Babies are sensitive to a number of cues that enable them to segment speech. These include transitional probabilities and stress.
- Babies are especially sensitive to the prosodic properties of languages. This can be seen in their ability to distinguish between two languages on the basis of their characteristic prosody.

3 Understanding first words

3.1 Linking sounds to meaning

So far in this chapter you have learned about how children perceive and recognize spoken language and divide the speech stream into discrete 'words'. I have put the term 'words' inside quotation marks because a sequence of sounds does not, of course, become a word until it acquires a meaning.

In order to begin to understand words, young children not only have to identify a 'word' in the speech stream but they also have to detect a consistent relationship between the appearance of the 'word' and some event that occurs at the same time. You will know from the previous chapter that children have a head start in detecting relationships between 'words' and objects because they are able to group similar objects into a single category. However, while this ability is crucial, a child at the very beginning of language development still has to link a 'word' with a particular object category. Also there are many cases in early word comprehension where children learn about personal names and words that describe actions, which cannot be linked to concrete objects. So what general mechanisms might underlie the way that children discover the meaning of first words?

Bruner's theory

One theory that provides a useful framework for thinking about early word learning was put forward by Bruner (1975, 1993). His key insight was that young children encounter language in highly familiar social contexts because people generally talk to them about familiar events and objects. So they hear speech that relates to events, objects and people that they are already familiar with and that are quite likely to be present or happening along with the speech.

To illustrate Bruner's theory, consider the following specific example of the way that early word meanings arise from a familiar social routine. The example comes from the diary records I kept of my daughter, Francesca, as she began to master her first words.

Francesca always lay on a changing-table in her bedroom while her nappy was changed. From about 3 months of age, when Francesca had her new nappy on and her clothes re-fastened, I would take her by the hands and ask 'Are you ready?'. Then I would gently pull Francesca up into a sitting position. When Francesca was 4 months old, I noticed that she would start to lift her head from the changing-table when I asked, 'Are you ready?'. What was striking was that Francesca did not try to lift her head as soon as I took hold of her hands but she actually waited for the crucial question. At first, Francesca would try to lift her head only when I asked the question in the specific context of nappy changing. However, 1 month later, Francesca's understanding had increased so that she responded both when her father asked the question and in other situations. Indeed the whole routine developed into a game in which Francesca lay on her back and her father or I took hold of her hands. She would then look intently up at our faces and, as she heard 'Are you ready?', she would attempt to pull herself up. This game was repeated many times on each occasion to our mutual delight.

Francesca's understanding of 'Are you ready?' grew directly out of the routine that took place at the end of nappy changing. It is clear from this example that, by 4 months of age, she had become sufficiently familiar with this routine to be able to predict what came next. She was then able to associate the question 'Are you ready?' with being raised into a sitting position and so to anticipate this event by raising her own head from the changing-table when she heard the familiar question. This instance of language comprehension, which arose directly in the context of a highly familiar social routine involving the infant and adult, is an example of what Bruner describes in his theory.

If first words grow out of familiar social contexts it should be possible to show that there is a close relationship between what parents say to their children and the events that are occurring at the time. The next activity gives you an opportunity to examine this relationship in detail.

Activity 4   The social context of early language experience

Allow about
30 minutes

This will help you to examine the way in which things that are said to young children often relate closely to what they are doing, and how this impacts on language development.

The following is part of a transcript made in a study by myself and two colleagues (Harris, *et al.*, 1983). It records a conversation between a mother and her 10-month-old daughter.

When the transcript begins, the child (who is just learning to walk) is standing holding onto the arm of a chair with one hand. The mother is sitting on the floor next to her child.

The first column of the transcript shows the time (in minutes and seconds) at which a particular utterance was made during the session. The second column records the mother's utterances and activity, and the third column describes what the child was doing and saying. If you look at the child's column you will see that she is not yet saying any words but she is babbling (recorded as 'vocalizes' on the transcript). Where an utterance is shown on the same line as an activity, they happened at the same time.

Look at the mother's utterances in the transcript (numbered 1–13) and work out what she is talking about in each case. Then draw a table as shown in the illustration below the transcript. In your table, write each of the mother's utterances in the appropriate numbered row in the second column. Then, in the third column write a brief description of the topic of each of the mother's utterances. Be sure to include the following information:

- Is the mother responding to something that has just happened?
- Is the mother describing something that the *child* is doing?
- Is the mother talking about something that *she* is doing?

There are two example answers shown in Figure 4 to help you.

Transcript of a conversation between a Mother (M) and her 10-month-old child (C). Utterances are shown in bold type

Time	Mother	Child 10 months old
		touches teddy on floor
00.01	(1) That's your teddy yeah.	
	(2) That's your teddy.	
		picks up small teddy
		puts it next to toy emu on floor
00.05	(3) And that one as well?	
	picks up emu	
	(4) That's a very strange looking thing.	
	making emu peck C	
		vocalizes, points at emu
		vocalizes
	sits big teddy up	
		turns to look at teddy
00.24	(5) There he is.	
	(6) He's bigger than you.	
		picks up small teddy then drops it
	rubs nose of small teddy on big teddy	
	(7) Yes look.	
		takes arm from chair
00.38	puts hand out to C	
	(8) Are you balanced?	
	(9) Come on then.	
	(10) Are you coming?	
		puts out hand to M then steps back to chair
00.50	(11) No all right.	
		bends down and points to small teddy
	picks up small teddy and shows to C	
	(12) There's yours.	
	rubs nose of small teddy on big teddy	
00.59	(13) Are they rubbing noses?	
		vocalizes, pointing to teddy bears

Source: Harris et al., 1983.

No	Mother's utterance	Topic of utterance
1	That's your teddy yeah.	Mother responding to child touching teddy.
2		
3		
4	That's a very strange looking thing.	Mother is talking about something she is doing – making the emu peck the child.
5		

Figure 4   Example answers for Activity 4.

Comment

In our study we found that the majority of a mother's utterances referred to objects or events that her child was *currently* attending to. The extract that you have just analysed was typical of what we found. All of the mother's utterances refer to something that has just happened, to something that the child is attending to, or the utterance actively directs the child's attention onto a particular object. The first two utterances occur immediately after the child has touched a teddy on the floor. Then the child picks up the teddy and puts it next to a toy emu (which was a glove puppet). The mother immediately responds by saying, 'And that one as well?'. She then picks up the emu, puts her arm inside it and says, 'That's a very strange looking thing'. As she says this, she makes the emu peck the child.

You will see that most of the mother's utterances follow on from something the child had done immediately beforehand. However, as well as taking her lead from the child, the mother also provides supporting actions of her own that serve to make her general meaning clear.

Notice that utterances 8–11 are all concerned with the child's attempts to walk towards her mother, hence they are focused on the child's current actions rather than objects. The conversation then returns to the topic of the toy animals.

Bruner himself does not give many specific examples of exactly how familiarity with the social context might help young children to understand what adults are saying to them. It is clear, however, that different kinds of words place different demands on young children. Like the child's attempts at walking in the activity above, Francesca's understanding of 'Are you ready?' was not focused on a particular object since she was learning to associate a question ('Are you ready?') with an action (lifting her head in anticipation of being pulled up). However, in many other cases, a young child has to learn that a particular personal name (such as 'mummy') is associated with the presence of a particular person, or that a particular object name (such as 'ball') is associated with the presence of a particular object.

Cues to reference

The development of an understanding of associations of this kind – between sounds and personal names or objects – is only possible if a child has some way of deciding *what* an adult is talking about. There are two specific cues that seem to be significant. These are gaze direction and pointing. Gaze direction alone can be difficult to interpret. However, when someone turns to look at a particular object or person, they often turn their head. Together, gaze, head turning and pointing can provide invaluable cues to reference, that is, what someone is referring to when they use a particular word.

Activity 5   *Cues to reference*

Allow about
5 minutes

This activity will help you to evaluate the different cues to reference that people use.

Imagine that you are listening to an unfamiliar language and have begun to recognize the sounds of a few words. Now you want to know they mean. Think about how much you could tell from where a speaker is looking or from where they are pointing. Which is the better cue? Can you think of any other cues that might be used? Make a brief note of your answer before reading further.

Comment

It turns out that pointing provides a more accurate cue to reference than either gaze or head movement alone. This is true for both infants and adults. Adults are better at working out what another person is referring to when the other person points than when they merely turn to look at a particular object, and infants can locate an object more accurately when someone points at it rather than merely looking at it (Butterworth, 1998). Another cue that people sometimes use is to touch or pick up an object that is being named. Parents sometimes pick up and animate objects that they are naming for children.

Pointing

Baldwin (1995) looked at the significance of pointing in the acquisition of new vocabulary. She studied the amount of time that infants looked at a novel object when an adult pointed to it and compared this with the time spent looking at an object when there was no pointing. Infants, who were as young as 10 months of age, spent significantly longer looking at objects when an adult pointed. When an adult named an object, as well as pointing to it, the amount of looking was even greater, suggesting that the young child is most predisposed to look at objects that are singled out both through pointing and through naming.

However, there appears to be an even closer relationship between pointing and first words than that illustrated by Baldwin. In a longitudinal study, Harris, *et al.*, (1995a) found that the age at which children first pointed – which was around

10 months – was highly correlated with the age at which they first showed signs of understanding the names of objects. This close relationship between pointing and the understanding of object names is well illustrated by another example from Francesca. Again, the example comes from the detailed diary records that I kept.

> The first object name that Francesca understood was 'nose'. She began by touching the nose on a toy koala bear when asked and then, the following day, she was asked 'Where's mummy's nose?' and 'Where's daddy's nose?'. Francesca reached out and touched her parents' noses. This first occurred when she was just over 9 months old. The very same day she pointed at a plant in the conservatory. This was the first time that she pointed.

This close relationship in time between first referring to objects in the world by pointing at them and first understanding an object name suggests that these are closely interlinked processes that may well have a common origin. For example, when sighted children read picture books with their care-givers, there is a shared attention to individual objects and animals through pointing. This seems to be one way in which infants acquire object names. However, since using pointing in this way obviously depends on a child's vision, it is relevant to ask what happens if an infant is blind and this activity is not accessible in the same way. Blind children have been found to produce significantly fewer words for discrete objects than sighted infants (Norgate, 1997) and this supports the importance of pointing in acquiring object names.

3.2 Early word comprehension

Most infants begin to comprehend words when they are around 7 or 8 months old. The first words to be understood are typically the child's own name and the names of other family members such as *mummy* and *daddy* and the names of familiar objects such as *clock*, *drink* and *teddy* (Harris *et al.*, 1995b).

   Much of the evidence about the development of comprehension comes from parental reports. More recently, researchers have been able to gain more standardized information from parents by asking them to use a checklist of the words that a young child might understand. The MacArthur Communicative Development Inventories (Fenson *et al.*, 1994) have been used extensively to gather data about early language development in children between 8 and 28 months.

Reading

SG

At this point you should turn to the end of this chapter and read Reading B, 'Developments in early lexical comprehension: a comparison of parental report and controlled testing' by Harris and Chasin (1999). This paper considers the accuracy of parental reports of early comprehension and compares data collected using the MacArthur checklist with data derived from experimental testing of comprehension. As you read this paper, think about the factors that might contribute to the accuracy of parental reports about vocabulary.

Figure 5 shows the average number of words understood by boys and girls between 8 and 16 months of age as reported by their parents who completed the MacArthur checklist. You can see two clear patterns. Girls are generally ahead of boys in the number of words they can understand. However, for both boys and girls, the overall pattern of development is essentially similar. The total number of words comprehended grows fairly slowly up to about 12 months of age. Then there is a sudden increase in vocabulary size.

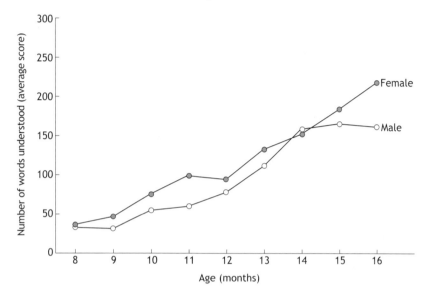

Figure 5   Average numbers of words understood by boys and girls between 8 and 16 months of age (adapted from Fenson et al., 1994, p. 74).

The vocabulary spurt

This increase in comprehension vocabulary size has been noted in many studies, and, as you will see below, there is a similar increase in production vocabulary as well. The increase is usually described as a 'vocabulary explosion' or 'vocabulary spurt'.

There are several different theories about why this spurt appears. One early theory was that it reflects the development of a 'naming insight' (Dore, 1978; McShane, 1979). The idea is that children suddenly realize that all objects have a name. However, this theory does not stand up to inspection because, as I have already mentioned, children understand some object names very early on. Another possible explanation is that the vocabulary spurt is a sign of a more general change in cognitive development. Again there seems to be a problem with this explanation for two reasons. Not all typically developing children show a vocabulary spurt and the spurts in comprehension and production do not usually occur together. In most cases the comprehension spurt occurs before the spurt in production.

Connectionist model
A computer simulation with many nodes and connections between them. As stimuli are presented, the activation levels of the nodes change, as do the weightings of the connections between the nodes. Such models can be 'trained' to learn about and recognize particular stimuli, and are often seen as useful models for how brains learn.

SG

Connectionist models of vocabulary learning

One recent explanation for the vocabulary spurt comes from *connectionist modelling*. Connectionist models make use of computers to simulate learning and they have been used to model a number of developmental processes including vocabulary learning.

One of the important developmental findings to emerge from connectionist modelling is that sudden changes in the rate of learning often emerge as the computer learns. These changes occur even though the process of learning continues in exactly the same way from beginning to end. It is as though learning becomes easier simply because a significant amount has already been learned.

Plunkett and Marchman (1993) developed a connectionist model of vocabulary learning in which the computer's task was to match labels to images. The computer's learning demonstrated the typical 'spurt' that has been found in many studies of early vocabulary development in children. In the connectionist model, success at matching labels to images was rather low for the first 20–30 label–image matches but after that there was a dramatic increase in the success rate. You can see the results of the Plunkett and Marchman study in Figure 6.

Clearly young children and computers do not behave in exactly the same way when they are learning. For one thing, computers have access to the memory of all that they have ever experienced while children do not. However, the central concept that comes from connectionist modelling is probably not specific to computers and could also apply to children's learning. This is that the rate of learning increases rather suddenly once a certain point in the learning process has been reached. If this concept is applied to early vocabulary it is no longer necessary to posit an additional ability to account for the vocabulary spurt. The idea that an increase in the rate of learning is a function of learning itself also means that it is not necessary to propose two separate mechanisms to underpin the spurt in comprehension and production.

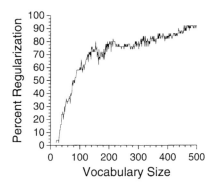

Figure 6   Changes over time in the success rate of a connectionist model matching labels to images. The vertical axis indicates the degree of success at matching. The horizontal axis shows the increase over time in the number of label–image pairs presented to the module (Plunkett and Marchman, 1993).

Summary of Section 3

- Children hear language in familiar social contexts. Such contexts provide them with familiar and predictable settings in which they can link often repeated adult words to familiar events or objects. Adult pointing serves as a useful cue when a word refers to a familiar object.
- Comprehension of words begins at around 7 months of age and the initial rate of word learning is slow. This is typically followed by an increase – or spurt – in the rate of learning.

4   Learning to say words

4.1 Babbling

Phonetic contrasts
Differences between the individual sounds that make up speech.

SG

Very young infants can distinguish a wide range of phonetic contrasts and, over the first year of life, they gradually lose the ability to discriminate contrasts that are not present in the language they hear around them (Werker and Tees, 1984).

Over the same time period, significant developments are taking place in infants' abilities to produce the sounds that they can hear. The development of 'babbling' – as this early sound-making is called – is divided into a number of stages.

- At first, babies do not produce speech-like sounds but they do make a number of different sounds. By 3 months, these sounds begin to be used communicatively and special sounds are used when babies are interacting with other people. This is known as *cooing*.
- By about 4 months, babies begin to engage in *vocal play* when they experiment with the loudness and pitch of their vocalizations and the position of their tongue. This experimentation gradually allows infants to produce adult-like vowels and some of the features of adult-like consonants.
- Around 6 months, another important change occurs in babbling. At this age, babies first begin to produce recognizable syllables. These are made up of a consonant sound and a vowel. Very early sounds include *da* and *ba*. Oller (1980) describes this 'prototypical' or 'basic' stage as *canonical babbling*.
- A little later, at around 8 months, babies begin to produce *reduplicated babbling* in which the same sound is repeated as in *da-da* and *ba-ba*.
- Around 10 months there is another change as babies become capable of *variegated babbling* (Oller, 1980). At this final stage, babies begin to follow one sound with another, similar sound such as *ba-da* or *da-de*.

4.2 Development of the vocal tract

In the early months, babies' vocalizations sound distinctively different from the speech sounds that we make as adults. One way to understand what gives babbling its characteristic sound is to look at the structure of the infant vocal tract. You can see a picture of the infant vocal tract in Figure 7.

Activity 6   *Why do babies sound different from adults?*

Allow about 15 minutes

This will help you to compare the physical characteristics of the adult vocal tract with those of the infant vocal tract and reflect on how such differences might impact on the production of speech sounds.

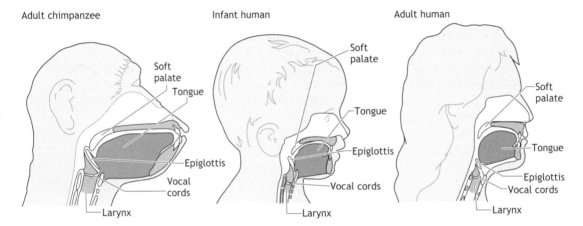

Figure 7   The anatomy of the vocal tract of chimpanzees and infant and adult humans.

Look at the three pictures in Figure 7 which show the vocal tracts of an adult chimpanzee, an infant human and an adult human. Look carefully at the size and position of the tongue and the position of the larynx (voice box) in each picture. Next, draw and fill in a table like the one below and use the information you have gathered to decide whether the infant is more like an adult human or more like a chimpanzee in the structure of its vocal tract. In order to compare the position of the tongue and larynx you may find it helpful to draw a line from the lips to the larynx and look at the angle that is created.

	Chimpanzee	Infant human	Adult human
Size of tongue relative to mouth			
Position of tongue relative to lips			
Position of larynx relative to lips			

Comment

The infant human's vocal tract is not simply a miniature version of the adult human tract and, up to the age of 3 months, it actually resembles the vocal tract of a chimpanzee more closely than that of an adult human. The infant's larynx is positioned high up so that the epiglottis nearly touches the soft palate at the back of the mouth. The baby's tongue is large in relation to the size of the mouth, nearly filling the oral cavity, while the pharynx is very short compared to that of an adult, allowing little room for the back portion of the tongue to be manipulated.

▲

The reason for the characteristic shape of the infant vocal tract at birth becomes clear once you realize that the main purpose of the infant's tongue in the first weeks after birth is to enable the strong piston-like movements that are essential for sucking. Once the first 4 months are over, and the baby has gained in weight, sucking becomes less of a priority. At this point, the vocal tract gradually changes into a more adult-like form so that infants can produce the complex range of movements that will be required for speech. Changes in the anatomy of the vocal tract are accompanied by neural maturation of the related motor areas in the brain. Together these developments enable infants to develop increasing control over the fine motor movements that are essential for producing the full range of speech sounds.

4.3 Early word production

The sounds that children produce towards the end of the first year, such as *ba* and *da*, feature in their first words. Children's early words are almost always phonetic simplifications of adult forms and it is not until the age of 5 or 6 that they can accurately produce all of the phonemes and combinations of phonemes that are used in a particular language.

Figure 8 shows how production vocabulary develops up to the age of 16 months. As with the graph that you looked at earlier for comprehension (Figure 5), the data

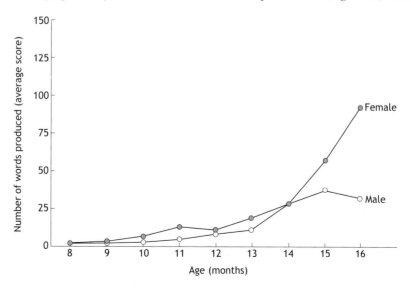

Figure 8   Average numbers of words produced by boys and girls between 8 and 16 months of age (adapted from Fenson *et al.*, 1994, p. 75).

are taken from the MacArthur study (Fenson *et al.,* 1994). Although parents are often unsure about children's early understanding of words, they can usually provide very reliable information about the new words that their children are producing. When collecting such data it helps to provide parents with clear instructions about what counts as a word. This is important because young children often simplify and shorten long words (e.g. saying *nana* for banana or *mama* for mummy), and hence such utterances, although not strictly words, need to be counted as such.

The MacArthur data show that most children produce their first word at around 10 months and gradually produce more words over the next few months. As with comprehension, there is a sudden increase in the rate of learning new words. This occurs around 13 months, and at this point girls are, on average, significantly ahead of boys in the number of words they are able to produce.

4.4 A comparison of comprehension and production vocabularies

Compare Figures 5 and 8 which show the graphs for comprehension and production vocabularies over the same period. You will see that the number of words children produce tends to be smaller than the number that they can comprehend. As you might expect, there was a significant correlation between comprehension and production in the MacArthur study. To put it another way, the greater the number of words children produce, the greater the number they understand. However the correlation was only 0.45 after age was removed from the analysis. (It was necessary to remove the age factor from the correlation since both comprehension and production vocabularies are likely to increase with age.) Although the correlation of 0.45 was highly significant with a large sample of children, the correlation accounts for only 20 per cent of the total variability. This means that there is a lot of independent variation in production and comprehension vocabulary size during development. This suggests that, while there is a general relationship between the size of children's comprehension and production vocabularies, this relationship is not the same for all children.

The MacArthur data show there is a clearly identifiable sub-group of children who have a large comprehension vocabulary (more than 150 words) but few if any words in their production vocabulary. Children like this acquire a very large comprehension vocabulary before saying their first word. I have also found a third, less frequent pattern in a longitudinal study of six children (Harris *et al.,* 1995a). Two of the children (Ben and Katy) understood only one or two words before they said their first word. Also the gap between the children understanding their first word and producing their first word was less than one month. If you look back at Figures 5 and 8 and compare them you will see that the usual lag is around 3 months.

Summary of Section 4

- Babbling goes through a series of stages from vocal play at 4 months to variegated babbling at 10 months.
- During this period the infant's vocal tract changes into a more adult-like form. This enables infants to produce a wider range of speech sounds.
- Children show variation in the age at which they first begin to produce words. Precocious talkers may produce their first word as early as 9 or 10 months but many children do not produce their first word until well into their second year. Some children understand as many as 150 words before they produce their first word.
- The size of children's production vocabularies is generally related to the size of their comprehension vocabularies. However the same relationship does not hold for all children.

5   The meaning of children's first words

So far you have read about the growth in children's comprehension and production of first words. However, I have not yet said anything about what first words *mean*. Early word meaning has been a topic of considerable debate among child language researchers and there has been a significant shift in the prevailing view.

5.1 Types of words

The most common view of early word meaning in the mid 1980s was that children's first words are *context-bound*. Context-bound words are produced in only one specific situation or context (Barrett, 1986). This very restricted use contrasts strongly with the way in which adults and older children use words naming objects or actions. For them, if a word serves as a name for something it will be used in a variety of different situations.

Here are some examples of context-bound words taken from a study that I carried out with a number of colleagues to look at the factors associated with children's production of first words (Harris *et al.*, 1988). James, one of the children we studied, initially used *mummy* only when he was handing a toy to his mother and *there* only when pointing up to a picture on a frieze. Another child, Jenny, initially used *bye-bye* only when she was waving goodbye.

Although young children do use some words in a single context, there is now extensive evidence that not all early words are used in this way. Bates *et al.* (1988) describe some very early words as being *contextually flexible* because children produced them in more than one context.

You have just read about James's use of *mummy* and *there* which were both context-bound. However, it is notable that James also used words in a contextually flexible way. He used *teddy* to refer to one particular teddy in a variety of different contexts (for example, when he was sitting on a teddy and when he was pointing to the teddy's reflection in a mirror). He also used the word *more* when he was reaching into a toybox for some bricks, taking another drink from his cup or holding out an empty bowl. Another child in our study, a girl called Madeleine, first used the word *shoes* in a range of situations including looking at pictures of shoes in a book, pointing at her own shoes and also when holding her doll's shoes.

In our study (Harris *et al.*, 1988), we looked at the first ten words produced by four different children. Table 1 shows the number of context-bound and contextually flexible words that the children produced.

Table 1   The number of context-bound and contextually flexible words produced by four children. Words in bold type were initially used as names for objects

Type of word	James	Jacqui	Jenny	Madeleine
Context-bound	Mummy Go Quack There Buzz Moo Boo	Wee Hello Mummy Here No Down More Go	Choo-choo Bye-bye There	There Hello Here Bye-bye
Contextually flexible	**Teddy** **Ball** More	Jacqui **Bee**	**Teddy** **Doggy** **Moo** **Shoe** **Car** Mummy No	**Teddy** **Shoes** **Brum** **Woof** **Baby** Yes

Source: Harris et al., 1988.

You will see from the table that all the children produced words of both types although there was variation from child to child in the relative number of each type. Jenny and Madeleine produced more contextually flexible words, whereas James and Jacqui both produced more context-bound words.

You will also see that several of the words in the table – the ones in bold – were initially used as the names for objects. This is consistent with the view that children do not suddenly develop a 'naming insight' but in fact use object names right from the beginning. Data from a study by Goldfield and Reznick (1990) support this view. In a longitudinal study of 24 children, starting from the age of just over 1 year, they found that half of the early words used by the children before the vocabulary spurt were object names.

SG

However, this same study also found that a small number of children showed a more gradual rate of lexical growth. These children seemed to be acquiring a broader range of different word types, while most of the children, who were acquiring mainly object words in their early language development, were more likely to show the rapid increase in rate of learning. This suggests that there may be different pathways in early language development, but a common feature for many children is a period when learning names for things is a dominant strategy. Issues relating to individual variability and their links to the vocabulary spurt will be discussed further in Section 6.

5.2 The role of experience

First words

Earlier in this chapter you read about Bruner's theory and saw that children's early experience of language occurs within the context of familiar social routines. Our study explored the extent to which children's first words grow directly out of their experience (Harris *et al.*, 1988).

You saw the first words that were produced by the children in our study in Table 1. We had two ways of finding out about how these first words were used. We asked the parents to keep a record of all the occasions when a child used a word. We also filmed the children and their mothers talking and playing together in a laboratory. These two sources of information allowed us to maintain a very accurate record of the children's first words so that we could see precisely how they were using them.

We made recordings of the mothers and children in the laboratory every 2 weeks. This meant that we also had a detailed sample of the mother's utterances over the course of the study. We started filming when the children were 6 months old and carried on until they were 2 years old. As soon as we were sure that a child was using a word, we looked at the mother's utterances that we had recorded in the previous month. We identified all the mother's uses of that word. Then we found out how many times she had used the word and in how many different ways she had used it.

We found that the children's use of their first words bore a very close resemblance to the mother's use of these same words. Of the 40 words that we studied (shown in Table 1) there were only three cases where there was no apparent relationship between a child's use and the mother's use of that word in the preceding month. Furthermore, for 33 out of the 40 words, the child's use was *identical* to the mother's most frequent use. For example, the first word used by James was *Mummy* but, rather puzzlingly, he initially restricted its use to situations where he was holding out a toy for his mother to take. This apparently idiosyncratic use of *Mummy* was explained when we found that his mother had most commonly used this word when holding out her hand to take a toy saying, 'Is that for Mummy?'.

Table 2 gives some other examples of the children's first words and their mothers' use of the same word.

You can see from these examples that *hello* was rather like *Mummy* in that the child had a single use that corresponded exactly to the mother's use. As in the case of James's use of *Mummy*, the corresponding mother's use was her most frequent use of *hello* when talking to her child. The other two examples are more complex because the first use of these words is contextually flexible. *Teddy* is an object name that the child first used only to refer to one particular teddy. (We know that it was an object name rather than a personal name because the child rapidly used it to refer to other teddies.) The mother's use was similar because she also used *teddy* to refer to a particular big teddy. *No* was used by Jenny in a range of situations where an anticipated action was not going to be carried out. Interestingly Jenny used *no* both to refuse an action that was requested by her mother and also in connection with her own action. Again you can see that the mother's own use of this word covered a similar range.

Table 2   Examples of four children's first words and their mothers' use of the same word

Word	Child's initial use	Mother's most similar use
Hello (Context-bound)	Child speaking into telephone receiver	Child speaking into telephone receiver (Mother says 'Say Hello')
Teddy (Contextually flexible)	Child labelling big teddy	Mother pointing at or holding big teddy Child playing with big teddy
No (Contextually flexible)	Child refusing an offered drink Child crawling to step which she is forbidden to crawl down Child refusing to comply with Mother's request	Mother telling child not to suck toy Mother commenting on child's refusal Child putting shape into incorrect hole of shape sorter

Source: Harris et al.*, 1988.*

The development of word meaning

It is important to note that the very close relationship between children's words and their mother's speech is limited to the first uses of first words. When a child subsequently acquires a new use of the same word, we found a much weaker relationship between the child's use and the mother's use (Barrett *et al.*, 1991). For example, James's use of *Mummy* expanded from being used only when he was handing a toy to this mother to being used only when he was cuddling her. We found that, for second uses, the proportion of cases where the child's use had a precedent in the mother's own use dropped to 45 per cent. This compared to the figure of 93 per cent that we had found for initial uses of the first ten words.

A study by Hart (1991) also shows that the importance of direct experience becomes much less important as children acquire more words. Hart compared early vocabulary with later vocabulary to see whether there was a difference in the frequency with which children heard the words that they acquire early on. Hart found that there was a difference. Children's first words tended to be the ones that their parents frequently used when talking to them – on average these words occurred 30 times in a monthly observation session. However, when the children were 6 months older, the words that they were acquiring had typically been used only twice in parental speech during an observation session.

Some effects of language experience do, however, appear to be of longer duration. Children learning English have a predominance of object names in their early vocabulary and relatively few verbs. In contrast, Gopnik and Choi (1995) found that verbs appear earlier, and form a greater proportion of early vocabulary in the speech of children acquiring Korean, while Tardif (1996) found that 21-month-old children who were learning Mandarin Chinese had as many different verbs as nouns in their vocabulary. These patterns reflect the fact that Korean- and Mandarin-speaking mothers use relatively more verbs than English-speaking mothers when they are talking to young children. It is thought that this is a result of the difference in structure between Korean and Mandarin (both of which emphasize verbs), and English (which emphasizes nouns).

Language experience and language delay

SG

If first words are rooted so firmly in children's early language experience then there should be some evidence that children's first words can be delayed if there is insufficient opportunity to identify words and to link them to a familiar event, person or object.

For children with typically developing language, there is a close correspondence between what mothers say and what is happening. As you saw earlier, the study by Harris *et al.* (1983) found that 78 per cent of maternal utterances to 16-month-old infants referred to objects on which the child was currently focusing attention.

In a later study, we had an opportunity to compare mothers' speech to typically developing children with the speech used to a small group of children with delayed language at 2 years. It turned out that the mothers of the children with delayed language referred far less often to objects that the child was attending to. For them, the proportion was just under 50 per cent.

The difference between the groups was even greater when we looked at the way that mothers referred to objects. For the children with typical language development at 2 years, almost half of the mothers' utterances contained at least one specific object name (where the object mentioned was one that the child was attending to). However, this proportion of specific object references was only 25 per cent for the children with slower language development. Mothers of children with delayed language were more likely to refer to objects using general names, such as *one* or *thing*, rather than specific names, such as *ball* or *teddy.*

Activity 6   *Differences associated with language delay*

Allow about
5 minutes

This will help you to think about possible reasons why mothers' speech to their children with language delay is different.

Read the four paragraphs above on language experience and language delay again. Note down at least two contrasting explanations for the differences in the speech of mother's of children with language delay, as compared with mothers of children with typical language development.

Comment

There are at least two possible explanations for the relationship between the mothers' speech and the children's language.

One possibility is that the differences in the mothers' speech in the two groups arose *because* of differences in the language ability between the groups. In other words, the two groups of mothers might have been talking differently because the two groups of children responded in different ways to what they were saying.

Another possible explanation is that these differences in maternal speech were responsible, at least in part, for the differences in the children's language ability.

There is good reason to prefer the second of the explanations offered above. When we sampled the speech of the two sets of mothers, both groups of children, who were then 16 months old, were producing similar speech. Evidence of differences among the children did not appear until several months later. At 2 years of age, the slower developers were still producing single words but the typical developers were producing utterances that were several words long. The groups also differed in their vocabulary size, with the typical developers producing significantly more words than the slower developers. Because these differences between the groups did not emerge until several months *after* the mothers' speech was sampled, it seems unlikely that the speech style of the mothers was influenced by the speech of their children, but rather that the maternal speech style was influencing the language development. These findings can therefore be seen as evidence that the close tying of maternal speech to the current social context is an important factor in early language development.

However, the issue of the causes and effects of language delay is complex. For example, it is possible that the 16-month measures of children's speech did not capture some aspects of the children's speech that were differentially affecting the mothers' behaviour. It is also possible that the children with language delay were less able to make use of their mothers' speech to them. What we can be sure of is that there is an interactive relationship between mothers' speech and their children's language development.

Summary of Section 5

- First words can have a variety of meanings. Some are context-bound and are used only in a single context. Others are contextually flexible which means they are used in a less restricted way. Some of these contextually flexible words are object names or the names of people. Others are used to describe events.
- There is a close relationship between children's use of first words and their experience of hearing words being used by adults in conversation with them. Early words arise from situations where children hear the same words being used in a consistent way to describe particular objects and events.
- As children acquire more words, they soon become less dependent on their experiences. Later words have to be heard less often in order for children to acquire them.
- Children who do not have the opportunity to hear words being used consistently in familiar situations can find that the process of acquiring first words is more difficult.
- Whereas it was once thought that children's first words were always context-bound, there is now evidence to suggest that this is not always the case.

6 Individual differences in first words

6.1 Variations in the rate of development

The graphs in Figures 9 and 10 are similar to the graphs you looked at earlier for the MacArthur norms for children's early comprehension and production vocabularies (Figures 5 and 8). However, this time they show not only the average (mean) numbers of words reported by parents but also the variation in vocabulary size. This is depicted by the lines that mark one standard deviation above and below the mean (labelled +1 SD and −1 SD on the graph).

The MacArthur data show that children vary considerably in the rate at which they understand and produce new words. The children's comprehension at 16 months ranges from 100 to 270 words whereas their production vocabulary at the same age ranges from 0 to 130 words.

This high degree of variability in vocabulary size at a given age means that it is rather misleading to talk about the 'average child'. Many children do not start to produce words until they are 18 months old as indicated in Figure 9 by the large number of children who are not saying any words at all at 16 months of age. However, in spite of this variability, parents and health professionals still need to know when a young child is showing signs of language delay.

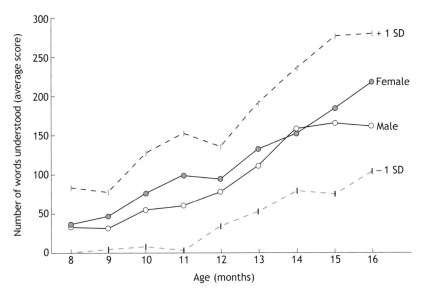

Figure 9   Amount of variation in the numbers of words understood between the ages of 8 and 16 months by boys and girls (Fenson *et al.*, 1994, pp. 74–5).

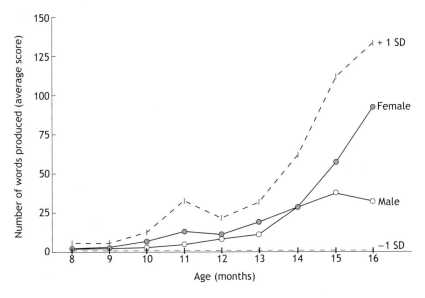

Figure 10   Amount of variation in the numbers of words produced between the ages of 8 and 16 months by boys and girls (Fenson *et al.*, 1994, pp. 74–5).

Although not all children will be producing words by 18 months of age, most will comprehend a considerable number of words at this age. This suggests that the first thing to look for when a child is not yet talking is vocabulary comprehension. If comprehension is poor relative to the norms, this could well be a sign of language delay. Another indication that can be used in younger children is babbling. The stages of babbling that you read about in Section 4 are fairly similar for all children. If a child is not producing canonical babbling by 10 months of age, this is a strong indication of a specific language problem.

6.2 Variations in vocabulary content

Children also show individual variation in the proportions of different kinds of words that make up their vocabulary. Most children have more object names in their early vocabulary than any other kind of word. However, the actual proportion of object names varies, with some children having many more such words. Nelson (1973) identified two distinctive styles in early language development which she labelled *expressive* and *referential* styles. Children who adopted the referential style had a large proportion of object names in their first 50 words, while expressive children had fewer object names but more action words and people's names.

Nelson argued that the kind of words that children produce is related to their overall rate of language development. Her argument was supported by data from a study by Bates *et al.* (1988). They found that the children who acquire a greater proportion of object names tended to build up a vocabulary more quickly than children who have fewer object names in their early vocabulary (up to the age of about 18 months). This supported Nelson's argument that children who adopted a referential style would have faster vocabulary development.

More recently, however, data collected using the MacArthur checklist (Fenson *et al.*, 1994) have shown that the relationship between vocabulary content and the rate of vocabulary development is more complex than Nelson had suggested. Fenson *et al.* considered children who had vocabulary sizes of between 20 and 50 words. This is the same range of vocabulary that Nelson considered, so it is legitimate to compare her conclusions with those of Fenson *et al.*

Fenson *et al.* found that the proportion of object names in this vocabulary size varied considerably with a range from 12 per cent to 100 per cent. As Nelson had argued, there was a link between vocabulary size and vocabulary content. For children with a small vocabulary, the proportion of object names was under 24 per cent. However, for children who had a large vocabulary, this proportion was at least 62 per cent. These two most extreme groups were clearly very different and could unambiguously be classified as having expressive and referential styles according to the proportion of object names. However, close analysis showed that the children with a more referential style were actually *older* than children with a less referential style. So this did not support the view that children who produced a large proportion of object names were more precocious in their language development.

Fenson *et al.* (1994) did, however, find that girls typically had more object names in their early vocabulary than boys. Since girls tend to be ahead of boys in the development of first words, it may be that there is something in Nelson's theory. It is also worth mentioning that the MacArthur data reported by Fenson *et al.* are not longitudinal. The average values for vocabulary size were derived from different children at each age point so it is still possible that individual rates of development may be linked to vocabulary content.

Summary of Section 6

- Children vary in the rate at which they acquire first words and also in the age at which they produce their first word. There are smaller differences in early comprehension.
- Children also show variation in the content of their early vocabularies. Some children, who adopt a referential style, have a large number of object names in their first 50 words. Other children, who have an expressive style, have a relatively low number of object names.

7 Conclusion

At the beginning of this chapter, I outlined a number of essential steps that are necessary for children to understand and produce their first words. You have now learned about each stage in this complex process and I want to end by asking you to reflect on the wide range of skills that come together when young children begin to build up a vocabulary.

Look again at the chart of component skills that you saw in Section 1.

Learning first words: stages in learning

	WORD COMPREHENSION	WORD PRODUCTION
Identify a word from the speech stream		
Remember what the word sounds like so that you can recognize it when you hear it again		
Link the word with some consistent event e.g. an object or action		
Repeat the sound of the word		
Say the word in an appropriate context		

When you consider all the skills that come together in learning first words, you can begin to appreciate what an extraordinary achievement it is when children first comprehend and produce words. And that, as you will see in Chapter 4, is only the beginning of a learning process that continues for many years until children become fully competent in their native language.

References

Baldwin, D. A. (1995) 'Understanding the link between joint attention and language', in Moore, C. and Dunham, P. J. (eds) *Joint Attention: its origins and role in development*, pp. 131–58, Hillsdale, NJ, Erlbaum.

Barrett, M. D. (1986) 'Early semantic representations and early word usage', in Kuczaj, S. A. and Barrett, M. D. (eds) *The Development of Word Meaning*, pp. 313–34, New York, Springer-Verlag.

Barrett, M. D., Harris, M. and Chasin, J. (1991) 'Early lexical development and maternal speech: A comparison of children's initial and subsequent uses of words', *Journal of Child Language,* vol. 18, pp. 21–40.

Bates, E., Bretherton, I., and Snyder, L. (1988) *From First Words to Grammar: individual differences and dissociable mechanisms*, Cambridge, Cambridge University Press.

Bruner, J. S. (1975) 'The ontogenesis of speech acts', *Journal of Child Language,* vol. 2, pp. 1–19.

Bruner, J. S. (1993) *Child's Talk: learning to use language*, New York, Norton.

Butterworth, G. (1998) 'What is special about pointing in babies?', in Simion, F. and Butterworth, G. (eds) *The Development of Sensory, Motor and Cognitive Capacities in Early Infancy*, pp. 63–88, Hove, Psychology Press.

Christophe, A. and Morton, J. (1998) 'Is Dutch native English? Linguistic analysis by 2-month-olds', *Developmental Science,* vol. 1, pp. 215–19.

DeCasper, A. J. and Fifer, W. (1980) 'Of human bonding: newborns prefer their mothers' voices', *Science,* vol. 208, pp. 1174–6.

DeCasper, A. J. and Spence, M. J. (1986) 'Prenatal maternal speech influences newborns' perception of speech sounds', *Infant Behavior and Development,* vol. 9, pp. 133–50.

DeCasper, A. J., Lecanuet, J.-P., Busnel, M.-C., Granier-Deferre, C. and Maugeais, R. (1994) 'Fetal reactions to recurrent maternal speech', *Infant Behavior and Development,* vol. 17, pp. 159–64.

Dore, J. (1978) 'Conditions for the acquisition of speech acts', in Markova, L. (ed.) *The Social Context of Language*, pp. 87–111, New York, John Wiley.

Elman, J., Bates, E., Johnson, M., Karmiloff-Smith, A., Parisi, D. and Plunkett, K. (1996) *Rethinking Innateness: a connectionist perspective on development*, Cambridge, MA, MIT Press.

Fenson, L., Dale, P., Resnick, S., Bates, E., Thal, D. and Pethick, S. J. (1994) 'Variability in early communicative development', *Monographs of the Society for Research in Child Development,* vol. 59, pp. 1–73.

Goldfield, B. A. and Reznick, J. S. (1990) 'Early lexical acquisition: rate, content, and the vocabulary spurt', *Journal of Child Language,* vol. 17, pp. 171–83.

Gopnik, A. and Choi, S. (1995) 'Names, relational words and cognitive development in English and Korean speakers: nouns are not always learned before verbs', in Tomasello, M. and Merriman, W. E. (eds) *Beyond Names for Things: young children's acquisition of verbs*, pp. 83–90, Hillsdale, NJ, Lawrence Erlbaum Associates.

Harris, M. and Chasin, J. (1999) 'Developments in early lexical comprehension: a comparison of parental report and controlled testing', *Journal of Child Language*, vol. 26, pp. 453–60.

Harris, M., Jones, D. and Grant, J. (1983) 'The nonverbal context of mothers' speech to infants', *First Language*, vol. 4, pp. 21–30.

Harris, M., Barlow-Brown, F. and Chasin, J. (1995a) 'The emergence of referential understanding: pointing and the comprehension of object names', *First Language*, vol. 15, pp. 19–34.

Harris, M., Yeeles, C., Chasin, J. and Oakley, Y. (1995b) 'Symmetries and asymmetries in early lexical comprehension and production', *Journal of Child Language*, vol. 22, pp. 1–18.

Harris, M., Jones, D., Brookes, S. and Grant, J. (1986) 'Relations between the non-verbal context of maternal speech and rate of language development', *British Journal of Developmental Psychology*, vol. 4, pp. 261–8.

Harris, M., Barrett, M., Jones, D. and Brookes, S. (1988) 'Linguistic input and early word meaning', *Journal of Child Language*, vol. 15, pp. 77–94.

Hart, B. (1991) 'Input frequency and children's first words', *First Language*, vol. 11, pp. 289–300.

Johnson, E. K. and Jusczyk, P. W. (2001) 'Word segmentation by 8-month-olds: when speech cues count for more than statistics', *Journal of Memory and Language*, vol. 44, pp. 548–67.

McShane, J. (1979) 'The development of naming', *Linguistics*, vol. 13, pp. 155–61.

Mehler, J. and Dupoux, E. (1994) *What Infants Know*, Oxford, Blackwell.

Mehler, J., Jusczyk, P. W., Dehaene-Lambertz, G., Dupoux, E. and Nazzi, T. (1994) 'Coping with linguistic diversity: the infant's viewpoint', in Morgan, J. L. and Demuth, K. (eds) *Signal to Syntax: bootstrapping from speech to grammar in early acquisition*, pp. 101–16, Millsdale, NJ, Lawrence Erlbaum Associates.

Nelson, K. (1973) 'Structure and strategy in learning to talk', *Monographs of the Society for Research in Child Development*, vol. 38, no. 136.

Norgate, S. H. (1997) 'Research methods for studying the language of blind children', in Hornberger, N. H. and Corson, D. (eds) *The Encyclopedia of Language and Education, Volume 8: research methods in language and education*, the Netherlands, Kluwer Academic Publishers.

Oller, D. K. (1980) 'The emergence of speech sounds in infancy', in Yeni-Komshian, G. H., Kavanagh, J. F. and Ferguson, C. A. (eds) *Child Phonology, Volume 1: Production*, New York, Academic Press.

Peters, A. (1985) 'Language segmentation: operating principles for the perception and analysis of language', in Slobin, D. I. (ed.) *The crosslinguistic study of language acquisition*, vol. 2, Hillsdale, NJ, Lawrence Erlbaum Associates.

Plunkett, K. and Marchman, V. (1993) 'From rote learning to system building: acquiring verb morphology in children and connectionist nets', *Cognition,* vol. 48, pp. 21–69.

Richards, D., Frentzen, B., Gerhardt, K., McCann, M. and Abrams, R. (1992) 'Sound levels in the human uterus', *Obstetrics and Gynaecology,* vol. 80, pp. 186–90.

Tardif, T. (1996) 'Nouns are not always learned before verbs: evidence from Mandarin speakers' early vocabularies', *Developmental Psychology,* vol. 32, pp. 492–504.

Werker, J. F. and Tees, R. C. (1984) 'Cross-language speech perception: evidence for perceptual reorganization during the first year of life', *Infant Behavior and Development,* vol. 7, pp. 49–63.

Readings

Reading A: Is Dutch native English? Linguistic analysis by 2-month-olds

Anne Christophe and John Morton

Abstract

A variant of the non-nutritive habituation/dishabituation sucking method was used to test 2-month-old English infants' perception of languages. This method tests for the spontaneous interest of the baby to a change in the stimulus. English and Japanese were clearly discriminated. The difference between French and Japanese was equally clearly not of interest to babies using this procedure, the babies behaving as though both languages were classified simply as 'foreign'. In order to further specify babies' representation of native and foreign language, we used Dutch, which shares a number of suprasegmental features with English. The results from our last 2 experiments indicate that a portion of our 6–12 week-old babies consider Dutch as native, suggesting that we tapped in a transition period where the babies are still refining the suprasegmental specification of their native language.

One of the most important tasks for a new-born infant is to learn its native language. The majority of babies grow up in a multi-lingual environment and must learn some characteristics of their mother tongue as early as possible so as to distinguish it from other languages. This is a particularly crucial ability, since infants could not possibly learn the syntax of a language (that is, discover the regularities shared by a number of sentences) if they worked on a database containing sentences from several different languages (Mehler *et al.*, 1994).

It has been shown that newborns can discriminate between their mother tongue and a foreign language. Mehler, Jusczyk, Lambertz *et al.* (1988) found that 4-day-old French infants discriminate between French (their mother tongue) and Russian stimuli, showing a preference for their native language (see also Moon *et al.* 1993, for equivalent results with English and Spanish). In addition, newborns are able to discriminate between utterances in two foreign and unfamiliar languages (Mehler and Christophe, 1995; Nazzi, Bertoncini, and Mehler, 1998). Most of these studies have been replicated successfully using speech which has been low-pass filtered at 400 Hz. Under these conditions, prosodic features such as intonation and rhythm are preserved, whereas most phonemic information is missing. It is therefore probable that babies' ability to discriminate between languages is based on a representation of speech prosody. It is very likely that the infant's preference for their native language comes from their having learned its prosody in utero. However, we still do not know the precise nature of the prosodic representation that babies use to classify languages.

Babies of 2 months of age behave slightly differently from newborns. They still discriminate between their native language and other languages but they fail to show any recovery of interest when switched from one foreign language to another. Thus, Mehler *et al.* (1988) showed that while 2-month-old American babies were able to discriminate between English (their mother tongue) and Italian, they did not discriminate between French and Russian. A possible interpretation of this counter-intuitive result is that, while newborns still attempt to analyse in detail any speech sample they are exposed to, 2-month-old infants have sufficient knowledge of their mother tongue to be able to filter out any foreign language as being not relevant.

Hesketh, Christophe and Dehaene-Lambertz (1997) developed a variant of the contingent sucking response method which has the advantage that it can be used both with new-borns and with 2-month-old infants and can be used with extended segments of speech. With this technique, 2-month-old English babies distinguished clearly between English and Japanese. It is this technique which we used to explore the infants' abilities further.

Method

The method for the Hesketh *et al.* experiment will first be briefly described (see Hesketh *et al.*, 1997, for details). The other experiments to be reported used the same technique apart from changes in language. The stimuli consisted of 80 sentences, half in English, half in Japanese, between 15 and 21 syllables long. These were recorded by four female native English speakers and four female native Japanese speakers respectively. Speakers were naïve as to the aim of the experiment and were instructed to read as naturally as possible. Ten sentences from each speaker were selected and matched for syllabic length (17.8 syllables) and duration (3.1 seconds). Each infant underwent two changes in stimulation, one experimental (language) change, the other control (or speaker) change. The key measure was the difference between these two changes.

Half the babies received the experimental change first and the control change second. In addition, the order of presentation of languages and of speakers was counter-balanced across subjects. This yielded eight conditions. In each of the three phases the baby heard sentences from two speakers with the idea of making speaker change mundane.

Subjects were seated in a car seat placed in a sound-proofed chamber and offered a standard (steam sterilised) pacifier. One experimenter, out of view of the baby and deaf to the stimuli, checked that the pacifier stayed in the baby's mouth throughout the experiment. A second experimenter monitored the experiment on the computer outside the chamber. The computer recorded the pressure of the infant's sucks via an analogue-digital card (NIDAQ), detected the sucking responses and delivered the sentences through a ProAudio 16 sound board according to the reinforcement schedule (see below). The computer also saved both the moment and amplitude of each suck as well as the stimuli triggered by the sucks. Hesketh *et al.* (1997) reported that the number of sentences triggered was a cleaner measure than the number of sucking responses. Only this measure will be reported here.

The experiment started with a short period without stimulation (about 30 secs) to settle the infants. The first phase of the experiment then began, during which infants heard sentences in either English or Japanese contingently upon their high-amplitude (HA) sucks. After a short 'shaping' phase, three HA sucks were required to trigger each sentence (such that there was less than one second between two consecutive sucks). There was an ISI of at least 600 ms between consecutive sentences. When reaching the end of an ISI period after presentation of one sentence, the program looked back to see if HA sucks had occurred recently: any sequence of three HA sucks such that the last one occurred within the last 600 ms was used to instantly trigger a new sentence. This procedure ensured fluent presentation of sentences in case of sustained sucking activity. Within each phase of the experiment, the order of presentation of the sentences was quasi-random for each baby.

A switch in stimulation occurred after a predefined habituation criterion had been met. For two consecutive minutes the infant's HA sucking rate had to be less than 80% of the maximum sucking rate from the beginning of the experiment. Each phase of the experiment lasted at least 5 full minutes. Sixteen babies aged between 6–12 weeks participated in the study, mean age 8 weeks 6 days. Subjects were randomly assigned to one of the eight conditions prior to testing.

To assess the effect of the experimental manipulation, two kinds of analyses were performed on the data: ANOVAs and non-parametric tests. For each baby we counted the number of sentences triggered during the two minutes before and after the experimental (language) switch. The difference between these two values gives us a measure of dishabituation to the language shift. The equivalent measure was computed for the control (speaker) switch. The difference between these two dishabituation scores represents a *discrimination index* for each baby: whenever this value is positive, the baby reacted more to the language change than to the speaker change. These values are shown in Figure 1 (left hand column).

A Wilcoxon signed ranks test showed that the median of the discrimination index for the number of sentences triggered was significantly above zero ($Z = 3.4$, $p < 0.001$). In the ANOVAs, the dependent measure was the dishabituation scores for the Experimental and Control switches. There was one within-subject factor (Experimental vs Control switch) and two between-subject counterbalancing factors, Order (experimental switch first, versus control switch first), and Language (English first vs Japanese first). There was a main effect of the Experimental factor ($F (1,12) = 11.6$, $p < 0.01$), no significant effect of any of the counterbalancing factors, and no interactions between the Experimental and counterbalancing factors.

Discrimination of two foreign languages: French vs Japanese

Previous experiments using other techniques have indicated that 2-month-old infants discriminated their native tongue from other languages, but that they failed to distinguish between pairs of unfamiliar languages.

Our next experiment, then, involved testing English babies on French and Japanese. These languages are very different from each other as well as from English; for instance, French has fixed word stress, and rather simple syllabic structure through resyllabification; Japanese exhibits pitch accent, is left-recursive (while both French and English are right-recursive), and prohibits consonant clusters (Dupoux *et al.*, submitted). Sixteen babies took part in this experiment, mean age 9 weeks, 5 days.

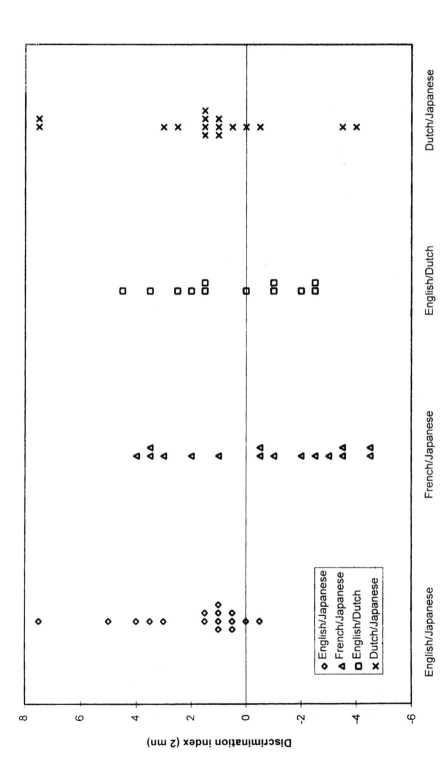

Figure 1 *Results of four language discrimination experiments using the modified non-nutritive sucking method (Hesketh et al., in press) where sentences are presented contingently upon sucking responses and each baby is submitted to two shifts of stimulation, one experimental (language change) and one control (speaker change). A discrimination index is computed for each baby: it represents the difference between the increase in the number of sentences triggered for the language change and the increase for the speaker (or control) change. Whenever this value is positive, the baby showed more interest in the language change than in the speaker change. Increases in the number of sentences triggered are computed using two minutes before and after each shift of stimulation.*

The distribution of the discrimination index can be seen in the second column of Figure 1. The infants gave no indication of being more interested in language change than in speaker change (Wilcoxon, $Z < 1$; ANOVA: $F(1,12) < 1$). This result is significantly different from the results of the experiment with English and Japanese. In an ANOVA contrasting the distribution of discrimination indices in these experiments, $F(1,28) = 8.32$, ($p < 0.01$).

The lack of interest shown by 2-month-olds in the differences between foreign languages is in line with previous work. Paired with Nazzi et al.'s (1998) confirmation that newborn infants can discriminate between sentences belonging to two foreign languages (with the same experimental technique as here), this result confirms the developmental trend already described. Our best interpretation is that 2-month-old infants have enough knowledge of the properties of their native language to be able to filter out foreign input as being irrelevant to their language learning. In that case, both French and Japanese would simply be classified as 'foreign' and would not be analysed to a sufficient depth to allow the differences to be detected.

The results of the first two experiments immediately pose a new question: how specified is the 2-month-olds' representation of their mother-tongue? What do they consider native, and what do they filter out as being foreign? To answer this question, we picked a language which shares with English a number of prosodic properties. Dutch, like English, has vowel reduction, complex syllabic structure, and the same sort of word stress as English. These factors lead to both English and Dutch as being heard as stress-timed (Cutler et al., 1997). In fact, Dutch and English have already been shown to be rather similar to babies' ears: Nazzi et al. (1998) demonstrated that French newborns do not distinguish between Dutch and English filtered sentences.

Discrimination of two stress-timed languages: English vs Dutch

There are two main possibilities for this experiment. On the one hand, it is possible that English 2-month-olds would behave exactly like the French newborns, and confuse the two languages. On the other hand, they may be able to discriminate Dutch from English, thanks to their exposure to English. Unlike Nazzi et al. (1998), we decided to use unfiltered sentences, as in our previous experiments. This means that, as Dutch and English differ widely in their phonemic inventories and phonotactics, being very distinct for adult listeners, these factors could give the infants additional cues for making the discrimination. Sixteen babies participated in the study, mean age 10 weeks 1 day.

The data are shown in the third column of Figure 1. The group showed some interest in the shifts between Dutch and English but the relative increase in sucking rate was only marginally significant (ANOVA: $F(1,12) = 4.17$, $p = 0.064$; Wilcoxon, $Z = 1.85$, $p = 0.065$). The distribution of the discrimination index scores for English/Dutch was not significantly different from that for English/Japanese (ANOVA $F(1,28) < 1$, $p = 0.10$) and was marginally different from that for French/Japanese ($F(1,28) = 3.97$, $p < 0.06$).

Is Dutch native English? Dutch vs Japanese

The previous experiment indicated that some babies of 2 months find it hard to discriminate between English and Dutch sentences. This cannot be attributed to a lack of interest of infants, since their mother tongue is present in the experiment. Instead, this result indicates that at least some of the infants confuse sentences from the two languages. In addition, it is possible that we tapped in a transition period where babies start paying attention to cues that distinguish Dutch from English (which might be phonemic). Taken to its limit, this result implies that our babies, or at least some of them, consider Dutch sentences as belonging to their native language. If this is truly the case, we predict that these infants should discriminate between Dutch (assimilated to native) and Japanese. This is what we tested in the next experiment. Sixteen babies, mean age 9 weeks 4 days, participated in the study.

The distribution of discrimination index scores is shown in the fourth column of Figure 1. A majority of the infants were more interested by the language change than by the speaker change. Just like in the previous experiment, we observed marginally significant discrimination ($F (1,12) = 3.4$, $p = 0.09$, $Z = 1.9$, $p = 0.054$). The distribution of the discrimination index scores for this experiment was not significantly different from English/Japanese ($F (1,28) < 1$), was marginally different from French/Japanese ($F (1,28) = 3.89$, $p = 0.06$), and was not different from English/Dutch ($F < 1$). Inspection of Figure 1 shows that there is a wide distribution of data, suggesting that the group is not homogeneous. In other words, some infants have specified *native* sufficiently to exclude Dutch, whereas the rest have not.

Discussion

Using the modified contingent sucking response we have shown that English 2-month-olds discriminate English from Japanese but not French from Japanese. Given that this habituation–dishabituation technique measures infants' interest in changes in auditory stimulation, it allows us to evaluate their spontaneous partitioning of perceptual space into categories. In the present case, the results suggest that babies form two major categories, one for English, which could be termed 'native' or 'mother tongue', and one, with French and Japanese, of 'foreign languages'.

In the last 2 experiments of this paper, we studied English infants' perception of Dutch, a language that is prosodically very similar to English. We contrasted Dutch to English and to Japanese. If English babies treat Dutch as native, they should not be able to discriminate between English and Dutch, but should readily distinguish Dutch from Japanese; in contrast, if they have already set up their *native* category such that Dutch is excluded, they should distinguish between Dutch and English but ignore the difference between Dutch and Japanese, both of which would be in the category *foreign*. Both experiments gave marginally significant results, indicating that some English babies consider Dutch as native but others do not. The former would distinguish Dutch from Japanese but not from English; the latter group would distinguish Dutch from English but not from Japanese. If we tested babies in both conditions, we predict that whenever one condition works the other would not. What factors may account for this individual variation? The most obvious candidate is age. At one month, all infants might regard Dutch as native, whereas by four months they might all have excluded it. Further, we would expect early exposure to different languages to affect the speed of setting up a tight specification of *native* but it is unlikely to be a factor in our experiments since we selected the babies to come from monolingual English households.

Eventually we will need to distinguish between environments where second languages are addressed to the infant from those where second languages are present but not directly addressed. The second case might accelerate the definition of *native* whereas the first case, true bilingualism, might lead to confusion. Recent experiments by Bosch and Sebastian (1997) showed that by four months of age, bilingual Spanish/Catalan babies already behaved differently from monolingual babies (either Spanish or Catalan). Monolingual babies oriented faster to their mother tongue than to English. In contrast, bilinguals orient to Spanish or to Catalan significantly more slowly than to English. Is this because of confusion? Apparently not, since in more recent and still unpublished work, these authors showed that, although Spanish and Catalan are close, both monolingual and bilingual 4-month-olds can discriminate between them. Of course the gap between these 4-month-olds and our 2-month-olds is enormous and it could be that at 2 months bilingual babies are confused. At any rate, it has become clear that, from birth, infants work hard at learning what language is native.

Acknowledgements

The work reported in this paper was assisted by a grant from the Human Frontiers Science Programme, the Human Capital and Mobility Programme, and the European Science Foundation. We especially want to thank Sarah Hesketh, Jon Bartrip and Sarah Minister for their help in recruiting and testing subjects.

References for Reading A

Bosch, L., & Sebastian-Galles, N. (1997). Native-language recognition abilities in four-month-old infants from monolingual and bilingual environments. *Cognition, **65***, 33–69.

Cutler, A., Dahan, D. & van Donselaar, W. (1997). Prosody in the comprehension of spoken language: a literature review. *Language and Speech, 40, 141–201.*

Dupoux, E., Kakehi, K., Hirose, Y., Pallier, C., Fitneva, S., & Mehler, J. (submitted). Epenthetic vowels in Japanese: A perceptual illusion. *Journal of Memory and Language.*

Hesketh, S., Christophe, A., & Dehaene-Lambertz, G. (1997). Non-nutritive sucking and sentence processing. *Infant Behavior and Development, **20**,* 263–269.

Mehler, J., & Christophe, A. (1995). Maturation and learning of language in the first year of life. In M. S. Gazzaniga (Ed.), *The Cognitive Neurosciences: A handbook for the field (pp.* 943–954). Cambridge, Mass.: MIT Press.

Mehler, J., Dehaene-Lambertz, G., Dupoux, E., & Nazzi, T. (1994). Coping with linguistic diversity: The infant's viewpoint. In J. L. Morgan & K. Demuth (Eds.), *Signal to Syntax: Bootstrapping from speech to grammar in early acquisition* (pp. 101–116). Mahwah, New Jersey: LEA.

Mehler, L., Jusczyk, P. W., Lambertz, G., Halsted, G., Bertoncini, J., & Amiel-Tison, C. (1988). A precursor of language acquisition in young infants. *Cognition, **29**,* 143–178.

Moon, C., Cooper, R., & Fifer, W. (1993). Two-day-olds prefer their native language. *Infant Behavior and Development, **16**,* 495–500.

Nazzi, T., Bertoncini, J., & Mehler, J. (1998). Language discrimination by newborns: Towards an understanding of the role of rhythm. *Journal of Experimental Psychology: Human Perception and Performance, **24**, 1–11.*

Source: Christophe, A. and Morton, J. (1998) 'Is Dutch native English? Linguistic analysis by 2-month-olds', *Developmental Science*, vol. 1, pp. 215–19.

Reading B: Developments in early lexical comprehension: a comparison of parental report and controlled testing

Margaret Harris and Joan Chasin

Abstract

Six children were studied from the age of 0;6 to 1;6 in order to chart their developing comprehension vocabularies from the first to the 100th word. Observational data were used in the first instance to identify newly comprehended words and then controlled testing was carried out for each word to confirm and expand the observational data. Comprehension of words was divided into four categories – object names, context-bound object words, action words and personal names. The relative frequency of the different categories of word was found to change with the size of the comprehension vocabulary as personal names decreased in importance and both object names and action words became increasingly more common. There was considerable variation among the six children especially in the proportion of object names and action words that they understood but vocabulary composition became highly stable between 60 and 100 words.

Introduction

This paper compares data on early lexical comprehension derived from parental report with that from systematic experimental testing. A major source of data on the composition of early comprehension vocabularies comes from Fenson, Dale, Reznick, Bates, Thal & Pethick (1994) who describe an extensive sample of children whose vocabulary was assessed with the MacArthur Communicative Development Inventories (Infant Scale). These data are cross-sectional rather than longitudinal but they do provide important evidence about the first 50 words that children understand.

Pooling data across subjects, Fenson *et al.* found that the words understood by the youngest children (aged 0;8) were the names of people or were related to games or routines. At 50 words, the main category was nouns (comprising household items, animal names, toys, clothing, food and drink, body parts, furniture and rooms) which accounted for 48% of items. The other categories were games and routines (20%), actions words (16%), personal names (10%) and sounds (6%). By 1;4 – when mean comprehension vocabularies were reported as 192 words – 52% of words understood were nouns, 19% were verbs, 9% were words stemming from games and routines and 3% were personal names. (For a complete list see Fenson *et al.* (1994) table 16.)

The use of the MacArthur Communicative Development Inventory for the assessment of early comprehension vocabulary has been questioned since it relies exclusively on parental report. Although there is a long tradition of using parental report for reliable assessment of production it is less clear that this can provide equally reliable assessment of early comprehension since it is often difficult to determine from observation alone whether a child understands a word or is, instead, responding to non-verbal cues. As a result there may be a tendency for parents to over-report comprehension, particularly in the first year of life. Fenson *et al.* are aware of this potential criticism and they provide several arguments in favour of their data. However, as Tomasello & Mervis (1994) note, these arguments are not entirely convincing particularly in the case of very early development and there is good reason to suppose that the Fenson *et al.* (1994) data over-estimate early comprehension. Another potential problem is that parental reports – even when supplemented with an interview – do not necessarily provide detailed information about the precise context in which a word is comprehended. Without such information it is difficult to determine accurately which category a particular word falls into. In particular, a word may appear to be an object name but, in fact, understanding may be restricted to a single behavioural context in which case the word is context-bound rather than referential. There are many examples of such context-bound word use in early production (Bates, Benigni, Bretherton, Camaioni & Volterra, 1979; Dore, 1985; Nelson & Lucariello, 1985; Barrett, 1986; Harris, Barrett, Jones & Brookes, 1988; Barrett, Harris & Chasin, 1991) and so there is every reason to suppose that comparable patterns will be evident in early comprehension.

The aim of the present study was to chart the development of comprehension of the first 100 words using observation and controlled testing as well as parental report. It was predicted that, overall, the rate of development of comprehension vocabularies would be significantly slower than that reported by Fenson *et al.* (1994). It was also predicted that, although the proportion of object names understood would increase with age, the mean proportion would be lower than that reported by Fenson *et al.* (1994) since genuine object name comprehension would be distinguished from context-bound comprehension of object words.

Method

Participants
Six children took part in the study, four boys (Ben, Andrew, Sebastian and George) and two girls (Katherine and Katy). All the children were first born and English was the only language spoken in the home. At the time of the first observation the children were 0;6 (range 0;5.24–0;6.06). Observation continued until the children were 2;0 although all children had attained a comprehension vocabulary of at least 100 words by 1;6. Data for the early production and comprehension of these children have been reported in Harris, Yeeles, Chasin & Oakley (1995a) and Harris, Barlow-Brown & Chasin (1995b).

Procedure
Assessment of comprehension
Full details of the procedure used to assess comprehension can be found in Harris *et al.* (1995a). Briefly, three different sources of evidence were used in the first instance. These were parental diary records, home observation (supplemented by videotaping) and a comprehension checklist which contained the most commonly understood words organized into categories (e.g. toys, food and drink, people, games, actions). The checklist was a modified version of the one used by Benedict (1977).

Once a new word was identified as appearing in comprehension, controlled testing was carried out to confirm parental reports and to determine the range of contexts in which a word was understood, most notably to distinguish between context-bound object words (which were understood only in a single behavioural context) and object names (which were understood in more than one context).

Classification of words
The first 100 words in comprehension for each child were divided into the four categories of personal names, object names, context-bound object words and action words. The criteria for this classification and examples of words in each category are shown in Table 1.

Table 1   Examples of categorization of early comprehension vocabulary

Category	Definition	Examples
Personal name	Unique name for people, family pets, favourite toys	*Lamby* – toy lamb used as comforter *Dylan* – family cat
Object name	Corresponding to Nelson's (1973) 'general nominal' category; only including words that were understood in at least two different behavioural contexts	*Cat* – family cat, novel picture of cats *Nose* – teddy's nose, own nose, mother's nose
Context-bound object word	Object words that were understood in only one behavioural context	*Bird* – when indoors, looks out of window to garden *Car* – waves on hearing word or sound of car
Action word	All words or phrases that were associated with actions rather than with objects	*Down* – squats down on haunches *Lunch* – goes to kitchen and attempts to climb into high chair

Assessment of production
The development of production was monitored through diary records, maternal interviews, home observations and video recordings. Details of the procedure are set out in Harris *et al.* (1995a). Briefly, a vocalization was counted as a word if it was reported in the diary record and observed either during home observation or in a videorecording. If there was no maternal report, three observations were required before a vocalization was counted. Unlike comprehension, controlled testing was only carried out if there was some ambiguity about the range of contexts in which the child produced a word as, for example, where a diary entry and an observation were not identical.

Results

The proportion of words comprehended in each of the four categories was calculated for vocabulary sizes of 20, 60 and 100 words. The proportion of words in each category was found to change as the size of comprehension vocabulary increased (see Table 2). At the 20-word level, the number of personal names and object names was almost equal and together they accounted for two thirds of the total. The remaining two categories – context-bound object words and action words – each made up about one sixth of the total. At 60 words, the proportion of object names and action words had both increased while there was a marked decrease in the proportion of personal names. By the 100-word level the proportion of personal names had decreased even further and there was a corresponding rise in the proportion of object names. The proportion of action words remained the same as at the 60-word level as did the proportion of context-bound object words which was identical at all three points.

Table 2   Mean percentage (and range) of words in each category in relation to size of comprehension vocabulary

Vocabulary size	Personal names	Object names	Context-bound object words	Action words
20	32.5 (20–60)	35 (15–60)	15 (0–30)	17.5 (10–25)
60	18 (12–23)	40 (30–52)	15 (8–23)	27 (15–37)
100	15 (10–19)	43 (30–56)	15 (11–20)	27 (13–37)

Table 3   Total comprehension and production vocabulary at 1;4

Child	Gender	Comprehension	Production
Andrew	M	59	11
Ben	M	48	46
George	M	52	5
Sebastian	M	80	39
Mean Fenson et al.	M	150	30
Katherine	F	224	65
Katy	F	111	25
Mean Fenson et al.	F	210	95

Individual data for the six children reflected the overall pattern. The number of object names understood by each child generally increased with the size of their comprehension vocabulary. However there was considerable individual variation in the number of different categories of word understood at each stage. A summary of the range in proportion for each category is shown in brackets in Table 2.

Although there was considerable individual variation in the composition of early comprehension vocabulary, there was great stability from 60 words to 100 words. The correlation for proportion of object names at these two points reached the maximum value ($R = 1.00$, $p < 0.001$) and for action words it was also significant ($R = 0.82$, $P = 0.04$). The corresponding correlations between 20 and 60 word vocabularies were not significant ($R = 0.49$, $p = 0.33$ for object names, $R = 0.75$, $p = 0.09$ for action words).

Table 3 shows the relative size of comprehension and production vocabularies at 1;4. Most of the children had many more words in comprehension than in production with the exception of Ben, whose comprehension and production developed more or less in parallel. Katherine's comprehension vocabulary was well past the 100-word level by this time and she had such a fast rate of acquisition that it was impossible to test all the later words that she understood. However, as very good observational and interview records were kept for her, the figure in Table 3 can be taken as an accurate estimate of the size of her comprehension vocabulary. The mean level of comprehension vocabulary at 1;4 was 96 words – considerably lower than the median of 169 words reported by Fenson *et al.* (1994). However, Katherine's vocabulary of 224 words did come close to the figure of around 250 reported by Fenson *et al.* as cutting off the 75th percentile. Table 3 also shows the extent of the range of vocabulary size at 1;4 and provides further evidence that, in this early period of acquiring language, children show highly individual patterns of development.

Discussion

Our data support the finding of earlier studies that the proportion of different classes of words comprehended changes with vocabulary size (Benedict, 1977; Bates, Bretherton & Snyder, 1988; Gunzi, 1993; Fenson *et al.*, 1994). Personal names figured prominently in early vocabulary but they made a relatively smaller contribution as the total number of words understood by the children increased. This decrease in the importance of personal names occurred as the proportion of both object names and action words increased. The proportion of context-bound object words remained stable throughout the period of development.

At 60 words, the mean proportion of object names was 40%. This is very comparable to Benedict's (1977) data for 50 words but somewhat lower than the 48% reported by Fenson *et al.* (1994). The mean proportion of action words at the same vocabulary size was 27% which was considerably lower than the proportions reported by both Benedict and Gunzi for 50 words but very similar to the total proportion reported by Fenson *et al.* for action words plus words related to games and routines (both of which were classified as action words in the present study). Our data suggest that some early words that appear to be object names are, in fact, context-bound object words and that a parental checklist may, therefore, over-represent the number of object names. There is also some suggestion from our data that parents over-estimate the number of words that children understand since even the most precocious child that we tested attained a score that was under the 75th percentile on the Fenson *et al.* norms; and there was a considerable discrepancy between the mean comprehension scores of our sample and that of the Fenson *et al.* sample even when scores for girls and boys were treated separately.

There was wide individual variation in the frequency with which both object names and action words were understood, confirming the findings of both Bates *et al.* (1988) and Fenson *et al.* (1994). Furthermore, by 60 words, a stable pattern of comprehension vocabulary style was established such that there was a very close relationship between the relative composition of vocabulary at the 60- and 100-word level.

In the six children studied there was a weak relationship between lexical comprehension and production. This dissociation between comprehension and production appears to be due in part, as Bates *et al.* (1988) and Fenson *et al.* (1994) have reported, to children who understand a great deal but say very little. Katy fits into this pattern (see Table 3). At 1;4 she understood over 100 words but had produced only 25. Table 3 also shows that another child, Ben, showed an equally exceptional pattern in that he understood and produced a similar number of words. He was also exceptional in showing a lag of only 14 days between comprehension and production of his first word (Harris *et al.*, 1995a) and these two modalities continued to be mirror images of each other until at least 1;4.

One final issue that is worthy of comment concerns the existence of a spurt in the development of comprehension and production vocabularies. Reznick & Goldfield (1992) have claimed that, for many children, a spurt in comprehension vocabulary occurs at the same time as a spurt in production. Their evidence for the timing of the spurt came from children's performance in a visual preference task in which comprehension of 15 selected words was tested at two-monthly intervals. There was an increase in the number of words understood from the start of the study at 1;2 to the end at 2;0 with individual children showing an apparent spurt in the number of words understood somewhere between 1;4 and 1;10. This age range is considerably later than that for the comprehension spurt shown by the children in the present study which occurred between 0;11 and 1;3. This age range (which is a conservative estimate given that it is based on testing rather than observation) is in line with the mean age of around 1;0 reported in the Fenson *et al.* (1994) data. The similarity of our own findings to those of the parental report data from Fenson *et al.* strongly suggests that the spurt reported by Reznick & Goldfield is some months later than the primary spurt in the development of comprehension vocabulary.

There are two possible explanations for the later increase in rate of development of comprehension vocabulary reported by Reznick & Goldfield. One possibility is that they are reporting a secondary increase in the rate of comprehension vocabulary development. The alternative explanation is that the exacting demands of the visual preference technique underestimated children's ability to understand words. Neither our own data nor those of Fenson *et al.* provide evidence about the development of comprehension beyond 1;4 so they do not rule out the possibility that after an initial spurt around 1;0, there is a secondary and later increase in the rate at which new words are understood in the age range that Reznick & Goldfield investigated. However, as Reznick & Goldfield only began testing at 1;2, their study does not provide evidence about developments in the earlier period that we investigated.

References for Reading B

Barrett, M. (1986). Early semantic representations and early word usage. In S. A. Kuczaj & W. Wannenmacher (eds), *Concept development and the development of word meaning*. Berlin: Springer.

Barrett, M., Harris, M. & Chasin, J. (1991). Early lexical development and maternal speech: a comparison of children's initial and subsequent uses. *Journal of Child Language* **18**, 21–40.

Bates, E., Benigni, L., Bretherton, L., Camaioni, L. & Volterra, V. (1979). *The emergence of symbols: cognition and communication in infancy*. New York: Academic Press.

Bates, E., Bretherton, I. & Snyder, L. (1988). *From first words to grammar: Individual differences and dissociable mechanisms*. Cambridge: C.U.P.

Benedict, H. (1977). *Language comprehension in the 10–16-month-old infants*. PhD Thesis. Yale University.

Dore, J. (1985). Holophrases revisited: their 'logical' development from dialogue. In M. D. Barrett (ed.), *Children's single-word speech*. Chichester: Wiley.

Fenson, L., Dale, P., Reznick, J. S., Bates, E., Thal, D. & Pethick, S. J. (1994). Variability in early communicative development. *Monographs of the Society for Research in Child Development* **59**, No. 5, 1–173.

Gunzi, S. (1993). Early language comprehension and production. Unpublished PhD thesis, University of London.

Harris, M., Barlow-Brown, F. & Chasin, J. (1995). The emergence of referential understanding: pointing and the comprehension of object names. *First Language* **15**, 19–34.

Harris, M., Barrett, M., Jones, D. & Brookes, S. (1988). Linguistic input and early word meaning. *Journal of Child Language* **15**, 77–94.

Harris, M., Yeeles, C., Chasin, J. & Oakley, Y. (1995). Symmetries and asymmetries in early lexical comprehension and production. *Journal of Child Language* **22**, 1–18.

Nelson, K. & Lucariello, J. (1985). The development of meaning in first words. In M. Barrett (ed.), *Children's single-word speech*. Chichester: Wiley.

Reznick, J. S. & Goldfield, B. A. (1992). Rapid changes in lexical development in comprehension and production. *Developmental Psychology* **28**, 406–13.

Tomasello, M. & Mervis, C. B. (1994). The instrument is great, but measuring comprehension is still a problem. *Monographs of the Society for Research in Child Development* **59**, No. 5, 174–9.

> Source: Harris, M. and Chasin, J. (1999) Developments in early lexical comprehension: a comparison of parental report and controlled testing', *Journal of Child Language*, vol. 26, pp. 453–60.

Chapter 3
Brain and cognitive development

Denis Mareschal, Mark H. Johnson and Andrew Grayson

Contents

Learning outcomes

After you have studied this chapter you should be able to:

1 describe the developmental origins of specialist areas of the cerebral cortex;
2 evaluate arguments for and against the notion of innate modularity;
3 discuss the case for and against innate specification of cortical function;
4 identify some special functions of the prefrontal cortex in children's cognitive development;
5 outline some aspects of the relationship between brain development and cognitive and language development.
6 In addition you should have:
   - enhanced your understanding of principles of self-organization;
   - further developed your understanding of plasticity;
   - reinforced your understanding of nativism and constructivism;
   - extended your knowledge of research methods.

1   Introduction

This chapter is about the development of the human brain in infancy, and about how changes in the physical structure of the brain can be related to children's cognitive and language development. In the course of this chapter we will address the following questions.

- What is the basic course of pre- and postnatal brain development? (Section 2)
- How do different areas of the brain come to perform different functions? (Sections 3 and 4)
- Are different areas of the brain innately pre-specified to take on their respective cognitive functions? (Sections 3 and 4)
- How can cognitive function be related to the development of brain structure? (Section 5)
- How much can be learned about cognitive development from studying brain development? (Sections 4 and 5)
- How is it possible to study brain function? (All sections)

We start in Section 2 by taking a brief look at some basic features of brain development in the child before birth and in the first few months after birth. A key idea in this section is that some brain development goes on postnatally, maximizing the opportunities for brain and cognitive development to be influenced by both genes *and* environment, in interaction with each other.

Cerebral cortex
The layer of cells on the outer surface of the forebrain; only found in mammals, and particularly well developed in humans.

SG

Epigenesis
Development by means of interaction between genes and their environment.

In Section 3 we examine the idea that different areas of the *cerebral cortex* (see Figure 1, p. 118) specialize in performing different cognitive functions. One way of thinking about this 'functional specialization' within the human brain is in terms of cognitive modules. Cognitive modules are hypothetical constructs that help to map what we know about brain *function* (what the brain does) to brain *structure* (its physical make-up). Section 3 considers the debate about how the cognitive functions performed by such modules might develop. Do they unfold from a predefined genetic blueprint, or are they dependent upon the child's interactions with the environment? We conclude that these cognitive functions develop according to epigenetic principles, with genes and environment inextricably linked. Section 4 considers this argument in detail in relation to language development.

In Section 5 we look at how psychologists relate knowledge about children's cognitive development to knowledge about the developing structure of the cortex. This section focuses on the *prefrontal cortex* (see Figure 1, p. 118) because of its importance within the field of developmental psychology. The prefrontal cortex has received considerable attention from psychologists because of its involvement in higher mental functions, such as the planning and initiation of actions, and the inhibition of irrelevant behaviour (so called 'executive functions'; see Chapter 5).

The chapter as a whole is about the relatively new field of 'developmental cognitive neuroscience' (Johnson, 1997). This interdisciplinary field has emerged partly as a result of new and improved ways of investigating brain structure and function (such as advances in neuroimaging) which have led to significant progress in understanding how brains are constructed during development. These methods will be described and illustrated throughout the chapter. Their importance for the psychological study of child development is that they allow us to investigate the relationship between the development of brain structure on the one hand and cognitive and behavioural development on the other.

1.1 Innateness and epigenesis

Neuroimaging
The use of various technologies for the non-invasive measurement of brain activity, aimed at specifying the functions of different brain regions. Also referred to as 'brain mapping'.

An important aim of this chapter is to address the question of whether the development of brain structure (its physical make-up) and function (what it does) are innately pre-specified, or whether the brain develops in response to the environment of the child. It is worth spending a few minutes thinking about what 'innate' means before we begin the discussion proper.

The term 'innate' is rather ill defined. Sometimes it is used interchangeably with the phrase 'genetically determined' to refer to an aspect of development being exclusively determined by genes. In this sense of the term it refers to 'nothing that exists in the natural world, except for genes themselves' (Johnson, 1997, p. 8). Genes *always* interact with their environment, so they can never be the sole determining factor in development. At the most basic level, the way that genes operate is affected by their local molecular and biochemical environment. There is no aspect of development that is purely genetically determined, so 'innateness', in this strong sense, is not a useful term.

SG

What psychologists usually mean by innateness is something like 'affected by factors intrinsic to the developing organism rather than by factors that are external to it'. Aspects of development that are affected by factors intrinsic to the child, that seem to apply to all children no matter what their environment, are likely to be strongly related to the child's genetic make-up. But even these aspects of development cannot be said to be innate in the strong sense of the word. So if the term 'innate' is to be meaningful, it has to be used in this looser sense, with a recognition that there is no such thing as an aspect of development that is purely genetically determined. This is the sense in which the term 'innate' and the phrase 'genetic determination' will be used in this chapter.

For the purposes of this chapter, then, genetic determinism is the view that there is a pre-specified 'genetic blueprint' which imposes itself on the developing child in a direct way, and which is minimally affected by environmental factors. Specifically, genetic determinism holds that brain development is the unfolding of a genetic plan, and that maturation in particular regions of the brain causes or allows specific advances in cognitive, perceptual or motor abilities in the child. This represents a classically nativist perspective on development.

SG

Genetic determination can be contrasted with epigenesis. This is the view that there are two-way interactions at all levels of development. For the purposes of this chapter, epigenesis refers to the way in which development may *not* be exclusively to do with factors that are intrinsic to the child. An epigenetic view suggests that brain development occurs as a result of the child developing in an external environment which affects the course of brain development. In other words it refers to the notion of genes and environment interacting to influence the course of development. In this respect it represents a potentially constructivist perspective.

While most people would acknowledge that there are complex interactions between genes and environment, the view of genetic determinism still tends to dominate common assumptions about the relation between brain development and cognition. But as you will see, this overly passive view of brain development fails to capture the importance of two-way interactions between brain and behaviour and the importance of the environment in neural development.

Activity I   *Thinking about innateness*

Allow about 10 minutes

This activity is a gentle introduction to some of the complex issues you will encounter concerning genetic and environmental influences on child development.

Think of ways in which someone you know well is psychologically similar to their parents. You might focus on personality traits, skills, interests, habits and so on. Write down a list of two or three examples.

For each example, think about the following questions and make brief notes.

- What factors have caused this person to be like this? Has this trait been developed through experience, or has it been inherited from their parents?

- Was it inevitable that this person would develop in this way, or could other choices or experiences have produced different outcomes?

- At what age was this similarity first evident?

Comment

At the very least this activity should highlight some of the complexities (perhaps the impossibility) of trying to separate 'genetic' and 'environmental' influences on human development. If children grow up to be like their parents in some ways, is this because they learned to be like this from them (an 'external' factor) or because they inherited these similarities from them (an 'intrinsic' factor)?

Plasticity
The ability of a system (such as a human brain) to change and adapt to circumstances.

SG

2 Prenatal and postnatal brain development

This section outlines some basic physiological features of early brain development. You will see that the changing physiology of the brain provides clues as to its changing functions, and how these functions relate to cognition and behaviour. Key processes in pre- and postnatal brain development are outlined and the crucial notion of plasticity is examined.

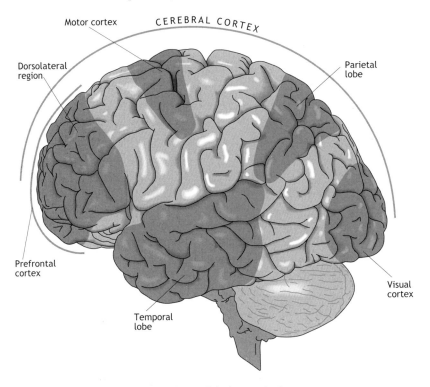

Figure I   Side view of the left hemisphere of the human brain.

The sequence of events that goes towards building human brains is very similar to that observed in other mammals, but the timescale over which these events occur is significantly more extended. This slower timescale has two major consequences. First, there is a prolonged period of postnatal development during which the later stages of brain development can be influenced by interaction with the outside environment. If the timescale of human brain development were quicker, and babies were born with more mature brains, then much more of their brain development would take place in the relatively limited environment of the mother's womb.

Second, the more delayed the general time course of the development of a species, the larger the relative volume of the later developing areas of the brain. In humans, the slowed rate of development is associated with a relatively larger volume of cerebral cortex, and an especially large *prefrontal cortex* (see Figure 1). The prefrontal cortex is considered by most investigators to be critical for many high-level cognitive abilities (Milner, 1982; Goldman-Rakic, 1987; Fuster, 1989) which you can read about in Section 5, and in Chapter 5 of this book. It is significant that the region of brain that undergoes most postnatal development, in interaction with the rich, external environment, is the region most closely associated with high-level cognitive abilities such as the planning and execution of complex sequences of behaviour.

Activity 2   The prenatal environment

Allow about 10 minutes

This activity explores what psychologists mean by the term 'environment', and emphasizes that environmental influences on child development operate before birth.

Imagine for a minute the prenatal environment of the child (the mother's womb). In what ways do you think it is similar to the child's postnatal environment? In what ways is it different? Write a list of characteristics under the headings as suggested below. See Figure 2 for an example to start you off.

Prenatal environment	Postnatal environment
1 Constant temperature	More varied temperature
2	
3	

Figure 2 Example answers for Activity 2.

Comment

'The environment' in developmental psychology means 'everything outside the child'. So, postnatally, children's environments include all aspects of their physical and social worlds. Clearly this is considerably richer in many ways than the restrictive environment of the mother's womb. The sample answer in Figure 2 indicates that the postnatal environment is much more variable, even at a simple physiological level. In addition, in the mother's womb the child cannot move easily, and has very limited access to information from the senses (which are also at an early stage of development). However, it is important to realize that the mother's womb *is* an environment, so even prenatal development cannot be put down exclusively to the unfolding of a genetic blueprint. Look back at the work of DeCasper and Spence (1986) and DeCasper *et al.* (1994) in Chapter 2 (Section 2) of this book to see examples of how the environment impacts on the prenatal child.

2.1 Prenatal brain development

Neurons are nerve cells that receive information and pass it on to other nerve cells in the form of electrochemical impulses. They are the basic building blocks of the brain. The prenatal development of the brain can be summarized in terms of the three stages that take place in the development of neurons. First, neurons are *born* through the process of cell division. Second, they *migrate* from the place of their birth to their final locations in the brain. Third, they *differentiate*, or take up their final form.

A few weeks after conception the human embryo develops a structure called the neural tube that will eventually transform into the different parts of the human brain. Neurons are born along the inner surface of this tube and then migrate to their final locations in the developing brain. Cells that will contribute to the cerebral cortex are formed around 6–18 weeks after conception. In the cerebral cortex, neurons move to their correct position in a process that is called active migration. This creates an 'inside-to-outside' pattern in which the newest cells move past older cells towards the surface of the brain to find their appropriate position. Active migration eventually creates the distinctive layered structure of the cerebral cortex. Some other parts of the brain are formed by passive migration in which the most recently born neurons simply push their older cousins further away from the location where they were all born.

Once neurons have migrated to their final positions, they take on their mature shape and form, completing the process called 'differentiation'. One aspect of differentiation is the growth and branching of dendrites. The dendrites of a neuron are like antennae that pick up signals from many other neurons and, if the circumstances are right, pass the signal down the neuron's axon and on to other neurons. The pattern of branching of dendrites is important, because it affects the amount and type of signals the neuron receives. The points of communication between neurons are called *synapses* (see Figure 3). Synapses begin to form in the brain in the early weeks of gestation. The generation of synapses occurs at different times in different areas of the cortex.

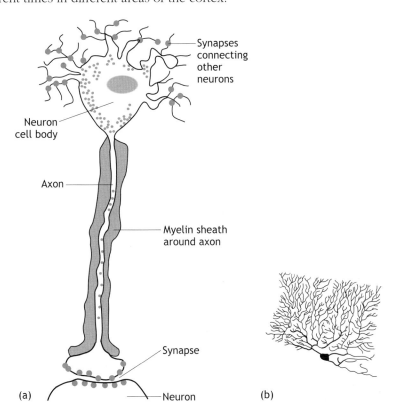

Figure 3   (a) A diagram of a neuron showing an axon (much shortened) with axon terminal (synapse) and dendrites with synaptic connections to other neurons; (b) a more realistic picture of the density of a dendritic tree in a human neuron (adapted from Stewart, 1991).

A second aspect of differentiation that occurs in most neurons is myelination. Myelin (see Figure 3) is a fatty sheath that forms around neurons and helps them to transmit signals more quickly. It begins to form around neurons before birth and continues to do so for many years, even into adulthood in some areas of the cortex. When myelination is delayed, a delay in development can also occur,

Motor cortex
The section of the cortex that is associated with the control of movement.

because the conductivity of the neurons is affected. For example, delayed formation of myelin sheaths in the *motor cortex* (see Figure 1, p. 118) is associated with delayed acquisition of motor milestones such as crawling and walking.

At the same time that the brain is growing and increasing in size and complexity, regressive events are also occurring. For example, it is estimated that 20–50 per cent of neurons die during development (Oppenheim, 1981; Cowan *et al.*, 1984) because of errors in cell division, because they were only temporarily needed, or because they are simply surplus to requirements. In adults, the brain has a very specific pattern of branching of dendrites and synapses between cells. This involves a large number of cells and connections. There are about 100,000,000,000 (one hundred billion or 10^{11}) neurons that make up the brain, each with one thousand connections. There simply is not enough space in the human genome to encode all of this information. Instead, this specificity is achieved partly by means of selective 'pruning', through which useful connections remain and surplus ones are eliminated.

Human genome
The complete set of genetic information contained in human chromosomes.

2.2 Postnatal brain development

As you learned in Section 2.1, there is a comparatively long phase of postnatal brain development in humans, which means that the brain is still undergoing major structural change and growth at the same time as the infant is perceiving and acting in (and on) the rich, complex, external environment. The most obvious aspect of postnatal brain development is an increase in its volume, which quadruples between birth and adulthood. This increase comes from a number of sources such as more extensive nerve fibre bundles, and neurons becoming covered in myelin. But perhaps the most remarkable sign of postnatal neural development is the increase in size, complexity and reach of the dendritic tree of many neurons (see Figure 4). There is also a corresponding increase in the number of synapses. Since synapses are the points of contact, or communication, between neurons, this indicates that the number of neural connections within the brain is increasing.

Visual cortex
The region at the rear of the brain that processes visual information.

Huttenlocher (1990) has reported a steady increase in the number of synapses in several regions of the human cerebral cortex. For example, in parts of the *visual cortex* (see Figure 1, p. 118) the generation of synapses begins around the time of birth. By the end of their first year of life children typically have 50 per cent more synapses in this area of the cortex than adults. In the prefrontal cortex the peak of synaptic density occurs later, typically at around 24 months of age. Although there is variation in the timetable, in all regions of cortex studied to date, the generation of synapses begins around the time of birth and increases to a peak level well above that observed in adults. A characteristic feature of the later stages of brain development, then, is a *decrease* in the overall number of connections among nerve cells from about the first year of life onwards. This pruning of connections is important because it may be one mechanism by which specialization of function in different regions of the cortex is achieved (see Section 2.4).

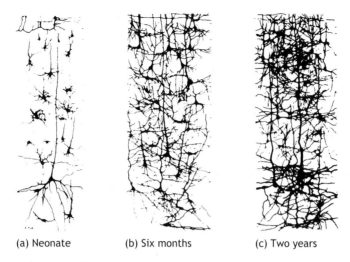

(a) Neonate   (b) Six months   (c) Two years

Figure 4 Dendrites in the visual cortex of human infants. As the dendritic trees of neurons extend, so the overall connectivity in the brain increases (adapted from Conel, 1939–63).

2.3 Plasticity

Plasticity is an inherent property of the developing brain. At birth the brain appears to be highly adaptable or 'plastic'. If one area is damaged, perhaps through a localized brain injury, or a stroke, other brain regions can take over the processing from the damaged region. In adult life, the brain is considerably less plastic, and localized brain damage is much harder to overcome.

Brain growth involves a process of increasing specialization in the sense that tissue and cells become more differentiated in their structure and functioning as development progresses. Sometimes this increased specialization is referred to as a 'restriction of fate' because at the outset of its life a cell might take on any number of forms and functions, but as development progresses, and as it assumes its mature form and connectivity, its 'fate' becomes increasingly specified. Plasticity simply represents the state of not yet having achieved specialization at some level. As an example, consider a piece of tissue from the cerebral cortex that may not yet have developed its specialization for processing a certain category of information when a neighbouring region is damaged. The same developmental mechanisms that would have ensured specialization for one type of processing may now bias the tissue towards the type of processing normally undertaken by its damaged neighbour. Thus in many instances, atypical patterns of brain specialization in developmental disorders may reflect the action of normal developmental processes following some earlier disturbance to the typical developmental pathway. Identifying and understanding the mechanisms underlying specialization, particularly in postnatal life, remains one of the major challenges for developmental cognitive neuroscience.

2.4 Increasing specialization of structure

As you will see in Section 3, the adult brain is characterized by cortical regions that are dedicated to different types of information processing and different cognitive functions. As neurons become increasingly differentiated, their fate is restricted, and their function becomes more specialized. But how does this happen? What processes are involved in the development of specialist cortical regions?

There is no clear agreement on this matter, so we will briefly look at one possible view of these processes, called 'selectionism' (Changeux, 1985). Remember that cortical development sees a rise in the number and density of synaptic connections, followed by a fall. The time course of this rise and fall differs from region to region. According to selectionism the decrease in synaptic connectivity that can be observed is a function of a kind of Darwinian selection. Neural circuits that are used more frequently (perhaps in response to stimuli from the environment) are preserved, and those that are activated less frequently are weakened. As the selective loss of redundant pathways increases, so does the separation of the surviving pathways. In the long term only neural circuits that are actively employed remain intact, and these become increasingly encapsulated (separated off from other pathways, and specialized in function). In essence, selectionism holds that increased specialization of cortical structure comes about through selective *loss* of connectivity. Note that stimulation from the environment is one determinant of which pathways are employed and ultimately preserved, so these processes can be thought of as a type of learning.

There is some evidence to support this account. For example, there is evidence to suggest that information from different senses (touch, vision, hearing) may not be clearly differentiated at a perceptual level in very young infants. For example, Lewkowicz and Turkewitz (1981) showed that a newborn infant's visual preference for looking at a bright or dim visual stimulus was affected by prior exposure to an auditory stimulus. Such confusion of different modes of sensory input ('cross-modal transfer') indicates a relatively unspecialized sensory cortex; perhaps one with a proliferation of somewhat haphazard connections, which is not yet able to transmit information across specialized neural pathways without triggering activity in other pathways.

Similarly, Stetri (1987) found evidence of cross-modal transfer of tactile and visual information at 3 months of age, but no such transfer at 5 months of age. Meltzoff and Borton (1979) found that 1-month-old infants preferred to look at the shape of a dummy which they had previously been given to suck. This cross-modal effect could not be detected in a sample of 3 month olds (Maurer, 1993). These studies suggest that infants become increasingly able to differentiate between information from the various senses. Perhaps the relevant pathways have, in these older infants, become sufficiently encapsulated to allow the processing of information from one sensory input to be undertaken relatively independently of other sensory pathways.

Darwinian selection
The process of natural selection identified by Darwin and also known as 'survival of the fittest'. When applied to a population of neural pathways in the brain, this concept suggests that the strongest, most active pathways survive at the expense of weaker, more infrequently used ones.

Encapsulation
The process by which a neural pathway comes to have a specialized function that is relatively unaffected by the activities of other neural pathways.

SG

These patterns of findings are consistent with selectionism. The explosion of neural connectivity which happens around birth supports somewhat random patterns of neural activity within the immature brain, with sensory information being processed by relatively undifferentiated pathways. As experience of sensations increases, so pathways that are unused are weakened, and gradually the encapsulation of neural circuits increases. Johnson (1997) notes that the adult experience of synaesthesia may result from a failure to lose neural connectivity, such that different sensory pathways do not become sufficiently separated. However, it is important to stress that the precise nature of the processes by which cortical specialization occurs are not all well understood, so the ideas of selectionism involve some speculation.

SG

Synaesthesia
The occurrence of multi-channel sensory experiences. The way in which some people 'taste' colour, or 'hear' visual stimuli.

Summary of Section 2

- A prolonged period of postnatal development in humans maximizes the possibilities for interaction between the young developing brain and the rich environment in which the infant grows.
- During early postnatal development there is a dramatic increase in the number of neural connections in the brain.
- After the first year of life the number of connections begins to decrease in most brain regions. In the prefrontal cortex the peak is reached at around 24 months.
- Plasticity is an inherent property of the developing brain. As specialization of brain structure and function increases, so plasticity decreases.
- Specialization of structure may be a function of a Darwinian-type process of selection, whereby unused neural connections die out, leaving increasingly encapsulated (separated) pathways intact.

3 Functional specialization of the cortex: modules

Neuro-psychology
The branch of psychology that specializes in the study of the brain and behaviour.

The twentieth century saw considerable advances in the field of neuropsychology. One thing that has become clear is that the majority of adults who have followed typical developmental pathways have similar perceptual, motor and cognitive functions associated with approximately the same regions of cortex. In other words, the differentiation of the cerebral cortex into different *structural* areas (as described in Section 2) results in a brain that may have different *functional* units – units that specialize in processing particular types of information, in particular ways. These functional units are called 'modules'.

This section will examine how such modules develop. Are they genetically pre-specified, simply unfolding as the child matures? Or are the functions and underlying structures of modules influenced by interactions with the environment?

Activity 3   The shared environment

Allow about
20 minutes

This activity encourages you to reflect on the way in which psychologists reason about genetic and environmental influences on development. It also aims to get you thinking about how the different functional areas of the brain might develop.

The fact that most typically developing children and adults end up with the same sort of perceptual, cognitive and motor functions performed by the same regions of cortex seems to suggest that the brain develops according to a genetic blueprint (in the same way that other features of the human body develop in similar ways in different people on the basis of a genetic blueprint). But such reasoning is not really sound.

To understand the problem with this reasoning it is necessary to consider the shared environment in which people develop. At one level it would seem that people's environments are unique to each individual. But if you take a few steps back and look at the bigger picture, you should realize that typically developing children and adults live in very similar environments. Spend a few minutes thinking about the following questions and write down your answers before reading further.

1   In what ways can one person's environment differ from the environment of another?

2   In what ways can it be said that people share a common environment?

Comment

People's environments vary in all sorts of ways, and it should not be difficult to list just a few of these. However, at a more global level there are also many ways in which it can be said that people's environments are alike. For example, typically developing people are surrounded by very similar perceptual worlds, with similar physical constraints (owing to the laws of physics and biochemistry) on what they perceive and what they do. They live in a world of shared objects that behave in certain predictable ways. It is necessary to think at this more global level to understand why similar cortical structures and functions do not necessarily imply that genes are the only factor involved in brain development. Genetic determination may play a part, but they may also be the result of a shared environment. It is more likely that the cortical structures and functions that typically developing adults have in common are a result of epigenetic processes which involve the interaction of genetic and environmental factors.

3   Some people experience atypical patterns of development; for example people with motor disabilities such as cerebral palsy, or sensory disabilities such as hearing loss or visual impairment. Can you think of ways in which people with these kinds of disabilities might not share a similar environment with typically developing children and adults? What implications might this have for our understanding of brain structure and function in atypical development?

Comment

People with different kinds of sensory disabilities operate in a world in which they rely on different kinds of sensory input. For example, people with an autism spectrum disorder may live in rather distinctive sensory worlds (Williams, 1996). Children with motor disabilities may not act in and on their environment in the same way as typically developing children. If the epigenetic view is correct we might expect such factors to have an effect on brain structure and function. In other words, if differences in brain structure and function are detected when comparing typically and atypically developing people, we should not assume that these differences are the cause of the disability; they might result from the disability.

3.1 Innate modularity versus modularization

Modularity
In this context, this refers to the notion that the brain comprises modular 'units' that perform different functions.

Before we start the discussion of how modules develop, we need to make a very important conceptual distinction – one that was alluded to in the introduction to this chapter. This distinction is between 'neural modules' and 'cognitive modules'. Neural modules are real, structural units of the brain. There is plenty of evidence for their existence. Cognitive modules, on the other hand, are hypothetical constructs that provide a way of thinking about how the different functions of the brain might be performed. There is considerable debate about whether cognitive modules 'exist' (that is, whether the brain works in a modular way), and if they do, what sorts of functions they perform. Developmental cognitive neuroscience can illuminate the extent to which functions of the brain (cognitive modules) map onto structures of the brain (neural modules). Some of this work is described in Section 5. It is important to realize that, unless otherwise stated, whenever the word 'module' is used in this chapter it is being used to refer to cognitive modules. The debate that we shall look at in this section is between two theorists – Fodor and Karmiloff-Smith – who share a view that the brain does function in a modular fashion. Their disagreement is with regard to how modules develop. One theorist holds that they are innately specified; the other holds that modularization occurs as the brain develops.

Fodor (1983) is the key advocate of innately specified modularity. Arguing from a nativist standpoint, he asserts that humans are born with the innate capacity to develop information processing systems that allow them to make sense of the world in which they have evolved. In this way he is affording the environment a crucial role in the development of cognitive modules in one sense, but not in another. To Fodor, the environment influences the structure and function of modules over the course of evolution in a 'phylogenetic' sense (to do with the long-term development of a species over many generations). In other words human brains have become modular through adaptations to the environment, during the course of evolution.

In contrast he does not believe that the environment plays a crucial role in their development in an 'ontogenetic' sense (that is when it comes down to understanding the development of a given individual child). Fodor's argument is summarized in Box 1.

Comment

Phylogenesis is to do with the development of a species. Ontogenesis is to do with the development of an individual member of a species. When discussing the role of the environment in development, it is important to be clear about whether one is talking 'phylogenetically' (that is, about the development of a species through evolution over many generations of individuals) or 'ontogenetically' (about the development over one lifespan of one or more members of the species from the same evolutionary stage).

BOX 1

Fodor's modularity of mind

Fodor's model of the mind has three major components: transducers, input systems, and central systems. *Transducer* is the name that Fodor gives to organs that process sensory information about the outer world. Transducers are to do with sensation rather than perception. Their function is simply to translate stimulus information into a format with which the perceptual system can work. Cognition proper begins with the perceptual *input systems*. They carry out specialized processing of the stimulus information and deliver representations of the world to the higher thought processes of the *central processor*. The central processor is concerned with higher cognitive functions (planning, problem solving, abstract thought and so on). It is the input systems, Fodor's middle stage of cognitive function, that he refers to as *modules*. Note that according to Fodor, higher cognitive functions are not modular.

The input systems (modules) are at the heart of Fodor's theory of innate modularity of mind. They have a number of key properties. Firstly, they are *domain-specific*. They take as input a limited set of stimuli (from the appropriate transducers), and the processing they perform is highly specialized. For example, the visual input system may perform computations that convert a two-dimensional set of sensations into a three-dimensional representation of an object. This three-dimensional representation is then passed onto the central processor.

The second essential property of the input system modules is information *encapsulation*. This means that each module works independently, unaffected by the operations of other modules. Each module gets on with its own task, in its own way, regardless of what is going on elsewhere in the system. Continuing with the example of the visual input system, the three-dimensional representation is created exclusively from the two-dimensional sensory input; that is, without reference to information from other modules.

The third property is that they are *mandatory*. Their processing *must* happen; it is automatic and not subject to conscious control. We cannot help but see an object in our visual field as a three-dimensional object rather than a two-dimensional array of varying colours and lines.

The fourth property is that they are very rapid processors. This follows from the first three properties, because information processing systems that are domain-specific, encapsulated and mandatory are extremely efficient.

Reading

Now read Reading A 'The fragmented mind' from *What Infants Know* by Mehler and Dupoux (1994). This excerpt further illustrates the notion of cognitive modularity by drawing on some clinical case studies. As you read the descriptions of the cases, consider how they relate to Fodor's model of the mind.

Fodor's ideas on innately specified modularity have been hugely influential among cognitive developmental theorists, but they have been vigorously contested. One critic is Karmiloff-Smith (1992), who accepts the basic notion of encapsulated cognitive modules, but who questions whether such modules are innately pre-specified. The more highly pre-specified a cognitive system is in its infancy, she argues, the less creative and flexible it can become as it develops. She suggests that because human minds are remarkably creative and flexible, a high level of innate specificity in brain function is unlikely.

Working within a broadly constructivist framework, Karmiloff-Smith proposes that modules are the *product* of development; that the human mind *becomes* modular as a result of development. A relatively limited number of innately pre-specified 'constraints' on the kind of information that is dealt with by the different parts of the infant brain would, she reasons, be enough to produce modular adult minds. 'I argue for innately specified predispositions that are more epigenetic than Fodor's nativism.' (Karmiloff-Smith, 1992, p. 5). You can read more about her perspective, and the type of evidence that supports it, in Reading B.

Reading

Now read Reading B 'Is the initial architecture of the infant mind modular?' from *Beyond Modularity* by Karmiloff-Smith (1992). This summarizes Karmiloff-Smith's objections to Fodor's nativist views, and sets out some features of her constructivist alternative. While reading, focus on the notions of *domain-specificity* and *domain-generality*, and on her argument that the brain becomes modular as a result of development.

What does the wider research evidence have to say on the matter of *innate modularity* (Fodor) versus *modularization* (Karmiloff-Smith)? As ever the picture is complex and incomplete. Some researchers (for example, Rakic, 1988) argue that the structural differentiation of the cortex could be explained in terms of a molecular and genetic specification (just as other organs in our body, such as the heart, lungs and liver, are differentiated one from another, without particular reference to interactions with the environment). If, once differentiated, the various structures of the cortex always took on the same cognitive functions in the developing child's mind, then this would support Fodor's position.

However, the balance of evidence (O'Leary, 1989; Elman *et al.*, 1996; Katz and Shatz, 1996; Johnson, 1997) suggests that for most regions of the cortex differentiation of function results from an epigenetic system. That is, differentiation results from an interaction between molecular and genetic factors

Neural activity
The electro-
chemical activity
of neurons as they
transmit
information from
one to another.

on the one hand and environmental factors on the other. This view holds that neural activity, itself the product of both biological and environmental factors, is the key to understanding differentiation of function in the cortex. Before birth, this neural activity is probably largely a spontaneous and intrinsic process, driven by genetic and molecular factors (though note our earlier reminder that the mother's womb provides an 'environment' in which the baby can, for example, hear). After birth, however, neural activity is substantially influenced by sensory and motor experience as well as by intrinsic factors.

What evidence can be cited to support this view? Petersen *et al.* (1990) used positron emission tomography (PET) (see Box 2) to study the responses of native English speaking adults to written stimuli in the form of (a) English words, (b) 'pseudowords' that obeyed English spelling rules (for example *floop* and *toglo*), (c) nonsense strings of letters (such as *pxqlo*) and (d) letter-like forms (false fonts). They found that a specific region of the left visual cortex only responded to the English words and to the pseudowords. It is implausible to suggest that native English speakers are genetically programmed to develop an area in the brain that will respond to the shapes of letters, but *only* when they are grouped together to form English words or words that follow the rules of English spelling (note that the activation was in *visual* areas, so the findings are unlikely to be to do with the 'pronounceability' of the different types of letter strings). A much better explanation of this finding would be that experience of a particular language environment has influenced the development of this specialist area of cortical function. The fact that the location of this specialist area is shared by native English speakers suggests that there are similar genetic and molecular processes *working in harmony* with a similar language environment, to produce a similar structural and functional outcome.

There are many more studies that provide evidence for the effect of experience on cortical structure and function. One example is Neville's (1991) work using scalp recorded event-related potentials (ERPs) with congenitally deaf participants (see Box 2). For these participants she found that regions of the temporal lobe (see Figure 1, p. 118) which in typical development respond to auditory, or multi-modal input (input from more than one of the senses) had become dominated by responses to visual input. This suggests that the function of these regions had been influenced by the distinctive sensory experiences of the participants.

BOX 2

Brain imaging methods used in developmental studies

One reason for the recently renewed interest in relating physical brain development to cognitive change comes from advances in methods which allow hypotheses to be generated and tested more readily than previously. One set of tools relates to brain imaging – the creation of 'functional' maps of brain activity based on either changes in cerebral metabolism, blood flow, or electrical activity. Some of these imaging methods, such as PET, are of limited usefulness for studying changes in behavioural development in typically developing infants and children due to their invasive nature (requiring the intravenous injection of radioactively labelled substances) and their relatively coarse temporal resolution (whereby measurements are taken in chunks of minutes, rather than seconds). However, two brain imaging techniques which can be used to study typical development are event-related potentials (ERPs), and functional magnetic resonance imaging (fMRI).

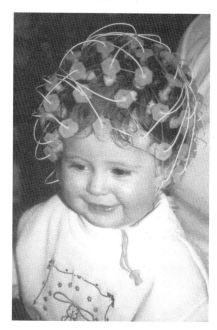

Figure 5   ERPs: sensitive electrodes are attached to the surface of the scalp (courtesy of Leslie Tucker, Centre for Brain and Cognitive Development, Birkbeck College).

Event-related potentials involve using sensitive electrodes on the scalp surface to measure the electrical activity of the brain that is generated as groups of neurons fire at the same time (see Figure 5). These recordings can either be of the spontaneous natural rhythms of the brain electroencephalogram (EEG), or the electrical activity induced by the presentation of a stimulus (ERP). Normally the ERP from many trials is averaged, in order to screen out the natural rhythms of the brain that are unrelated to the presentation of the stimulus. With a high density of electrodes on the scalp, algorithms (mathematical procedures) can be employed which infer the position of the sources of electrical activity in the brain from the particular pattern of electrical activity on the scalp surface (see Figure 5). Recent developments of the ERP method allow relatively quick installation of a large number of sensors thus opening new possibilities in the investigation of infant brain function.

Functional MRI allows the non-invasive measurement of cerebral blood flow (Kwong et al., 1992), with the prospect of (a) millimetre spatial resolution, and (b) temporal resolution in the order of seconds. In other words, very accurate 'maps' of moment-by-moment brain activity can be built up. Although this technique has been used with children (Casey et al., 1997), the distracting noise and vibration, and the presently unknown possible effects of high magnetic fields on the developing brain, make its usefulness for healthy children under 4 or 5 years of age uncertain. However, there has been at least one fMRI study of infants initially scanned for clinical reasons (Tzourio et al., 1992), and the advent of 'open' scanners in which the mother can hold the infant may increase possibilities further.

A further example, also from Neville and her colleagues (Mills *et al.*, 1993) shows how, with experience, certain types of processing are performed by progressively smaller (more localized) regions of cortex. For instance, data from scalp-recorded ERPs suggest that processing of known words and control stimuli is initially spread over a relatively large area of cortex. This processing narrows to an area over the left temporal lobe only when the child's vocabulary reaches about 200 words, irrespective of maturational age. We will look at further evidence relating to whether modularization occurs as the brain develops when we discuss the specific case of language in Section 4.

Comment

The area of the brain shown by Neville and colleagues (Mills *et al.*, 1993) to process some aspects of word recognition appears to change at a certain point in vocabulary development, rather than at a certain age. How can we interpret these findings? If this 'narrowing' of function to the left temporal lobe happened for all children at a similar age, it could be argued that this was due to an innate 'pre-programmed' specification of function that was simply unfolding with maturity. Indeed this could still be the case if it happened at different ages, given that children mature at different speeds. The fact that it happens at different ages for different children, and that it relates to something so dependent on experience (vocabulary development) suggests that the environment is playing a part and supports the modularization position.

3.2 Self-organization

Section 3.1 provided some evidence to support the view that the environment plays a part in the development of the structures and functions of the brain. If this is the case, how might it happen? What processes might be involved in this gene–environment interaction that we are invoking? One answer lies with the concept of *self-organization.*

Self-organization occurs when structure emerges in response to a system's dynamic interactions with an environment. All stages of brain development involve an element of self-organization (Keslo, 1995; Johnson, 1997). Initially the neural system is relatively undifferentiated (randomly organized) but, as a result of small adaptive changes, an order begins to emerge among the elements of the system. In the brain, synaptic adjustment rules (such as the Hebb rule; see Box 3) can lead to ordered connection patterns that in turn lead to structured behaviours. In arguing that cognitive modules emerge as a result of development, Karmiloff-Smith (1992) is proposing that the brain is a self-organizing system. The child interacts with its environment, and as a result particular neural structures and modules emerge. Self-organization is regarded by many researchers as a fundamental characteristic of the brain (Changeux *et al.*, 1984; von der Malsburg, 1995).

BOX 3

The Hebb rule

Donald Hebb has been hugely influential in neuropsychology because of his early attempts to link psychological processes to properties of nerve cells. He developed an approach to understanding learning at the level of the neuron which is generally referred to as the Hebb rule (Hebb, 1949). 'This states that when two adjacent neurons are repeatedly activated then contingent metabolic changes lead to a lowered synaptic resistance between the two cells. This in turn increases the probability that activity in one cell will cause activity in the other' (Quinlan, 1991, p. 4).

What this rule says is that activity between connected neurons tends to increase the ease with which one can activate the other. According to Hebb there are metabolic (biochemical) reasons for this. So the more a pathway of interconnected neurons gets used (activated), the more robust the activation can be along that pathway. Thus learning, at the level of the neuron, can be regarded as the strengthening of neural pathways through repeated usage. You might like to refer back to Section 2.4 to see how this fits in with the 'selectionism' view of increased cortical specialization.

SG

Self-organization occurs in systems with a large number of degrees of freedom; that is, in complex systems where there are seemingly endless possibilities for how things might 'turn out'. In such systems it is difficult to see how all the elements can be following a predetermined plan. For example, in the case of brain development, the cerebral cortex alone contains some 100,000,000,000,000 (also written as 10^{14}) synapses. It is unlikely that the genes can (in any direct way) encode the full information necessary to generate this level of complexity according to a predetermined plan (Elman *et al.*, 1996). This is another argument in favour of an epigenetic view of brain development, and in favour of Karmiloff-Smith's argument that modularization happens as a *product* of development.

There are many well-studied examples of self-organization in the physical and biological sciences. For example, in snowflakes and in many other crystals, a complex structure emerges from the apparently random addition of new material (see Figure 6). Simple local rules of where new material can be added result in intricate global patterns appearing in the final crystal. Processes of self-organization can explain many complex patterns in nature, from the shape of storm clouds to the spots on a leopard (Goldfield, 1995).

Figure 6   A snowflake is a complicated, non-random shape that looks 'designed', yet it arises from a very simple process; there is no design for a snowflake built into water molecules. When an ice crystal starts to form it initially takes a simple hexagonal shape. With the crystal suspended in humid, cold air, water molecules join on more easily at the corners, starting to form a star. Alternate melting and freezing then creates more corners where molecules join, leading to the crystal becoming more and more complex.

A fundamental characteristic of self-organizing systems is that global order can arise from local interactions. In other words, the overarching functional units of the brain about which you have been reading and which involve the development of massively complex structures, arise from the ongoing, small-scale activities of sets of neurons interacting with each other in local sets of connections and networks. In the brain, local interactions between neighbouring neurons create states of global order that ultimately generate coherent behaviour. Note that it is important to be careful about how 'local' is understood in this context. Because nerve cells are connected by long axons, local neural interactions are not necessarily topologically (spatially) arranged. Connected cells can be neighbours although they are physically located at other ends of the brain. One implication of this is that some ordered structures in the brain may not initially 'look' ordered, because the units of the structure can be spatially distributed across different areas of the brain.

SG   Principles of self-organization as they relate to brain development can be illustrated using computer models of networks of interconnected neurons (called connectionist or neural network models). Connectionist models simulate the way in which networks of neurons can 'learn' to process certain stimuli. The activity levels and connectivity of the simulated neurons are adjusted according to simple rules, and the self-organization that occurs leads to a network that can process the stimuli appropriately. In this way connectionist modelling can help psychologists to understand how brain structure (networks of interconnected neurons) might link to cognitive function (in this case, the processing of stimuli). It can also help psychologists to learn more about the processes of self-organization in the brain.

Summary of Section 3

- Cognitive modules are hypothetical constructs that may help psychologists to understand the relationship between the brain's structure and its functions.

- Fodor argued from a nativist perspective that modules are innately specified and develop as the child matures, relatively unaffected by the environment.

- Karmiloff-Smith argued from a more constructivist perspective, asserting that modules are a result of development; a result of children interacting with a complex environment.

- The empirical evidence is complex, but on balance supports the epigenetic view of theorists such as Karmiloff-Smith, that cognitive development is characterized by a process of modularization, rather than by a predefined structure of modularity. More relevant evidence will be examined in Section 4.

- Self-organization is a key concept in understanding how genes and environment can interact to affect the development of brain structures and their functions.

4 Language

This section extends the argument from Section 3. It looks in more detail at evidence relating to the question of whether specialist brain functions are genetically predetermined, or the result of a more epigenetic system in which genes and environment interact. We will focus on the case of language. Of all human abilities, language has been regarded as the most 'biologically special' (Johnson, 1997, p. 137). It is in this domain that the strongest nativist case for innateness of function has been made, notably by Chomsky (1965, for example). Chomsky's ideas have been further developed in the persuasive arguments of Pinker (1994), which are the topic of this section of the chapter.

4.1 An instinct for language?

SG

Like Chomsky, Pinker can be characterized as a nativist. Indeed, the title of his book *The Language Instinct* (Pinker, 1994) already gives a strong indication of his theoretical perspective. In this book Pinker makes a highly readable and convincing case for the innateness of language. The case begins with observations about the universality of language among humans. But Pinker acknowledges that these observations, in themselves, do not constitute proof that language is an innate quality.

The ubiquity of complex language among human beings is a gripping discovery and, for many observers, compelling proof that language is innate. But to tough-minded skeptics ... it is no proof at all. Not everything that is universal is innate.

(Pinker, 1994, p. 31)

It is important to understand why Pinker has to go beyond the observation of the universality of language among humans in order to sustain an argument that language is an innate quality. The fact that highly structured, complex language is found in every human group, without exception, *can* be taken as an indicator that it is an innate characteristic of the human species. Anthropologists and linguists have often noted that the linguistic sophistication of people never varies from group to group. Neither is there any evidence of a region acting as the origin of language, from which it developed and spread to other, previously languageless groups. Language seems as inevitable a part of the human condition as any innate physiological characteristic one could think of. However, Pinker acknowledges that this observation alone cannot be taken as proof that language is innate. It may be that people have evolved as intelligent problem-solvers who as children have the information processing capability to learn their language from adults. If this were the case, it would not be necessary to invoke any special innate status for language; language could just be regarded as a by-product of human information processing. So Pinker acknowledges that in order to make the case for the innateness of language he must draw on several other lines of evidence.

Pidgin
A 'make-shift jargon ... choppy strings of words borrowed from the language of [others] ... highly variable in order and with little in the way of grammar' (Pinker, 1994, p. 33).

There are four basic components to Pinker's argument: the existence of pidgins and creoles, observations regarding the so-called 'poverty of the input', the commonality of certain grammatical formulations across different languages, and evidence about brain structure and function. We will now look at each of these four elements in turn. First, Pinker draws on the work of the linguist Derek Bickerton who studied the development of pidgins and creoles. Pidgins (you may have come across the term 'pidgin English') are non-grammatical forms of communication that are cobbled together by adult speakers who share no common native language but who nevertheless learn to communicate. At the beginning of the twentieth century many migrant workers collected in Hawaii to work on booming sugar plantations. They developed a pidgin to communicate with each other. But the children who grew up in this pidgin-speaking community ended up speaking a fully fledged creole. A creole is a grammatical language, with all the structures and constructions of a 'conventional' language.

Creole
A fully grammatical language developed out of a pidgin.

According to Pinker's interpretation of Bickerton's work, the children simply could not help creating a grammatically well formed language, even though they had not been exposed to one. A similar effect can be observed in deaf children of hearing adults, or deaf children of deaf adults who learned sign language late in life. The sign language that the children are exposed to is like a pidgin; it is relatively ungrammatical and poorly structured. However, the children themselves learn a genuine sign language with all the grammatical complexities of any other language. In doing this, Pinker argues, the children of the immigrant communities and of the non-native signers, are actually doing no more than every child does – they are reinventing language anew as they use it. He sees this as compelling evidence for a language instinct:

> ... *children actually reinvent [language]* generation after generation – not because they are taught to, not because they are generally smart, not because it is useful to them, but because they just can't help it.

(Pinker, 1994, p. 32; emphasis as in original)

The second element of Pinker's case is drawn from Chomsky's own 'argument from the poverty of the input' (Pinker, 1994, p. 42). The core of this argument is that children produce language that they can never have heard before, indicating that they are not 'learning' or imitating it, but generating it anew. Pinker gives the example of how children are able to produce grammatically correct questions, even though they will not have heard these questions asked before, and even though the rule that they have to follow is comparatively complex, and one that they are unlikely to have learned.

Activity 4   How are questions formed?

Allow about 10 minutes

This activity will help you to reflect on Pinker's second piece of evidence for the innateness of language – the fact that children formulate sentences correctly, even when the rules they are using are complex. Pinker's evidence is based on Chomsky's classic illustrations of how children appear to know the deep structure of their language.

1   Turn the following statement into a question: 'A unicorn is in the garden'. Can you devise a rule that you could follow to convert a statement like this into a question?

Comment

You should have come up with something like 'Is a unicorn in the garden?' or 'Is there a unicorn in the garden?' The rule that you followed might have been 'take the first "is" and move it to the beginning of the sentence, and add a question mark'. (Whether or not you added 'there' is not relevant to this activity.)

2   Now formulate a question from the following sentence: 'A unicorn that is eating a flower is in the garden'. Write your question down. Does your original rule still work?

Comment

Your original rule would produce the non-grammatical (in fact nonsensical) question 'Is a unicorn that___ eating a flower is in the garden?'. This is clearly not correct. This time you have to take the second 'is' and move it to get 'Is (there) a unicorn that is eating a flower in the garden?'.

Pinker's and Chomsky's observation is that children have no difficulty in formulating such questions, even though the rule they have to follow is not superficially easy, and despite probably never having heard such a construction before. 'Surely not every child learning English has heard Mother say *Is the doggie that is eating the flower in the garden?* (Pinker, 1994, pp. 41–2). According to the nativists, children achieve the right grammatical form for the question because they have an innate grasp of the deep structure of language and its units of meaning.

The third element of Pinker's argument is related to the second. Pinker asserts that many languages around the world use auxiliary verbs and that these languages move the auxiliary to the beginning of the sentence to formulate a question. (The 'is' in the sentences in Activity 4 is an English auxiliary verb.) If you think about it, there are limitless ways in which a question might be formulated. Why not turn the sentence backwards, or exchange the first and last words? So why have all these languages hit upon the same way of doing this? 'It is as if isolated inventors miraculously came up with identical standards for typewriter keyboards or Morse code or traffic signals.' (Pinker, 1994, p. 43). Pinker's answer to this question is that it is *not* miraculous, and it is not a coincidence; rather, it reflects a commonality in the structure of the human brain.

The final and fourth part of Pinker's argument brings us back to the specific topic of this chapter; that is, to studies of brain and cognitive development. He argues that there is 'an identifiable seat [for language] in the brain, and perhaps even a special set of genes that help wire it into place' (Pinker, 1994, p. 45). We will look in more detail at this claim, but now from the perspective of the wider developmental cognitive neurosciences literature.

4.2 The evidence from developmental cognitive neuroscience

One way of tackling the issue of innateness from the point of view of cognitive neuroscience is to ask whether there are any areas of cortex that are *critical* for language processing or acquisition. If there are such areas, without which language simply cannot happen, then a working assumption would be that these areas have an innate, language-specific processing capacity. If, on the other hand, there are a variety of cortical regions that can support language acquisition, then this would suggest that areas of language specialization emerge from more general structures, connectivity and processes within the developing brain, in concert with the rich language environment.

Hemisphere
The cerebral cortex is divided into two halves, known as the left and right hemispheres.

Sometimes this debate is framed in terms of the concept of 'equipotentiality'. This refers to the hypothesis that at birth the left and right hemispheres of the brain both have 'equal potential' for developing language. Evidence in favour of equipotentiality would seriously undermine the nativist case for innate language-specific areas of the cortex. Bear in mind that in typically developing adults, areas of the left hemisphere are strongly associated with language processing, and damage to those areas in adulthood can cause a variety of lasting language difficulties. There is no doubt that by adulthood there are specialist cortical regions that are devoted to language processing (language modules). The question is whether language processing *must* be carried out by these areas, or whether early damage, or indeed atypical developmental pathways, (for example, through deafness) can lead to other cortical regions performing the same functions.

On balance, the evidence from neuroscientific studies points to the conclusion that several cortical regions are capable of supporting the development of language, but does not support the hypothesis of full equipotentiality. For example, Neville *et al.* (1998) used the fMRI technique (see Box 2, Section 3.1) to examine the brain regions that are involved in language processing in deaf and hearing participants. When the deaf participants viewed American Sign Language (ASL) sentences (see Figure 7b) they showed activation in language areas in the left hemisphere, as did the hearing participants on reading English sentences (see Figure 8a). However, the deaf participants (who were all native ASL signers) also displayed a level of activation in the right hemisphere that was *not* observed for the hearing participants (compare Figure 7b with Figure 8a).

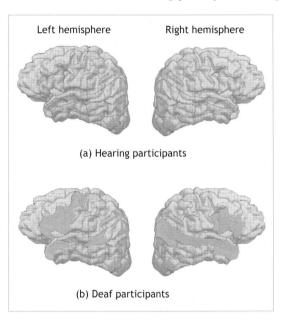

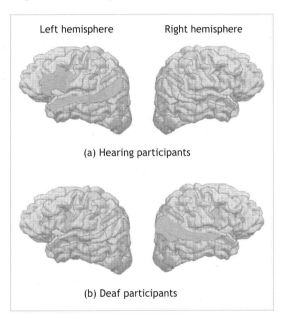

Figure 7 Images of left and right hemispheric activation in response to American Sign Language (adapted from Neville et al., 1988).

Figure 8 Images of left and right hemispheric activation in response to written English (adapted from Neville et al., 1988).

Activity 5   *Equipotentiality: evaluating the evidence*

Allow about 10 minutes

This activity encourages you to think about the implications of Neville et al.*'s pattern of findings.*

Look carefully at the findings reported for Neville *et al.* (1998) (see Figures 7 and 8). You will see that they found that both hearing and deaf participants in their study showed activation in language areas of the left hemisphere when processing language stimuli in their native language (ASL for deaf participants, written English for the hearing participants). In addition, the level of right hemisphere activation was higher for the deaf participants than for the hearing participants. What implications do these findings have for the hypothesis of equipotentiality? Make brief notes before reading further.

Comment

Bearing in mind that these findings are from just one study (and you should therefore exercise caution in interpreting them) they indicate the following:

1   The language areas of the left hemisphere are prepared in some way to process language-related information, irrespective of the form of the language. Both signed and written sentences were processed by the classic language areas of the left hemisphere.

2   Some areas of the right hemisphere had been 'captured' for language processing in the deaf participants, perhaps because of the role of visuo-spatial information in sign languages.

Both these findings suggest some kind of bias towards language processing in areas of the left hemisphere, but also that other areas in the right hemisphere are capable of supporting language-related information processing. Note also the right hemisphere activation for deaf participants when reading English sentences (Figure 8b).

Semantic
To do with meaning.

Neville and her colleagues (Neville *et al.*, 1992) also noted *different* patterns of cortical response (as measured by ERPs) in hearing and deaf participants whilst reading *grammatically* significant words in sentences, but noted *similar* patterns of response across the two groups when they were reading *semantically* important words. So perhaps the question of how biologically special language is may require different answers for different aspects of language processing and acquisition. Neville *et al.*'s findings indicate that grammatical aspects of language may be more sensitive to experience than semantic aspects, because hearing and deaf participants (who have a different experience of language) responded in different ways to the grammatical information. After summarizing a decade of their research, Neville and Bavelier conclude that the evidence supports the hypothesis that 'there are constraints on the organisation of the neural systems that mediate formal language ... however, it is clear that the nature and timing of sensory and language experience significantly affect the development of the language system of the brain' (Neville and Bavelier, 2001, p. 283).

Further evidence to support the hypothesis that different areas of the cortex are capable of supporting language processing comes from studies of children with localized brain damage (focal lesions) that happened either before or during birth. In a sample of children aged between 3 and 9 years, Reilly and colleagues (Reilly *et al.*, 1998) found that the group of participants with a focal lesion performed worse on a series of language tasks than the group of typically developing control participants (see Research summary 1). However, the children with a focal lesion showed a pattern of catching up on these measures, then lagging behind at the next stage of language development, then catching up again. The crucial points here are: first, functional recovery from a focal lesion appears to be an ongoing process in childhood, and second, there is an implication that functions affected by the original damage to a localized area of the cortex were taken over in later development by undamaged areas of the cortex.

In study children were asked to tell a story from a 24-page picture book about a boy, a frog and a dog. The researchers aimed to examine the effects of focal lesions which happen before 6 months of age on children's subsequent narrative language skills. The study involved 62 children, of which thirteen had right-hemisphere damage (RHD), eighteen had left-hemisphere damage (LHD) and 31 were typically developing (neurologically intact) control participants. All the RHD and LHD children had focal lesions in one hemisphere only, which had occurred before 6 months of age. The age range of participants was 3 years and 5 months (3;5) to 9 years and 4 months (9;4), with a mean age of just over 6 years. The participants were also subdivided into two age levels: younger than 5 years (seven LHD, four RHD and eleven controls) and older than 5 years (eleven LHD, nine RHD and 20 controls). This gave the researchers an experimental design that allowed them to test hypotheses relating to age (comparing the younger group with the older group), neurological status (comparing the children with focal lesions with the neurologically intact group), lateralization (comparing RHD with LHD), and interactions among all these factors. This is known as a factorial design.

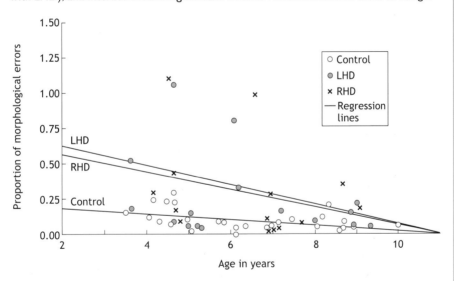

Figure 9   Grammatical errors of participants (adapted from Reilly et al., 1998).

The researchers collected both quantitative and qualitative data. The quantitative data involved systematic measurements of various features of the narrative account of the story produced by each child.

The researchers found that the children with brain injury showed some delays in grammatical and narrative skills when compared to their control group. But the data also showed 'clear evidence of change and development on all fronts' (Reilly et al., 1998, p. 358). For example, Figure 9 plots a measure of grammatical errors ('morphological errors') on the vertical axis against age on the horizontal axis. Each child is represented by a marker within the graph. The higher up the marker is, the more errors the child made. The 'regression' lines (or 'lines of best fit') for the three groups, all of which slope downwards from left to right, show that in all groups (LHD, RHD and control) older children did, on average, better than younger children. Note how the lines converge with age; at 4 years of age there is quite a gap between the performance of the control group, on the one hand, and the LHD and RHD groups on the other. By 6 years of age this gap in performance had narrowed, and by 9 years of age it had narrowed even further.

The qualitative data were used to analyse the nature of any grammatical errors. From this analysis the researchers were able to conclude that for the brain injured group 'the raw data suggest ... a delay in morphological development, but there is no evidence here for a qualitative deviation from the normal pattern' (Reilly et al., 1998, p. 360). The younger children in the LHD and RHD groups made significantly more errors than their age-matched controls, but the errors that they made were 'normal' errors.

Like Reilly and colleagues (1998), Stiles and Thal (1993) also studied children with focal lesions that had occurred either to the left or right hemisphere before 6 months of age. The children were examined longitudinally, and were found to have language delays irrespective of which hemisphere had been damaged. Surprisingly, though, the most significant delays in word comprehension were found among the right hemisphere lesion group. In adults one would expect to see this kind of problem when an area of the left hemisphere becomes damaged. This suggests that the regions responsible for language acquisition are not necessarily the same as those used for language processing in the adult.

The evidence presented in this section does not in itself rule out the proposition that the left hemisphere is innately 'pre-wired' for language. It only shows that other areas of the brain can 'do' language, if necessary. However, there is a proposition that fits the evidence a little more securely than this. This is that the architecture and connectivity of the left temporal lobe (the region most clearly related to language processing in adults) biases the system towards building neural modules that specialize in language processing in these regions. These regions may be slightly better suited to processing rapidly changing information than other areas of the cortex, and so can develop more efficient computational properties for processing language. However, the regions are not the only place where language processing can find a home. There is sufficient plasticity in the developing child's cortex to enable other regions to take on these functions, perhaps with some loss of efficiency. 'While regions of the left temporal lobe may be best suited to language processing, they are not critical since language can develop in a close to normal way without [them]' (Johnson, 1997, p. 141). Overall, therefore, the evidence from developmental cognitive neuroscience supports a compromise position somewhere between equipotentiality on the one hand, and genetically predetermined language-specific cortical regions on the other.

4.3 An instinct for language: review

Where does this leave the arguments of Chomsky, Pinker and the nativists? In some respects, the evidence from developmental cognitive neuroscience supports their position. There is clearly some kind of predisposition in human infants to develop language. Even if there is damage to some of the brain structure that typically goes on to support language in adults, the plastic, self-organizing infant brain will find another way of dealing with it. As Pinker says, children cannot help but develop language.

However, the fact that early damage to structures that usually go on to develop language can be overcome suggests that there are general properties of brain structure and connectivity that are suited to processing language, without being pre-specified to do so.

If an innate, specialized cortical region for processing language were *necessary* for the developing child to acquire language (as the strong version of the nativist argument maintains) one might expect more disruption to language development if this region were damaged in early pre- or postnatal development. It would be unlikely that other cortical regions would also have a specialized capacity for processing language just in case they are needed (these other regions normally go on to process other kinds of information). So the fact that other regions can support language adequately well if they are employed sufficiently early, suggests that the brain's ability to process language has more to do with the general properties of its structure and connectivity, than it has to do with innate, language-specific regions.

Furthermore, if one region of the cortex always went on to support language, it could be argued that it is innately predetermined to do so. But if, as you have seen, other regions can support language when necessary, then this suggests that there is some other factor that influences the development of these brain regions, above and beyond an innate blueprint. If the fate of these regions has not been determined by a genetic blueprint, then what else is there to feed into the equation? The answer is, surely, the environment; specifically, the child's language environment. These regions have genetic constraints on what they can and cannot do, in terms of innately pre-specified principles of neural connectivity and structure. But within these constraints the different cortical regions can self-organize through interaction with a complex environment to develop their ultimate cognitive function. All this takes us back to the argument of Section 3 in favour of the epigenetic basis for the development of specialized cognitive modules. It suggests that both in typical and atypical development, what drives the development of brain function is a potent mix of genes and environment, and that specialist cognitive modules are a *product* of development. This is a rather more constructivist position than the one adopted by Chomsky and Pinker.

▼

Activity 6   *Evidence for and against a language 'instinct'*

Allow about
30 minutes

This activity encourages you to review the debate about 'the language instinct', and to weigh up the evidence for and against the nativist approach.

Review the nativist arguments of Chomsky and Pinker in Section 4.1 in the light of the evidence presented in Section 4.2, together with the evidence presented in Section 3. Does the evidence support or refute their position? As usual, the answer is probably not clear cut. To help you carry out your review, construct a list of points in favour of the nativist stance, and points against it. Structure your list as shown in Figure 10, remembering to cite evidence wherever possible (we have provided some examples to get you started).

For the nativist position	Against the nativist position
1 Universality of language	Ability of different cortical regions to process language e.g. Neville et al. (1988).
2	
3	

Figure 10   Example answers for Activity 6.

▲

Summary of Section 4

- Pinker and Chomsky are key advocates of the nativist position on language development, which prioritizes the role of genetic determination.
- In support of his case, Pinker uses arguments from (a) the development of pidgins into creoles, (b) the 'poverty of the input', (c) the universality of potentially arbitrary grammatical rules, and (d) neuropsychology.
- Equipotentiality is an epigenetic proposition that the left and right hemispheres are equally equipped for language development at birth.
- Evidence from developmental cognitive neuroscience suggests that there is sufficient plasticity in the infant's brain to enable several regions of cortex to support language development and processing.

- In typically developing adults, areas in the left temporal lobe deal with many language-specific functions. Damage to these areas in adulthood can seriously disrupt key language functions.
- It is likely that the left temporal lobe becomes the 'seat of language' because of slight advantages in its capacity for processing complex, rapidly changing information, rather than because it has an innate capacity to process language.
- Broadly speaking, the neuroscientific evidence supports an epigenetic view of the development of language-specific functions in the adult brain.

5 The emergence of specialized cortical function: the case of the prefrontal cortex

In this section we leave behind arguments about the origin of cognitive modules, and turn more directly to the question of how the development of brain structure can be related to the development of cognition and behaviour in infants and children. We focus on the case of the prefrontal cortex for the reasons outlined in Section 5.1. Thereafter, Sections 5.2 and 5.3 provide two competing views of how structural developments in this area of the brain can be related to advances in cognitive ability.

5.1 The prefrontal cortex

The region of the frontal lobe in front of ('anterior to') the primary motor and premotor cortex, the *prefrontal cortex* (see Figure 1), accounts for almost one-third of the total cortical surface in humans and is considered by most investigators to be critical for many higher cognitive abilities (Milner, 1982; Goldman-Rakic, 1987; Fuster, 1989). The types of cognitive processing that have been associated with the prefrontal cortex concern the planning and execution of sequences of action, the maintenance of information over short delays in working memory, and the ability to inhibit a set of responses that are appropriate in one context but not another. Collectively these cognitive processes are known as 'executive function'. This aspect of cognitive function will receive more detailed treatment in Chapter 5 of this book.

The prefrontal cortex is the part of the brain that shows the most prolonged period of postnatal development, with changes in synaptic density detectable even into the teenage years (Huttenlocher, 1990). For this reason it has been the part of the brain most frequently associated with cognitive development.

Working memory
The part of the memory system that deals with the active manipulation of information (as opposed to long-term memory which is more to do with 'storage' of information).

There is disagreement among psychologists about exactly how the development of the prefrontal cortex relates to cognitive development. The two main approaches to this question are presented in the following sections.

5.2 Relating structural change to cognitive development

One approach to understanding the relationship between cognitive development and structural developments in the prefrontal cortex is to chart advances in cognitive abilities at a given age, and to try to relate these advances to observed changes in the prefrontal cortex. Does the emergence of a particular ability happen at the same age as an observed change in brain structure? (Bear in mind that if a change in cognitive ability does occur at the same time as a change in brain structure, this does not necessarily mean that the two things are directly related; instead it indicates relationships that are worthy of further investigation.)

An example of this approach is found in the work of Diamond and Goldman-Rakic (Diamond and Goldman-Rakic, 1986, 1989; Goldman-Rakic, 1987). On the basis of their research with monkeys they argue that the maturation of the prefrontal cortex between 6 and 12 months of age accounts for a number of transitions observed in infant behaviour on object permanence and object retrieval tasks. One such task was based on Piaget's (1954) observation that infants younger than 8 months often fail to retrieve a hidden object (from under 'cloth B') after a short delay period if the object's location had been changed from one where it had previously been successfully retrieved (from under 'cloth A'). Infants often make a particular error (the 'A-not-B error') in which they reach to the hiding location where the object was found on the immediately preceding trials, even though they have seen the object being moved to the other location. By around 9 months infants begin to succeed on the task with successively longer delays between the presentation of the hidden object and the point at which they are allowed to respond (Diamond, 1985).

Diamond and Goldman-Rakic (1989) tested monkeys on a version of this task. Consistent with the observations of human infants, infant monkeys failed to retrieve the hidden object. Further, adult monkeys with lesions to the dorsolateral region of the prefrontal cortex (DLPC) (see Figure 1, p. 118) were also impaired on this task. Lesions to some other parts of the brain did not significantly impair performance, suggesting that the DLPC plays a central role in tasks which require the maintenance of spatial or object information, or information about objects, over short periods of time.

Evidence linking success on the object permanence task to prefrontal cortex maturation in human infants comes from a number of sources. One of these is a series of EEG studies (see Box 2, Section 3.1) with typically developing infants (Fox and Bell, 1990; Bell, 1992; Bell and Fox, 1992). These showed that increases in EEG responses recorded from over the prefrontal cortex were correlated with the ability to respond successfully over longer delays in delayed response object permanence tasks; the more activation there was in the prefrontal cortex, the longer the infant's response could be delayed and still be successful.

A second source of evidence is work on cognitive development in children with phenylketonuria (PKU). Even when treated, this inborn condition can cause a reduction in the levels of a neurotransmitter, dopamine, in the prefrontal cortex. Neurotransmitters are chemicals that enable neurons to communicate with each other across their synapses, so a reduction in the level of a neurotransmitter will affect the efficiency of neural connections. In these cases, reductions in dopamine levels in the DLPC result in impairments on tasks thought to involve parts of the prefrontal cortex such as object permanence and object retrieval tasks. The affected infants show no impairment on tasks thought to depend on other regions of cortex.

Phenyl-ketonuria
An inborn condition which affects the infant's ability to process a protein (phenylalanine) and which can lead to severe learning difficulties if untreated by a dietary intervention.

Neuro-transmitters
Chemicals that are released by neurons and which affect the transmission of information between neurons.

5.3 The prefrontal cortex and the acquisition of new skills

An alternative perspective on the role of the prefrontal cortex in cognitive development has been proposed by several researchers who have suggested that the region may play a role in organizing other parts of cortex (for example, Thatcher, 1992), and that it plays a critical role in the acquisition of new knowledge and skills. According to this view, regions of the prefrontal cortex play an important role in the early stages of the development of a new skill. As mastery of the skill increases, so involvement of the prefrontal cortex decreases, and other specialist areas of cortex take over. The processing resources of the prefrontal cortex are then switched to some other newly developing skill. In contrast to the perspective presented in Section 5.2 this view leads to the prediction that the involvement of the prefrontal cortex in a particular task or situation will *decrease* with increased experience or skill in the domain.

Two recent lines of evidence are consistent with the view that regions of prefrontal cortex play a key role during the earlier stages of skill acquisition during infancy. Johnson and colleagues (1998) studied infants with localized damage to parts of their cortex in a visual attention task. They found that only infants with damage in the prefrontal regions of cortex were impaired on the task. In adults one would expect those with damage to parietal regions (see Figure 1, p. 118) to show such an impairment. Similarly, a recent study involving visual attention and eye movement planning in infants showed suggestive evidence of prefrontal cortex involvement (Csibra *et al.*, 1998). The same effect was not observed in adults. You can read about Johnson *et al.*'s research in more detail in Research summary 2.

RESEARCH SUMMARY 2

Johnson, Tucker, Stiles and Trauner, 1998

Milliseconds
There are 1000
milliseconds (ms)
in a second.

When an adult is looking at something, and a brief visual stimulus is displayed elsewhere in their field of view, their attention is drawn momentarily to that stimulus. If, within about 150 milliseconds (ms) (nearly one seventh of a second), this stimulus is shown again in the same location, together with a competing visual stimulus elsewhere in their field of view, the adult will look at it more readily than they will at the competing stimulus. If there is a gap of around 700 ms before the second presentation, the adult will be *less* likely to look at it than at the competing stimulus. The first effect is called 'facilitation of detection' (because the first showing of the stimulus helps detection of the same stimulus the second time round). The second effect is called 'inhibition of return' (the first showing seems to inhibit attention to the stimulus when it is shown for a second time). Both effects have been well documented in studies of attention shifting. By about 7 months of age, typically developing infants also display these patterns of attention shifting (Johnson and Tucker, 1996).

Johnson et al. set out to discover what areas of the brain are involved in these patterns of attention shifting. They studied seven, 7-month-old infants who had sustained localized damage to an area of their brain during or shortly before birth. Three of these infants had damage on the left-hand side of the prefrontal cortex, and four had damage in other regions of the cortex.

The infants were seated in front of three computer screens, positioned side by side. On the middle screen a visually interesting pattern was played which engaged their attention. At a given point in time a stimulus was flashed onto either the right-hand or left-hand screen. After a set interval (133, 200, 700 or 1200 ms) the same stimulus would be flashed onto both side-screens. Each infant experienced 32 trials, eight at each of the four different intervals. Video recordings of the infants' looking behaviour were made from a camera located above the middle screen, and a record was made of which way the infant looked on each occasion that the double stimulus was displayed.

The researchers found that the infants without left side damage to the prefrontal cortex showed similar patterns of attention shifting behaviour to the typically developing infants from the Johnson and Tucker study (1996). The infants with left side damage, on the other hand, showed no sign of the 'facilitation of detection' effect for the 133 ms interval. This suggests that the prefrontal cortex plays a role in visual attention tasks in infancy. In adults only those with damage to the parietal lobe (see Figure 1, p. 118) show such a pattern of results.

The findings from the Johnson *et al.* (1998) study, and from Csibra *et al.* (1998) are consistent with the view that the cortical regions that are crucial for a particular ability change with the stage of acquisition of that ability. Perhaps there is greater prefrontal activity on visual attention tasks in infancy than in adulthood because infants are still at an early stage of developing visual attention skills. By adulthood the skills have been learned and have 'moved' to a different, more specialized area of the cortex.

Activity 8 *The role of the prefrontal cortex*

Allow about
15 minutes

This activity will help you to review the material presented in Section 5 of this chapter.

Summarize the evidence that supports each of the two perspectives presented in Section 5 on prefrontal cortex development in infancy. The two perspectives are:

1   Various aspects of the cognitive and behavioural development of infants can be related to structural changes in the prefrontal cortex.

2   The prefrontal cortex is specifically associated with the early stages of the development of a new skill, and its involvement decreases with the development of that skill.

5.4   A note on relating brain structure and function

Section 5 has been about efforts to bridge the conceptual gap between brain structure (how the different regions of the brain are physically organized) and function (what these regions do). This is a major challenge for developmental cognitive neuroscience. Much is known about the brain at a structural level. Much is also known about behaviour and cognition. But there is still a great deal to learn about how structures underpin behaviours and cognitive functions, and about how behaviours and cognitive functions influence the development of structures. One tool for investigating the relationship between structure and function in this respect is connectionist computational modelling (neural networks). One aim of connectionist modelling is to see how the brain structures that we know about could possibly give rise to human behaviour and cognition. You will encounter more about connectionist modelling in Chapter 4.

SG

Summary of Section 5

- The prefrontal cortex is associated with higher cognitive functions, and because of its prolonged postnatal development, it is the area of the brain most closely associated with cognitive development.
- There is evidence to suggest that developments in the prefrontal cortex are associated with the developing abilities of the infant, as measured by performance on object permanence tasks.
- Alternatively, the prefrontal cortex may play a more organizing function with respect to cognitive development, and its role in the acquisition of skills may diminish as other more specialist cortical regions take over.
- Linking cortical development to cognitive and behavioural development is a complex, inexact process. Connectionist computational models are one set of tools for trying to bridge the gap.

6   Conclusion

This chapter has introduced you to the field of developmental cognitive neuroscience. It has described some aspects of early brain development, and discussed notions of innate modularity and modularization. Particular attention has been paid to language and to the prefrontal cortex. The chapter has taken an epigenetic view of brain development, arguing that children's brain structures and functions develop out of potent interactions between intrinsic (for example, genetic) and external (environmental) factors. It is evident from the material presented in this chapter that the major challenge for researchers in the field of developmental cognitive neuroscience is to find ways of enhancing our understanding of the complex relationship between brain structures and functions.

Further reading

Elman, J. L., Bates, E. A., Johnson, M. H. *et al.* (1996) *Rethinking Innateness: a connectionist perspective on development*, Cambridge, MA, MIT Press.

Johnson, M. H. (1997) *Developmental Cognitive Neuroscience*, Oxford, Blackwell.

Nelson, C. A. and Luciana, M. (2001) *Handbook of Developmental Cognitive Neuroscience*, Cambridge, MA, MIT Press.

References

Bell, M. A. (1992) 'A not B task performance is related to frontal EEG asymmetry regardless of locomotor experience', in Rovee-Collier, C. (ed.) *Proceedings of the VIIIth International Conference on Infant Studies 15 (Special ICIS Issue)*, p. 307, Miami Beach, FL: Infant Behavior and Development.

Bell, M. A. and Fox, N. A. (1992) 'The relations between frontal brain electrical activity and cognitive development during infancy', *Child Development*, vol. 63, pp. 1142–63.

Casey, B. J., Trainor, R. J., Orendi, J. L. *et al.* (1997) 'A developmental functional MRI study of prefrontal activation during performance of a go-no-go task', *Journal of Cognitive Neuroscience*, vol. 9, pp. 835–47.

Conel, J. L. (1939–63) *The Postnatal Development of the Human Cerebral Cortex*, Vols I–VI, Cambridge MA, Harvard University Press.

Changeux, J.-P. (1985) *Neuronal Man: the biology of mind*, New York, Pantheon.

Changeux, J.-P., Heidman, T. and Patte, P. (1984) 'Learning by selection', in Marler, P. and Terrace, H. S. (eds) *The Biology of Learning*, pp. 115–33, Berlin, Springer-Verlag.

Chomsky, N. (1965) *Aspects of the Theory of Syntax,* Cambridge, MA, MIT Press.

Cowan, M. W., Fawcett, J. W., O'Leary, D. M. and Stanfield, B. B. (1984) 'Regressive events in neurogenesis', *Science,* vol. 225, pp. 1258–65.

Csibra, G., Tucker, L. A. and Johnson, M. H. (1998) 'Neural correlates of saccade planning in infants: a high-density ERP study', *International Journal of Psychophysiology,* vol. 29, pp. 201–15.

DeCasper, A. J. and Spence, M. J. (1986) 'Prenatal maternal speech influences newborns' perception of speech sounds', *Infant Behavior and Development,* vol. 9, pp. 133–50.

DeCasper, A. J., Lecanuet, J-P., Busnel, M-C., Granier-Deferre, C. and Maugeais, R. (1994) 'Fetal reactions to recurrent maternal speech', *Infant Behavior and Development,* vol. 17, pp. 159–64.

Diamond, A. (1985) 'Development of the ability to use recall to guide action, as indicated by infants' performance on AB', *Child Development,* vol. 56, pp. 868–83.

Diamond, A. and Goldman-Rakic, P. S. (1986) 'Comparative development of human infants and infant rhesus monkeys of cognitive functions that depend on prefrontal cortex', *Neuroscience Abstracts,* vol. 12, p. 274.

Diamond, A. and Goldman-Rakic, P. S. (1989) 'Comparison of human infants and infant rhesus monkeys on Piaget's AB task: evidence for dependence on dorsolateral prefrontal cortex', *Experimental Brain Research,* vol. 74, pp. 24–40.

Elman, J. L., Bates, E. A., Johnson, M. H., Karmiloff-Smith, A., Parisi, D. and Plunkett, K. (1996) *Rethinking innateness: a connectionist perspective on development,* Cambridge, MA, MIT Press.

Fodor, J. A. (1983) *The Modularity of Mind: an essay on faculty psychology,* Cambridge, MA, MIT Press.

Fox, N. A. and Bell, M. A. (1990) 'Electrophysiological indices of frontal lobe development', in Diamond, A. (ed.) *The Development and Neural Bases of Higher Cognitive Functions,* pp. 677–98, New York, New York Academy of Sciences.

Fuster, J. M. (1989, 2nd edn) *The Prefrontal Cortex,* New York, Raven Press.

Goldfield, E. C. (1995) *Emergent Forms: origins and early development of human actions and perception,* Oxford, Oxford University Press.

Goldman-Rakic, P. S. (1987) 'Development of cortical circuitry and cognitive function', *Child Development,* vol. 58, pp. 601–22.

Hebb, D. O. (1949) *The Organisation of Behavior: a neuropsychological approach,* New York, Wiley.

Huttenlocher, P. R. (1990) 'Morphometric study of human cerebral cortex development', *Neuropsychologia,* vol. 28, pp. 517–27.

Johnson, M. H. (1997) *Developmental Cognitive Neuroscience,* Oxford, Blackwell.

Johnson, M. H. and Tucker, L. A. (1996) 'The development and temporal dynamics of spatial orienting in children', *Journal of Experimental Child Psychology,* vol. 63, pp. 171–88.

Johnson, M. H., Tucker, L. A., Stiles, J. and Trauner, D. (1998) 'Visual attention in infants with perinatal brain damage: evidence of the importance of anterior lesions', *Developmental Science*, vol. 1, pp. 53–8.

Karmiloff-Smith, A. (1992) *Beyond Modularity: a developmental perspective on cognitive science*, Cambridge, MA, MIT Press.

Katz, L. C. and Shatz, C. J. (1996) 'Synaptic activity and the construction of cortical circuits', *Science*, vol. 274, p. 1133–38.

Keslo, S. (1995) *Dynamic Pattern: the self-organization of brain and behavior*, Cambridge, MA, MIT Press.

Kwong, K. E., Belliveau, J. W., Chesler, D. A. *et al.* (1992) 'Dynamic magnetic resonance imaging of human brain activity during primary sensory stimulation', *Proceedings of the National Academy of Sciences*, vol. 89, pp. 5675–9.

Lewkowicz, D. J. and Turkewitz, G. (1981) 'Intersensory interaction in newborns: modification of visual preferences following exposure to sound', *Child Development,* vol. 52, pp. 827–32.

Maurer, D. (1993) 'Neonatal synesthesia: implications for the processing of speech and faces', in de Boysson-Bardies, B., de Schonen, S., Jusczyk, P. *et al.* (eds) *Developmental Neurocognition: speech and face processing in the first year of life*, pp. 109–24, the Netherlands, Kluwer.

Mehler, J. and Dupoux, E. (1994) *What Infants Know*, Oxford, Blackwell.

Meltzoff, A. N. and Borton, R. W. (1979) 'Intermodal matching by human neonates', *Nature,* vol. 282, pp. 403–4.

Mills, D. M., Coffey, S. A. and Neville, H. J. (1993) 'Language acquisition and cerebral specialization in 20-month-old infants', *Journal of Cognitive Neuroscience*, vol. 5, pp. 326–42.

Milner, B. (1982) 'Some cognitive effects of frontal-lobe lesions in man', *Philosophical Transactions of the Royal Society of London*, vol. 298, pp. 211–26.

Nelson, C. A. and Bloom, F. E. (1997) 'Child development and neuroscience', *Child Development*, vol. 68, pp. 970–87.

Neville, H. J. (1991) 'Neurobiology of cognitive and language processing: effects of early experience', in Gibson K. R. and Peterson A. C. (eds) *Brain Maturation and Cognitive Development: comparative and cross-cultural perspectives*, pp. 355–80, New York, Aldine de Gruyter.

Neville, H. J. and Bavelier, D. (2001) 'Variability of developmental plasticity', in McClelland J. L. and Siegler, R. S. (eds) *Mechanisms of Cognitive Development: behavioral and neural perspectives*, pp. 271–87, London, Lawrence Erlbaum Associates.

Neville, H. J., Mills, D. and Lawson, D. (1992) 'Fractionating language: different neural subsystems with different sensory periods', *Cerebral Cortex,* vol. 2, pp. 244–58.

Neville, H. J., Bavelier, D., Corina, D. *et al.* (1998) 'Cerebral organisation for language in deaf and hearing subjects: biological constraints and effects of experience', *Proceedings of the National Academy of Science, USA*, vol. 95, pp. 922–9.

O'Leary, D. D. M. (1989) 'Do cortical areas emerge from a protocortex?', *Trends in Neuroscience*, vol. 12, pp. 400–6.

Oppenheim, R. (1981) 'Neuronal death and some related regressive phenomena during neuro-genesis: a selective historical review and progress report', in Haith, M. M. and Campos, J. (eds) *Infancy and the Biology of Development: vol. 2 Handbook of Child Psychology*, pp. 273–97, New York, Oxford University Press.

Petersen, S. E., Fox, P. T., Snyder, A. Z. and Raichle, M. E. (1990) 'Activation of extrastriate and frontal cortical areas by visual words and word-like stimuli', *Science*, vol. 249, pp. 1041–4.

Piaget, J. (1954) *The Construction of Reality in the Child*, New York, Basic Books.

Pinker, S. (1994) *The Language Instinct: the new science of language and mind*, London, Penguin.

Quinlan, P. T. (1991) *Connectionism and Psychology: a psychological perspective on new connectionist research*, London, Harvester Wheatsheaf.

Rakic, P. (1988) Specialization of cerebral cortical areas, *Science*, vol. 241, pp. 170–6.

Reilly, J. S., Bates, E. A. and Marchman, V. A. (1998) 'Narrative discourse in children with early focal brain injury', *Brain and Language,* vol. 61, pp. 335–75.

Stetri, A. (1987) 'Tactile discrimination of shape and intermodal transfer in 2 to 3 month old infants', *British Journal of Developmental Psychology*, vol. 5, pp. 213–20.

Stewart, M. (1991) (ed.) *Animal Physiology*, London, Hodder and Stoughton/The Open University.

Stiles, L. and Thal, D. (1993) 'Linguistic and spatial cognitive development following early focal brain injury: patterns of deficit and recovery', in Johnson, M. H. (ed.) *Brain Development and Cognition: a reader*, pp. 643–64, Oxford, Blackwell.

Thatcher, R. W. (1992) 'Cyclic cortical reorganization during early childhood', *Brain and Cognition*, vol. 20, pp. 24–50.

Tzourio, N., de Schonen, S., Mazoyer, B. *et al.* (1992) 'Regional cerebral blood flow in two-month old alert infants', *Society for Neuroscience Abstracts*, vol. 18, p. 1121.

von der Malsburg, C. (1995) 'Self-organization in the brain', in Arbib, M. A. (ed.) *The Handbook of Brain Theory and Neural Networks*, pp. 840–46, Cambridge, MA, MIT Press.

Williams, D. (1996) *Autism: an inside-out approach,* London, Jessica Kingsley.

Readings

Reading A: 'The fragmented mind' from *What Infants Know*

Jacques Mehler and Emmanuel Dupoux

Like vision, language also appears to us to be a whole. It even seems indissociable from the other higher faculties. But we have known for more than a century that certain cortical lesions localized particularly in the left hemisphere can have specific effects on linguistic capacity. Some patients lose the ability to understand language, while others lose the ability to produce sentences. Others, more seriously affected, lose both abilities. Neuropsychologists have been trying to link these symptoms with the affected areas of the cortex since the nineteenth century. Thus it was believed that anterior lesions in particular caused problems with production of speech, *Broca's aphasia*, and that lesions of the posterior parts of the cortex tended to create difficulties in language comprehension, *Wernicke's aphasia*. Today, thanks to a better description of these symptoms and deficiencies, this gross classification has proved to be of limited interest. On the other hand, a more specific description has permitted us to show how traumas can cause a loss that remains limited to a very specific component of the linguistic system. Thus, some patients experience difficulty identifying words, while others have problems with grammar, reading, or writing. Without enumerating all the different forms of aphasia, it is possible to say that clinical studies have facilitated the relatively precise description of the various stages of linguistic data processing. They seem to be specific and modular.

As Broca discovered, certain cerebral traumas can cause loss of language without affecting other faculties. Aphasics suffering from a serious lesion in the left hemisphere thus can still reason and calculate. However, one might think that since both language and music are auditory, patients who have a hard time understanding what is said to them would also have a problem recognizing a piece of music. But this is not true, as several celebrated cases demonstrate.

At the age of seventy-seven, a well-known composer and organist, who was blind, suffered a stroke. A cerebral lesion of the left hemisphere left him aphasic. He could no longer speak words or utter sentences. And yet his musical abilities were unaffected: he could still decipher scores by ear. But above all, and even more astonishingly, while he could read music in braille, the accident had left him almost unable to read braille texts. This discrepancy was all the more surprising since the symbols representing notes and letters are identical in braille. The nature of the system used was therefore not a factor. Musical ability would then be a function of the right hemisphere, while linguistic competence would be handled by the left one.

A, a musical score; B, the same score in braille; C, a transcription of the braille score with the letters used. The patient can play the score presented in braille, but has great difficulty reading E, which represents ... "le père" [the father]. He reads: "Le ... Pa ... le ... ta ... le frère [the brother] ... la ... le par ... il y a [there is] pé." (Signoret *et al.*, 1987).

The example of another patient, also a professional musician, bears out this theory. It concerns a right-handed conductor who had led the La Fenice orchestra in Venice and the La Scala orchestra in Milan for many years. At sixty-seven, a stroke injuring his left cerebral hemisphere caused the loss of all linguistic aptitude, and he was unable to speak for the next six years. On the other hand, his musical capacities remained almost intact. He was incapable of naming notes, but could sing or play them. He made such rapid progress that, despite his inability to communicate with an orchestra except by gestures, he continued to be a completely professional conductor capable of detecting the most subtle musical errors. His interpretation of Verdi's *Nabucco* was especially appreciated by critics.

The lesion resulting from his first stroke therefore affected only his left hemisphere, the seat of language. Six years later, a second vascular accident partly destroyed his right hemisphere. Unfortunately, this time he did not recover and his death prevented our testing his musical capacities. Other cases of lesions suppressing the aptitude for music confirm, however, that musical ability has its seat in the right hemisphere of the brain.

As indicated above, commissurotomy cases illustrate the dissociation that exists between language and other mental functions, for in these patients we can present data to one hemisphere only. For example, we can arrange for the image of a word to reach the left hemisphere only. Subjects can read it and even point to the corresponding object. But this is possible only if they use their right hand. This hand is directly linked to the left hemisphere, in other words, to the one that "saw" the word.

If, on the contrary, we present a word to the opposite hemisphere, subjects are unable to read it, and even claim not to have seen anything. However, they can locate the object, with their left hand. In these cases, the left hemisphere, which is responsible for language, has not "seen" the word presented, and subjects are therefore unable to formulate a verbal response. To summarize, if we analyze the subjects' behavior in terms of what they perceive and produce with their right hemispheres, we conclude that they have a very diminished linguistic capacity similar to that of certain aphasics. Yet if we analyze their behavior in terms of what they control with their left hemisphere, we conclude that they are in full possession of their linguistic capacities.

How is this possible? How can one both be and not be aphasic? In fact, this discrepancy between mental faculties in the same person is only partial and manifests itself only in very specific experimental situations. Under normal conditions, both hemispheres function in a coherent fashion, for they have many means of communicating with another. For example, eye movements permit the duplication of visual data in both hemispheres, and information can also circulate through the intermediary of motor activity. For instance, we have observed a subject give an incorrect verbal response, raise his eyebrows, and then immediately correct himself. No doubt the right hemisphere, which knew the correct answer, prompted the raised eyebrows, which informed the left hemisphere of its error and led him to change his response. It is also possible that such phenomena sometimes occur in healthy individuals.

Be that as it may, these surprising observations clearly show that it is counterproductive to see our mental faculties as an inseparable whole. In the light of neuropsychological studies, our psychological mechanism seems rather to be composed of independent and autonomous faculties like the perception of faces and of language. And language itself is not all of one piece either. Very specific afflictions illustrate this. Some patients, for example, lose the use of conjunctions but not of nouns and adjectives, or even the use of a whole semantic group like fruits and vegetables, or trees. An apparently simple and homogeneous task therefore calls upon many distinct and specialized submechanisms, which can break down while the rest of the system continues to function normally.

Commonsense psychology, as we clearly see, cannot explain this type of phenomenon. Nor is the perspicacity forged by years of experience of any use. We therefore must assume that a part of our cognitive system is divided into functional units, or modules, which are responsible for a given aptitude and operate in an autonomous fashion oblivious to what is happening elsewhere in the system. The more research advances, the less our intelligence seems to resemble a whole with indistinct equipotential parts, rather like a bowl of jello, and the more it seems to be subdivided into a great number of functions which have a certain autonomy. Gall's intuition has proven to be right. As we already mentioned, it was taken up again in more modern form by Jerry Fodor.

According to Fodor's formulation, we can compare a function, or module, to a physical organ. Our body is made up organs which have their specific functions and which, through their interaction, contribute to the functioning of the whole. However, modules do not exchange fluids or energy, but information. Thus each module constitutes an abstract organ which we could describe, at least in a rough approximation, in terms of concepts borrowed from computer science (representation, structure of data, manipulation of symbols, etc.). In a sense, then, a module is closer to a computer program than to a heart or liver. However, like its physiological counterpart, it has a specific function: it only processes a fragment of the information circulating through the whole psychological mechanism and can only use rather restricted, predetermined channels of communication. Conscientious, but rather limited, it is an expert in its field. Furthermore, just as in the case of physical organs, the growth and organization of cognitive modules is guided by genetic program specific to the species. And finally, as the example of language shows, a module is not distributed throughout the entire brain, but involves a specific nervous structure, circuit, and/ or cortical area.

From this perspective, we can no longer imagine that our psyche is controlled by a central intelligence. The data used by each module are limited and its field of operation is restricted. A so-called superior intelligence is no longer necessary. It is the system as a whole that exhibits a behavior we can term intelligent, not its parts taken separately, and not just one part in particular.

How many modules are there? How are they organized? According to one of Fodor's hypotheses, there are many specialized systems which are consolidated into large modules, each specialized in the rapid and automatic processing of one type of data (e.g., language). Each module delivers information to a central processing unit which compares the different entries as well as all the other knowledge available to the organism, making it possible to elaborate the long-term planning of actions.

It is quite obvious that we have not yet been able to explore this extremely complex modular architecture in detail. We are still taking the first baby steps in a discipline which is centuries behind the natural or exact sciences. This functionalist representation of the psychological mechanism is above all a guideline: it enables us to formulate hypotheses and submit them to experimental verification. The actual existence of a particular system or a particular exchange of data is not a metaphysical postulate. The beauty and perfection of the theory matter less than its ability to raise questions that experiments can then proceed to answer.

Reference for Reading A

Signoret, J.-J., Van Eeckhout, Ph., Puncet, M. and Castigne, P. (1987). Aphasie sans amusie chez un organiste aveugle. *Revue de Neurologie, 143*, pp. 182–88.

Source: Mehler, J. and Dupoux, E. (1994) *What Infants Know: the new cognitive science of early development*, tr. Southgate, P., pp. 146–50, Oxford, Blackwell.

Reading B: Beyond modularity

Annette Karmiloff-Smith

Is the initial architecture of the infant mind modular?

Fodor's 1983 book *The Modularity of Mind* (which I later criticize) made a significant impact on developmental theorizing by suggesting how the nativist thesis and the domain-specificity of cognition are relevant to constraints on the architecture of the human mind. For Fodor, the notion of 'architecture' refers to the organization of relatively fixed and highly constrained innate specifications: the invariant features of the human information-processing system. Unlike Bruner (1974–75) and Piaget (1952), who argue for domain-general development, Fodor holds that the mind is made up of genetically specified, independently functioning, special-purpose 'modules' or input systems. Like Fodor, I shall use the terms 'module' and 'input system' as synonyms. Each functionally distinct module has its own dedicated processes and proprietary inputs.

[...]

Each module is like a special-purpose computer with a proprietary database. By 'proprietary' Fodor means that a module can process only certain types of data and that it automatically ignores other, potentially competing input. A module computes in a bottom-up fashion a constrained class of specific inputs; that is, it focuses on entities that are relevant to its particular processing capacities only. And it does so whenever relevant data present themselves – that is, an input system cannot refrain from processing. This enhances automaticity and speed of computation by ensuring that the organism is insensitive to many potential classes of information from other input systems and to top-down expectations from central processing.

Input systems, then, are the parts of the human mind that are inflexible and unintelligent. They are the stupidity in the machine – but they are just what a young organism might need to get initial cognition off the ground speedily and efficiently.

[...]

Prespecified modules versus a process of modularization

Fodor's detailed account of the encapsulation of modules focuses predominantly on their role in on-line processing. There is little discussion of ontogenetic [developmental] change, except to allow for the creation of new modules (such as a reading module). Fodor takes it as demonstrated that modules for spoken language and visual perception are innately specified. By contrast, I wish to draw a distinction between the notion of prespecified modules and that of a process of *modularization* (which, I speculate, occurs repeatedly as the *product* of development). Here I differ from Fodor's strict nativist conception. I hypothesize that if the human mind ends up with any modular structure, then, even in the case of language, the mind becomes modularized *as development proceeds*. My position takes account of the plasticity of early brain development (Neville, 1991; Johnson, 1993). It is plausible that a fairly limited amount of innately specified, domain-specified predispositions (which are not strictly modular) would be sufficient to constrain the classes of inputs that the infant mind computes. It can thus be hypothesized that, *with time*, brain circuits are progressively selected for different domain-specific computations; in certain cases, relatively encapsulated modules would be formed. Thus, when I use the terms 'innately specified' ..., I do not mean to imply anything like a genetic blueprint for prespecified modules, present at birth. Rather, ... I argue for innately specified predispositions that are more epigenetic than Fodor's nativism. The view that I adopt ... is that Nature specifies initial biases or predispositions that channel attention to relevant environmental inputs, which in turn affect subsequent brain development.

[...]

Development from a domain-general perspective

Fodor's nativist thesis is in sharp contrast with domain-general theories of learning, such as Piaget's constructivist epistemology, which were once popular in the development literature. Piagetian theory argues that neither processing nor storage is domain specific. Of course, implicitly at least, a Piagetian must acknowledge that there are different sensory transducers for vision, audition, touch, and so forth. They do not accept, however, that the transducers transform data into innately specified, domain-specific formats for modular processing. For Piagetians, development involves the construction of domain-general changes in representational structures operating over all aspects of the cognitive system in a similar way.

[...]

Neither the Piagetian nor the behaviourist theory grants the infant any innate structures or domain-specific knowledge. Each grants only some domain-general, biologically specified processes: for the Piagetians, a set of sensory reflexes and three functional processes (assimilation, accommodation, and equilibration); for the behaviourists, inherited physiological sensory systems and a complex set of laws of association. These domain-general learning processes are held to apply across all areas of linguistic and nonlinguistic cognition. Piaget and the behaviourists thus concur on a number of conceptions about the initial state of the infant mind. The behaviourists saw the infant as a *tabula rasa* with no built-in knowledge (Skinner, 1953); Piaget's view of the young infant as assailed by 'undifferentiated and chaotic' inputs (Piaget, 1955) is substantially the same.

Needless to say, there are fundamental differences between these two schools. Piagetians view the child as an active information constructor, behaviourists as a passive information storer. Piagetians conceive of development as involving fundamental stage-like changes in logical structure, whereas behaviourists invoke a progressive accumulation of knowledge. However, in the light of the present state of the art in developing theorizing, Piagetians and behaviourists have much in common in their view of the neonate's 'knowledge-empty' mind and their claims that domain-general learning explains subsequent development across all aspects of language and cognition.

Development from a domain-specific perspective

The nativist/modularity thesis projects a very different picture of the young infant. Rather than being assailed by incomprehensible, chaotic data from many competing sources, the neonate is seen as preprogrammed to make sense of specific information sources. Contrary to the Piagetian or the behaviourist infant, the nativist infant is off to a very good start. This doesn't, of course, mean that nothing changes during infancy and beyond; the infant has much to learn. But the nativist/modularity stance posits that subsequent learning is guided by innately specified, domain-specific principles, and that these principles determine the entities on which subsequent learning takes place (Gelman, 1990; Spelke, 1991).

The domain specificity of cognitive systems is also suggested by developmental neuropsychology and by the existence of children in whom one or more domains are spared or impaired. For example, autism may involve a single deficit in reasoning about mental states (theory of mind), with the rest of cognition relatively unimpaired. Williams Syndrome, by contrast, presents a very uneven cognitive profile in which language, face recognition, and theory of mind seem relatively spared, whereas number and spatial cognition are severely retarded. And there are numerous cases of idiots-savants in whom only one domain (such as drawing or calendrical calculation) functions at a high level, while capacities are very low over the rest of the cognitive system. By contrast, Down Syndrome is suggestive of a more across-the-board, domain-general deficit in cognitive processing.

Adult brain damage points to domain specificity, also. It is remarkably difficult to find convincing examples in the neuropsychological literature of an across-the-board, domain-general disorder (Marshall, 1984), although a case might be made for an overall deficit in planning in patients with prefrontal damage (Shallice, 1988). But in many instances, disorders of higher cognitive functions consequent upon brain damage are typically domain specific – that is, they affect only face recognition, number, language, or some other facility, leaving the other systems relatively intact.

So if adults manifest domain-specific damage, and if it can be shown that infants come into the world with some domain-specific predispositions, doesn't that mean that the nativists have won the debate over the developmentalists still ensconced on the theoretical shores of Lake Geneva (Piaget's former bastion of anti-nativism and anti-modularity)? Not necessarily, because it is important to bear in mind that the greater the amount of domain-specific properties of the infant mind, the less creative and flexible the subsequent system will be (Chomsky, 1988). Whereas the fixed constraints provide an initial adaptive advantage, there is a tradeoff between the efficiency and automaticity of the infant's input systems, on the one hand, and their relative inflexibility, on the other. This leads me to a crucial point: *The more complex the picture we ultimately build of the innate capacities of the infant mind, the more important it becomes for us to explain the flexibility of subsequent cognitive development.* It is toward such an end – exploring the flexibility and creativity of the human mind beyond the initial state – that my work in language acquisition and cognitive development has been concentrated, in an attempt to determine both the domain-specific and the domain-general contributions to development. It is implausible that development will turn out to be entirely domain specific *or* domain general. And although I will need to invoke some built-in constraints, development clearly involves a more dynamic process of interaction between mind and the environment than the strict nativist stance presupposes.

References for Reading B

Bruner, J. S. (1974–75) 'From communication to language: a psychological perspective', *Cognition*, **3**, pp. 255–87.

Chomsky, N. (1988) *Language and Problems of Knowledge*, MIT Press.

Fodor, J. (1983) *The Modularity of Mind*, MIT Press.

Gelman, R. (1990) 'First principles organize attention to and learning about relevant data: number and animate–inanimate distinction as examples', *Cognitive Science*, **14**, pp. 79–106.

Johnson, M. H. (1993) 'Constraints on cortical plasticity' in Johnson, M. H. (ed.) *Brain Development and Cognition: a reader*, Blackwell.

Marshall, J. C. (1984) 'Multiple perspectives on modularity', *Cognition*, **17**, pp. 209–42.

Neville, H. J. (1991) 'Neurobiology of cognitive and language processing: effects of early experience' in Gibson, K. R. and Petersen, A. C. (eds) *Brain Maturation and Cognitive Development: comparative and cross-cultural perspectives*, Aldine deGruyter.

Piaget, J. (1952) *The Origins of Intelligence in Children*, International University Press.

Piaget, J. (1955) *The Child's Construction of Reality*, Routledge and Kegan Paul.

Shallice, T. (1988) *From Neuropsychology to Mental Structure*, Cambridge University Press.

Skinner, B. F. (1953) *Science and Human Behaviour*, Macmillan.

Spelke, E. S. (1991) 'Physical knowledge in infancy: reflections on Piaget's theory' in Carey, S. and Gelman, R. (eds) *Epigenesis of the Mind: essays in biology and knowledge*, Erlbaum.

Source: Karmiloff-Smith, A. (1992*) Beyond Modularity: a developmental perspective on cognitive science,* Cambridge (MA.), MIT Press.

Chapter 4
The development of children's understanding of grammar

Kim Plunkett and Clare Wood

Contents

Learning outcomes

After you have studied this chapter you should be able to:

1   describe the key stages in children's grammatical development;
2   understand Chomsky's theory of 'Universal Grammar';
3   show familiarity with methodological approaches to studying children's grammatical development;
4   offer a critical account of single and dual route explanations of grammatical development;
5   compare and contrast nativist and empiricist accounts of grammatical development.

1   Introduction

If you have ever tried to learn a foreign language as a teenager or an adult, you will know that one of the most complex aspects is understanding and remembering its grammatical rules. Learning vocabulary is a relatively simple affair, but knowing how to combine those words to form legitimate sentences that are an accurate representation of what you want to communicate is a more sophisticated skill. Moreover, the fact that languages can differ greatly from each other in their grammatical rules further emphasizes the complexity of the task. So, consider how much more difficult it would be if you were never explicitly taught what these rules were, and were left to discover them for yourself. Think also about how difficult this task would be if you were not already fluent in a language of your own. And yet, this is exactly the position that infants are in during the first few years of life.

In Chapter 2, 'First words', you read about how children come to acquire their spoken vocabulary. In this chapter the focus is on how children achieve the apparently insurmountable task of acquiring grammatical understanding. We will consider the nature of spoken language and how it is constructed before looking at methodological approaches to this area of research. We will then examine two approaches to explaining how children acquire knowledge about the grammar of their first language. The two approaches reflect and further develop the long-standing debate over the fundamental source of human knowledge, be it linguistic or non-linguistic, between nativists and empiricists.

What you will also notice while reading this chapter is how children's grammatical development further illustrates an underlying theme of this book: that cognitive development is characterized by a progression from a piecemeal knowledge of the environment to an organized, systematic understanding that imposes structure on what is experienced.

SG

Nativists
Theorists who argue that development is primarily driven by innate (inborn) constraints.

Empiricists
Theorists who argue that development is primarily driven by factors in the environment.

Summary of Section 1

- Acquisition of grammar is a complex and sophisticated process.
- Nativist and empiricist explanations of grammar acquisition have been proposed.

2 The nature of spoken language

Before engaging with the question of how young children acquire grammatical understanding, it is first necessary to appreciate the complexity and the significance of spoken language as a structure. When people speak, they are producing and combining sounds to communicate their ideas. The capacity to combine sounds in different ways enables the speaker to communicate different ideas. The capacity to combine sounds in novel ways enables the language user to communicate ideas that have never been expressed before. So, the creative use of language is entirely dependent on the ability to assemble simple building blocks of sound into the complex structures we call sentences. Speakers of a language appreciate the organization of their systems of linguistic combination. They recognize when a sentence is spoken incorrectly, say by a child or a foreigner. Speakers can even classify the type of mistake in an erroneous utterance. For example, they may comment that it was not correctly pronounced, that it contained an unknown word, or that it was grammatically incorrect. See Box 1 for a reminder of some grammatical terms.

In learning to combine sounds in a way that is appropriate, children develop a largely implicit understanding of *phonology, morphology* and *syntax* (see Figure 1).

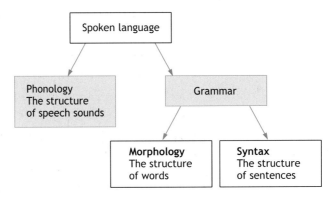

Figure I   The structure of language.

BOX 1

Grammatical terms: a reminder

Noun: a word that 'names' something, somewhere or someone. For example, in the sentence 'The child is riding the bike', the nouns are 'child' and 'bike'.

Verb: a word that describes an action, such as 'ride'.

Auxiliary verb: a verb that precedes the main verb in a sentence in order to 'complete' the main verb. For example, the verb *to be* is the auxiliary verb in our example: 'The child *is* riding the bike'.

Subject: the person or thing that is performing the action in the sentence. For example, in 'The child is riding a bike', it is 'the child' who is doing the riding, and is therefore the subject of the sentence.

Object: the person or thing that is the recipient of the action in the sentence. In our example 'the bike' is the object.

Active and passive sentences: 'The child is riding the bike' is an *active* sentence, as the verb is being directly executed by its subject. The *passive* version of the sentence is 'The bike was ridden by the child'. Note the change in wording: the object now appears first, and to accommodate this change we now have to use an auxiliary verb and the word 'by' has also been added (the presence of these factors indicates a passive statement). The object of the sentence (the bike) now has prominence over the subject (the child).

2.1 Phonology

Phonology and *phonotactics* are terms that are used to refer to the knowledge that a speaker possesses about the sound patterns of his or her native language. For example, in English, speakers readily distinguish sounds like [b] as in 'bat' from sounds like [p] as in 'pat', whereas Arabic speakers ignore this distinction.

Activity 1
Allow about
5 minutes

Phonological distinctions

This activity will help you appreciate the subtlety of the phonological distinctions that are made in understanding language.

Say 'pig' and 'big' out loud, paying attention to the very beginning of each word, and what your mouth and throat have to do to produce these sounds. In what way are they the same, and what is the crucial difference?

Comment

For both words, the mouth, lips and tongue are in the same position. The main difference is that the /p/ in 'pig' is 'voiceless' (i.e. the vocal chords do not move as the initial sound is made) but for the /b/ in 'big' voicing starts sooner. If you put your hand on your throat while saying just the words you will notice this more easily. Other sounds, such as [t] and [d], and also [k] and [g], differ in the same way. Although the difference between these two sounds is subtle, the impact that it has on the meaning of an utterance is huge (e.g. 'big' and 'pig' simply differ in whether the first brief sound in the word is voiced or voiceless, but they have very different meanings!).

Similarly, other languages such as Thai, recognize other subtle distinctions which English speakers ignore; the aspirated [pʰ], as in 'pit', versus the unaspirated [p] as in 'spit', are treated as the same sound by English speakers, but signal a difference in meaning to speakers of Thai. To notice the difference between the aspirated and unaspirated [p], try saying 'pit' while holding your hand in front of your face; you should feel a burst of air on your hand. Now do the same as you say 'spit'. You will notice that the burst of air is absent, or at least a great deal weaker.

Aspirated
These are phonemes that are accompanied by a 'puff of air' as they are spoken.

Likewise, there are combinations of sounds that English speakers would regard as 'foreign'. For example, the /p/ sound cannot be followed by the /s/ sound at the beginning of a word in English but it is permitted in French. So, in the English word 'psychology', the letter 'p' is silent, but in the French word 'psychologie' the /p/ and the /s/ sounds are both pronounced. Speakers who are not careful in articulating these subtle cues, or listeners who do not pay attention to them, are likely to be misunderstood or to misunderstand the communications of others. Indeed, as you saw in Chapter 2, much of language development during the first year of life is concerned with mastering the mechanics of speech production, or deciphering the sound patterns of the language that dominate the infant's acoustic environment.

2.2 Morphology

Morphology is the term used to refer to the knowledge a speaker possesses regarding the manner in which new words can be created from existing words or other meaningful units of language. There are many aspects to morphology, so we will introduce you to just two here for the purposes of illustration. The first of these is known as *compounding*. This is the combinatorial capacity in a language whereby two existing words are glued together to form a new word. For example, in English the nouns 'lady' and 'bird' can be combined to form the new word 'ladybird'. Sometimes, as with this example, the meaning of the new word is not predictable from its origins. In other cases, the meaning of the newly created word is more transparent, like 'lighthouse'.

Young children frequently demonstrate sensitivity to morphology in the way that they invent their own compound words that are meaningful to them. For example, one child that we know spontaneously invented the noun 'moregranny' to refer to one of her grandmothers, and to differentiate her from her other 'granny'. The logic of 'granny' and 'moregranny' is undeniable and appealing, and all the more remarkable because this shows us that children are not merely imitating what they hear adults saying: they are generating their own ideas about the rules that govern how language is constructed.

Grammatical morpheme
A 'morpheme' is a unit of speech that has meaning. A grammatical morpheme is a unit of speech that modifies the meaning of the word to which it is added, such as 'ed' when added to the end of a word like 'kick'.

Language users exploit another combinatorial device in which existing words are joined together with other sounds that do not have meaning in-and-of themselves. These other sounds, referred to as grammatical morphemes, modify the meaning of the words with which they combine: the morpheme /s/ in the word 'boy*s*' indicates plurality (*more than one* boy); the morpheme /ed/ in the word 'kick*ed*' indicates that the action was performed in the past. The use of grammatical morphemes such as word endings in this way is known as *inflection*.

English-speaking children begin to use plurals early in their third year. Most children will also have used some past tense verbs by about 30 months of age (see Table 1, Section 3.3). In English, plural and past tense forms are marked either by a process of adding an ending (dog → dog*s*, walk → walk*ed*) or through some change of the word stem (man → m*e*n, see → s*a*w). The process whereby an ending is added is known as *suffixation*. This is the *regular* (typical) way of forming plurals and past tenses in English. Other changes are called *irregular* (though do note that some nouns, for example 'deer', and verbs, for example 'hit', do not change their form at all in the plural or the past tense). Although a wider range of nouns and verbs are inflected through suffixation, irregular plurals and past tenses are commonly used in everyday adult language. Indeed, irregular plural and past tense forms are amongst the earliest acquired by young children.

Again, it can be inferred that children have a developing sensitivity to inflections from their early utterances. That is, initially children produce plural and past tense verb forms perfectly. However, towards the end of their third year they start to make errors like these:

My teacher holded the baby rabbits and we patted them.

I love cut-upped egg.

(Pinker, 1995, p. 109)

Instances where children incorrectly add /s/ to the end of a word to indicate plurality (e.g. 'sheep*s*'), or apply the 'add /ed/' rule for indicating that something has happened in the past are known as *over-regularization* errors. These types of error continue for several years. However, such errors are relatively rare, with over 95 per cent of irregular past tense verb use continuing to be perfect (Pinker, 1995; see also Figure 2). The incidence of over-regularization then decreases as children get older before gradually returning to 100 per cent performance in adulthood. The reason behind this 'U-shaped development', as it is termed by psychologists, is linked to children's increasing sensitivity to morphological rules (see Figure 2). That is, initial 'perfect' production of past tense verbs is likely to be due to children simply copying the speech that they hear. The period of over-regularization suggests that children have inferred a rule about how to indicate that things happened in the past – 'add /ed/' to the end of the verb – which they then have to learn to apply appropriately. We will discuss different explanations of how children learn to do this later in the chapter.

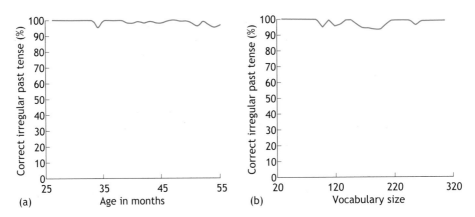

Figure 2 Graphs showing the percentage of irregular verb errors (a) observed in the speech of Adam (one of the children from Brown's study, 1973), and (b) made by a computer model that is learning how to produce irregular verbs (Plunkett and Marchman, 1993). Note that in both cases the overall rate of correct responses is high, but both are characterized by a small 'dip' in performance over time and as vocabulary increases. This is the so-called 'U-shaped' pattern of development.

2.3 Syntax

Syntax is the term used to refer to the knowledge that a speaker possesses regarding the manner in which words can be combined to form sentences. In English, syntax provides the information needed to determine *who did what to whom*. For example, English speakers have no difficulty distinguishing the meanings of the two sentences:

(1) John gave Mary the flowers.

(2) Mary gave John the flowers.

In the first sentence, John does the giving whereas in the second sentence it is Mary. The meanings of the words by themselves do not yield this information. It is necessary to pay attention to their position in the sentence. It might be tempting on the basis of this simple observation to conclude that syntax is synonymous with word order. For example, we might infer that the noun that occurs first is always the subject of the sentence. However, it is relatively easy to show that syntax is more complicated than this. In the sentence,

(3) Mary was given the flowers by John.

the subject of the sentence is the *last* noun mentioned, yet it is not difficult to understand that John did the giving. Figuring out who does what to whom requires the listener to be sensitive to the cues that indicate the type of sentence used. The language learner must decipher these cues – in this case, whether it is a passive (as in example (3) above) or an active sentence (as in example (1)). In general, this means paying attention to the structure of the sentence.

One of the achievements of grammarians has been to discover the kinds of structures listeners must recognize when understanding sentences. For example, passive sentences are easily identified by the presence of the word 'by'. However, sometimes the structural cues are far more subtle. In Chapter 3, Activity 4, you considered the example,

(4) A unicorn is in the garden.

and how easy it is to turn this into a question by moving the word 'is' to the front of the sentence. However, you also noted that this simple 'rule' does not apply when a sentence such as (5) is converted into a question.

(5) A unicorn that is eating a flower is in the garden.

Such examples demonstrate people's sensitivity to more complex aspects of sentence structure.

2.4 Learning morpho-syntax

Different languages vary in the extent to which they rely on morphology and syntax to signal who did what to whom. For example, as you have seen, English tends to rely on word order (syntax) to indicate this. In contrast, Turkish permits more variation in word order because it relies instead on special word endings (morphology) to indicate who did what to whom. These differences present children who are learning their first language with a problem: how are they to discover the extent to which their native language relies on either syntax or morphology? Most of the time, speakers produce multi-word sentences, irrespective of the language they are using, so both morphological and syntactic cues might be present. How is the child to learn which type of cue is important?

Theorists have offered two types of solution to this problem. One solution is that children have to work out the significance of morphology and syntax on the basis of their experience with linguistic forms and the objects and events that those linguistic forms describe. For example, if the child hears the sentence,

(6) Mary chases John.

used to describe the event <Mary chasing John> but hears the sentence,

(7) John chases Mary.

used to describe the event <John chasing Mary>, then there is good reason to suppose that syntactic cues (word order) are important in the language. On the other hand, if the child hears the sentence,

(8) John chases Mary-da.

used to describe the event <John chasing Mary> but hears the sentence,

(9) John-da chases Mary.

used to describe the event <Mary chasing John>, then there is good reason to suppose that morphological cues are important in the language (the suffix 'da' is indicating the *object* of the sentence: the person or thing that is on the receiving end of the action in the sentence). This solution to the problem presupposes that children can remember the word sequences or identify the inflections on the words and then work out how they relate to the events described by the speaker.

An alternative solution is that young children already 'know' that languages can be syntactically or morphologically oriented. That is, they are born with an implicit understanding that languages can signal who did what to whom through syntactic or morphological devices. In Chapter 3 you were introduced to the idea of language development being underpinned by an innate predisposition to acquire it; a position advocated by the work of Noam Chomsky, and further developed by Steven Pinker. With respect to acquiring grammatical understanding, Chomsky (1965) argued that humans have an innate knowledge of *potential* language structures, which he refers to as *Universal Grammar*. Universal Grammar contains a set of constraints on language processing that can be switched on or off through exposure to spoken language. Languages which exploit morphological cues 'switch on' the morphological constraints, whilst those which exploit syntactic cues switch on the syntactic constraints.

Chomsky argued that this kind of innate knowledge is necessary because children are rarely presented with coherent, grammatically complete speech that maps directly onto things happening in their immediate environment. For example, speakers might say a variety of different things in the context of <John chasing Mary> such as 'Look' or 'Not him again', or the conversation may be about something that happened in the past that the child knows nothing about. How are children to know which are the important parts of language to focus on? Chomsky's answer to this question is that it is Universal Grammar that directs the child's linguistic attention to the right kind of information.

Reading

At this point you should read Reading A, which is an extract from *The Articulate Mammal* by Jean Aitchison. This reading offers a simple introduction to Chomsky's notion of a Universal Grammar which we will return to later in this chapter.

SG

Summary of Section 2

- Phonology refers to the knowledge that a speaker possesses about the sound patterns of his or her language.
- Morphology refers to the knowledge a speaker has about the manner in which new words can be created from meaningful units of language, such as words, and grammatical morphemes.
- Syntax refers to the knowledge a speaker has about the ways in which words may be combined to form sentences.
- Languages differ in the extent to which they rely on either morphology or syntax to indicate who did what to whom.
- English speaking children pass through a U-shaped pattern of development in their understanding of morphology. This is where they

initially produce grammatically perfect utterances, and then pass through a period of making errors, before eventually regaining high levels of accurate language production.

- Universal Grammar refers to the idea that children may have an innate cognitive mechanism that represents 'knowledge' of how languages can be constructed. Through linguistic exposure, constraints that relate to their language are 'switched on' and others that do not apply are 'switched off'.

3 The development of spoken language

So far we have talked generally about the complex nature of acquiring grammatical understanding and introduced you to the idea of Universal Grammar. This section will offer a brief account of the patterns of grammatical development that are observed in young children who learn to speak English, as an illustration of how a clear developmental sequence in children's use of certain grammatical forms can be observed in any language.

3.1 One word at a time

As you saw in Chapter 2, many children produce their first recognizable words shortly after their first birthday. In addition to the most welcomed forms – 'mama' and 'dada' – other object words that are frequent and salient to children may be quickly mastered (e.g. 'cup', 'bottle', 'shoe'). Words that are suited to interacting with and directing a conversational partner also appear early in the child's lexical repertoire (e.g. 'look', 'no', 'more'). Sometimes, children use words in unusual ways, such as saying 'up' to request being picked up. Or (more embarrassingly) 'Daddy' is uttered when the postman or milkman delivers in the morning. One year olds are able to make effective use of a limited vocabulary to achieve a remarkable number of goals. This communicative flexibility is all the more surprising given the fact that early utterances usually consist of just a single word.

The utility of single word utterances derives from the manner in which the one year old manages to exploit the context in which the words are produced. Saying 'up' while making eye contact with an adult and reaching out her hands provides the child's conversational partner with unambiguous cues as to her intention, even though she has simply uttered a single word that describes a direction of movement. Intonation is also used to enhance or modulate the communicative force of the utterance: 'More!' may be produced in a demanding tone or a more enquiring tone ('More?'), perhaps depending on the child's confidence that she is going to get what she is asking for. Manual gestures and facial expressions combine with the utterance, assisting the listener's comprehension of the child's intended communication.

3.2 Early combinations

As indicated in Chapter 2, vocabulary development proceeds slowly between 12 and 18 months of age. At around 21 months of age many infants show a 'vocabulary spurt' where the rate of vocabulary growth increases dramatically. Shortly before this developmental landmark the earliest word combinations begin to appear. Some of these combinations are markedly hesitant – 'Look … Doggy' – as if they were two single word utterances strung together. Indeed, the disconnected intonation of these early two-word phrases reinforces their disjointed character. Each word is produced with its own rise-and-fall contour. The words bond together through their appropriateness to the communicative situation. They also usually conform to the word order constraints honoured by adult speakers, although they lack the function words ('the', 'of', 'is', 'and', etc.) that act as the grammatical glue in adult speech. These early word combinations are often referred to as *telegraphic speech*.

However, not all early word combinations are disfluent. Common phrases used by adults are often used by children too. 'What's that?' may be uttered fluently in an appropriate context and with a questioning intonation by pre-vocabulary spurt children, suggesting a greater mastery of multi-word combinatorial speech than their telegraphic utterances reveal. Often these expressions are produced in a rather inarticulate manner by children, as if they are trying to squeeze more sounds into an utterance than their memory will allow. However, the multi-word status of these fluent productions is open to question. They are frequently referred to as *formulaic speech* or *amalgams*, the prevailing assumption being that they constitute chunks of speech that have simply been memorized by the child as a single unit. For example, the child who says 'What's that?' may be treating this phrase as if it were one word. By the time children pass through their vocabulary spurt, telegraphic speech is produced in a more fluent manner, and formulaic expressions become less abundant in their productions.

3.3 Utterance length as a measure of complexity

The standard way of measuring the grammatical complexity of children's language is called Mean Length of Utterance (MLU) and was introduced by Brown (1973) in his pioneering study of three children's early linguistic development. Brown and his colleagues studied regular samples of the language produced by Adam, Eve and Sarah, all of whom were just beginning to produce utterances that were longer than one word at the beginning of the study, although their ages differed. This enabled Brown and his colleagues to engage in a highly detailed analysis of the changes that occur in children's use of language over time.

MLU is calculated by taking the first 100 utterances from a transcription of a child's speech and then finding the average length of those utterances in morphemes (units of meaning). Consequently, if a child is producing exclusively single-word utterances, his or her MLU will be just 1.0 (the minimum level of complexity). Once he or she begins to combine words and other morphemes, his or her MLU will be greater than 1.0 (see Figure 3).

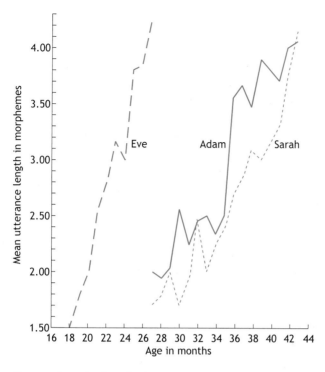

Figure 3 Mean utterance length and chronological age for three children. Brown (1973) observed that children's MLU increases with age. (Adapted from Brown, 1973, p. 55.)

Brown (1973) identified stages in language development in terms of the child's MLU. For example, when children have an MLU of 1.75, they are still in the telegraphic stage. By the time they have an MLU of 2.25 – that is when most of their utterances are multi-morphemic – children's speech will contain examples of the plural and continuous present forms (e.g. 'Boys walk*ing*') as well as words like 'in' and 'on'. Table 1 lists other landmarks in language development that Brown identified as characteristic of various levels of MLU. It should be kept in mind that the MLU of spontaneous adult conversation is usually in the range of 4.0–5.0. Hence, you should not expect MLU to offer a discriminating measurement of grammatical competence beyond early language development.

Table 1   Stages of linguistic development as defined by Brown (1973)

Stage	MLU	Forms
I	1.75	Telegraphic speech
II	2.25	Use of -*ing*, plural endings, *in*, and *on*
III	2.75	Some specific uses of the verb 'to be', 'the', 'a', irregular past tenses of verbs, use of -'s to indicate ownership
IV	3.5	Regular past tense of verbs (add /ed/), use of the 'third person'
V	4.0	Use of auxiliary verbs

Individual variation in patterns of linguistic development also cautions against using MLU as an unambiguous indication of the emergence of particular words or grammatical forms in the way implied by Table 1. For example, not all children will learn irregular past tense forms (e.g. 'went') before they learn regular ones (e.g. 'walked'). Likewise, some children may use the indefinite or definite articles ('a' and 'the' respectively) before they use plural forms. Nevertheless, Brown's observations offer a useful rule of thumb for gauging the emergence of different grammatical forms during the second and third years of life.

You may have noticed that the facts presented in this section have been based entirely on children's expressive language. This is largely due to the techniques that have been used to investigate children's grammatical development. The primary method that has informed these accounts is that of systematic transcription (see Box 2).

Expressive language
The language that a person actually produces.

BOX 2

Systematic transcription

Systematic transcription is a process whereby periods of speech are recorded and then transcribed. The recording almost invariably includes excerpts of speech from the child's conversational partner, thereby providing a context in which to interpret the child's utterances. The continuous collection of data (sometimes over several hours) offers the investigator a representative sample of the child's language. Indeed, recording in different situations allows the investigator to determine how speech varies from one context to another. The cost of this enriched source of data is the time taken to collect and transcribe the material. For example, a single hour's talk can take many hours to transcribe.

There are two ways that speech can be transcribed. The first of these is *phonetic transcription* which involves representing each utterance using a special phonetic alphabetic. This differs from standard alphabets, which may use the same letter symbol to represent more than one sound (e.g. in English the letter 'c' can represent the sound [k] or [s]), or more than one symbol to represent the same sound (e.g. in English the letters 'f' and 'ph' both represent the sound [f]). Moreover, each language only uses a proportion of all the sounds that it is possible to produce. In contrast, the phonetic alphabet has one symbol each for all the sounds that could possibly be produced by the human voice and also distinguishes between sounds that a speaker of a single language may not recognize (see Section 2.1). This makes it ideal for transcribing the talk of young children whose early utterances can include 'foreign' sounds.

Many researchers opt instead for the second way, that is producing *orthographic transcriptions*. This form of transcription glosses over the peculiarities of the child's pronunciation, and identifies words from adult language that the investigator believes that the child is attempting to produce. The addition of video-recording methods and digital enhancements provides investigators with even richer sources of information to interpret and analyse children's utterances. For example, it is now possible to view on a computer screen a digital video recording of a child simultaneously with a transcription of what the child or his or her conversational partner is saying.

However, systematic transcription records do not necessarily offer an accurate reflection of what children *know* about language. After all, children may know a lot more about language than they actually say. Also, given the naturalistic situation in which the data are typically collected, it can be very difficult to assess what could be contributing to a child's linguistic behaviour. Take, for example, the case of a child who produces an especially complex utterance, potentially indicative of a sophisticated knowledge of language. Was it, in fact, only produced because of something an adult has just said or done, or because of the presence of other objects and events at the time? Consequently, investigators have turned to more experimental methods to assess children's comprehension of linguistic forms, which offer the investigator more control over the situation in which the children's talk occurs.

Receptive language
The language that a person actually understands, but that may not necessarily feature in their own language use.

Relatively little work has been done to determine the grammatical abilities present in one year olds' receptive language. In general, the ability to comprehend language is better developed than the ability to produce language. For example, children are unlikely to produce the word 'dog' unless they are able to understand it. Consequently, there is good reason to believe that the developmental profile of speech presented in this section may underestimate the grammatical abilities of the one year old.

Experimental procedures have been developed to enable investigators to better assess young children's potential to understand grammatical rules. One such procedure is the *inter-modal preferential looking task*. This procedure was first developed by Spelke (1979) who used it to investigate infants' perceptual abilities. She showed infants two events (e.g. something being dropped or hands clapping) but only played the sound associated with one of those events (e.g. clapping). The children were found to spend more time looking at the event that was consistent with the sound that they heard, their extended gaze suggesting that they correctly associated the sound with the event. This technique has since been adapted to analyse very young children's understanding of grammar and how this might facilitate the acquisition of new words (see Research summary 1).

RESEARCH SUMMARY 1

The inter-modal preferential looking task

Naigles (1990) used the inter-modal preferential looking task in a study to look at whether young children (aged approximately 2 years and 1 month) were able to use the grammatical context of a sentence to work out the meaning of a new word. During the task, each child sat on his or her mother's lap in front of two television monitors that were 12 inches (30 cm) apart. Between the two monitors was a concealed speaker. Above the speaker was a light that attracted the child's attention back to the centre of the display between trials. The mother was instructed not to look at the screens and her eyes were covered. This was to ensure that the child could not follow her gaze or body position to locate the correct screen (see Figure 4).

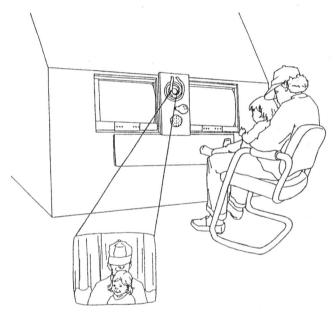

Transitive verb
A verb that must refer to an object in a sentence. For example the verb 'to hit' is transitive – it is not legitimate just to say 'I am hitting'. It is necessary to say *what* is being hit.

Intransitive verb
A verb that does not require its object to be specified in a sentence. For example, 'to read' is intransitive as it is possible to say 'I am reading'. It is not necessary to say what is being read.

Figure 4 Experimental set-up of the preferential looking task (from Naigles and Kako, 1993, p. 1670).

The child was shown actions where one actor had an effect on something (causative actions) and actions that had no effect on another thing (non-causative actions). So the child saw, for example, footage of a duck making a rabbit bend over (a causative action) while both animals were making arm movements (the non-causative actions). This scene was paired with a nonsense verb (e.g. 'gorp') which was presented in one of two sentences. One sentence, 'The duck is gorping the bunny', implied that the nonsense word was a transitive verb (one that requires a corresponding 'object'). The other sentence, 'The duck and the bunny are gorping', implied that the nonsense word was an intransitive verb (one that does not require an object).

Then the actions were shown separately. On one screen the duck was shown bending the rabbit over; on the other screen the duck and the rabbit were shown just moving their arms (see Table 2).

Naigles found that the children looked at the causative actions, such as the duck forcing the rabbit to bend over, for longer than they did at the other screen when they heard the phrase 'The duck is [word]-ing the bunny!'. They looked at the non-causative actions, such as the duck and rabbit making arm movements, for longer when they heard the phrase 'The duck and the bunny are [word]-ing!'. These results were taken as evidence that children are able to use their sensitivity to grammatical forms to learn about verb meanings.

Table 2   Structure of the stimulus video tapes for the verb 'gorp'

Video tape 1	Audio	Video tape 2
The duck is forcing the rabbit into a bending position; both are making arm gestures	Look! The duck is gorping the bunny!	Black screen
Black screen	Look! The duck is gorping the bunny!	Duck is forcing the rabbit into a bending position; both are making arm gestures
Duck is forcing the rabbit into a bending position; both are making arm gestures	Look! The duck is gorping the bunny!	Duck is forcing the rabbit into a bending position; both are making arm gestures
Duck is forcing the rabbit into a bending position	Oh! They're different now!	The duck and rabbit are making arm gestures
Duck is forcing the rabbit into a bending position	Where's the gorping now?	The duck and rabbit are making arm gestures
Duck is forcing the rabbit into a bending position	Find gorping!	The duck and rabbit are making arm gestures

Source: adapted from Naigles, 1990, p. 374.

3.4 Full blown grammar

The transition from early child-like word combinations to full blown grammar is rapid. By the time children reach their fourth birthday, they have mastered an impressive range of grammatical devices. For example, they know how to ask questions, make statements and issue commands. The dramatic nature of this development is well illustrated by the extracts below from Adam, one of the children that Brown (1973) studied longitudinally.

Age 2;3: Play checkers. Big drum … A bunny-rabbit walk …

Age 2;6: What that egg doing? No, I don't want to sit seat …

Age 2;9: Where mommy keep her pocket book? Show you something funny …

Age 3;0: I going wear that to wedding … Those are not strong mens … You dress me up like a baby elephant …

Age 3;2: So it can't be cleaned? I broke my racing car. I want to have some espresso … Can I put my head in the mailbox so the mailman can know where I are and put me in the mailbox? …

(Pinker, 1994, pp. 269–70)

Activity 2   *Reflecting on grammatical development*

Allow about
5 minutes

This activity will help you to reflect on the ways in which children's grammatical competence changes over time.

Look back at the examples of Adam's speech. What do you notice about the way that Adam forms his utterances over this period?

Comment

The most obvious thing to note is the change in the length of Adam's utterances. His attempts to combine words are not always grammatical, but they do increase in length over time. The early utterances omit function words ('the', 'a', 'on', etc.) as expected. He attempts to formulate questions quite early on in his multi-word utterances although 'is' is often omitted. He also makes an interesting error – 'mens', where he correctly inflects the noun 'man', but still adds the conventional /s/ ending to indicate that there is more than one. The later utterances are more in line with adult speech ('I want to have some espresso') although they are not always error free ('… the mailman can know where I are …'). The main source of error throughout is from omitting words, rather than getting them wrong. You can see that simply by inserting the missing words the sentences become grammatical: the actual order of the words that are produced is correct, suggesting that Adam shows some grasp of syntax.

Even when they make errors, children still show sensitivity to correct forms, even though their own productions may be flawed.

Child: You readed some of this too … She readed all the rest.

Parent: She read the whole thing to you, huh?

Child: Nu-uh, you read some.

Parent: Oh, that's right, yeah. I readed the beginning of it.

Child: Readed? (*annoyed surprise*) Read! (*pronounced 'red'*).

Parent: Oh, yeah, read.

Child: Will you stop that, Papa?

(Pinker, 1995, p. 119)

Although children are continuously bombarded during their waking hours with a stream of richly structured linguistic input, they seem to assimilate the structures of their native language without explicit instruction or correction (Brown and Hanlon, 1970). The ease with which all this seems to occur belies the underlying complexity of the skill acquired. As is often the case with many complex abilities, a lot can be learned from observing the order in which parts of the skill are acquired, and tracking down the rare mistakes that individuals make in exercising their skills. This is precisely what will be discussed in the next two sections. The discussions in these sections will help you to evaluate the extent to which it can be said that language acquisition is driven by innate cognitive mechanisms (like Universal Grammar) or experience of a linguistic environment.

Summary of Section 3

- One-word utterances typically appear shortly after a child's first birthday and are effectively combined with intonation and gesture to make a meaningful utterance.
- Formulaic speech refers to the way in which children who are at the one-word stage may use a longer adult phrase appropriately, but without necessarily realizing that it consists of more than one word.
- Mean Length of Utterance (MLU) is used as a measure of grammatical complexity in young children's emerging speech, and refers to the average number of morphemes used by the child in an utterance.
- Systematic transcription is a technique used to study children's expressive language development. Extracts of children's speech are regularly sampled and transcribed either phonetically or orthographically.
- Experimental methods can be used to examine the determinants of children's linguistic behaviour. They are also increasingly used to assess children's receptive language abilities.
- Where children make linguistic errors, they are typically omissions of function words or over-generalizations of rules. Word order is normally appropriate.

4   'I readed the beginning of it …': learning about word endings

As illustrated in Section 2.2., inflectional morphology refers to the way that inflections (the 'outer layers' of a word, e.g. -ed or -s) are used in language to provide additional information about the meaning of an existing word. For example, as discussed earlier, when /ed/ is added to a word, it indicates to an English speaker that an action was performed in the past.

As already noted in Section 2, the development of plural and past tense inflection is characterized by surprisingly few errors. The developmental profile thus proceeds from a period of error-free performance, through a period where some errors are observed, to a later stage of adult-like performance (the U-shaped development referred to in Section 2).

The traditional explanation for this pattern of development is that initially young children simply memorize the plural and past tense forms of nouns and verbs. They do not make mistakes because they only repeat words that they have heard and memorized. However, when children first discover the underlying regularities associated with plural or past tense formation, such as the 'add /ed/' rule, they are prone to overextend these regularities even to words which do not adhere to the regular pattern: for example 'shake' becomes 'shaked'. Later, as they gain more experience with the language, children are able to produce reliably both the regular and irregular forms of plural and past tense words.

However, there is disagreement as to how the processes of memorization and inflection operate to produce the U-shaped pattern of development that is observed in English-speaking children. One view assumes that early learning is dominated by a general memory system and that the discovery of the regularities in plural and past tense forms requires a separate system of linguistic rules. This is referred to as the *dual route theory*. A second view assumes that a single memory system is sufficient to explain the whole profile of inflectional development, which is known as the *single route theory*.

4.1 Dual route theory

Dual route theory (Pinker and Prince, 1988) proposes that plural and past tense inflection is achieved through two cognitive systems operating in parallel with each other:
* a rule system adding the appropriate ending to the word stem; and
* a memory system containing a record of all the irregular and most common inflections in the language.

According to this model, when an individual attempts to inflect a word, the memory system is consulted to determine whether there is a corresponding irregular past tense form stored. Simultaneously, the rule system is engaged, and the appropriate regular ending is added to the word. If the memory system fails to find a stored record that corresponds to the word, the rule system succeeds and the regular form of the word is produced. If the memory system finds a stored record, the rule system is 'blocked' and the memorized (irregular) form is produced. For example, in an attempt to inflect the word 'go', the language user will discover that the memory system contains 'went', which blocks the application of the 'add /ed/' rule, preventing the error 'goed'.

Activity 3   *Dual route theory*

Allow about
5 minutes

This activity will enable you to assess how well you understand dual route explanations of inflection.

Assume that a boy's 'memory system' contains only the following irregular past tense verb forms: went, broke and held. What does the dual route theory predict the child will say when he is required to produce the past tense of the following words: go, want and eat?

Comment

According to the dual route model, he would be expected to say 'went' rather than 'goed' because he has a representation of this irregular form in his memory system. He should say 'wanted' because if there is no corresponding irregular representation in the memory system the 'add /ed/' rule will be applied. However, the boy will say 'eated' instead of ate, because there is no stored representation of the irregular form, and so the 'add /ed/' rule will, once again, be applied in this case.

According to this account, the development of the memory system is critical to the proper operation of the inflectional process. In order to identify an irregular inflection such as 'went' or 'men', the irregular forms need to be stored and retrievable from memory. Failure to retrieve exceptions from memory will result in a failure of blocking and hence an over-regularization error. Memory failure is most likely due to lack of knowledge of particular words. Hence, irregular words that only rarely occur in speech are most susceptible to over-regularization. With greater experience (as the child gets older) memories for rare types of inflection are consolidated and errors diminish. Dual route theory suggests that the inflection that occurs across the greatest number of words is established as the *default* rule (Marcus *et al.*, 1992); for example -ed is the most common type of past tense inflection in English, so it becomes the 'rule'.

4.2 Single route theory

Single route theory proposes that regular and irregular inflections are produced by a *single* system that stores *all* of the inflections in the language (Rumelhart and McClelland, 1987). At first this may seem a preposterous claim since there are many thousands of noun and verb inflections which language users would need to remember. However, Rumelhart and McClelland (1987) demonstrated that a simple connectionist network has a formidable capacity to remember a wide range of inflections (see Box 3).

BOX 3

Connectionism

Connectionist networks are computer models loosely based on the principles of neural information processing. They are sometimes referred to as *neural networks*. It is only necessary to have a basic knowledge of how connectionist models work in order to understand what they can tell us about cognitive processes (such as language understanding and memory) and cognitive development.

A connectionist model consists of 'units', which can be thought of as roughly analogous to neurons. A typical network is organized as follows. A set of units is designated as *input units*. These can be thought of as equivalent to human *sensory neurons* which are activated by a stimulus from the environment. Another set of units is designated as *output units*. It might be helpful to think of these as the equivalent of *motor neurons*, which produce a behaviour. In between the input and output units are various configurations of *hidden units*. These can be thought of as equivalent to all the neurons which are part of the 'black box' of cognition; everything that goes on between input (stimulus) and output (response).

A connectionist network needs to be able to accept an input (a stimulus), make various computations, and produce an output (a response). The job of a connectionist network when it is being used as a *model* of human information processing, is to accept a stimulus and to learn to make the response that a person would make to that stimulus. For example, if a connectionist network were being built to model a child's developmental mastery of the English past tense it would be provided with the stimuli of English verb stems. It would need to learn to respond to each verb with the appropriate past tense form. Its behaviour would be observed as it learned (developed) and then compared to the course of development that can be observed in children.

Plunkett and Juola (1999) trained a connectionist network on some 5,000 different English inflections. They found that, like children, their network went through an initial period of producing nouns and verbs correctly, which was then followed by a period of intermittent over-regularization. They also found that the network 'learned' plural inflections before past tense inflections. If you look back at Table 1, you will see that this is consistent with the results of Brown's (1973) study of children's grammatical development. Given the small scale of these networks compared to a human brain (see Chapter 3, Section 2.1), the proposal that a single system might memorize all of the inflections in the language does not seem so unlikely after all.

Single route theory differs from dual route theory in its account of why children begin to make over-regularization errors. The explanation is this. As more and more inflections are stored in memory, competition for memory resources increases. This competition between words results in *interference effects*, where words that are very similar to each other are easily confused. For example, 'fan' and 'man' sound very similar to each other but one has a regular plural inflection ('fan*s*') and the other has an irregular inflection ('m*e*n'). In the case of the irregular word 'man', if there are lots of regular words stored that have a similar phonological structure (e.g. 'fan', 'ban', 'van' and 'span') then 'man' may be accidentally treated as if it too has a regular inflection ('mans').

This is exactly what Rumelhart and McClelland (1987) found when they trained their connectionist network on regular and irregular verb inflections. Early in training, the network only had a few verbs to memorize and so it managed to inflect the verbs correctly. However, as its vocabulary grew, competition for network resources intensified and over-regularization errors were found. With further training, the irregular verbs became more robustly stored in the network and were able to resist the interference effects of regular neighbours.

Activity 4   *Computational modelling*

Allow about
5 minutes

This activity will encourage you to reflect on the advantages of computational modelling as a technique in research into child development.

Why would you want to model a developmental process? What would be the aim of such a model?

Comment

The aim of any model is to test specific predictions about the mechanisms that underlie the developmental process in question. It is one thing to propose a model on paper, but quite another thing to build a computational model that actually has to function. For one thing it forces researchers to be explicit about how all the different structures and processes that they are proposing work. If the finished model shows patterns of behaviour that are similar to those shown by children, then perhaps the structures and processes built into the model are similar to those going on in the developing child. 'Perhaps' should be emphasized because even if two systems (in this case a child and a computer model) produce the same behaviour, that does not necessarily mean they are doing it in the same way. If you search your memory for a piece of information, and a computer searches its memory for the same piece of information, the output from you and the computer may be the same, but the search process may have been completely different.

4.3 Comparing single and dual route approaches

Single route and dual route theories both explain U-shaped development in terms of competition effects. However, dual route theory supposes that over-regularization errors result from a competition between two different cognitive *mechanisms*, namely a memory system and a rule system. In contrast, single route theory claims that it is competition between *words* within a single memory system that is the cause of over-regularization errors in children's utterances. Both theories explain the eventual disappearance of over-regularization errors as a by-product of the strengthening of the memory traces of irregular inflections. Indeed, both theories predict that inflected words that are common in the language (including many irregular words) are least likely to be over-regularized.

Given that both theories predict the same developmental patterns of grammatical development, how can researchers determine which theory offers the *better* account? Fortunately, the two theories predict different types of errors, and the occurrence of certain types of mistakes in children's speech strengthens the evidence in favour of one account over the other.

Activity 5   *Predicting errors from the models*

Allow about 10 minutes

This activity will give you another opportunity to test your understanding of single and dual route accounts.

As discussed earlier, single route theories and dual route theories differ in the types of mistakes that they predict children will make when learning about inflections. Here are two types of child-like inflection errors [with the correct form of the verb in brackets]:

(a)   I holded [held] the books for my teacher.

(b)   The paperclips were lank [linked] together.

Can a dual route account explain both these types of error? Can a single route account explain both these types of error?

Comment

Sentence (a) is an example of an over-generalization error, and hopefully you remembered that both theories can explain this sort of mistake. Sentence (b) is an example of what happens when a regular word takes an irregular inflection. While very rare, these do occur in children's speech. Dual route theory predicts that regular words are not susceptible to interference effects from irregular words in the way illustrated by sentence (b). So errors like 'lank' should not occur. However, single route theory predicts that interference effects will impact on children's production of both regular and irregular words. That is, just as regular inflections interfere with the production of irregular words (just as 'fold' becomes 'folded' in the past tense, so 'hold' wrongly becomes 'holded'), so should irregular words interfere with the production of regular inflections (just as 'sink' becomes 'sank', so 'link' wrongly becomes 'lank', instead of 'linked'). Consequently, this kind of evidence favours single route theory.

The two theories also differ in their account of how children generalize inflections to new words. For example, given the novel word 'wug', children and adults would most likely use the word 'wugs' as its plural form. Dual route theory explains this creative use of inflections in terms of the operation of the rule, and there being no entry in memory to block the application of the rule. Single route theory explains generalization in terms of the *similarity* of the new word to existing words in the language ('mug', 'slug', 'hug', etc.).

There is controversy here as to what the language user does with words that are not similar to any other word stored in memory. This situation is particularly poignant in the case of children with relatively small vocabularies. Dual route theory predicts that the word will simply be inflected according to the default rule, whereas single route theory predicts that an educated guess will be made on the basis of a weighted similarity to all the other words in the individual's vocabulary. Experimental evidence provided by Marchman (1997) has examined just this question and favours the single route account (see Research summary 2).

RESEARCH SUMMARY 2

Evidence for the single route explanation

Marchman (1997) gave 74 children, whose ages ranged between 3 years and 8 months and 13 years and 5 months, a picture book. Each picture depicted everyday activities and the children were asked to say 'What happened yesterday'. For example, they were shown a picture of a boy walking down a street, and were told 'This boy is walking. He walks everyday. Yesterday he _____?'. Eleven regular verbs and 38 irregular verbs were used in the task. Each verb was evaluated in terms of how many neighbourhood 'friends' it had – in other words, how many other verbs that sound similar also change in the same way in the past tense (e.g. throw and blow are 'friends', as they become 'threw' and 'blew'). The number of 'enemies' each verb had was also counted (e.g. throw and mow are 'enemies' because mow becomes 'mowed', not 'mew' in the past tense). The frequency of the past tense form (i.e. how many words change in the same way) of the words in the task was also measured.

Single route theory predicts that irregular verbs that sound similar to regular verbs will be more prone to having '/ed/' added by the children when it should not be. For example, 'throw' might become 'throwed', because it is similar to 'row' which becomes 'rowed'. However, dual route models predict that these errors will occur in a way that is uninfluenced by the number of similar, regular word 'neighbours' that it has.

Marchman found that irregular verbs with many 'enemies' were more likely to have 'add /ed/' wrongly used as their past tense form by the children than verbs that had few regular verb enemies. She also found that irregular verbs that had highly frequent past tense forms were less likely to be given the regular past tense endings than those verbs whose past tense form was rare. These results are consistent with single route accounts.

Comment

So far, we have been careful not to relate either the dual or single route theories to either nativist or empiricist positions. This is because both theories are simply about specifying the nature of the cognitive mechanism that might account for the patterns of development observed in young children. This debate can be seen as separate from discussions of whether the mechanism is believed to be innately pre-programmed or to develop in response to experience with the linguistic environment. However, historically 'nativists' have aligned themselves with the dual route theories (note that Pinker is an advocate of dual route theory) and 'empiricists' (such as Marchman) have supported the single route position. The basic distinction is that dual route theorists generally propose that the rule mechanism is innate whereas single-route theorists contest this view. However, it is entirely possible to present a view in which a dual route system might arise as the result of learning.

4.4 Cross-linguistic evidence for single route theory

Another way of testing the viability of such ideas is to examine how well these theories can account for the use of inflections in other languages. One of the reasons for proposing a dual route account of inflections in English was that most nouns and verbs are regular and take a single ending, like '/ed/'. Irregular words are few in number and so can be readily stored in a system that memorizes their exceptional properties. The dual route account was seen as an efficient and economic solution available to the user of a highly regular language. However, other languages have multiple 'regular' endings. For example, the German plural system has eight ways of forming the plural, all of them well known to speakers of the language.

Dual route theory proposes that the rule system is dedicated to processing just one of the endings and that the majority of the regular inflections in these languages are stored in memory as if they were exceptions (Marcus *et al.*, 1995). For example, Marcus *et al.* (1995) argue that the default rule in German is the 's' plural (although it should be noted that it is *not* the most common of the plural endings, which *contradicts* the explanation offered by Marcus *et al.* (1992); see Section 4.1). Marcus *et al.* (1995) offer evidence that the default rules in these languages operate in the same way as the regular rule system does in English; that is, they cause over-regularization errors and are used for inflecting novel words (like wug). So, if 's' is the default rule in German, it should be over-represented in children's over-regularization errors.

However, recent longitudinal research on German (Szagun, 2001) has questioned the validity of these claims (see Research summary 3).

RESEARCH SUMMARY 3

Plural inflection errors in German-speaking children

Szagun (2001) conducted a longitudinal study of 22 German-speaking children from the age of 1 year and 4 months until they were 2 years and 10 months old. Two hours of the children's spontaneous speech was recorded on audio tape every 20 weeks. The parents' child-directed speech was also sampled at four points during the study. The purpose of this was to study the pattern of development in the children's use of plurals. In German there are eight different types of plural inflection, with '-n' and '-e' being the most frequent, and with '-s' and '-er' being relatively rare. In line with single route theory, Szagun predicted that the children's use of '-n' and '-e' endings will develop most rapidly and, that errors will be apparent from early on in the children's speech (not after a period of correct usage as observed in English-speaking children). Szagun argues that a single route explanation is better suited to learning languages with more than one regular inflection. That is, it is more advantageous for a German-speaking child to start out by generalizing from the different regularities of German inflection that they hear (in the way described by single route accounts), than if they were to learn the endings by rote and then generate rules to govern their use (as suggested by dual route theory).

Szagun found a much wider variety of errors in children learning German than that reported by Marcus *et al.* (1995) with little evidence of the 's' plural dominating in the way they suggested. The children's development in using the different plural inflections was consistent with the occurrence of those inflections in their parents' speech. The frequency of the children's use of the different inflections was the same as that of their parents by the time they were 3 years and 8 months old. Finally, the children made errors right from the beginning of their use of plural forms. These findings are consistent with a single route account of German inflectional morphology.

4.5 Evidence for dual route theory from studies of developmental disorders

Williams Syndrome
A non-hereditary syndrome caused by a chromosomal abnormality. Brain and physical development can be affected, and symptoms can include poor co-ordination, some muscle weakness, possible heart defects, occasional kidney damage and high calcium levels. Development is generally delayed in these children.

Specific language impairment (SLI)
A specific and severe difficulty in acquiring some aspect of language development, despite no apparent general cognitive or neurological impairment.

Another way of testing the strength of a theory is to see how well it can account for instances where the production of a behaviour is known to be problematic. So far you have seen that the pattern of typical development in English and other languages seems to favour the single route account. However, Pinker (1991) has argued that instances of the *breakdown* in usage of inflections favours the dual route account.

He cites two developmental disorders, Williams Syndrome and specific language impairment (SLI) where researchers have discovered different patterns of behaviour for regular and irregular past tense word forms. For example, some studies of children with Williams Syndrome (Bellugi *et al.*, 1990) show that these children are able to produce regular forms of past tense verbs, but their production of irregular past tense verbs is more problematic. In contrast, other studies of participants with SLI (e.g. Gopnik and Crago, 1991) show that *irregular* forms are relatively preserved. For example, one 10-year-old child with SLI wrote the following in his school notebook:

Monday 12th September

On Saturday I watch TV and I watch plastic man and I watch football. On Sunday I had pork and potato and cabbage.

(Gopnik and Crago, 1991, p. 39)

In this extract the regular verb 'to watch' is not marked for past tense, although the irregular verb 'to have' is produced correctly. Gopnik and Crago noted that the children were significantly more likely to make mistakes on regular verbs than on irregular ones. Moreover, there was evidence that when the teacher corrected past tense errors of this kind, the children did appear to learn the correct form in that case, but were unable to generalize the 'add /ed/' rule to other regular verbs.

This pattern of results reflects a *double dissociation* between regular and irregular inflection. Double dissociation refers to evidence that two cognitive processes appear to be unrelated to each other. This is because not only does one group of people show ability at A but impairment B (a single dissociation), but another group of people exists who show ability at B but impairment at A. The existence of both patterns is the double dissociation. Double dissociations are widely considered to be one of the most powerful tools in identifying the component parts of cognition (Shallice, 1988).

Dual route theory offers a simple explanation of the reported double dissociation between Williams Syndrome and SLI children. Impairment of the rule route will affect performance on regular verbs, but leave irregular performance intact (as is observed with SLI children). Impairment of memory will affect irregular verbs, but leave regular verb production intact (as is the case with people with Williams Syndrome). In contrast, the defining feature of single route theory is that regular and irregular inflections share the same processing resources. Therefore, impairment of one type of inflection should also appear together with impairment of the other type. The existence of double dissociations between regular and irregular inflection therefore seems to count against single route theory.

However, there are two considerations presented in the developmental disorder literature which caution against dismissing single route theory on the basis of these findings, one empirical and one theoretical. First, the evidence is not consistent. For example, Thomas *et al.* (2001) found no difference in performance between regular and irregular past tense verb forms in Williams Syndrome children. Similarly, Bishop (1997) did not find a straightforward dissociation between regular and irregular verbs in SLI children. Second, single route theorists have been able to replicate double dissociations between regular and irregular verbs in their connectionist models (Joanisse and Seidenberg, 1999; Juola and Plunkett, 2000). The reason single route theories can produce double dissociations is because the resources available to the system are not shared *equally* between regular and irregular inflections. Some parts of the system have more memory resources invested in regular verbs whilst other parts have more resources invested in irregular verbs (recall in Section 4.2 the discussion of competition for memory resources being affected by the nature and number of similar words in memory).

The implications of these developmental disorders for our understanding of how children learn about inflections are unclear and their investigation remains a topic of intensive research.

Comment

There are other arguments, aside from the linguistic evidence, that favour the single route model. Firstly, it is a parsimonious account; that is, it is a simple account, having only one component. It also appears to offer a biologically plausible account of how neural connections might operate in the human brain to produce the observed patterns of inflection use. Finally, the idea of distributed representation, that knowledge is not represented in one 'location' in the brain but is the product of a network of processing units (e.g. neurons) that is consequently resistant to minor damage, is one that has appeal.

Summary of Section 4

- There are two proposed explanations of the U-shaped pattern of development in children's acquisition of inflectional morphology: a dual route model and a single route model.
- Dual route theory proposes that inflection is achieved through two processing systems that operate in parallel: a rule system and a memory system containing irregular and high frequency inflections. This type of explanation has historically been associated with nativist explanations of language acquisition.
- Single route theory proposes that all inflections are produced by a single memory system. This type of explanation has historically been associated with empiricist accounts of language acquisition.
- Connectionist networks are computer models that are loosely based on principles of neural information processing. They can be used to 'test' theories of language acquisition by attempting to simulate how children learn to use language. Connectionist models support the plausibility of single route explanations.
- Evidence from children's production errors and from cross-linguistic research favours single route explanations.
- Evidence from studies of developmental disorders is ambiguous in its potential to support either dual or single route accounts.

5 'Where Mummy is going?': learning about word order

So far you have seen that there are two competing explanations of how children acquire inflectional morphology, and that historically they have been associated with either nativist or empiricist accounts of language acquisition. To extend and further illustrate the nature of the nativist–empiricist discussion, we will now introduce you to explanations of how children come to understand the significance of syntax for constructing meaningful sentences.

Telegraphic speech (children's early use of highly simplified sentences) offers the first opportunity to examine children's mastery of the syntax of their language. On the surface, children seem to be doing a pretty good job even by their second birthday. Words are produced more or less in the right order ('Mummy gone work'). They are creative in their combinations ('All gone Mummy') and they know how to use these sequences in conversation to ask questions, make statements and issue commands. All that seems to be missing are the function words that are characteristic of well-formed adult sentences ('Mummy *has* gone *to* work').

However, closer inspection of children's errors reveals that much linguistic work remains to be done. For example, consider the following ill-formed attempts to pose *Wh*-questions:

(10)   What Daddy is eating?

(11)   Where Mummy is going?

Subject-auxiliary inversion
The change in word order that is required to make a statement (e.g. 'Mummy is going') into a question (e.g. 'What is Daddy eating?'), which involves putting the auxiliary verb before the subject of the sentence (in this case, Daddy).

Notice that both sentences (10) and (11) contain the necessary ingredients for the correct formulation of questions. The child has simply failed to place the auxiliary verb 'is' in front of the subject ('Daddy' or 'Mummy'). Notice that sentences (10) and (11) stripped of their respective *Wh*-words constitute legitimate statements. Perhaps the first attempts to produce *Wh*-questions build upon the ability to make statements? At some point, however, the child must discover the importance of subject-auxiliary inversion for question formation. How is this achieved?

5.1 What, where, why and who: asking questions about syntax

A relatively straightforward and uncontroversial answer is that children must pay attention to the practices of question formation in their language. They are given ample opportunity to discover that *Wh*-words are often followed by a relatively small set of function words such as 'is', 'has' or 'does', and that these function words are related to the noun that follows ('Where *are* the boys going?'). Uncovering these regularities is presumably just like discovering the regularities of past tense and plural formation: looking for patterns in the language. Unfortunately, this supposedly straightforward answer disguises a theoretical hornet's nest!

The idea that a limited set of function words immediately follow after a *Wh*-word is not strictly true. For example, (12) is a perfectly legitimate question beginning with a *Wh*-word, but is followed by a noun, (13) does not have an auxiliary verb, and (14) is not even a question.

(12)   What colour is the grass?

(13)   What type of plane flies to New York in less than 4 hours?

(14)   What Stephen did is of no consequence.

The language learner has to cope with all these different usages of 'what'. Furthermore, a little imagination reveals that the range of possible 'What ...' sentences is almost endless. Chomsky (1965) proposed that speakers can produce and understand an indefinite number of sentences because they have mastered a set of grammatical rules for combining words and morphemes in their language. He also suggested that these rules cannot be extracted from the speaker's linguistic environment because there are simply too many possibilities to choose between. Therefore, he argued, the language learner must have some innate knowledge of the rules of language. This knowledge cannot be specific to a particular language, so this is why he called it Universal Grammar (see Section 2). Language learning therefore consists of finding evidence in the linguistic environment that will enable the learner to select from the range of potential grammatical rules that are made available by Universal Grammar.

5.2 A grammatical conundrum and a nativist solution

Consider the implicit knowledge that a speaker of English possesses in relation to a sentence like (15):

(15)   The girl gave the present to the boy.

In particular note that (16) is an entirely legitimate paraphrase of (15).

(16)   The girl gave the boy the present.

In fact, the verb 'give' seems to allow this kind of paraphrase (the technical term is *dative alternation*). Likewise, the verb 'tell' permits dative alternations:

(17)   The man told the story to the boy.

(18)   The man told the boy the story.

On the basis of exposure to these kinds of alternations, one might suppose that children infer a rule that would enable them to exploit this pattern creatively. However, care is required to avoid *over-generalizing* the rule. For example, although (19) is perfectly legitimate, (20) is not:

(19)   The man reported the accident to the police.

(20)   The man reported the police the accident.

Despite the fact that the verbs 'tell' and 'report' have similar meanings, one allows dative alternation and the other does not. Children need to be able to tune their grammar to these exceptions, rather like they must notice that 'went' is the past tense of 'go'. In fact, children make over-generalizations of dative alternations (Pinker, 1989) just like they over-regularize word endings. The problem facing children in this case, however, is somewhat more serious. With word endings, children will almost certainly hear counter-evidence that might persuade them to give up their mistaken hypothesis – if they think that the past tense of 'go' is 'goed', they will eventually hear 'went'. However, in the case of a mistaken dative alternation, children will never hear a sentence that directly contradicts their hypothesis (unless their parents produce negative evidence – see Box 4). They will only hear correct renditions of the unalternated form.

BOX 4

Negative evidence

Brown and Hanlon (1970) argued that parents do not seem to correct the grammatical errors of their children in a systematic fashion. They are more likely to correct the factual errors or meaning of their children's language. Explicit attempts to tell the young language user that they have made a mistake – 'No you said that wrongly' – are very rare indeed. Language researchers therefore assumed that any theory of language acquisition needs to be able to deal with an environment that does not provide the learner with *negative evidence*. This assumption has not gone unquestioned. For example, Demetras et al. (1986) suggested that indirect or implicit feedback to the child may occur when a grammatical mistake is made. Indirect feedback might take the form of clarification questions or repetitions. However, Marcus (1993) argued that indirect evidence of this kind is unlikely to be of much use to the child since it is unsystematic. It does not happen all the time. It does not only occur after grammatically incorrect utterances and it does not tell the child what he or she did that was ungrammatical. The issue as to whether negative evidence is available for natural language learning remains unresolved.

How then are children to correct their grammar? Two solutions seem possible here. First, the language learner 'knows' that certain types of verbs allow dative alternations and others do not. Second, the language learner only uses dative alternations on verbs for which there is evidence that they occur and refrains from using them elsewhere. However, both of these solutions beg the question of why children make the over-generalization in the first place and how are they able to correct themselves.

Pinker's solution is that language learners 'know' what verbs allow dative alternations, by virtue of their knowledge of a set of rules linking the *meaning* of the verb to the grammar associated with it. Subscribing to Chomsky's view that Universal Grammar is innate, Pinker (1989) proposes that dative over-generalizations are a consequence of imprecise knowledge about word *meanings*. For example, a child may think of 'report' as meaning the same as 'tell'. As a consequence, the same 'rules' of grammar might also apply to it. As the child's understanding of word meanings develops and the differences between the two verbs are refined, the meaning structures associated with 'report' will trigger a different set of rules in Universal Grammar which will prevent the inappropriate dative alternations.

The important feature of this solution to the problem of correcting over-generalization errors in syntax is that it assumes that the grammar is correct all along. It is just the semantics (word meaning) that the child has mistaken. This approach is entirely compatible with the view that Universal Grammar is innate.

5.3 Empiricist approaches to acquiring syntax

Other approaches to grammatical development do not assume that the child has innate knowledge of Universal Grammar. Tomasello (2000) presents such an argument, suggesting that children build up a knowledge of the structure of grammar in a piecemeal fashion based on regularities in the way words are used in the language. This is referred to as the *distributional* approach to syntax development. Tomasello suggests that verbs play a prominent role in structuring the child's developing syntactic knowledge because they place important constraints on utterances. For example, as discussed in Research summary 1, transitive verbs demand an object ('I am meeting ... X.') whereas intransitive verbs do not ('I am reading.'). Moreover, the meaning of verbs provide important clues as to the kind of sentence structures that are permitted. Early grammatical knowledge is piecemeal in the sense that the child does not possess knowledge of categories like 'noun' and 'verb', which are fundamental to the nativist, Universal Grammar account. If these categories exist at all in the mind of the child, they are *emergent* properties of the learning process, rather than prerequisites for it.

So, according to this approach, how do children extend their knowledge to new situations and new sets of words? It is not possible for children to memorize all the utterances they hear for later reproduction. However, a possible explanation for their creativity with language is analogy; children may initially memorize some of the utterances they hear and then adapt them as prototypes for the construction of new utterances. In fact, one of the earliest accounts of children's grammatical development (Braine, 1963, 1976) comes very close to adopting this position (see Box 5 for a discussion of early 'diary' methods of studying language development).

Braine (1963) examined his son Martin's early word combinations and found that they exhibited clear ordering patterns. Some words only ever occurred in one position in the utterance (initial or final). He called these words *Pivot* words. Other words were free ranging. He called these *Open* words. Of course, most words can occur in a wide range of positions in a sentence. However, Martin may have noticed that some words vary more in their distribution than others. For example, nouns move around a lot in the sentence (subject versus object position) whilst verbs tend to stay put. Did Martin observe his parents and other adults producing speech where the position of the Open words in sentences varied more than Pivot words and imitate these patterns to structure his own sentences?

BOX 5

Diary studies of grammatical development

The earliest attempts to study grammatical development in young children relied on the diary method. Investigators took notes of children's verbalizations and used this material to construct a profile of linguistic development. Clearly, investigators could not write down everything that their young participants uttered, which limited the sampling rate, but given the high level of repetition in the early stages of acquisition, this may not have been overly disadvantageous. Moreover, the object of the investigator's interest was typically their own child, so they were in a unique position to summarize the essential characteristics of the child's verbal repertoire. Up until the 1960s, when audio-recording methods became generally available, diary data constituted the primary source for studies of language acquisition.

Disadvantages of this approach stemmed directly from the time-consuming nature of the enterprise: investigators could only record a small amount of the child's verbalizations, making it difficult to judge whether the recorded material was representative of the child's overall level of performance. They tended to notice special events that perhaps were given undue weight in their interpretations, resulting in an anecdotal flavour to the investigation. It was also impossible to check on the accuracy of the information; for example, investigators might mishear the child's verbalization. Since there was no independent record of the utterance, corroboration of the event could not be achieved, even by the investigators themselves. Given the spontaneous nature of the material collected, it was also impossible to replicate a study.

According to distributional accounts of learning syntax (e.g. Tomasello, 2000) children should not systematically generalize word order from one learned word combination to all similar utterances. In early development, at least, creativity will derive from small 'pockets of knowledge' such that regularities that have been discovered for some combinations of words will not automatically be applied to other words. As these pockets of knowledge broaden, they can influence each other and lead to a systematic expression of grammatical regularities.

Since distributional approaches to grammatical development do not assume the existence of Universal Grammar, they have to offer different solutions to the problem of how children retreat from over-generalization errors such as those observed in dative alternations or question formation. Why should a child give up a generalization once discovered, particularly if there is no reliable evidence to contradict it? A possible solution to this problem is that as the child's isolated pockets of knowledge about word order become more integrated, a reduction in errors occurs. These errors could have been due to the *inappropriate extension* of a pocket of grammatical knowledge or an attempt to resolve conflicts *between* pockets of grammatical knowledge. In contrast to Universal Grammar based approaches, grammatical errors may be just inappropriate hypotheses about how words might be combined.

Elman (1990, 1993) has shown that a neural network trained simply to predict the next word in a sentence is able to use the information inherent in sentence structure to identify the grammatical categories of words (for example, whether it is a verb or a noun) and work out the correct sequence of those categories in a sentence. Such models do have apparent limitations as they are only able to work out regularities based on the sentences to which they are exposed. Interestingly, Elman (1993) found that the order in which the computer model was exposed to different sentence types had important consequences for its ability to learn the overall grammar. In particular, if the computer was exposed initially to simple grammatical sequences it was more successful in later training at learning complicated grammatical sequences, than if it had been exposed to complex grammar from the start of training. Some researchers have suggested that parents use a special style of speaking, variously known as *motherese,* or *child directed speech* (Snow, 1972) that constitutes a set of language lessons facilitating grammatical development (Furrow *et al.*, 1979). Although the 'motherese hypothesis' is speculative, it sits well with Elman's modelling experiments (as child-directed speech is characterized by simple grammatical sequences) and with the idea that grammatical development proceeds in a piecemeal fashion.

Summary of Section 5

- Chomsky's theory of Universal Grammar suggests that children must have some innate knowledge of syntax rules, because the linguistic environment is too complex and ambiguous to enable a child to extract these rules for themselves. Pinker further suggests that apparent grammatical 'errors' may derive from incorrect representations of word meaning, rather than being genuine mistakes of syntax.
- Distributional explanations of children's understanding of syntax suggest that it is possible to construct a knowledge of the structure of language in a piecemeal fashion based on regularities in the way words are used, and on the constraints associated with particular types of words. Neural networks can be trained to acquire grammar in this way.
- Diary studies were an early technique used primarily before the advent of appropriate recording equipment to collect data on children's language development. Typically this took the form of a study of the researcher's own child, as in the case of Braine's work.
- The motherese hypothesis, the idea that the way parents talk to their young children can facilitate grammatical development, is consistent with the results of distributional models of syntax development.

6 **Conclusion**

This chapter has introduced you to the complex nature of learning grammar as an infant, and to various theoretical explanations of how acquisition of grammar might be achieved. These explanations can be aligned to broadly nativist and empiricist accounts of development. Chomsky's Universal Grammar and Pinker's dual route explanation of inflection use suggest that children are born with innate cognitive mechanisms that enable them to acquire grammatical competence on exposure to the linguistic environment. In contrast, single route theories of inflection use and distributional accounts of syntax development suggest that children can acquire representations of grammatical forms and how to use them simply from exposure to the linguistic environment.

The balance of evidence presented in this chapter favours the more empiricist accounts. Single route theories appear to offer a more credible account of development across languages, and distributional accounts of syntax have the support of evidence from modelling studies. This theory is also consistent with observations of children's language production and the nature of parental speech to children. However, that is not to say that the idea of there being some form of innate predisposition to acquire language has been rejected. Theoreticians are in broad agreement that the *homo sapien* comes equipped with specialized machinery that permits the acquisition of language. The days of *tabula rasa* empiricism are long gone. Discussions are concerned with identifying the nature of the skills that the child brings to language learning, and whether those skills are specifically related to language, or part of a more general cognitive ability. The idea of a Universal Grammar, a detailed, innate knowledge of all types of grammatical rules, is still being considered and assessed, as is the idea of children having the ability to extract grammar from their environment as a result of the nature of their neural systems.

Throughout this chapter you should also have gained a sense of how methods of studying children's grammatical development have developed over time. Early diary studies were superseded by the use of recording equipment and commonly agreed methods of systematic transcription. However, as these methods only have the potential to inform discussions of expressive language use, experimental techniques have been used to assess the nature of children's expressive *and* receptive language abilities (for example, see Research summary 2 and Research summary 1 respectively). Finally, advances in cognitive science have led to the development of connectionist models that enable theorists to test the viability of their theories regarding the cognitive architecture needed to realize acquisition of grammar. As methods continue to develop in response to the theories, psychologists will move closer to a resolution to debates regarding the nature and extent of innate knowledge in children's grammatical development.

Further reading

Aitchison, J. (1998, 4th edn) *The Articulate Mammal: an introduction to psycholinguistics*, London, Routledge.

References

Bellugi, U., Bihrle, A., Jernigan, D., Trauner, D. and Dougherty, S. (1990) 'Neuropsychological, neurological and neuroanatomical profile of Williams Syndrome', *American Journal of Medical Genetics*, vol. 6, pp. 115–25.

Bishop, D. V. M. (1997) 'Cognitive neurospsychology and developmental disorders: uncomfortable bedfellows', *The Quarterly Journal of Experimental Psychology*, vol. 50, pp. 899–923.

Braine, M. (1963) 'On learning the grammatical order of words', *Psychological Review,* vol. 70, pp. 323–48.

Braine, M. D. S. (1976) 'Children's first word combinations', *Monographs of the Society for Research in Child Development, vol. 41*, Chicago, IL, University of Chicago Press.

Brown, R. (1973) *A First Language: the early stages,* Cambridge, MA, Harvard University Press.

Brown, R. and Hanlon, C. (1970) 'Derivational complexity and order of acquisition in child speech', in Hayes, J. R. (ed.) *Cognition and the Development of Language*, New York, Wiley.

Chomsky, N. (1965) *Aspects of the Theory of Syntax*, Cambridge, MA, MIT Press.

Demetras, M. J., Post, K. N. and Snow, C. E. (1986) 'Feedback to first language learners: the role of repetitions and clarification questions', *Journal of Child Language*, vol. 13, pp. 275–92.

Elman, J. (1990) 'Finding structure in time', *Cognitive Science*, vol. 14, pp. 179–212.

Elman, J. (1993) 'Learning and development in neural networks: the importance of starting small', *Cognition*, vol. 48, pp. 71–99.

Furrow, D., Nelson, K. and Benedict, H. (1979) 'Mothers' speech to children and syntactic development: some simple relationships', *Journal of Child Language*, vol. 6, pp. 423–42.

Gopnik, M. and Crago, M. (1991) 'Familial aggregation of a developmental language disorder', *Cognition*, vol. 39, pp. 1–50.

Hirsh-Pasek, K. and Golinkoff, R. M. (1996) *The Origins of Grammar: evidence from early language comprehension*, Cambridge, MA, MIT Press.

Joanisse, M. E. and Seidenberg, M. S. (1999) 'Impairments in verb morphology after brain injury: a connectionist model', *Proceedings of the National Academy of Sciences of the United States of America*, vol. 96, pp. 7592–7.

Juola, R. and Plunkett, K. (2000) 'Why double dissociations don't mean much', in Cohen, G., Johnston, R. A. and Plunkett, K. (eds) *Exploring Cognition: damaged brains and neural networks: readings in cognitive neuropsychology and connectionist modelling*, pp. 319–27, Hove, Psychology Press.

Marchman, V. A. (1997) 'Children's productivity in the English past tense: the role of frequency, phonology and neighborhood structure', *Cognitive Science*, vol. 21, pp. 283–304.

Marcus, G., Pinker, S., Ullman, M. *et al.* (1992) 'Overregularization in language acquisition', *Monographs of the Society for Research in Child Development*, *vol. 57*, Chicago, IL, University of Chicago Press.

Marcus, G. (1993) 'First contact in verb acquisition: defining a role for syntax', *Child Development*, vol. 64, pp. 1665–87.

Marcus, G., Brinkmann, U., Clahsen, H., Wiese, R. and Pinker, S. (1995) 'German inflection: the exception that proves the rule', *Cognitive Psychology*, vol. 29, pp. 189–256.

Naigles, L. (1990) 'Children use syntax to learn verb meanings', *Journal of Child Language*, vol. 17, pp. 357–74.

Naigles, L. and Kako, E. T. (1993) 'First contact in verb acquisition: defining a role for syntax', *Child Development*, vol. 64, pp. 1665–87.

Pinker, S. (1989) *Learnability and Cognition: the acquisition of argument structure*, Cambridge, MA, MIT Press.

Pinker, S. (1991) 'Rules of language', *Science*, vol. 253, pp. 530–5.

Pinker, S. (1994) *The Language Instinct*, New York, Morrow.

Pinker, S. (1995, 2nd edn) 'Why the child holded the baby rabbits: a case study in language acquisition', in Gleitman, L. R. and Liberman, M. (eds) *An Invitation to Cognitive Science, vol. 1: Language*, pp. 107–34 Cambridge, MA, MIT Press.

Pinker, S. and Prince, A. (1988) 'On language and connectionism: analysis of a parallel distributed processing model of language acquisition', *Cognition*, vol. 29, pp. 73–193.

Plunkett, K. and Juola, P. (1999) 'A connectionist model of English past tense and plural morphology', *Cognitive Science*, vol. 23, pp. 463–90.

Rumelhart, D. and McClelland, J. (1987) 'learning the past tenses of English verbs: implicit rules or parallel distributed processing?', in MacWhinney, B. (ed.) *Mechanisms of Language Acquisition*, pp. 195–248, Hillsdale, NJ, Lawrence Erlbaum Associates.

Shallice, T. (1988) *From Neuropsychology to Mental Structure,* Cambridge, Cambridge University Press.

Snow, C. E. (1972) 'Mothers' speech to children learning language', *Child Development*, vol. 43, pp. 549–65.

Spelke, E. (1979) 'Principles of object perception', *Cognitive Science*, vol. 14, pp. 29–56.

Szagun, G. (2001) 'Learning different regularities: the acquisition of noun plurals by German-speaking children', *First Language*, vol. 21, pp. 109–41.

Thomas, M. S. C., Grant, L., Barham, Z. *et al.* (2001) 'Past tense formation in Williams Syndrome', *Language and Cognitive Processes*, vol. 16, pp. 143–76.

Tomasello, M. (2000) 'The item-based nature of children's early syntactic development', *Trends in Cognitive Sciences*, vol. 4, pp. 156–63.

Reading

Reading A: An extract from *The Articulate Mammal*

Jean Aitchison

Chomsky's later views: setting switches

Suppose children knew in advance that the world contained two hemispheres, a northern and a southern. In order to decide which they were in, they simply needed to watch water swirling down the plug-hole of a bath, since they were pre-wired with the information that it swirled one way in the north, and another way in the south. Once they had observed a bath plug-hole, then they would automatically know a whole lot of further information: an English child who discovered bath-water swirling clockwise would know that it had been placed in the northern hemisphere. It could then predict that the sun would be in the south at the hottest part of the day, and that it would get hotter as one travelled southwards. An Australian child who noticed water rotating anticlockwise would immediately realize the opposite.

This scenario is clearly science fiction. But it is the sort of situation Chomsky now envisages for children acquiring language. They are pre-wired with a number of possible options which language might choose. They need to be exposed to relatively little language, merely some crucial trigger, in order to find out which route their own language has chosen. Once they have discovered this, they automatically know, through pre-programming, a considerable amount about how languages of this type work.

Let us consider how Chomsky hit on such an apparently bizarre idea.

Learnability remained Chomsky's major concern. How is language learnable, when the crumbs and snippets of speech heard by children could not possibly (in Chomsky's view) provide sufficient clues to the final system which is acquired? ... The learnability problem has also been called the 'logical problem of language acquisition': how, logically, do children acquire language when they do not have enough information at their disposal to do so?

The logical answer is that they have an enormous amount of information pre-wired into them: the innate component must be considerably more extensive than was previously envisaged. Children, therefore, are born equipped with *Universal Grammar*, or UG for short: 'UG is a characterization of these innate, biologically determined principles, which constitute one component of the human mind – the language faculty' (Chomsky 1986: 24). This is 'a distinct system of the mind/brain' (1986: 25), separate from the general intelligence...

In 1986, then, Chomsky viewed UG and language as something like an orchestra playing a symphony. It consisted of a number of separate components or *modules*, a term borrowed from computers. Chomsky noted: 'UG ... has the modular structure that we regularly discover in investigation of cognitive systems' (1986: 146). Within each module, there were sets of principles. Each principle was fairly straightforward when considered in isolation. The principles became complex when they interacted with those from other modules...

How many modules were involved, and what they all did, was never fully specified. But the general idea behind the grammar was reasonably clear. For example, one module might specify which items could be moved, and how far, as with the word WHO, which can be moved to the front of the sentence:

WHO DID SEBASTIAN SAY OSBERT BIT?

Another [module] might contain information as to how to interpret a sentence such as:

SEBASTIAN SAID OSBERT BIT HIM INSTEAD OF HIMSELF.

This would contain principles showing why SEBASTIAN had to be linked to the word HIM, and OSBERT attached to the word HIMSELF. These two types or principles would interact in a sentence such as:

WHO DID SEBASTIAN SAY OSBERT BIT INSTEAD OF HIMSELF?

Most of the principles, and the way they interleaved, were innately specified and fairly rigid.

However, a narrowly constrained rigid UG presented another dilemma. Why are not all languages far more similar? Chomsky argued that UG was only partially 'wired-up'. There are option points within the modules, with switches that can be set to a fixed number of positions, most probably two. Children would know in advance what the available options are. This would be pre-programmed and part of a human's genetic endowment. A child would therefore scan the data available to him or her, and on the basis of a limited amount of evidence would know which way to throw the switch. In Chomsky's words: 'We may think of UG as an intricately structured system, but one that is only partially "wired-up". The system is associated with a finite set of switches, each of which has a finite number of positions (perhaps two). Experience is required to set the switches. When they are set the system functions' (Chomsky 1986: 146).

Chomsky supposed that the switches must be set on the basis of quite simple evidence, and that a switch, once set in a particular direction, would have quite complex consequences throughout the language. These consequences would automatically be known by the child ...

UG, then, was envisaged as a two-tier system: a hard-wired basic layer of universal *principles*, applicable to all languages, and a second layer which was only partially wired in. This contained a finite set of options which had to be decided between on the basis of observation. These option possibilities are known as *parameters*, and Chomsky talks of the need 'to fix the parameters of UG' (Chomsky 1981: 4). The term *parameter* is a fairly old mathematical one, which is also used in the natural sciences. In general, it refers to a fixed property which can vary in certain ways. For example, one might talk of 'temperature' and 'air pressure' as being 'parameters' of the atmosphere. So in language, a parameter is a property of language (such as [word] ... position, discussed above) whose values could vary from language to language.

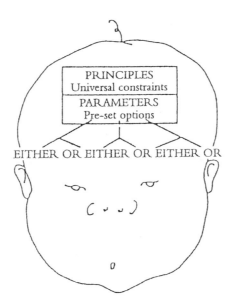

We are therefore dealing with 'a system of unifying principles that is fairly rich in deductive structure but with parameters to be fixed by experience' (Chomsky 1980: 66). The interlocking nature of the system will ensure that minor alterations will have multiple consequences: 'In a tightly integrated theory with a fairly rich internal structure, change in a single parameter may have complex effects, with proliferating consequences in various parts of the grammar' (Chomsky 1981: 6). In particular, 'a few changes in parameters yield typologically different languages' (Chomsky 1986: 152). This whole idea has become known as the 'principles and parameters' or 'P and P' approach ...

Children have relatively little to do in this new system: 'We view the problem of language acquisition as ... one of fixing parameters in a largely determined system' (Chomsky 1986: 151). Indeed, many of the old rules which children had to learn just appear automatically, because the principles underlying them are there already. ... If this minimal effort by the child is correct, then it makes sense to think of the language system as a 'mental organ', which grows mainly by itself, in the same way that the heart grows in the body. Chomsky is increasingly concerned to understand the principles which underlie this growth.

References for Reading A

Chomsky, N. (1980) *Rules and Representations*, Oxford: Blackwell.

Chomsky, N. (1981) *Lectures on Government and Binding*, Dordrecht: Foris.

Chomsky, N. (1982) *Some Concepts and Consequences of the Theory of Government and Binding*, Cambridge, MA: MIT Press.

Chomsky, N. (1986) *Knowledge of Language: Its Nature, Origin and Use*, New York: Praeger.

Chomsky, N. (1995a) 'Bare phrase structure', in G. Webelhuth (ed.) *Government and Binding Theory and the Minimalist Program*, Oxford: Blackwell.

Source: J. Aitchinson (1998, 4th edn) 'A blueprint in the brain?', in *The Articulate Mammal: an introduction to psycholinguistics*, pp. 109–29, London and New York, Routledge.

Chapter 5
Executive functions in childhood: development and disorder

Claire Hughes, Andrew Graham and Andrew Grayson

Contents

Learning outcomes

After you have studied this chapter you should be able to:
1 provide a working definition of executive function;
2 evaluate the developmental significance of executive function;
3 describe the development of one aspect of executive function in children;
4 identify some key implications of executive dysfunction.

1 Introduction

Behaviour
The public side of human life: anything that a person does that is observable by a third party.

Experience
The private side of human life: internal cognitive and emotional processes that cannot be observed from the outside.

One way of thinking about the developmental story that we have told so far in this book is in terms of the progressive organization of children's behaviour and experience.

Chapter 1 discusses ways in which infants organize their understandings of the world in terms of categories. Chapter 2 shows how this organizational framework underpins, and is developed by, language. Chapter 3 examines ways in which brain development can be seen in terms of increasing levels of organization in both structure and function. The theme is extended further in Chapter 4 by looking at how language itself develops into an organized system of linguistic structures. Why is this developmental trajectory towards organization in the growing child of such interest to psychologists?

One answer to this question is that organization of behaviour and experience is a necessary pre-condition for intelligent, aware, planned action. It is a pre-condition for children having control of their own actions. If a child (or indeed a person of any age) has no way of organizing their understanding of the world around them, then they will be unable to behave appropriately or effectively. Imagine, for a moment, being unable to comprehend that the next person you meet is a person, that they have things in common with other people, and that they differ in significant ways from things that are not people. Alternatively imagine knowing that people differ in significant ways from each other, and from things that are not people, but not being able to control your actions in a way that acknowledges these differences. In both cases there would simply be no basis for anything other than chaotic behaviour.

The term 'executive function' (EF) is used to refer to the set of high-level cognitive functions that enable people to plan, initiate and carry through goal-directed behaviour in an organized and 'thought out' way. This definition reflects the contrast between high-level cognitive functions such as integration, synthesis, planning, organizing and so forth with more basic, 'low-level' cognitive functions such as processing auditory, visual and tactile sensations. This distinction maps onto the model proposed by Fodor in Chapter 3, Section 3, which sees the lower-level cognitive functions as being organized in a modular fashion in such a way as to feed the higher-level, and more global 'executive' functions.

Executive function is an important topic in child development for a number of reasons. First, the executive control of action is something that a child *develops*. A newborn baby has very little control of his or her behaviour, whereas a 10-year-old child has a great deal of control (although not always as much as parents and teachers would like!). Developmental psychologists ask the same questions about how this control of behaviour develops as they ask, for example, about how language develops. What course does this development take? Are there important milestones along the way? What are the consequences for children whose development is atypical in this respect? And how can all this be studied empirically?

Second, impairments in the control of action, or failure to develop sufficient levels of executive control, are generally thought to contribute to behavioural problems that adversely affect social relationships, cognitive development and learning. Knowledge of age-related improvements in executive function in typically developing children will therefore help to identify children with poor regulatory control who might benefit from intervention programmes, or from more structured environments that place fewer demands on executive function.

Third, understanding the capacities of children of different ages to learn and remember information is vital for developing effective methods of teaching that maximize the potential of typically developing children. Similarly, deficits in strategic processes and organizational capacities may underpin many different profiles of learning disability. Thus, understanding the exact nature of these deficits helps psychologists to target children in need of remedial support and to develop new techniques that open up their learning opportunities.

Summary of Section 1

- One crucial aspect of development is the way in which children are progressively able to organize their experiences and behaviour.
- 'Executive function' is an umbrella term that is used to refer to the high-level processes that govern flexible, goal-directed behaviour.
- Impairments of executive control can contribute to difficulties in social relationships, in cognitive development and in learning.

2   History and definition

It is Debbie's fifth birthday party. A group of children stand facing her mother at the front of the room. She is leading them in a game of 'Simon says'. In this game she models simple actions, like putting her hands on her head, or jumping up and down. The children must either copy these actions, or ignore them. Each action is accompanied by a verbal instruction. If Debbie's mother says 'Simon says, do this' then the children must copy the action that follows. If she says only 'do this' then the children must stay still and not copy her.

Debbie's mother says 'Simon says, do this' and sits on the floor. All the children sit down as quickly as they can. She then says 'Simon says, do this', and jumps up again. All the children follow. Immediately she says 'do this' and sits down again. Half the children sit down. The other half put their hands over their mouths and giggle. The children who have sat down quickly realize their mistake and jump to their feet again.

The behaviour of the children who mistakenly sat down may be attributed to a number of factors. They may not have listened to or understood the instructions of the game, for example. But first and foremost their behaviour can be attributed to a failure of executive function. Their behaviour was automatic and momentarily beyond their conscious control. They acted first, and thought later. Note that within seconds of sitting down (perhaps even in the same moment as they sat down) the children probably realized their mistake. Conversely, the children who ignored the adult model were able to resist what was most likely a strong urge to sit down. Their behaviour was guided by a greater level of 'executive' control.

There are several things to note about this example that will help you to relate the abstract concepts that will be covered in this section of the chapter to everyday experiences (see Box 1).

BOX 1

A guide to causing breakdowns in executive function in 'Simon says' games

1   Play the game with young children. The older children get, the easier they find it.
2   Use simple actions, for example sit down, jump up, touch your nose.
3   Maintain a quick pace, so that the actions come thick and fast.
4   Lull the children into a false sense of security. Perform many repeated 'Simon says do this' actions before a 'do this' action.
5   Repeat the same action several times before performing it as a 'do this' action.

2.1 Executive function in cognitive psychology

In cognitive psychology there is a classic distinction between two types of human action. The first type includes habitual actions (for example, driving along a well-known route) that involve automatic responses and require very little or no effortful (conscious) processing. The second type includes flexible adaptive responses to novel or difficult situations (for example, driving while struggling to navigate in an unknown city) requiring effortful control. Executive function is an umbrella term used to refer to the processes underlying this second type of action. More specifically, executive function is thought to be necessary in situations that involve:

- the learning of new skills;
- planning and decision making;
- error correction or troubleshooting;
- initiating novel sequences of actions;
- danger or technical difficulty;
- conscious moment-to-moment control of behaviour;
- the need to overcome a strong habitual response.

The 'Simon says' example is most relevant to the last two situations listed above, where conscious control of behaviour is necessary, and where there is a need to overcome a strong, habitual response. The adult leads the children into a sequence of behaviour in which they are behaving automatically. The actions are simple so the children do not need to engage in 'effortful processing' in order to copy them. They may start to watch others, become distracted by other thoughts and experiences, and forget to monitor what the adult is saying. Suddenly, and with minimal warning (by means of a minor alteration to the verbal cue), the automatic response is no longer the correct one. In order to succeed the children have to *inhibit* the habitual response of copying.

An early example of the distinction between automatic and controlled actions in the psychological literature was given by one of the founding fathers of psychology in the USA, William James. He described how he went upstairs to change his clothes and then found that he had got into bed instead. This kind of automated, unmonitored action can be contrasted with actions that are 'preceded by an additional conscious element' (James, 1890, p. 522). Note how the children who succeed at 'Simon says' need to attend to the precise wording of the instructions, and have to monitor their behaviour consciously in order to avoid slipping into thoughtless imitation.

Activity 1   Slips of action

Allow about 10 minutes

This activity illustrates the distinction between automatic, habitual behaviour on the one hand, and consciously planned behaviour, on the other. It will enable you to use this distinction to analyse familiar everyday mistakes.

Identify examples from your own experience of 'slips of action', when something that you meant to do was overridden by automatic, habitual behaviour. One example might be dialling a familiar telephone number, only to realize when the person answers that you had meant to telephone someone else.

Comment

Here are some examples that we came up with:

- finding yourself taking the turning that you usually take every day on your way to work, when you were meant to be driving somewhere else;

- writing last year's date on a cheque on 2nd January;

- going upstairs to fetch something, getting distracted by something else, and going back downstairs without the thing that you went to get in the first place;

- clicking the 'OK' button on the computer to ignore, as usual, a warning when *this time* you should have pressed 'Cancel'. You realize this as your finger clicks the mouse button. Your whole assignment has been deleted!;

- making coffee for four people. One of them does not take milk. You intend to leave one cup black, but you end up putting milk in all of them.

Everyday mistakes such as these appear to result from strongly automated behaviours taking over from a conscious plan to do something else. They are examples of momentary failures of executive function. The mistakes children make in the 'Simon says' game also result from a strongly automated set of behaviours (copying the adult again and again) overriding conscious planning.

It is important to note that for an act to be automatic it does not necessarily need to be simple, such as copying an adult putting one hand in the air. Driving a car is a complex skill but it is one which can become almost automatic if it is sufficiently well learned. So, what does distinguish controlled actions from automatic actions? Controlled actions involve three important features:

1   The execution of *novel* as distinct from familiar action sequences.
2   Making a choice between *alternative* responses in opposition to the execution of a single action sequence.
3   The execution of acts that are accessible to *consciousness*, as opposed to those that are not.

Again you will see that the 'Simon says' example fits with at least two of these three features. We have already noted how the actions of the successful children are at least momentarily accessible to consciousness (they are aware of what they are doing), when the decision as to whether to copy or not is made. In addition, these children have to make a choice between alternative responses (to copy or not to copy) each time the adult performs an action. Children who mistakenly imitate a 'do this' action probably intend to make a choice when they start the game, but quickly forget and end up simply executing a single action sequence (copying every move).

2.2 Executive function in clinical psychology

The examples of executive function in the previous section are drawn from familiar, day-to-day experiences. However, the concept is also of particular interest to clinical psychologists who study the effects on behaviour of injuries and insults to the brain. In this respect damage to the prefrontal cortex (see Figure 1) appears to be associated with impairments in the ability to plan and to think in an abstract fashion, in addition to changes in personality.

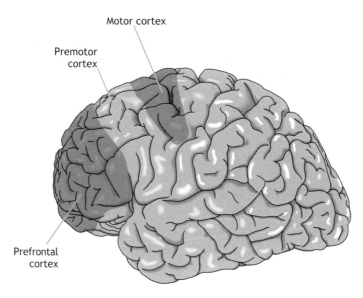

Figure 1   The prefrontal cortex.

A particularly dramatic example of damage to the prefrontal lobes is provided by the case of Phineas Gage (see Box 2). This and other nineteenth-century studies of people who had suffered similar injuries documented changes in mood and attention, and apathy and impulsivity, rather than specific consequences for cognition. However, this picture changed in the light of medical evidence from large numbers of soldiers in the First World War (1914–18) who sustained bullet wounds where the location and extent of the damage to the brain could be analysed with greater precision. Where damage was restricted to the frontal lobes it was noted that the soldiers were unimpaired in familiar, routine matters but had difficulty in grasping the whole of a complicated task or mastering new tasks. One investigator (Goldstein, 1944) put forward the concept of 'abstract attitude' – similar in many respects to the contemporary notion of general intelligence – which he saw as being deficient in some aspect or other in all of his patients with frontal lesions.

BOX 2

Phineas Gage

In 1848 Phineas Gage, a railway worker in the USA, was using an iron rod to tamp down gunpowder for blasting when a spark caused an explosion and the rod was propelled straight up through one eye socket and both left and right frontal lobes (see Figure 2). Initial interest was focused on the remarkable fact that he had survived this injury at all, and the wider implications of the case were not appreciated until a follow-up report 20 years later. In this report, Harlow drew attention to the fact that whilst Gage had indeed recovered from the accident with his speech, learning and memory intact, he was left with such a profound impairment of social behaviour and personality that according to friends and co-workers 'he was no longer Gage'. Changeux quotes from Harlow's account of Gage:

> He is fitful, irreverent, indulging at times in the grossest profanity ... impatient of restraint or advice when it conflicts with his desires ... capricious and vacillating, devising many plans of future operations, which are no sooner arranged than they are abandoned in favor of others.

(Harlow, quoted in Changeux, 1985, pp. 158–9)

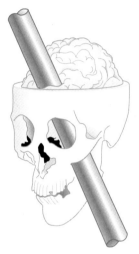

Figure 2   The skull of Phineas Gage.

2.3 Components of executive function

As you may have already begun to appreciate, 'executive function' is not a single, easily identifiable cognitive function. The term actually describes a set of related cognitive functions. For this reason executive function is referred to as *fractionated* (Shallice and Burgess, 1991); that is, it subdivides into different component processes. There are many competing models of executive function, which describe these component processes in different ways, but commonly distinctions are made between *cognitive flexibility, planning and working memory* and *inhibitory control*. Each of these subcomponents can be further divided, but extensive coverage of all aspects of executive function is beyond the scope of this chapter. We will briefly outline the characteristics of *cognitive flexibility* and *planning and working memory* here, before moving onto a more detailed analysis of the development of *inhibitory control* in Section 3.

Cognitive flexibility

Cognitive flexibility refers to the aspect of executive function that enables people to think and behave appropriately according to the changing needs of a complex environment, and in line with their plans and goals. One of the hallmarks of mature human behaviour is its flexibility and responsiveness to the constantly changing features and demands of the environment, particularly of the social environment. Executive function is concerned with how people organize their thinking and behaviour in order to act intelligently and flexibly in the face of complexity. Researchers sometimes conceptualize this in terms of the 'orchestration' of different elements of cognition and behaviour (Cavanagh and Perlmutter, 1982).

The ability to switch flexibly between planned actions and different approaches to a task, without losing sight of the goals that are being aimed for, is a high-level cognitive function that is critically important in everyday life. Take reading, for example. The goal of reading is to extract meaning from a text. This is a highly complex process. Sometimes a skilled reader can read text relatively automatically, accessing the meaning without conscious effort. On the other hand, sometimes even skilled readers have to work at decoding the words, perhaps when they are unfamiliar or unusually complex. At other times, even though the words might be familiar, the meaning of the text has to be consciously worked at. If readers are unable to switch from automated reading of simple passages to effortful control of reading for more complex passages they are likely to find themselves just decoding the words, and not attending to their meaning. How often have you got to the end of a page in a book and realized that you have not taken anything in, even though you have 'read' all the words?

For young readers the executive control demands of reading are high. Cognitive resources have to be allocated to the business of decoding the text (identifying the sounds associated with the letters and then reading the words), at the expense of extracting meaning. Indeed, the basic demands of decoding the words are such that young readers often do not even realize that they are meant to be trying to understand what the words mean (Baker and Brown, 1984). Furthermore, an experienced reader may be able to switch flexibly between reading and other tasks (getting a drink, taking notes, answering the door) whilst still being able to achieve the goal of understanding the text that they are tackling. An inexperienced reader may find such orchestration of resources highly problematic.

Planning and working memory

'Planning', in this context, is about intending to do something that will achieve a goal. Much human behaviour is goal-directed. People are able to organize their cognitive and behavioural resources in ways that enable them to achieve goals that are not the immediate consequence of one simple action. Take, for example, the case of communicating with someone. Effective communication requires that there is an intention to say something. A lot of the time people are not aware of these intentions because the interactions are so over learned, as in the case of rather automated exchanges such as greetings and farewells. Sometimes, however, communicative intentions are more explicit, as in the case of planning to say something emotionally difficult or complex to someone. But in both cases there is some sort of goal in mind, and the communicative behaviour has to be organized in such a way as to achieve that goal (words have to be selected and ordered in well-formed sentences; see Chapter 4). Note how cognitive flexibility operates in tandem with planning to facilitate the achievement of the goal. Imagine needing to say something awkward to someone close to you. Bear in mind that communication is a fast-moving, on-going, two-way process. As soon as you start communicating, the other person will respond to you in a way that requires you, in real time, to adjust your plan flexibly in order to take account of what they are saying, and of their perspective. If you are unable to show sufficient cognitive flexibility – for example, if you continue remorselessly with your plan to say something in a certain way irrespective of the contributions of the other person – the communication is likely to be ineffective. Hughes and colleagues (2000) undertook a study which sought to investigate links between the planning component of executive function and social and communication skills (see Research summary 1).

RESEARCH SUMMARY 1

Antisocial behaviour, communication skills and executive function

In this study Hughes and colleagues (2000) compared a group of 40 'hard-to-manage' pre-school children with a group of 40 control children. The hard-to-manage children were identified with a screening questionnaire that had been completed by parents. All children were between the ages of 3 years and 6 months and 4 years and 6 months.

The researchers filmed each child playing with a friend in a room at school and then transcribed the video tapes in order to code various aspects of social and communicative behaviour. They also gave the children tests of verbal ability, executive function and theory of mind (see Chapter 6). One of the executive function measures was the Tower of London task (Shallice, 1982). This task uses three differently coloured balls, and a set of three pegs that vary in length, allowing each peg to take one, two or three balls. The tester, who has their own set of these materials, shows the child a particular pattern of balls on pegs. Working from a specific starting position, and moving one ball at a time from one peg to another, the child has to copy the demonstrated pattern in as few moves as possible. There is an ideal solution for each pattern, in terms of the minimum number of moves that are needed to copy it. The key performance measure on each trial is the number of extra moves, above the minimum, that the child needs to complete the task. The better the child's planning skills, the fewer extra moves they will take.

The researchers found that in the hard-to-manage group, there was significantly more antisocial behaviour (e.g. hurting, bullying, snatching) than in the control group and also more violent pretend play (Dunn and Hughes, 2001). Those children who engaged in antisocial acts showed the poorest communication skills when playing with their friend. Furthermore, both violent pretend play and antisocial behaviour showed a significant correlation with performance on the Tower of London task (poorer performance on the Tower of London task was associated with higher levels of antisocial behaviour). These findings suggest the existence of a set of inter-relationships among play, communication skills and planning skills that are worthy of further investigation.

Activity 2

Allow about
5 minutes

The Tower of London task

This activity gives you practical experience of doing the Tower of London task and illustrates how it measures planning.

Look at Figure 3. Moving one ball at a time, what is the minimum number of moves that is needed to change the pattern of balls in the 'initial position' into the pattern shown as 'goal position no. 1'? Starting from the initial position in each case, work out the minimum number of moves needed for goal positions no. 2 and no. 3.

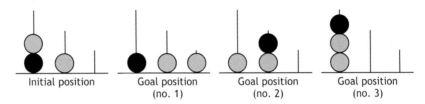

| Initial position | Goal position (no. 1) | Goal position (no. 2) | Goal position (no. 3) |

Figure 3   Tower of London task (Shallice, 1982).

Comment

Turn to the end of the chapter to find out the answers. The real task is somewhat easier to do because it involves real pegs and balls that can be moved around (or ones that can be moved around on a computer screen). Using static pictures, as you have been, places an additional load on 'working memory', because for every move that you make you must actively hold in your memory the position to which each ball has been moved.

As you can see from Activity 2, working memory is related to planning in this view of executive function. Working memory refers to that aspect of remembering that involves holding things actively in mind in support of ongoing plans of action. For example, in the previous example of conversing with someone, working memory would be used to maintain a representation of what the other person is saying, or has just said, while planning a response to them. Working memory is in itself a huge area of psychological research, which is beyond the scope of this chapter. It is important to recognize, however, that it can be regarded as a component of executive function.

Summary of Section 2

- Executive function refers to the processes that underlie flexible, planned, conscious actions that require effortful control.
- Executive function has been studied in both cognitive and clinical psychology.
- The prefrontal cortex is the area of the brain most closely associated with executive function.
- *Cognitive flexibility, planning and working memory* and *inhibitory control* are three major subcomponents of executive function.

- Executive functions are a set of high-level cognitive functions that play a crucial role in the organization of everyday behaviour and experience, and as such they underpin intelligent human action in a complex world.

3 The development of executive function in children

For much of the twentieth century, research on executive function centred almost exclusively on adults. This was mainly because the prefrontal cortex was thought to become functionally mature only late in development, around adolescence (Luria, 1973). However, it has become increasingly clear that the onset of the development of executive function occurs much earlier than was previously thought. This has become apparent following the appearance of more appropriate tools for studying it at earlier ages. In this section we will look at the course of one aspect of early executive function development; inhibitory control.

3.1 Inhibitory control

We have seen in other chapters in this book that one aspect of child development concerns the progressive organization of children's behaviour and experience. One factor that underpins this is a developing ability to *inhibit* responses to stimuli. Why is this so important?

Activity 3

Allow about 5 minutes

The richness of the sensory world

This activity encourages you to reflect on the complexity of your everyday environment.

Consider your sensory world. Look around the environment you are in. Try to observe *everything* you can see. Then sit back, shut your eyes and listen to *everything* that you can hear. After that, focus on what is touching you. Attend to each part of your body in turn. What can you feel? It takes a few minutes to get the most out of this activity, so do not hurry it.

Comment

The richness and complexity of the assaults on your senses are considerable. However, it is hard to experience this complexity to its full extent because the mature human mind is so expert at filtering out irrelevance, and building stimuli into simpler, more meaningful (and organized) patterns. If this 'filtering' did not take place, and you gave equal weight to all incoming sensory information, it would be impossible to behave in anything but a chaotic manner.

Your current plan of action probably revolves around reading this section of the chapter. In order to do this successfully you have to be able to ignore most of the sensory world around you. You have to be able to prioritize the meaningful stimuli – the print that makes up words on the page – and inhibit responses to irrelevant stimuli, in order to enact your plan of reading the current paragraph, and to achieve the goal of finishing it. What if you were unable to do this? What if you could not give the words on the page any greater priority in cognition than the grain of the wood on the table on which your book is resting? What if you were unable to inhibit responses to the sound of the computer fan as it whirrs in the background, or the feel of your feet on the carpet?

If you were unable to inhibit responses to stimuli that do not relate to the task that you have planned to do, then it would probably be impossible to complete it and achieve your goal. You would be drawn from one stimulus to another, in a haphazard fashion, and it would be impossible to undertake any coherently organized action. This is a rather extreme way of conveying the point, but young children and people with executive function related disorders of inhibitory control do have difficulty in prioritizing their response to task-related stimuli, and do have difficulty in inhibiting responses to what are referred to as 'prepotent' stimuli.

A prepotent stimulus is a stimulus that draws a person's attention towards it, and which seems to cause the person to behave in a particular way (the prepotent response). Prepotency is a very important feature of effective everyday functioning. It is to be hoped, for example, that a red traffic light would draw a driver's attention towards it, and cause the driver to behave in a certain way. The sight, smell and feel of the mother's breast are the most likely prepotent stimuli for the young breast-feeding infant.

In the course of typical development it is possible to observe infants and young children being distracted by inappropriate prepotent stimuli. By 'inappropriate' we mean stimuli that are nothing to do with the child's current plan of action. For example, one might observe an 8-month-old infant catch sight of a toy on the other side of the room and begin crawling towards it. It is clear to an observer that they are enacting a plan to get the toy, but halfway across the room the infant notices a scrap of paper on the floor. This seems to 'capture' their behaviour and their attention. They pick it up, sit down and inspect it. The original plan is now lost and they have been catapulted onto another stream of behaviour, which might involve another plan, which might itself get interrupted by another prepotent stimulus, and so on and so forth. This executive function analysis of a familiar scene offers one explanation of why infant behaviour sometimes appears somewhat haphazard and disorganized to an adult onlooker – according to this view it is because executive functions are as yet undeveloped.

One aspect of child development that psychologists have become interested in, then, is the way in which children develop an ability to inhibit responses to stimuli that are nothing to do with their current plan of action. Put another way, this amounts to an ability to prioritize responses to task-relevant (as opposed to task-irrelevant) stimuli. When children begin to be able to do this, their behaviour becomes less haphazard, and progressively more strategic and *organized*.

3.2 Measuring the development of inhibitory control

Psychologists use a number of methods to measure the development of inhibitory control. One widely used technique is known as the Stroop task.

Activity 4

Allow about
15 minutes

The Stroop task

This activity allows you to do the Stroop task and gives you a way of experiencing prepotency directly.

Get three coloured pens – perhaps a blue one, a red one and a black one. Write down a list of fifteen words as follows (using the names of the colours that you have chosen). Note that each word is written in the *wrong* colour.

BLUE	(write in red ink)
RED	(write in black ink)
BLACK	(write in blue ink)
RED	(write in blue ink)
RED	(continue writing each word in the 'wrong' colour, sometimes writing 'RED' in blue, sometimes in black)

BLUE

BLACK

BLUE

RED

BLACK

BLACK

BLUE

RED

BLUE

BLACK

Now, out loud, and working as accurately and as a quickly as you can, call out the colour of the *ink* in which each word is written. What happens?

Comment

You should find that after a few words you start to get confused, wanting to call out the word that you are reading, rather than the colour of the ink in which it is written. The meaning associated with the word is acting as a powerful prepotent stimulus. You have to inhibit everything you have learned about words and their meaning in order to call out the colour of the ink. You could take two measures of performance from this, each of which would give some information about inhibitory control: speed of completion, and number of errors made. Why do you think that this task is not suitable for children of, say, 3 years of age?

The Stroop task tends to be used with older children and adults because of the demands it makes on literacy skills, which in themselves are not a component of executive function. Indeed young children's limitations with respect to language processing pose a problem in finding age-appropriate executive function tasks. Children's levels of verbal comprehension may influence their overall performance on tasks that have complex instructions or written stimuli, and this decreases the validity of such tasks as measures of executive function. Consequently, tests for young children need to be kept as simple as possible. The Handgame and the Knock/Tap game (see Box 3) are good examples of some tasks that have been designed to minimize the importance of written language skills.

SG

BOX 3

The Handgame

The Handgame is a task that has the same basic structure as the Stroop task from Activity 4. The child must inhibit a prepotent response in order to execute a rule-guided action. Specifically, the child is first asked to imitate two hand actions (making a fist and pointing a finger). Then, in the conflict condition, children must make the opposite responses (making a fist when the experimenter points their finger and vice versa). This involves:

* inhibiting the prepotent response to imitate; and
* performing an action guided by the rule 'do the opposite of what the experimenter is doing'.

The measure of executive function that this task provides is the number of errors in the conflict condition. The task is based on work by Luria and has been used with preschool children. Other variants of this task include Luria's Knock/Tap game (in which the child must knock when the experimenter taps the table and vice versa), the Opposite Worlds task (in which school-aged children are asked to say 'one' when they see a '2' and to say 'two' when they see a '1'), and the Day/Night Stroop task (Gerstadt *et al.*, 1994; see Figure 4) in which children are instructed to say the word 'day' when shown a line drawing of the moon and stars, and 'night' when shown a line drawing of the sun. You should be able to see how these tasks relate conceptually to the Stroop task, and how they are better suited to minds that are not yet at the stage of having overlearned (automated) the ability to read words.

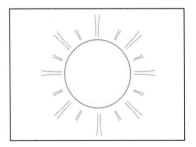

Figure 4   Images from the Day/Night Stroop task.

Measuring the development of inhibitory control in infancy is particularly challenging. One method that is used is the structured observation of infant performance on certain tasks. Inferences are then made from these observations about inhibitory control. An example of this is the work of Diamond (2002). They observed infants of 8–11 months performing problem-solving tasks such as retrieving an object from an open box. They concluded that 9–10-month-old infants show evidence of inhibitory control, and that even in this narrow age band there was already evidence of older infants maintaining their attention on-task longer than the younger infants.

Another indicator of inhibitory control in infancy is provided by the A-not-B task (Piaget, 1954) which is described in Chapter 3, Section 5. It is unclear whether the 8-month-old infant who makes the classic A-not-B error, by persistently looking for the object under cloth A, when they have seen it move to under cloth B, is being drawn back to the prepotent stimulus of the place they previously found the object (a lack of *inhibitory control*), or is unable to switch strategy from searching under cloth A to searching under cloth B (displaying a lack of *cognitive flexibility*). It is likely that both of these aspects of executive function are involved in this task. What is clear is that by 12 months of age infants are able to succeed on the task, so if cloth A does act as a prepotent stimulus, by 12 months of age infants are able to inhibit any response to it.

Commission errors
Giving a response when no response is required (on the Go/NoGo task this is when the child 'Goes' on the NoGo stimulus). Commission errors can be interpreted as a failure to inhibit.

Most work on inhibitory control in childhood has focused on children who are 3 years of age and over. A range of tasks has been developed that is suitable for use with children of different ages. One of these is the Go/NoGo task (Drewe, 1975). In one version of the task different letters are displayed, one after the other, on a computer screen. The child is instructed to press the space bar as quickly as they can whenever a letter is flashed onto the screen (Go), *except* when that letter is an 'X' (NoGo). Errors of commission, when a child presses the space bar mistakenly in response to the letter 'X', indicate a failure to inhibit. A variant of this task uses pictures of planes with a cartoon bomb as the 'NoGo' stimulus (Rubia *et al.*, 2001). Note that in the 'Simon says' game, 'do this' (without the preceding 'Simon says') is equivalent to a NoGo stimulus.

Using tests such as these researchers have found that there are significant improvements in task performance between the ages of 3 and 6 years. In a study by Mahone *et al.* (2001) 87 typically developing children completed a computerized Go/NoGo task. Even though the 3-year-old children managed the task with few omission or commission errors, the researchers noted a developmental trend across their sample: increasing age was associated with steady and significant improvements in performance.

Omission errors
Missing a response when one is required (on the Go/NoGo task this is when the child does not 'Go' on the Go stimulus). Omission errors can be interpreted as a failure to attend to the task.

More complex inhibitory control functions are tapped by non-verbal Stroop tasks (for example, Luria's Day/Night, Handgame, Knock/Tap; see Box 3). These require children not only to inhibit a response (as in the Go/NoGo task), but also to execute a rule-guided action. The majority of 3 year olds fail the Day/Night task (Gerstadt *et al.*, 1994), the Handgame (Hughes, 1996; Hughes, 1998a and b) and the Knock/Tap game (Perner and Lang, 2002). However, the majority of 4 year olds pass these tasks. Thus significant improvements in both simple and complex inhibitory control are evident in the pre-school years.

Developmental improvements in inhibitory control also continue throughout childhood, as demonstrated by findings from studies with school-aged children using the Go/NoGo tasks (for example, Manly *et al.*, 2001). Interestingly, findings from a brain imaging study by Casey *et al.* (1997) that used functional magnetic resonance imaging (fMRI; see Chapter 3, Box 1) suggest that children and adults show similar patterns of brain activation during the Go/NoGo task, and that this activation is in the prefrontal cortex (see Research summary 2).

RESEARCH SUMMARY 2

Inhibitory control and brain activation

Casey *et al.* (1997) used an fMRI scanner to examine patterns of brain activation during a Go/NoGo task. Nine children and nine adults took part. The children were between the ages of 7 and 12 years, and the adults were between the ages of 21 and 24 years.

The participants undertook a Go/NoGo task that involved responding to any letter that was presented to them on a screen inside the scanner, except for the letter X. Functional MRI scanners are like a large, narrow tube into which the participant is slid on their back, so a hand-held device was specially constructed to record the participants' responses.

The researchers found that during the task adults and children showed the same location of brain activation within the prefrontal cortex. However, they also observed that the *amount* of activation was significantly greater for the children. The interpretation of this finding is complex, but it is likely to relate to the fact that the task places more demands on executive functions for children than for adults. For adults the executive demands of the task are probably lower. This interpretation is supported by the fact that the adults performed better than the children on the task. So as suggested in earlier sections of this chapter, and in Chapter 3, Section 5, *increasing* skill in a task is associated with *decreasing* involvement of the prefrontal cortex and executive function. The association between the prefrontal cortex and executive function is shown in the correlation reported by the researchers between levels of prefrontal activity and success on the task. Specifically it was found that *increasing* levels of prefrontal activity were associated with greater accuracy of performance (fewer errors of commission).

3.3 Inhibitory control in child development

The picture of development that has been built up in this section is one that shows the child gradually mastering the inhibitory control component of executive function. Development in this respect is already detectable in infancy (for example, on the A-not-B task), and continues well into the school years. Although it is not sensible to ask at what age this development is 'complete' (development does not just stop when a child becomes an adult), we can ask at what age it becomes impossible to distinguish between child and adult performance on standardized measures. In this respect Chelune and Baer (1986) have reported a steady improvement in performance on the Wisconsin Card Sorting Test (WCST; see Box 4) from 6 years of age, with participants achieving adult levels of performance by around 10 years of age. This finding has been replicated in subsequent studies (for example, Levin *et al.*, 1991; Welsh *et al.*, 1991).

Executive function plays a crucial role in the early stages of mastering new skills. When a child is learning to read, the executive demands of the activity are high. A great deal of conscious effort is required on the part of the novice reader simply to decode the written symbols into words. So much conscious effort is required that, as was noted earlier, there may be insufficient cognitive resources to interpret the meaning of the text that is being read. Gradually, as reading skill increases, the executive demands of decoding diminish. The child becomes able to read the words 'automatically' and can allocate more resources to the business of constructing meanings. If you consider the development of any skill you will see that the involvement of executive function is greatest when the actions involved are still novel (see Chapter 3, Section 5). As mastery of the skill develops, so the role of executive function diminishes, and automated action takes over. There is something of a paradox here: executive function is least well developed in the very people who need it most in order to develop new skills – young children.

BOX 4

The Wisconsin Card Sorting Test

The most widely used measure of executive function is Grant and Berg's (1948) Wisconsin Card Sorting Test (WCST). The WCST involves a set of four target cards, and a deck of stimulus cards, each with a picture that varies in colour, shape, and number (for example, two blue stars, or three black squares; see Figure 5). The child is asked to sort each card onto one of the target cards, and is told whether or not they have placed the card correctly. Feedback is given after each card is sorted. By a process of trial and error the child should be able to work out the rule according to which they should sort the stimulus cards (for example, by colour or by shape). After six consecutively correct responses the sorting rule is changed and the child must discover the new rule. The two key measures from the WCST are (i) the number of 'rules' for which a child achieves a run of six correct trials; and (ii) the number of post-rule-change trials for which the child makes a perseverative error (that is, continuing to sort according to the previously correct, but now incorrect rule). Like other traditional executive function tasks, the WCST actually taps into several different aspects of executive function and so provides an index of overall executive function development. For example, because the same set of cards is used for each sorting 'rule' (and the child is not told that the rule has changed), it is unclear whether perseverative errors reflect a failure to shift to the newly relevant rule (thus demonstrating cognitive inflexibility) or a failure to inhibit a previously reinforced response to a specific card type (thus demonstrating a failure of inhibitory control).

Perseveration
The continuous, insistent performance (repetition) of a behaviour.

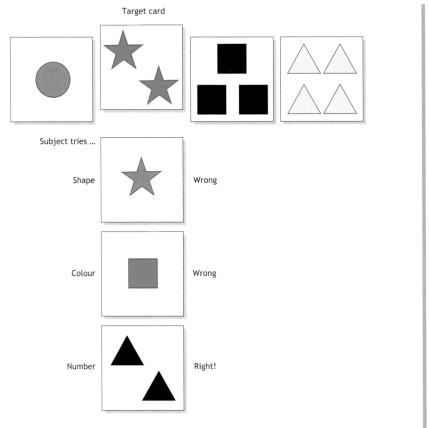

Figure 5   The Wisconsin Card Sorting Test.

As executive function develops, so children's abilities to learn new skills improve, and they are increasingly able to behave in a planned, strategic and organized manner. They are able to stay 'on-task' longer. They are able, when necessary, to override habitual responses to prepotent stimuli. They become more skilled and flexible in 'orchestrating' elements of their thinking and behaviour, and they are able to engage in increasingly sophisticated planning and decision making. Inhibitory control is only one component of this developmental trajectory, but it is of fundamental importance. One way to assess this importance is to look at the implications for child development of a failure to develop typical levels of inhibitory control. This is the topic of Section 4.

Summary of Section 3

- The ability to inhibit responses to prepotent stimuli is a prerequisite for planned, intelligent action.
- Some components of executive function are already developing in pre-school children, and play a much greater role in early child development than previously thought.
- Adult levels of performance on a standard measure of executive function (for example, the Wisconsin Card Sorting Test) are achieved by around 10 years of age.
- Executive function plays a crucial role in the initial mastery of new skills, before the skills become automated.

4 Executive dysfunction

This section looks at executive function from a different perspective. What might the consequences be if the development of executive function were impaired? This is an important question to ask for two reasons. The first of these is to understand the experiences and needs of those children and adults who are directly affected. The second reason is that investigating the dysfunction of cognitive processes is one way of increasing psychological knowledge about how the processes work, and of finding out about what contribution they make in typical development. We will focus on problems in the development of inhibitory control, but you should bear in mind that executive dysfunction can also take the form of cognitive *in*flexibility, planning difficulties, and problems associated with working memory.

Activity 5

Allow about 10 minutes

Implications of under-developed inhibitory control

This activity encourages you to consider the developmental consequences of poor inhibitory control.

What would you predict to be the implications for a child of a failure to develop typical levels of inhibitory control? Note down possible consequences of under-developed inhibitory control with respect to cognitive, social and emotional development.

Comment

If you were to compare a group of children with poor inhibitory control with a group of typically developing children of the same ages, you might expect the former group to be, on average:

- more distractible;
- less able to undertake tasks and learn skills that require sustained levels of concentration;
- more socially awkward (perhaps saying things at inappropriate moments; 'blurting' out);

- more impulsive (socially and emotionally);
- less able to regulate emotions (more prone to mood swings and fits of anger);
- more prone to obsessions and the later development of addictions;
- more susceptible to peer pressure (less able to inhibit, or say 'no').

This is by no means an exhaustive list. You may have come up with more ideas than this. The activity should give you some indication of the importance of inhibitory control in child development.

Difficulties with inhibitory control may have a pervasive impact on the developing child. The difficulties experienced by the child are likely to become more pronounced as development progresses; this is because in early childhood a relative lack of inhibitory control is characteristic of *typical* development.

One group of children who have particular difficulties with inhibitory control are children with attention deficit hyperactivity disorder (ADHD) (Barkley, 1997). ADHD is a syndrome with three subtypes reflecting the relative severity of its main symptoms: distractibility, hyperactivity and impulsivity. It is difficult to diagnose before age 6 (perhaps because its three main symptoms are features of very typical behaviour in young children!). Distractability and impulsivity may be very strongly related to poor inhibitory control. Children who do not inhibit responses to inappropriate prepotent stimuli will find it very hard to stay on-task, and will get distracted by things around them. They would also present as impulsive because of the way in which poor inhibitory control would lead to a shifting of attention, apparently haphazardly, from one thing to another.

Note that inhibitory control is not all-or-nothing. There is a continuum from typical development to the symptoms of a 'condition' (such as ADHD). You will doubtless find that there are times when you find it difficult to stay on-task with your studies, and fail to inhibit a response to the prepotent stimulus of the washing-up, or some other task that for some reason simply has to be done now. Whether or not a failure to inhibit should be regarded as part of a 'condition' or not really depends on the extent to which it interferes with the business of getting on with one's life, and on the socio-cultural context of diagnosis.

There is good evidence for executive dysfunction involvement in ADHD. At the level of brain structure and function there is evidence of delayed myelination in the prefrontal cortex, and depletion of the neurotransmitter dopamine (Levy and Swanson, 2001). Delayed myelination and dopamine depletion affect the speed and efficiency with which nerve impulses are transmitted within the brain, so findings such as these suggest some kind of dysfunction in the prefrontal cortex, which is known to play a crucial role in executive function and in inhibitory control. Increasingly, children with ADHD are medicated with amphetamine-based stimulants (most commonly methylphenidate) which affect the levels of dopamine in the brain and which reportedly lead to some improvements in both behaviour and cognitive performance (Kempton *et al.*, 1999).

Rubia *et al.* (2001) observed significantly poorer performance of children with ADHD (aged 7 to 15 years) than the typically developing control children on a set of computerized tests which included the Go/NoGo task. Furthermore, fMRI of a subset of participants during the response inhibition tasks revealed reduced prefrontal activation for the ADHD group. So, not only does this study demonstrate poorer performance on a test of inhibitory control among the ADHD children, but it also shows that this poorer performance is associated with less activation in a brain region that is known to be involved in executive function.

In terms of cognitive function and inhibitory control Manly *et al.* (2001) reported findings from 24 boys with ADHD (not yet receiving medication) tested on an age-normed battery of tests of attention and executive function. Compared with several comparison groups, the ADHD boys showed global deficits, but group differences were especially marked on the tests of sustained attention and suppression of prepotent responses. In contrast, a study using a computerized set of executive function tasks with the same group of 'hard-to-manage' children described earlier (see Research summary 1) but now aged 7 showed no deficits on any of the formal task measures (Brophy *et al.*, 2002). However, during the tasks elevated rates of rule-violations and perseverative errors (that were not recorded by the software) were noted by observers.

Although diagnosis of ADHD itself before age 6 is difficult, it is possible to look at inhibitory control in the behaviour of pre-school children who have been assessed as being disruptive. Hughes *et al.* (2000) did this in their study of 'hard-to-manage' children that you read about in Research summary 1. They point out that the poor peer relationships experienced by disruptive children have been linked to serious long-term consequences, including academic failure, criminality, drug abuse and psychiatric illness (Parker and Asher, 1987).

It is unclear whether inhibitory control problems cause ADHD, or are simply one feature of the condition. Indeed there is considerable debate about this in the literature (Barkley, 1997; Brown, 1999). But we do not need to be side-tracked by that debate here. In this context it is enough to note that the difficulties experienced by children with ADHD, which can be profound in terms of their impact on social, emotional and cognitive development, are strongly associated with poor inhibitory control.

Summary of Section 4

- Attention deficit hyperactivity disorder (ADHD) is associated with executive dysfunction.
- Poor inhibitory control is a feature of ADHD.
- Impulsivity and distractibility are strongly related to poor inhibitory control.
- Difficulties with inhibitory control may have a pervasive influence on the social, emotional and cognitive development of children.

5 Conclusion

The development of executive function is a process by which children come to be able to act effectively in a complex, and not entirely predictable world. It is about how children learn to organize – or 'orchestrate' – the cognitive and behavioural skills that they are developing, in order to be able to respond flexibly to the demands of the world around them, in line with their own plans and goals. As you have seen, executive function is particularly strongly associated with the early stages of learning new skills, and is involved in the effortful production of controlled (as opposed to automatic, or over learned) actions. As such, executive function depends on high-level cognitive processes. You will read about another aspect of high-level cognition in Chapter 6, which is about 'theory of mind'.

Answers to Activity 2

Goal position 1: two moves.

You would move the grey ball from peg 2 to peg 3 and the pink ball from peg 1 to peg 2.

Goal position 2: four moves.

You would move the grey ball from peg 2 to peg 3; the pink ball from peg 1 to peg 2; the black ball from peg 1 to peg 2 and the grey ball from peg 3 to peg 1.

Goal position 3: five moves.

You would move the pink ball from peg 1 to peg 2; the black ball from peg 1 to peg 3; the pink ball from peg 2 to peg 1; the grey ball from peg 2 to peg 1 and the black ball from peg 3 to peg 1.

References

Baker, L. and Brown, A. L. (1984) 'Metacognitive skills and reading', in Pearson, P. D. (ed.) *Handbook of Reading Research*, pp. 353–94, White Plains, NY, Longman.

Barkley, R. A. (1997) 'Behavioral inhibition, sustained attention and executive functions: constructing a unified theory of ADHD', *Psychological Bulletin*, vol. 121, pp. 65–94.

Brophy, M., Taylor, E. and Hughes, C. (2002) 'To go or not to go: inhibitory control in 'hard-to-manage' children', *Infant and Child Development, Special Issue on Executive Functions and Development*, vol. 11, pp. 125–40.

Brown, T. E. (1999) 'Does ADHD diagnosis require impulsivity-hyperactivity?: a response to Gordon & Barkley', *ADHD Report*, vol. 7, pp. 1–7.

Casey, B. J., Trainor, R. J., Orendi, J. L. *et al.* (1997) 'A developmental functional MRI study of prefrontal activation during performance of a Go-No-Go task', *Journal of Cognitive Neuroscience*, vol. 9, pp. 835–47.

Cavanagh, J. C. and Perlmutter, M. (1982) 'Metamemory: a critical examination', *Child Development*, vol. 16, pp. 11–28.

Changeux, J.-P. (1985) *Neuronal Man: the biology of mind*, Oxford, Oxford University Press.

Chelune, G. J. and Baer, R. A. (1986) 'Developmental norms for the Wisconsin Card Sorting Test', *Journal of Clinical and Experimental Neuropsychology*, vol. 8, pp. 219–28.

Diamond, A. (2002, 2nd edn) 'A model system for studying the role of dopamine in the prefrontal cortex during early development in humans', in Johnson, M. H., Munkata, Y. and Gilmore, R. O. (eds) *Brain Development and Cognition: a reader*, pp. 441–93, Oxford, Blackwell.

Drewe, E. A. (1975) 'Go-no go learning after frontal lobe lesions in humans', *Cortex*, vol. 11, pp. 8–16.

Dunn, J. and Hughes, C. (2001) ' "I got some swords and you're dead!": violent fantasy, antisocial behavior, friendship, and moral sensibility in young children', *Child Development*, vol. 72, pp. 491–505.

Gerstadt, C. L., Hong, Y. and Diamond, A. (1994) 'The relationship between cognition and action: performance of 3 –7 year old children on a Stroop-like day-night test, *Cognition*, vol. 53, pp. 129–53.

Goldstein, K. (1944) 'The mental changes due to frontal lobe damage', *Journal of Psychology*, vol. 17, pp. 187–208.

Grant, D. A. and Berg, E. A. (1948) 'A behavioral analysis of degree of reinforcement and ease of shifting to new responses in a Weigl-type card sorting problem', *Journal of Experimental Psychology*, vol. 38, pp. 404–11.

Harlow, J. M. (1868) 'Recovery from the passage of an iron bar through the head', *Publications of the Massachusetts Medical Society*, vol. 2, pp. 327–46.

Hughes, C. (1996) 'Control of action and thought: normal development and dysfunction in autism', *Journal of Child Psychology and Psychiatry*, vol. 37, pp. 229–36.

Hughes, C. (1998a) 'Executive function in preschoolers: links with theory of mind and verbal ability', *British Journal of Developmental Psychology*, vol. 16, pp. 233–53.

Hughes, C. (1998b) 'Finding your marbles: does preschoolers' strategic behaviour predict later understanding of mind?', *Developmental Psychology*, vol. 34, pp. 1326–39.

Hughes, C., White, A., Sharpen, J. and Dunn, J. (2000) 'Antisocial, angry, and unsympathetic: "hard-to-manage" preschoolers' peer problems and possible cognitive influences', *Journal of Child Psychology and Psychiatry*, vol. 41, pp. 169–79.

James, W. (1890) *The Principles of Psychology*, New York, Holt.

Kempton, S., Vance, A., Maruff, P., Luk, E., Costin, J. and Pantelis, C. (1999) 'Executive function and attention deficit hyperactivity disorder: stimulant medication and better executive function performance in children', *Psychological Medicine*, vol. 29, pp. 527–38.

Levin, H., Culhane, K. A., Hartmann, J. *et al.* (1991) 'Developmental changes in performance on tests of purported frontal lobe functioning', *Developmental Neuropsychology*, vol. 7, pp. 377–95.

Levy, F. and Swanson, J. M. (2001) 'Timing, space and ADHD: the dopamine theory revisited', *Australian and New Zealand Journal of Psychiatry*, vol. 35, pp. 504–11.

Luria, A. R. (1973) *The Working Brain: an introduction to neuropsychology*, New York, Basic Books.

Mahone, E., Pillion, J. and Hiemenz, J. (2001) 'Initial development of an auditory continuous performance test for preschoolers', *Journal of Attention Disorders*, vol. 5, pp. 93–106.

Manly, T., Anderson, V., Nimmo-Smith, I., Turner, A., Watson, P., and Robertson, I. H. (2001) 'The differential assessment of children's attention: the Test of Everyday Attention for Children (TEA-Ch), normative sample and ADHD performance', *Journal of Child Psychology and Psychiatry*, vol. 42, pp. 1065–81.

Parker, J. G. and Asher, S. R. (1987) 'Peer relations and later personal adjustment: are low accepted children at risk?', *Psychological Bulletin*, vol. 102, pp. 357–89.

Perner, J. and Lang, B. (2002) 'What causes 3-year olds' difficulty on the dimensional change card sorting task?', *Infant and Child Development, Special Issue on Executive Functions and Development*, vol. 11, pp. 93–106.

Piaget, J. (1954) *The Construction of Reality in the Child*, New York, Basic Books.

Rubia, K., Taylor, E., Smith, A., Oksanen, H., Overmeyer, S. and Newman, S. (2001) 'Neuropsychological analyses of impulsiveness in childhood hyperactivity', *British Journal of Psychiatry*, vol. 179, pp. 138–43.

Shallice, T. (1982) 'Specific impairments of planning', *Philosophical Transactions of the Royal Society London*, B298, pp. 199–209.

Shallice, T. and Burgess, P. (1991) 'Higher cognitive impairments and frontal lobe lesions in man', in Levin, H. S., Eisenberg, H. M. and Benton, A. L. (eds) *Frontal Lobe Function and Dysfunction,* pp. 125–38, Oxford, Oxford University Press.

Welsh, M. C., Pennington, B. F. and Groisser, D. B. (1991) 'A normative-developmental study of executive function: a window on prefrontal function in children', *Developmental Neuropsychology*, vol. 7, pp. 131–49.

Chapter 6
Understanding minds

Emma Flynn

Contents

Learning outcomes

After you have studied this chapter you should be able to:

1 understand and define what is meant by the term 'theory of mind';
2 understand the rationale underlying the tests used to establish whether young children have developed the ability to reflect on another person's mind;
3 recognize what a 'false belief' is and why it is important;
4 understand the difference between first-order and second-order theory of mind;
5 appreciate that the development of a theory of mind allows other skills to develop;
6 identify the relationship between skills which develop early in infancy and a subsequent appreciation of minds;
7 understand the relationship between children's cognitive development and their social environment;
8 understand the relationship between children's communication and the development of their theory of mind.

1 Introduction

1.1 The importance of understanding minds

You are gazing out of the window and see ten people standing in a line on the pavement by the side of a road. Most of them are facing in the same direction, looking towards the oncoming traffic. Beside the first person in the line is a pole with a sign at the top. What are they doing there?

You probably recognize, instantly, that this is a queue at a bus stop. In doing so, you identify that the people standing in the queue *intend* to catch a bus, *believe* that a bus will arrive and *hope* that it will arrive on time. In making that assessment you are demonstrating your understanding that other people – here the ones in the queue – have 'minds', and that what goes on in their minds dictates their behaviour. Without such an assumption you would only see these people standing, pointlessly, in a line. There would be no apparent reason for their behaviour because you would not appreciate their knowledge, desires, hopes and intentions; this, and all other human behaviour, would appear similarly unsystematic and meaningless.

As adults we appreciate that other people have minds like our own and that these contain both information and desires, intentions, hopes and beliefs (sometimes referred to as 'mental states') which inform and determine how they behave. It also follows that we appreciate that other people have the same

Theory of mind
The under-
standing that
other people have
minds which
inform their
behaviour.

understanding of what it is that informs and drives our own behaviour. Psychologists call this understanding *theory of mind*.

A theory of mind is made up of a number of different skills, and an understanding of what these are, how they develop and how they relate to other aspects of human development is the focus of this chapter. These skills are believed to develop in the first 4 years of life, and so it is children within this age range who will come under particular scrutiny.

1.2 Understanding minds and egocentrism

SG

There are parallels between the development of theory of mind skills and Piaget's theory of egocentrism in young children (Piaget, 1932; Piaget and Inhelder, 1968). Piaget believed that young children up to the age of about 6 or 7 years are unable to detach themselves from their own perspective about the world, and this causes them to be unable to reflect on other people's perspectives (see the introduction to this book). Similarly, more recent research proposes that it is only once children have a theory of mind that they have the ability to appreciate that other people have minds and that these minds contain different information from their own. Subsequent research into egocentrism (e.g. Donaldson, 1978) has led to the conclusion that young children are not as totally egocentric as Piaget believed them to be, and also that the ability to appreciate the contents of other people's minds occurs earlier than he suggested.

In order to appreciate the development of theory of mind skills it is important to understand how these skills are measured in young children. So, before explaining the consequences and processes of theory of mind development, the next section will describe the rationale behind the different tests that psychologists use to measure theory of mind skills.

Summary of Section 1

- People often explain the actions of another person by reflecting on that person's mental state.
- Psychologists use the term 'theory of mind' to refer to an appreciation of the psychological level of information (i.e. unseen and contained in the mind) which drives our behaviour.
- Theory of mind skills are believed to develop in the first 4 years of life.

2   What is a theory of mind?

> An individual has a theory of mind if he imputes mental states to himself
> and others. A system of inferences of this kind is properly viewed as a
> theory because such states are not directly observable, and the system can
> be used to make predictions about the behavior of others.

(Premack and Woodruff, 1978, p. 515)

Psychologists' interest in the development of theory of mind skills began, not with
human beings, but with research on chimpanzees. In a study which has since
become a classic (Premack and Woodruff, 1978), an adult chimpanzee called
Sarah was shown a series of videotaped scenes in which a human actor struggled
with problems of different kinds. Some of the problems appeared simple, such as
trying to get hold of bananas that were out of reach. Others were more complex,
such as trying to escape from a locked cage. For each scene Sarah was presented
with two photographs that showed different actions, only one of which was an
effective solution to the problem. So, for the scene in which the actor was locked
in a cage, Sarah was presented with a photograph of a key and a photograph of a
solution to a different problem, for example, a stick to get the out-of-reach
bananas. On the overwhelming majority of occasions (21 out of the 24) Sarah
selected the 'correct' solution. Premack and Woodruff concluded that the
chimpanzee 'understood' the actor's purpose and therefore 'understood' the
contents of the actor's mind.

Activity I   Understanding Sarah's mind

Allow about
10 minutes

This activity will help you identify possible explanations for Sarah's behaviour.

From what you have just read of the experiment involving Sarah, do you think the results
indicated that the chimpanzee understood the actor's purpose and the contents of the
actor's mind? What other interpretation might there be?

Comment

The philosopher Daniel Dennett (1978) has provided an important line of criticism of
Premack and Woodruff's conclusions. Dennett suggested that their evidence did not show
that chimpanzees have an understanding of other people's intentions, desires or knowledge.
Sarah could have shown that level of success on the task without reflecting on the actor's
mental states at all. Instead, she could have solved the problem by drawing on her knowledge
of the associations between objects in the real world, what is sometimes referred to as the
external contingencies of objects. So, for example, on seeing the actor in a cage, rather than
impute the actor's mental state, i.e. her desire and intention to escape from the cage, Sarah
could see the cage and match this to its common partner, a key, as shown in one of the
solution photographs.

2.1 Understanding other people's minds

How, then, can we distinguish between someone reflecting on another person's mind to explain that person's behaviour, as proposed by Premack and Woodruff, or relying on common connections in the world to predict behaviour, as Dennett proposes? Dennett himself suggested that one way of making that distinction would be by reference to situations where someone's knowledge about the world was different from the actual state of the world. In such situations, the prediction of behaviour would differ according to whether the observers were referring to what they knew about the contents of an individual's mind or relying on what they knew to be reality. One task that meets these requirements is variously known as the 'Sally/Anne task' or the 'Maxi task', after the characters involved in the scenario. More formally, it is known as the *unexpected transfer task* (see Box 1).

What happens when children are presented with the unexpected transfer task? Wimmer and Perner (1983) carried out the first study that examined theory of mind skills in children. Their unexpected transfer task was identical in its underlying structure to the Sally/Anne task described in Box 1, though its surface features were different. In their version a boy called Maxi puts his chocolate in the blue cupboard. Then, while he is playing outside, his mother moves the chocolate from the blue cupboard and places it in the green cupboard. Maxi comes inside and wants to get his chocolate. The children were asked where he would look for it.

Table 1 summarizes the data from this study. All the children in the youngest group said that Maxi would look for his chocolate in the green cupboard, where they knew it had been put. They were being informed by their perception of reality. Just over a half of the 4 and 5 year olds correctly identified that Maxi would look in the blue cupboard. Nearly all (22 out of 24) of the oldest group (6 to 9 year olds) were able to identify Maxi's false belief.

Table 1   Percentages of children aged 3 to 9 years correctly identifying where Maxi would look for the chocolate (i.e. in the blue cupboard)

3 year olds (n = 20)	4 and 5 year olds (n = 114)	6 to 9 year olds (n = 24)
0%	57%	92%

Source: Data from Wimmer and Perner (1983).

Extensive research on the development of theory of mind has been carried out since Wimmer and Perner's study. Improvements have been made to the tasks, such as reducing the linguistic demands (for example, using simpler test questions) which has resulted in enhanced performance particularly for younger children. However, regardless of these modifications, the age of 4 years still remains as the point at which the critical change in children's understanding of false beliefs appears to occur. Before 4 years, children rely on the current state of reality to answer questions in the unexpected transfer task. From about 4 years on, children begin to hold representations of people's mental states, reflecting on the belief of the story character and recognizing that that belief is false.

BOX I

The unexpected transfer task

The child is told a story concerning two characters, Sally and Anne (see Figure I, Frame I). Sally puts a ball in a basket (Frame 2) and then leaves the room (Frame 3). While Sally is out of the room, Anne removes the ball from the basket and puts it in a box (Frame 4). The child is then told that Sally has returned and wants to find her ball (Frame 5). At this point any child following the story knows that the ball is in the box. Sally, on the other hand, does not know the ball has been moved; she still thinks it is in the basket. Therefore Sally holds a *false belief*, i.e. a belief about the world that is incorrect.

In studies using this task, the child is first asked where the ball actually is; this shows whether they have been paying attention to the story. Then the child is asked where Sally will look for her ball. Children who rely on reality and are unable to hold a representation about people's mental states will say, incorrectly, that Sally will look for the ball in the box, i.e. where they know it to be. However, children who can hold and reflect on the representations that another person has about the world in order to predict that person's behaviour, will appreciate that Sally has a false belief about the location of the ball. They will say that Sally will search for the ball where she believes it to be, in the basket, and not where it really is, in the box.

This is Sally.      This is Anne.

Figure I
The unexpected transfer task (adapted from Frith, 1989, p. 160).

Much of the research on the development of theory of mind has been based on samples of children in Europe and North America. How do children in contrasting cultures fare on the unexpected transfer task? Avis and Harris (1991) investigated this with children of the Baka tribe, who live in the rainforests of south-east Cameroon. The Baka are non-literate pygmies who have a hunter-gatherer lifestyle with different values from those which predominate in Western societies. The researchers acted out a version of the unexpected transfer task, adapted to be more appropriate to the Baka children. In this version a member of the group cooks some mangoes and leaves them in a cooking pot. While the cook is absent the mangoes are transferred to a second, closed pot. The children were then asked where the cook would look for his mangoes when he returned. The 5 and 6 year olds judged that the cook would look for the mangoes in the cooking pot. Younger children made reality-based errors, saying that the cook would look for them in the closed pot. Avis and Harris's results are very similar to those found by Wimmer and Perner and other researchers, and they suggest that the development of an understanding of false beliefs is not specific to one culture and that important changes occur at a similar age for different children around the world.

2.2 Understanding our own minds

The evidence presented so far indicates that before the age of about 4 years children are unable to appreciate that other people can hold an incorrect representation of the world. Young children are realists and believe that everyone in the world behaves according to how the world truly is, rather than how each individual represents the world to be. At about 4 years, children appear to become able to hold a number of representations concerning a situation in their mind at the same time – that is they can *meta-represent*. For example, in the unexpected transfer task 4 year olds can hold a representation about the true state of reality (the ball is in the box) and also a different representation of a story character's beliefs about the state of reality (the ball is in the basket). They can compare and contrast these different representations and appreciate that someone can hold a representation about the world that is incorrect.

Meta-representation
The ability to hold a number of representations of a situation in mind at the same time.

False beliefs are a common feature of everyday life, for example searching for something in one location when it is actually in another. Before the age of 4 years, children observing such a scene would not appreciate why such mistakes occur. But if children do not understand other people's false beliefs, can they nevertheless understand their *own* inaccurate beliefs about the world? This question has been addressed using another ingenious procedure known as the 'Smarties task', for reasons that will become apparent from the description in Box 2. Less entertainingly, it is also referred to as the *deceptive box test*.

SG

BOX 2

The deceptive box test

A child is shown a tube of Smarties and asked what is inside. Nearly all children recognize the packaging and say that the tube contains sweets (see Figure 2, Frame 1). Then the experimenter opens the tube and shows the child that it actually contains pencils (Frame 2). Invariably, this comes as a surprise. The child is then shown the closed tube and asked, once again, what is inside (Frame 3). This is to check that they now know that there are pencils inside, even though they cannot see them. The child is then introduced to a Sooty puppet who has been asleep in the toy box. The child is asked, 'When Sooty wakes up and sees this tube all shut up like this, what will he think is inside?' (Frame 4). This has obvious similarities with the Sally/Anne task. Will the child answer 'pencils' (what he knows are in the tube) or 'sweets', (what Sooty might reasonably be expected to think are in the tube)?

Figure 2 The deceptive box test.

Gopnik and Astington (1988) found that children older than about 4 years were able to appreciate that Sooty would hold a false belief about the contents of the tube – that it contained sweets. However, younger children who are reality-biased, said that Sooty would say there were pencils in the tube. Ingeniously, the researchers then asked the children about their own, previous false belief, 'When you first saw this tube and it was all shut up like this, what did you think was inside?' (Frame 5). Again, children of 4 years or older were able to reflect on their own mental states, and even though they now knew the tube contained pencils, answered that they had previously believed that it contained sweets. By contrast, the younger children stated that originally, before the tube had been opened, they had believed that it contained pencils. These findings suggest that as well as being unable to reflect on other people's false beliefs, young children remain reality-biased and are unable to reflect on their own, previous false beliefs.

As is often the case with research of this sort, questions arise as to whether the results might be affected by the experimental procedures or other factors. So, further studies using the Smarties task have concluded that the young children's responses are not attributable to difficulties in understanding the specific moment of time to which the question refers. This was established by asking, 'What did you think was in the box before I took the top off?' (Lewis and Osborne, 1990). Nor were the results due to the children's embarrassment at admitting their original ignorance. Wimmer and Hartl (1991) introduced children to a silly puppet, who always made mistakes. Adding this element to the design of the experiment enabled the researchers to work out whether children's incorrect answers were caused by their embarrassment at admitting their previous ignorance, rather than lack of theory of mind skills. When the silly puppet was introduced, if children were simply embarrassed about getting the question wrong, they would fail questions about their own previous false belief by stating that they always knew the contents of the tube. However, they would be expected to pass questions regarding the false belief of the silly puppet, and to state that the puppet previously believed that the tube contained Smarties since they would not be expected to feel embarrassed about the silly puppet's false belief. However, young children without theory of mind skills were just as likely to get the false belief question wrong, irrespective of whether they were asked about their own previous false belief, or the false belief of the puppet.

The overall conclusion appears to confirm that before the age of about 4 years children rely on reality to predict their own and other people's behaviour. However, from about 4 years onwards, they begin to appreciate that a psychological level of information (the beliefs that people hold about the world) dictates people's behaviour and that sometimes these beliefs are wrong.

Summary of Section 2

- Theory of mind is measured using tests which involve false beliefs, for example the unexpected transfer task and the deceptive box test.
- Before about 4 years of age, children rely on reality to address questions of false belief. After 4 years, children are able to reflect on different people's representations of the world.
- Research suggests that the development of theory of mind occurs across cultures and at roughly the same age across the world.
- Research has shown that not only are young children unable to reflect on the mental states of other people, they are also unable to reflect on their own previous false beliefs.

3   Implications of developing a theory of mind

3.1   Understanding jokes, irony and sarcasm: second-order theory of mind

It is no coincidence that a number of other skills develop shortly after a child has acquired a theory of mind. Understanding the mental states of others opens up a new realm of information on which to draw. For example, jokes often contain a double meaning, one that is *explicit* and one that is only understood by reflecting on the teller's *intended* meaning. When the geography teacher asks a student, 'Where are the Andes?' and the student replies, 'At the end of my arm-es' the joke relies on the fact that we appreciate the answer that the teacher expects and that this is different from the answer given by the student who has interpreted the question differently.

A similar distinction occurs in sarcasm and irony. It is only by reflecting on an individual's mental states that we are able to identify the true meaning of a sarcastic or ironic statement. Consider a scenario in which a mother asks her son, Sam, to clean up his messy room. Sam forgets all about cleaning the room and reads his comic instead. After a while Sam decides he wants to play outside, and so asks his mother's permission. She sends his brother to check that Sam has cleaned his room. When he returns from the still messy room, Sam's brother tells his mother, 'Sam did a really great job of cleaning his room'. As adults we can appreciate that although the literal meaning of what he says suggests one thing, that the room is now clean, the brother's intended meaning is entirely different, that the room is still messy. We can even imagine the tone of voice in which the words would have been delivered. The understanding of jokes, sarcasm and irony requires a more complex level of theory of mind than that which has been discussed so far. This is known as *second-order theory of mind*.

Second-order theory of mind
The ability to attribute *beliefs about beliefs* or *beliefs about intentions.*

Thus far, this chapter has been about first-order theory of mind, that is the ability to appreciate and reflect on the contents of another person's mind. Second-order theory of mind is the ability to attribute *beliefs about beliefs*, or *beliefs about intentions*.

Figure 3 illustrates the difference between first-order and second-order theory of mind skills. The boy on the left is simply thinking about taking the girl's apple; he is not using theory of mind skills. The girl, by contrast, is using first-order theory of mind skills as she is thinking about the boy on the left's desire and intention (mental states) to steal her apple. Unfortunately for her, the boy on the right is using second-order theory of mind skills. He realizes that he can steal the girl's apple, for he believes (correctly, as it happens) that she is preoccupied with thinking about the other boy's intention to steal her apple.

Second-order theory of mind skills are believed to develop between the ages of 6 and 8 years.

Figure 3   First-order and second-order theory of mind (Whiten, 1991).

A lie or a joke?

Do children need to have attained second-order theory of mind skills in order to be able to distinguish lies from jokes? This question was answered by Sullivan *et al.* (1995) in a study in which 48 children, whose ages ranged from 5 to 9 years, were told four brief stories. Two of the stories assessed the children's second-order ignorance (for example, does John know that Mary knows X?) and second-order belief understanding (for example, what does John think Mary thinks?). The other two stories assessed the children's ability to discriminate between a lie and a joke. In one story a boy who did not clean his room lies to his mother by saying, 'I did a really good job cleaning my room'. In a second story a boy does not finish eating his dinner and jokingly says to his mother, while they both sit at the table, 'I did a really good job finishing my peas'. At the end of each story the participants were asked whether the story character was lying or joking. The results showed that children typically were able to distinguish a lie from a joke only after they could attribute second-order ignorance, but before they could attribute second-order false belief. Therefore, the skill that appears to be crucial when distinguishing a joke from a lie is the ability to appreciate and reflect on what different people know or do not know, rather than being able to reflect on the knowledge that people have about other people's minds.

Such conclusions seem to make sense, since jokes differ from lies in terms of the knowledge of the listener and the speaker. With jokes, the speaker knows that the listener also knows the truth. In the example, both the boy and his mother could see the peas remaining on his plate when he said, 'I did a really good job finishing my peas'. However, with lies the speaker and listener have different knowledge and the speaker is aware of this difference; the boy who did not clean his room knows that his mother does not know he has not cleaned his room when he says, 'I did a really good job cleaning my room'. Therefore, understanding lies and jokes requires an understanding of another person's knowledge or ignorance of facts rather than an understanding of someone's beliefs about beliefs.

3.2 Improved social interactions

It is clear that the development of a theory of mind goes along with an ability to appreciate a speaker's intentions. It also appears that being able to reflect on the needs, intentions, desires and beliefs of people provides children with information that helps to improve the quality of their interactions with others. Astington and Jenkins (1995) assessed the theory of mind skills of 30 children aged 3 to 5 years and also observed them while they took part in a 10-minute session of pretend play. One measure they made was of *joint proposals*, when a child made reference to another person and to himself or herself within the same turn, saying, for example, 'Pretend *you're* squirting *me* again'. The children with good theory of mind scores made more joint proposals with their partner in the play session than did the children with lower theory of mind scores. Astington and Jenkins concluded that there was an association between theory of mind skills and children's abilities to reflect on their own desires and also to incorporate their partner's desires during play.

Activity 2   *Cause and effect*

Allow about
5 minutes

This activity will help you to appreciate some of the difficulties in establishing cause and effect.
Would you say that Astington and Jenkins' conclusion was justified?

Comment

One problem with research that shows a correlation between two variables is that it is difficult, if not impossible, to identify with any certainty whether an increase in one variable *causes* an increase in the other. In this case, do enhanced theory of mind skills lead to an improvement in social interactions, or are children who are more socially skilled more likely to develop a theory of mind before those who are less socially skilled?

In a subsequent study (Jenkins and Astington, 2000) the researchers sought to shed light on the direction of causality by using a different research design. They carried out a longitudinal study that tested 20 children aged 3 and 4 on three occasions in the course of approximately 7 months. On each occasion the children were presented with a series of false belief understanding tasks, and they were video-recorded during play with a friend. The play sessions generated measures of the amount of pretend play, joint proposals, and explicit role assignment (where the child assigns a pretend role to himself or herself, or to another child, by suggesting, for example, 'Let's be firegirls now'). It was found that the children's performance on the theory of mind understanding tests taken during the first recording session predicted joint proposals and role assignment during play in the second session. However, there was no evidence that social behaviours predicted children's theory of mind. Therefore, it appears that the development of theory of mind skills brings with it a change in the quality of children's interactions.

3.3 Bullying

The previous example of the relationship between theory of mind skills and children's interactions during play is positive in every respect. It would be reassuring to think that the ability to appreciate the feelings and thoughts of others would make children more altruistic and sensitive to those around them. However, this is not always the case. The development of a theory of mind may also bring with it an improved capacity for children to bully others and also to lie and deceive. To be sure, children may lie, deceive or bully before they understand mental states, but once they have developed a theory of mind they become more sophisticated in the strategies that they can use. By being able to appreciate another person's mind, bullies are better able to identify their victim's weaknesses and vulnerabilities and use this understanding to refine their bullying strategies.

By contrast with the popular stereotype of an 'oafish' bully lacking in social skills and understanding, bullies may be manipulative experts in social situations, organizing gangs and using subtle, indirect methods to bully. One study examined the level of children's understanding of the emotional and cognitive content of other people's minds and related this to their role in bullying. 'Ringleader' bullies scored higher on both of these measures than 'follower' bullies (those who helped or supported the bully), victims and defenders of the victim (Sutton *et al.*, 1999).

Summary of Section 3

* The development of a theory of mind provides a new realm of information from which children can draw.
* There is a second stage to the understanding of mental states which is called *second-order theory of mind.*
* The development of theory of mind skills allows a number of other skills to develop, including the understanding of jokes, lies, irony and sarcasm. An understanding of mental states also improves social interactions.
* Theory of mind development can also have negative consequences, such as enhanced strategies in bullying.

4 Developing a theory of mind

The Sally/Anne task and the Smarties task have been devised by psychologists as techniques for studying the emergence of theory of mind in controlled, experimental settings. But they are not the only way of gaining access to this aspect of children's development; this and the following section consider three other methods.

1   Children's everyday behaviour can be observed and recorded to look for indications of theory of mind development. For example, does their talk include words and phrases that imply an awareness of other people's minds – so-called *mental state terms*?

2   The cognitive skills that provide the foundation for theory of mind development can be examined. Two of these skills will be considered here: joint attention and the understanding of intentions.

3   Research has looked at the relationship between children's theory of mind development and the environmental factors that might facilitate or hinder this development.

Although these three areas of investigation – observations of everyday behaviour, associated cognitive skills and social environment – are discussed separately, it is important to bear in mind that they are inextricably linked. The relationship between these different factors will be discussed at the end of this chapter.

4.1 Theory of mind in everyday life

Understanding and using mental state terms

What can we learn about how children understand and relate to the world around them by listening to what they say? Wellman and Bartsch (1994) gathered samples of the everyday speech of ten children. When the study began the children were under 2 years old and it continued until they were 5. The researchers examined over 200,000 utterances, looking in particular for *desire-based* terms (words such as 'want', 'wish', 'hope') and *belief-based* terms (words such as 'think', 'know', 'expect', 'understand'). They logged about 12,000 utterances of this sort (approximately 6 per cent of the total).

Activity 3   *Analysing young children's talk*

Allow about
10 minutes

This activity asks you to analyse short extracts of children's talk to identify patterns in their use of desire-based and belief-based terms.

Look at the following six examples from four of the children in the study by Wellman and Bartsch and identify which contain desire-based terms and which belief-based terms. Note the ages of the children at the time of the recording: does any pattern emerge?

I   Adam (2 years 7 months)

Adam: Eat mommy.

Mother: Eat?

Adam: Yeah.

Mother: I'm not hungry.

Adam: Want spoon?

Mother: No thank you.

Adam: OK. You don't want a spoon. You don't want a spoon.

2   Adam (3 years 3 months)

Adam: Can I put dis in de mail? Can I put my head in de mailbox ... so de mailman can know where I are?

3   Ross (2 years 6 months)

Ross: He scratched me.

Adult: Didn't it hurt?

Ross: Yeah. I want a band-aid. The boy hurt me.

Adult: The boy hurt you? How did the boy hurt you?

Ross: The boy wanted to.

4   Ross (3 years 3 months)

Ross: He was trying to rip it up, right?

Adult: No he won't rip it.

Ross: But I know he could rip it.

5   Abe (3 years 3 months)

Abe: I didn't get you a surprise

Adult: You didn't. I'm sad.

Abe: No don't be sad. I thought I would, 'cept I didn't see one for you.

6   Sarah (4 years 4 months)

Sarah: You put it ... see? You don't know where the pieces go. I know. An' that goes there, right?

(Adapted from Wellman and Bartsch, 1994, p. 334)

Comment

Extracts 1 and 3 contain desire-based terms – 'You don't want a spoon' and 'I want a band-aid'. Extracts 2, 4, 5 and 6 contain belief-based terms – 'so de mailman can know where I are', 'I know he could rip it', 'I thought I would' and 'You don't know where the pieces go'. The two examples of desire-based terms come from Adam and Ross when they were younger by several months than in the other extracts.

This hint of an age trend across these examples was borne out by the fuller analysis of the data. Wellman and Bartsch found that genuine reference to the subjective mental state of desire occurred around 2 years of age. At this age, not only do children refer to their own desires but they are also able to refer to other people's desires, as Adam does in Extract 1. This use is distinct from some early uses of the word 'want' – 'I want this', 'I don't want to'– that may not truly reflect a child's understanding of mind, but rather may simply be a tool they have learned to use in order to obtain desired objects or not to have to undertake undesired activities. These children may have no psychological understanding of the psychological state 'desire', but may simply be using 'want' because they have built up a conditioned response which achieves desired goals. The use of 'genuine reference' at the beginning of this paragraph distinguishes those 'learned responses' from uses which indicate a true understanding of the mental state of desire.

The Sally/Anne and Smarties tasks provide ways of establishing whether children really do understand the psychological consequences of mental states rather than simply rote learning mental state terms. Just as with analyses of everyday language, studies employing these tasks show that children pass tests for an understanding of desires *before* they pass tests for false belief understanding. Research summary 1 provides an example of one such study by Repacholi and Gopnik (1997).

RESEARCH SUMMARY 1

The joys of broccoli: the appreciation of different desires

In this study by Repacholi and Gopnik (1997), 81 children aged 14 months, and 78 children aged 18 months watched an experimenter express either disgust or pleasure as she tasted either a biscuit or broccoli. On half of the occasions with one sample of children, the experimenter pretended to like the biscuit and dislike the broccoli, and on the other half, with other children, she showed the opposite preference, liking the broccoli and disliking the biscuit. The children were also observed to see which of the foods they preferred; in nearly all cases it was the biscuit. When the child was not touching either food, the experimenter placed her hand between the two bowls of food, and said, 'Can you give me some?' The 14 month olds responded egocentrically, offering the food they themselves preferred – most often a biscuit. By contrast, the 18 month olds correctly inferred that the experimenter wanted the food associated with her positive behaviour, even though the experimenter's desires sometimes contrasted with their own preference. The older children not only inferred that the other person held a desire, but also recognized how desires are related to emotions and their expression.

As can be seen from these examples, both naturalistic observations and experimental paradigms have shown that there is a critical shift at about 18 months as children begin to appreciate that different people can have different desires. It is likely that this understanding is an important stepping stone to understanding false beliefs.

4.2 Associated cognitive skills

The abilities that help children learn about people are either inborn or develop early in life. Very young babies can discriminate between faces, voices and human movement and they seem compelled to interact with others, learning turn-taking procedures. Babies also induce in adults a desire to interact with them. These skills, together with a host of others including language development and *executive function* (see Chapter 5) form a foundation for developing an understanding of our own mind and the minds of others. Two important skills, here, are *joint attention* and the *understanding of intentionality*.

Joint attention

Dyadic joint attention
When child and adult are the focus of one another's attention

Triadic joint attention
Where child and adult interact around the focus of an object such as a toy.

A notable feature of all infants' experience is the conversation-like exchanges that they get into with adults, typically from the age of 2 months. Child and adult become the focus of each other's attention and take turns in exchanges of looks, mouth movements, noises and other recognizable expressions; psychologists call this *dyadic joint attention.*

From about 9 months onwards, these sorts of exchanges take on a third dimension, as objects – typically toys – are introduced into the conversation; this is *triadic joint attention.*

These exchanges play an important part in early language learning as adults use the names of the objects to which they are jointly attending – 'Where's teddy?', 'Give me the brick'. Within experiences like these, it is argued, the ability to focus attention on another individual or object at the expense of all other surrounding stimuli plays an important part in beginning to understand the causes of people's behaviour. The study by Charman *et al.* (2000) described in Research summary 2 is an example of an attempt to explore this relationship.

RESEARCH SUMMARY 2

Pay attention: the importance of joint social goals

Charman *et al.* (2000) tested thirteen infants when they were 1 year and 8 months and again at 3 years and 8 months. On the first occasion experimenters recorded the number of times the children switched their gaze between a noisy toy, activated by the experimenter, and an adult (either a parent or the experimenter). They also noted the number of times the children looked at an adult during a play session of fixed duration in which the adult either teasingly removed a toy from them or held their hands so that they could not manipulate the toy. These were both measures of joint attention.

The researchers also observed the extent to which the children engaged in pretend play when provided with props, such as a toy kitchen stove and accessories. The third type of measure was of imitation, observing the number of occasions on which the children imitated an action which they had just seen modelled by the experimenter.

Two years later the same children were tested on a battery of theory of mind tasks. Of the three measures taken at 1 year and 8 months, only the joint attention behaviours were associated with subsequent theory of mind ability. Why might joint attention abilities be more strongly related to later theory of mind development than play or imitation abilities? The researchers suggest that joint attention behaviours, in contrast to play and imitation, have a directly *social* goal, which is to share one's mental state of perception with others. Although play and the imitation of actions may involve similar goals, these behaviours are associated with the properties of objects rather than with one's perceptual awareness.

Understanding intentions

The example of the bus queue, which began this chapter, illustrated that in order to understand the intentions of another person it is necessary to impute desires and goal states to their actions – the people are standing, waiting, because they are hoping that a bus will arrive. In order to understand that people have minds and that their minds dictate their behaviour, it is necessary to appreciate that behaviours are purposeful. If behaviours are not seen as purposeful then there would be no need to try to explain them because they would appear to be unsystematic and therefore meaningless. When do children show evidence of beginning to understand the intentions behind people's actions? Research summary 3 describes a piece of research by Meltzoff (1995) which addresses this question.

RESEARCH SUMMARY 3

Doing what you think I want to do, rather than what I am doing: understanding intentions

In a study by Meltzoff (1995) 40 18-month-old children, individually, watched an adult act out a scene with a number of different objects. One was a dumbbell-shaped toy (Figure 4a) that could be pulled apart at its mid-point. Some of the children watched the experimenter try to pull the two halves apart but fail on each attempt when one of his hands slipped off the end. A similar number of children watched the same scene, but in their case the experimenter succeeded in pulling the two halves apart. All the children were then presented with the object and allowed to play with it. Would the children in the first group, who had not seen the act successfully accomplished, be able to infer the intended action from the actor's behaviour and therefore produce this act? The results showed that they could. Children who had watched the failed attempt were more likely to perform the intended action than children who either had not seen any demonstrations at all or had watched the experimenter perform actions which were unrelated to the key action, such as pushing the two ends of the dumbbell together.

A further experiment investigated whether 18-month-old children would infer intentions when the pulling apart of the dumbbells was done by an inanimate mechanical device with 'arms' and pincers for 'fingers' (Figure 4b). The children's reaction to the mechanical device was completely different from their reaction to the person. Again, the researchers noted what happened when the children were given the dumbbells. Those who had watched the human demonstration were six times more likely to complete the target act than those who had watched the mechanical device. The researchers concluded that 18-month-old children situate people, but not mechanical devices, within a psychological framework. At 18 months children are able to look beyond the surface behaviour people show and appreciate a deeper, psychological level involving goals and intentions.

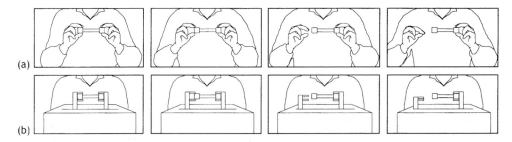

Figure 4   (a) The human experimenter attempts to pull the dumbbells apart but his fingers slip off the end. (b) The mechanical 'arms' and 'fingers' located in front of the human experimenter fail in a similar fashion to pull the dumbbells apart (from Meltzoff, 1995, p. 844).

Summary of Section 4

- Many techniques can be used to examine the process of developing a theory of mind including: naturalistic observations, investigation of the associated skills and an examination of the environmental factors affecting theory of mind development.
- Naturalistic observations, as well as experimental work, have shown that children understand desires before they understand false beliefs.
- There are a number of skills that are fundamental to the development of theory of mind skills. Two such skills are joint attention and the understanding of intentions.

5   Social factors affecting theory of mind development

In Section 1, the age of 4 years was identified as a significant point in the emergence of the ability to attribute mental states to others. But of course, children do not magically wake up on their fourth birthday with this new competence. Its development can begin at any time between the ages of 3 and 5 years and involves a continuous improvement rather than a sudden change. Numerous studies have shown that many factors in a child's environment can affect when the development of a theory of mind begins. From a Vygotskian perspective, the development of this fundamentally social skill, understanding other people, is seen as being inextricably linked to a child's social world.

Activity 4

Allow about 10 minutes

How do we learn to think about others?

This activity will help you think about experiences that might encourage an understanding of other people's minds.

Think of some experiences within a young child's day-to-day environment that might encourage the development of an understanding of other people's minds. What might assist them to 'stand in another person's shoes'? And how, in turn, might these different factors affect children's cognitive development?

Note down your thoughts and review them as you read the rest of this section.

5.1 Social interaction

Interaction with siblings

You may have thought of a number of ways in which theory of mind skills might be developed. One possibility is that having older siblings is significant because of the nature of the interactions that they encourage. When 68 children aged 3 to 5 years were given four tasks as a test of false belief understanding, Jenkins and Astington (1996) found that the children's false belief understanding scores increased with the number of siblings they had. A further interesting finding from this research concerned the relationship between family size, false belief understanding and language development. The data in Table 2 are the average scores on the tests of false belief understanding, for children with low and high levels of language ability, related to the number of siblings they had. These scores are based on the number of tests passed; the higher the scores, the better the level of understanding.

Table 2   **Mean false belief understanding score (possible score 0–4) according to children's language ability and the number of siblings they have**

Number of siblings	Low language ability group	High language ability group
0	0.3 (n = 13)	2.9 (n = 9)
1	1.4 (n = 15)	2.9 (n = 17)
2	3.2 (n = 4)	3.6 (n = 10)

Source: Data from Jenkins and Astington (1996).

Activity 5   *The significance of siblings*

Allow about 5 minutes

This activity will give you further experience of analysing and interpreting data.

Study the scores shown in Table 2. What conclusions can you draw from these results?

Comment

Where children have no siblings there appears to be a relationship between their level of language ability and their competence at theory of mind tests – those with lower language ability do less well. However, when children have two siblings there is a clear indication that this difference is reduced – the presence of siblings appears to compensate for slower language development in developing false belief understanding.

If siblings make a difference in this way it would seem plausible that their age might be of significance. When Ruffman *et al.* (1998) examined the results of 444 English and Japanese children whose ages ranged from 3 years and 1 month to 6 years and 11 months, they found that the number of theory of mind tests that they passed increased with the number of older siblings a child had. However, there was no connection between children's success on the tests and either the number of younger siblings or the gender of the siblings (whether older or younger). How might the older siblings facilitate a child's theory of mind development? Ruffman *et al.* point to activities such as pretend play, deception, teasing and talk about feelings, all of which would feature less in interactions with younger siblings.

Interaction with adults

If older siblings can have this sort of influence, does the same apply to exposure to adults, both in and outside the family, who may also engage in pretend play, teasing and the like? In one study which addressed this question (Lewis *et al.*, 1996) 82 pre-school children living in Crete were questioned about their extended kin, and a further 75 children, this time from Cyprus, were questioned about the adults with whom they had daily contact. Both samples were also tested on a set of theory of mind tasks. As well as confirming Ruffman's findings on the relationship between theory of mind development and the number of older siblings a child had, Lewis *et al.* found that performance on the tests was improved by both the number of available adult kin (in Crete) and the number of adults the children interacted with daily (in Cyprus). So, children who interact on a daily basis with a number of different adults, whether related or not, appreciate other people's minds earlier than children who have contact with fewer adults. It might be expected that the amount of time spent in such interactions and the nature of the interactions would also be significant.

5.2 Communication

The role of language use in the family

What is it about the interactions with older siblings and adults that has a positive effect on young children's theory of mind development? Ruffman *et al.* (1999) investigated whether mothers in some way facilitate false-belief understanding in their children and, if so, what elements of their behaviour aid this facilitation. The researchers used a questionnaire to ask the mothers of 64 children aged 3 and 4 years about their own education and occupation, the number of younger and older siblings the child had, the time the child spent with them and how they dealt with disciplinary situations involving their child. Three factors were found to relate to the children's belief understanding: the age of the child, the number of older siblings, and the number of times mothers said they would respond to disciplinary situations by asking the child to reflect on the victim's feelings, for example 'Imagine how Billy feels when you hit him', or 'How would you feel if Billy hit you?' There was no effect for mothers who engaged their child in general discussion or exploration of the disciplinary issues, or who simply reprimanded the child without discussing the situation. This suggests that the way a mother approaches disciplining her child can have an effect on the child's understanding of feelings and mental states. It seems that asking children to reflect on mental states and feelings facilitates development, whereas general discussions of transgressions and discipline do not, irrespective of the amount of time children spend with their mother.

Other forms of communication

What happens to the development of theory of mind skills when a child is unable to use the usual forms of communication and so is not exposed, early in life, to the general discussions about mental states that occur in everyday interactions? Some research with deaf children sheds light on these questions. Woolfe *et al.* (2002) compared the performance of two groups of deaf children in tests of theory of mind. One group of children whose ages ranged from 4 years to 8 years and 6 months consisted of 'native-signing' children whose parents were deaf and used sign language; these children had therefore had communicative input from a young age. The others, aged between 4 years 6 months and 8 years 9 months, were 'late-signing' children who were raised by hearing parents and so were not immediately immersed in an environment where they had access to everyday communication.

Table 3   Performance in theory of mind tests by native-signing, late-signing and hearing children (the higher the scores, the better the level of understanding)

	Native signers (n = 19)	Late signers (n = 32)	Hearing 3 year olds (n = 20)	Hearing 4 year olds (n = 20)
Mean score on theory of mind tests	1.42	0.34	0.35	1.30
Standard deviation	0.61	0.65	0.86	0.35

Source: Data from Woolfe et al. (2002).

The data in Table 3 indicate that the children in the late-signing group showed less well-developed theory of mind skills than either the native-signers ($p < 0.001$) or a sample of 4-year-old hearing children ($p < 0.001$). It would appear that access to early conversation – through whatever medium – is an important factor in the development of a theory of mind.

5.3 Gender

There is much research to show that the gender of a child can affect the types of interaction they have with their environment. For example, mothers tend to talk about emotions more to their 2-year-old daughters than to their 2-year-old sons (Dunn *et al.*, 1987). Older siblings tend to mention feeling states more frequently to girls than boys (Brown *et al.*, 1996). Girls also tend to use words which signify emotional states earlier and more frequently than boys (Cervantes and Callanan, 1998). This suggests that girls might succeed on tests of false belief understanding before boys. Evidence from nearly 1,500 children, aged between 2 years and 4 months and 6 years and 3 months, indeed showed a slight advantage for girls on false belief understanding tests (Charman *et al.*, 2002). However, this was only so for children younger than 4 years and 8 months, not for children older than that, and in any event the researchers concluded that if there is an age-specific advantage for girls in the acquisition of false belief understanding it is only a very weak effect.

5.4 Summing up the significance of social factors

The selection of research presented above indicates that there is a strong relationship between children's surroundings and their cognitive development. Such evidence supports the Vygotskian approach that views a child as an apprentice in the world, learning much from those surrounding him or her. Yet Piaget's constructivist approach, which theorizes that a child acts on his or her own surroundings to change and actively learn from those surroundings, cannot be overlooked. When considering cognitive development it is important not to consider the different influencing factors in isolation from one another. Often, changes in one of the factors can have an effect on a second factor, which may in turn have a further effect on the original influencing factor. For example, there is a close link between children's theory of mind skills and the quality of interaction that they have with the people surrounding them. Having a mother who frequently uses mental state terms, an older sibling who teases, deceives or takes part in pretend play, and having regular contact with a number of other adults, will all facilitate the development of an understanding of people's minds. Once theory of mind skills have developed, a new realm of information is opened up to children and this will allow them, in turn, to improve the quality of the interactions that they have with others. This improved quality of interactions may then assist in developing more complex theory of mind skills, such as second-order theory of mind. In practice, there are some facilitatory factors that are unlikely to be related to one another. For example, it is impossible for a child's linguistic skills to influence whether he or she has any older siblings. However, interestingly, the number of older siblings a child has could affect his or her linguistic competence. On the whole, the complex transactional relationship between children's social environments and their cognitive development can be seen extremely clearly when considering the development of a child's understanding of minds.

Summary of Section 5

- There are many factors in children's environments which affect their theory of mind development including: the number of older siblings, exposure to early conversations, the number of adults with whom they have daily contact, their parents' communication style and their gender.

6 Conclusion

At the beginning of this chapter you were asked to imagine what the world would be like if we were not able to appreciate the minds of other people. It should now be clear that a theory of mind is an exceptionally important ability that allows us to perform complex behaviours and draws upon some fundamentally important skills. Before the age of about 4 years, children do not fully appreciate other people's mental states and so they are unable to use this rich source of psychological information to predict a person's behaviour. Young children believe that people behave according to how the world really is, rather than how each person believes the world to be. However, research using tests of false belief understanding has shown that, at about 4 years, children begin to appreciate the mental states of others. This change in cognitive skills appears not to be restricted to Western cultures.

Having a new realm of information upon which to draw allows children to develop many other skills, including improved interactions with others and the appreciation of intentions in lies, jokes, and ironic or sarcastic comments. The development of a theory of mind also provides children with the tools to bully and lie more effectively.

The development of theory of mind skills draws upon many cognitive abilities, including joint attention and the understanding of desires and intentions. Being able to share one's perceptual focus with another person and being able to appreciate the desires and intentions of others by watching their actions appear to underpin the development of an understanding of false beliefs. Furthermore, the environment within which a child lives can also affect theory of mind development. The interactions that children have with their siblings, friends, parents and other adults affect how they see other people. From about 4 years of age a child sees other individuals not just as people, but as people who have minds of their own.

References

Astington, J. and Jenkins, J. (1995) 'Theory of mind development and social understanding', *Cognition and Emotion,* vol. 9, pp. 151–65.

Avis, M. and Harris, P. (1991) 'Belief-desire reasoning among Baka children: evidence for a universal conception of mind', *Child Development*, vol. 62, pp. 460–7.

Brown, J., Donelan-McCall, N. and Dunn, J. (1996) 'Why talk about mental states? The significance of children's conversations with friends, siblings and mothers', *Child Development,* vol. 67, pp. 836–49.

Cervantes, C. and Callanan, M. (1998) 'Labels and explanations in mother–child emotion talk: age and gender differentiation', *Developmental Psychology*, vol. 34, pp. 88–98.

Charman, T., Baron-Cohen, S., Swettenham, J., *et al.* (2000) 'Testing joint attention, imitation, and play as infancy precursors to language and theory of mind', *Cognitive Development*, vol. 15, pp. 481–98.

Charman, T., Ruffman, T. and Clements, W. (2002) 'Is there a gender difference in false belief development?', *Social Development*, vol. 11, pp. 1–10.

Dennett, D. (1978) 'Beliefs about beliefs', *Behavioral and Brain Sciences*, vol. 1, pp. 568–70.

Donaldson, M. (1978) *Children's Minds*, Glasgow, Fontana.

Dunn, J., Bretherton, I. and Munn, P. (1987) 'Conversations about feeling states between mothers and their young children', *Developmental Psychology*, vol. 23, pp. 132–9.

Frith, U. (1989) *Autism: explaining the enigma*, Oxford, Blackwell.

Gopnik, A. and Astington, J. (1988) 'Children's understanding of representational change and its relation to the understanding of false belief and the appearance-reality distinction', *Child Development*, vol. 59, pp. 26–37.

Jenkins, J. and Astington, J. (1996) 'Cognitive factors and family structure associated with theory of mind development in young children', *Developmental Psychology*, vol. 32, pp. 70–8.

Jenkins, J. and Astington, J. (2000) 'Theory of mind and social behavior: causal models tested in a longitudinal study', *Merrill-Palmer-Quarterly*, vol. 46, pp. 203–20.

Lewis, C., Freeman, N., Kyriadidou, C., Maridaki-Kassotaki, K. and Berridge, D. (1996) 'Social influences on false belief access', *Child Development*, vol. 67, pp. 2930–47.

Lewis, C. and Osborn, A. (1990) 'Three-year-olds' problems with false belief: conceptual deficit or linguistic artifact?', *Child Development*, vol. 61, pp. 1514–19.

Meltzoff, A. N. (1995) 'Understanding the intentions of others: re-enactment of intended acts by 18-month-old children', *Developmental Psychology*, vol. 31, pp. 838–50.

Piaget, J. (1932) *The Moral Judgement of the Child*, New York, Harcourt Brace.

Piaget, J. and Inhelder, B. (1968) *The Psychology of the Child*, New York, Basic Books.

Premack, D. and Woodruff, G. (1978) 'Does the chimpanzee have a theory of mind?', *Behavioral and Brain Sciences*, vol. 1, pp. 515–26.

Repacholi, B. M. and Gopnik, A. (1997) 'Early reasoning about desires: evidence from 14- and 18-month-olds', *Developmental Psychology*, vol. 33, pp. 12–21.

Ruffman, T., Perner, J., Naito, M., Parkin, L. and Clements, W. (1998) 'Older (but not younger) siblings facilitate false belief understanding', *Developmental Psychology*, vol. 34, pp. 161–74.

Ruffman, T., Perner, J. and Parkin, L. (1999) 'How parenting style affects false belief understanding', *Social Development*, vol. 8, pp. 395–411.

Sullivan, K., Winner, E. and Hopfield, N. (1995) 'How children tell a lie from a joke: the role of second-order mental state attributions', *British Journal of Developmental Psychology*, vol. 13, pp. 191–204.

Sutton, J., Smith, P. and Swettenham, J. (1999) 'Social cognition and bullying: social inadequacy or skilled manipulation?', *British Journal of Developmental Psychology*, vol. 17, pp. 435–50.

Wellman, H. and Bartsch, K. (1994) 'Before belief: children's early psychological theory', in Lewis, C. and Mitchell, P. (eds) *Children's Early Understanding of Mind: origins and development*, pp. 331–54, Hove, Lawrence Erlbaum Associates.

Whiten, A. (1991) *Natural Theories of Mind: evolution, development and simulation of everyday mindreading*, Oxford, Blackwell.

Wimmer, H. and Hartl, M. (1991) 'Against the Cartesian view on mind: young children's difficulty with own false beliefs', *British Journal of Developmental Psychology*, vol. 9, pp. 125–38.

Wimmer, H. and Perner, J. (1983) 'Beliefs about beliefs: representation and constraining function of wrong beliefs in young children's understanding of deception', *Cognition*, vol. 13, pp. 103–28.

Woolfe, T., Want, S. C. and Siegal, M. (2002) 'Signposts to development: theory of mind in deaf children', *Child Development*, vol. 73, pp. 768–78.

Chapter 7
Mathematical and scientific thinking

Terezinha Nunes and Peter Bryant

Contents

Learning outcomes

After you have studied this chapter you should be able to:

1 understand the difference between *generative* and *reproductive* knowledge;
2 distinguish between the ways in which children think in mathematics and science;
3 understand the importance of situations, and not just of computations, in problem solving in mathematics;
4 assess the impact of cultural settings on mathematical and scientific thinking;
5 discuss possible connections between the development of intelligence and learning science and mathematics;
6 compare different theories about how children progress in their mathematical and scientific thinking and the implications of this analysis for education.

1 Introduction

1.1 Cognition and language in context

So far in this book you have seen that as children gain an increased understanding of their linguistic and physical environments they attempt to organize and systematize this knowledge in a number of important ways. They develop explicit categories that capture not just key characteristics of their environment, but also the similarities and differences between aspects of it. They apply verbal labels to them and to their own internal mental states. They learn how to use language to communicate their ideas and desires, and through this communication they acquire knowledge about how others think about and understand the world. This in turn pushes their own understanding of their environment to new levels of sophistication. They generate hypotheses about how language is formed, how the world 'works', and how other people think.

At each stage children are moving towards the ability to represent their world in symbolic ways. Words in language are used to represent real objects, events and feelings, and enable the discussion of things that can only be imagined. Through such discussions children begin to deal with unknown factors and hypothetical situations. This is especially true when they begin to acquire mathematical and scientific understanding of their environment.

This chapter will introduce you to the nature of mathematical and scientific understanding. We will introduce the idea that mathematical and scientific knowledge is not simply a 'collection of facts' but a 'way of thinking' and we will present you with an overview of the psychological research that has attempted to uncover how children come to acquire this way of thinking. What you will discover is that children often rely on their everyday understanding of the world to generate solutions to mathematical and scientific problems.

1.2 What is the nature of mathematical and scientific knowledge?

The learning of mathematics and science can sometimes be mistakenly characterized as the mastery of facts and procedures. For example, in mathematics young children learn to count, to write numbers, to do addition and subtraction, to say the multiplication table, to do long division, and so on. All these are either procedures (*how to ...*) or facts (for example, the number names, or the fact that 6 x 7 = 42). Similarly, in science children learn facts (for example, the world is round) and procedures (using formulae to solve problems in physics, chemistry or genetics). According to this characterization, it might be expected that children will know only what they have been taught and will not know what they have not been taught. Is this view of mathematical and scientific learning justified? Try Activity 1 now.

Activity 1

Allow about 5 minutes

Learning to count in Japanese

This activity will help you to appreciate the difference between reproductive and generative learning.

Study the numbers below, which are in Japanese but written phonetically in English.

1	ichi	10	ju	20	ni ju
2	ni	11	ju ichi	21	ni ju ichi
3	san	12	ju ni	22	ni ju ni
4	shi	13	ju san		
5	go	14	ju shi		
6	roku				
7	sichi				
8	hachi				
9	ku				

How do you say 15 in Japanese? How do you say 43? How do you say 67? Do you think you could count to 99? How did you get your answers?

Comment

Your performance in Activity 1 can show you that you know more facts about Japanese numbers than you were taught. Learning mathematics means understanding a system that goes beyond the examples you learn from. For this reason mathematics learning is said to be 'generative', that is, learning the system allows you to generate new facts that you were never taught about. If mathematical and scientific knowledge were simply reproductive (the repetition of what the person was taught), you could not have answered the questions in Activity 1.

As you saw in Activity 1, learning mathematics means understanding a system that allows you to generate new facts that you have not been taught. However, learners do not always grasp the system appropriately. Children form their own ideas about what they are taught in mathematics and science. Sometimes they are able to repeat some of the facts they are taught without integrating them in a way of thinking. Can you try to figure out the systems used by the four children whose writing of numbers is part of Activity 2?

Activity 2   Generating numbers

Allow about
5 minutes

This activity encourages you to consider the need to look at learning processes (how children come to understand something) rather than just at the outcomes (what they are able to do).

Look at Figure 1. It contains numbers written by four children aged between 5 and 6 years of age. They had not been taught how to write multi-digit numbers in school. However, they see numbers around them and do their own analysis of how numbers should be written. Can you figure out how each one generates the writing of numbers? Which children seem to think similarly about writing numbers? What similarities and differences are there?

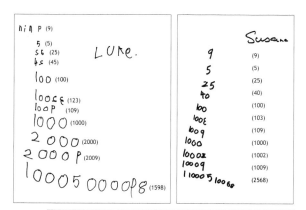

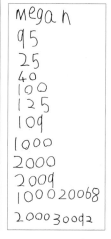

Figure 1   Four children's written productions of numbers.

Comment

In order to understand children's learning of mathematics, it is necessary to analyse their productions – the way they count, write numbers, solve problems and so on – and try to figure out how they think. It is not enough to try to find out what number facts they know or do not know. Consider first Alice's production. Alice seems to have the idea that, for each number word, you put down a digit. She does not know which digits she should put down for some words – for example, twenty, hundred and thousand – so she uses one line for twenty and two number-like shapes for hundred and thousand, respectively. Although not correct, her writing of numbers is not random and can be understood if you crack her system. Luke and Susanna seem to use similar systems. It is quite likely that they have learned how to write two digit numbers so they get these right (if you disregard Luke's inversion of the digit 2). For three digit numbers, they have created a system: they write each number in sequence, as if they wrote the words in sequence. Megan succeeds in keeping three digit numbers within the conventional writing but finds it hard to do so with four digit numbers. For these three children, number learning is not a simple sequence to be memorized, with the larger ones being learned later: they succeed with 2,000, yet do not write smaller numbers correctly. They have a system, but it happens not to be the one that adults use.

It may seem that this notion of generative knowledge applies more readily to mathematical than to scientific knowledge. It could be argued that there are many 'scientific facts' about the world that children can be taught in school and they will learn them without difficulty – and this is to some extent true. However, scientific information is often considered to be something that is transmitted in school as 'mere fact', when this information is not only that. Often what people call 'scientific fact' is important because it reflects a way of thinking. Try Activity 3 now and think about facts and ways of thinking in science.

Activity 3   Facts and ideas

Allow about
10 minutes

This activity will help you to consider the distinction between understanding a fact, and showing awareness of the underlying principles that explain that knowledge.

It has been known now for a long time that the world is round and not flat, as it was thought in the past. This is a fact. But is this a 'mere fact' or is it a way of thinking? This is what Nussbaum, Novack and their colleagues at the University of Cornell decided to figure out (Nussbaum and Novack, 1976; Nussbaum, 1985).

Look at the picture of the world in Figure 2. It illustrates the idea that there are two girls, one who lives at the North Pole and one who lives at the South Pole. They have two bottles each, one with a cork in and one that is open. Their bottles are half filled with juice. Can you draw in the juice in their bottles?

Look at the second picture of the world in Figure 3. It shows three boys, one living at the North Pole, one living on the Equator, and one living at the South Pole. They each have a ball in their hand. What will happen to the ball if they drop it? Can you draw in the path the ball will follow?

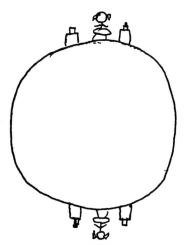

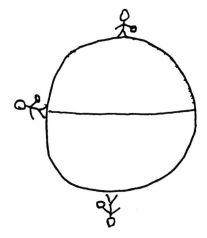

Figure 2   What will happen to the juice in the bottles?

Figure 3   What will happen to the ball if it is dropped?

Comment

As with mathematical knowledge, scientific knowledge is not the accumulation of facts but is defined by 'ways of thinking'. Most children in primary school will know and tell you (if asked) that the world is round. Yet, their thinking may be governed by the idea that the world is flat, with the sky above and the ground below. This is what their drawings of people on earth and of rain clouds suggest (see Figure 4). Their answers to the questions in Activity 3 (Figure 5) also indicate a way of thinking that is consistent with a flat world conception.

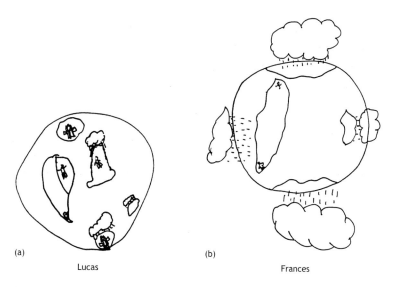

(a)

Lucas

(b)

Frances

Figure 4   Children's drawings of the earth and of rain clouds.

Lucas (6 years) and Frances (8 years) were asked (following Nussbaum and colleagues) to imagine that they were astronauts and were looking at the world from a distance. What would the world look like? The answer to this question typically is 'round' or 'like a ball' or something of the sort – and both Lucas and Frances answered in this way. They were then asked to draw the world as it would be seen from the spacecraft. After this was accomplished, they were asked to put in some people, some clouds and some rain in the picture. The children were also asked to indicate the North and the South Pole as a preparation for the next activity.

Both drew a round world and both decided to put in some countries. Lucas put in a rather good outline of South America and England plus what he thought was not a good outline of Australia, but he wanted to have it in anyway (see Figure 4a). Frances put in some countries but was not sure what they were supposed to look like (see Figure 4b). As you can see, apart from these similarities, their drawings of people on earth, clouds and rain differ in significant ways. For Lucas, each country had its own cloud 'on top' and its rain falling from top to bottom. His round world contains people all standing in one direction with clouds above and not all around. Even though 6-year-old children have been told that the world is round and draw it round when asked to, they place people, clouds and rain in a way that is more fitting with a belief in a flat world. They have learned the fact but not the way of thinking that goes with it. For Frances, the conception of the round world prevails in this drawing; she also put in some countries, each one with a rain cloud but the clouds are positioned all around the world.

INTERVIEWER TO FRANCES: ... Can you draw this for me?

FRANCES: Yes. [see (4b)] *(Later, as she draws the South Pole)* ... I used to think that people would fall off the earth. I didn't know why they wouldn't fall off when they were here.

INTERVIEWER: Do they fall off?

FRANCES: No *(laughing)*.

INTERVIEWER: Why not?

FRANCES: My father told me. It's because of gravity. *(She draws the rain falling on the South Pole and remarks that 'Isn't it funny to think of rain falling this way?')*

The drawings by the children are consistent with the solutions they give to the problems posed in Activity 3 – presented in Figure 5. Lucas's solution is typical for children of his age. The drink in the uncorked bottles owned by the little boys at the South Pole and at the Equator falls out of the bottles. The balls also fall the same way as the liquid. Frances thought that the liquid would stay in the bottles but was quite doubtful when giving her answer about the little girl's liquid at the South Pole. When asked about the ball, she commented it would go 'right down into space'. Frances seemed to alternate between a round and a flat world way of thinking.

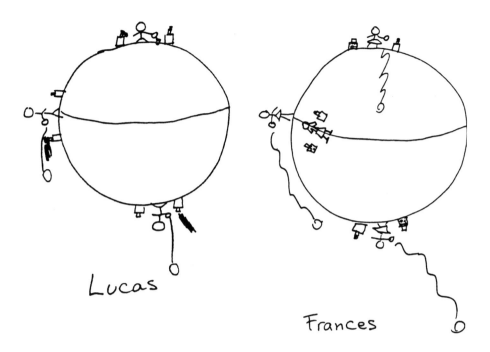

Figure 5 Drawings by the children in response to questions in Activity 3.

So, what can be seen from this example is that knowledge of mathematics and science is about knowing how to think appropriately about a problem, rather than repeating facts that have been learned by rote. Moreover the example shows that although children often know particular facts, they can be seen to apply their knowledge in a way that betrays a lack of understanding about the underlying 'laws' that account for those facts.

We will now consider children's development in understanding these laws in relation to specific aspects of mathematical and scientific reasoning. We will turn to mathematical reasoning first, and consider the question of whether children are always susceptible to these kinds of errors, or whether mathematical understanding is mediated by certain contextual factors.

Summary of Section 1

- Reproductive learning is comparable to learning facts: you only know what you have been taught. Generative knowledge allows you to come up with answers for things that you have not been taught. Generative knowledge is more like thinking than like knowing facts.
- Mathematics learning is *generative*; it enables you to use a system that will allow you to generate new facts that you were not taught.

- Sometimes children evolve their own way of thinking about what is around them. They generate answers that differ from adults' answers. They often merely repeat certain facts without being able to integrate them into a system.
- Scientific knowledge, similarly to mathematical knowledge, is defined by 'ways of thinking', not by just learning facts.

2   The development of mathematical understanding

From the examples in Section 1 you might conclude that children are likely to find the acquisition of mathematical understanding difficult. This is because they need to think about the facts and procedures that they know in a systematic way in order to reveal their underlying uniting principles and 'rules' in a way that will enable them to make predictions about their environment. This type of reasoning seems especially sophisticated. Jean Piaget's studies of mathematical reasoning appear to support this conclusion. However, subsequent research that has explored the role of factors that appear to mediate children's understanding of mathematical concepts tells a slightly different story.

2.1 Piaget's research into mathematical reasoning

Piaget developed a theory of how children learn that was an attempt to view knowledge as structured and generative. For example, children's understanding of number, according to Piaget, did not result from learning the number labels, but from the realization that the number of objects in a set was invariant (did not change) unless objects were added or taken away. Adding and taking away are actions that modify quantities. Even young children (4 or 5 years of age) realize that adding increases and subtracting decreases the number of bricks in a box, for example. However, Piaget argued, young children also believe that spreading a group of objects out means that there are now more of them and putting them closer together means that there are now fewer (Piaget and Szeminska, 1952). This is what he concluded from his studies of children's understanding of *conservation*. In these studies, children were shown two rows of coins with, for example, eight coins in each. It was established that there were as many coins in one row as in the other. They then saw the experimenter performing a transformation on one of the rows – for example, spreading the coins in one row further apart, so that one row was now longer than the other. Even young children who could count, and therefore ascertain that there were still eight coins in each row, still said that there was more money in the row where the coins had been spread apart. According to Piaget, these young children did not understand fully the results of their actions and did not realize that only the addition of more

Concrete operations
The stage at which children can think logically about objects and events in their environment, and represent them symbolically. However, they are still unable to generate hypotheses systematically combining possible different situations and outcomes.

coins would have increased the quantity. Through their own interactions with objects, by changing displays in several ways and checking the results of such changes, they would later on come to understand the invariance of number.

The discovery of the invariance of number in spite of spatial displacements that make sets look larger or smaller (around the age of 6 or 7) was considered so important by Piaget that it was taken as a mark of a new stage in children's intellectual development: the stage of concrete operations.

This was not the end point of development, though, for at this stage children's mathematical understanding was, according to Piaget, restricted to one-variable problems for which addition and subtraction are sufficient. If 7-year-old children have to solve a problem that requires establishing a proportional relationship between two different variables, they are not able to cope. An example of proportional relations is given in Activity 4 below.

Activity 4   *Proportional relationships*

Allow about 5 minutes

This activity will encourage you to test your understanding of the nature of proportional reasoning.

Here is an eel:

He is 10 cm long. He needs to eat 20 g of food a day to survive.

Here is another eel:

He is 20 cm long. He needs to eat 40 g of food a day to survive.

Here is my pet eel, Ernie:

He is just 5 cm long. How much food should I feed him each day?

Figure 6   How much food do these eels need?

Comment

The information in the first two examples should have indicated to you that there is an underlying ratio of eel length to amount of food of 1 cm: 2 g, and this should enable you to work out that Ernie needs 10 g of food each day. In a study by Inhelder and Piaget (1958) children were told that eels have to be fed amounts of food that vary with their size. They were asked to look at some values in both variables – length of the eel and amount of food it needed – and then say how much food an eel of a certain length should receive. Children at age 7 normally suggested higher values for longer eels but did not derive the values systematically. In contrast, older children (about 11–13 years of age) tried to establish a relationship between the two variables and to use this relationship to deduce how much food the longer eel would need.

Piaget and his colleagues (Inhelder and Piaget, 1958; Piaget *et al.*, 1968) considered the achievement of *proportional* reasoning as another landmark in the development of intelligence. Proportional reasoning involves the recognition that the *relationship between two variables remains the same (invariant) although the values in both variables are changed*. This ability to establish an invariant relation among relations is a higher order operation that, according to Piaget, indicates the achievement of a new level of thinking, that of formal operations.

Formal operations
The stage at which children are able to reason in an abstract way without reference to concrete experience. They can tackle problems in a systematic and scientific manner and are able to generate hypotheses about the world based on their accumulated knowledge.

2.2 Limitations in Piaget's ideas

Although Piaget's contribution to current approaches to the study of children's mathematical and scientific thinking is broadly recognized, some aspects of his work have been criticized.

The most serious criticisms have been directed at his idea that children's intellectual structures determine how they think, above and beyond any other influences. Much of the recent research on mathematical reasoning seems to suggest that both children and adults show different levels of success when solving problems that involve the same intellectual structures but differ in other respects, such as the *content* of the problem, the particular *mathematical representation* they are using, or the *social situation* in which they are engaged.

With respect to the *content* of the problem, for example, it is easy to imagine that someone may grasp that the relationship between quantity purchased and amount of money that has to be paid is proportional. In other words, the more sweets you buy, the more you pay, and the amounts vary in a fixed ratio – for example, 5 p per sweet. Yet, this same person may not realize that, if you enlarge a rectangle, the ratio between length and width must be kept constant for the figure to look similar – if the length is twice the width in the small rectangle, it must also be twice the width in the larger one, otherwise the figures look different.

With respect to the type of *mathematical representation,* Nunes (1993) has shown that pupils (of approximately 12–13 years) who were able to solve problems with negative numbers orally made significantly more errors if they were asked to write the information down before solving the problem. Although the content of the problem and the social situation were the same, the written representation had characteristics that confused the pupils when they were solving the problems.

Lave (1988) showed that adults in California performed very differently when solving the same type of proportion problems in different *social situations*. They were much more successful in the supermarket than in a written test. Thus it now seems clear that while intellectual structures may influence performance in problem solving, they do not directly determine what a person will actually do. Other aspects of the problem situation need consideration.

Gérard Vergnaud, a French developmental psychologist who studied with Piaget, synthesized these ideas in his theory, which is known as the theory of conceptual fields. According to Vergnaud (1985), in order to analyse mathematical concepts, the *invariant* properties of the concept must be considered, as Piaget proposed, and also the *situations* that give meaning to the concept and the *symbols* used in its representation. He further proposed that in mathematics one should think not of isolated concepts, but of *conceptual fields* where the different concepts are connected to the same core invariants, situations and symbolic representations. For example, he distinguished between the conceptual field of additive reasoning and the field of multiplicative reasoning. Although there are connections between these two domains of reasoning, Vergnaud's view was that the differences between them are important enough to require that children's understanding in these two domains must be analysed separately. We will use additive reasoning as an example to illustrate our discussion of mathematical development.

2.3 Understanding addition

In everyday life addition and subtraction may appear to be two distinct operations. This is to some extent justifiable because there are situations in which addition can be understood without reference to subtraction – for example, when two groups of things are put together or when more things are added to a group of objects. However, a careful analysis of other addition problems shows that some problems can only be understood in relation to subtraction. Similarly, there are 'subtraction problems' that can only be understood in relation to addition. Try Activity 5 now.

Activity 5

Allow about 5 minutes

How difficult are these problems?

This activity will encourage you to reflect a little on the nature of addition problems, and in particular what makes some addition tasks difficult for young children.

Read the arithmetic problems presented below. They have different levels of difficulty for young children. Try to figure out which one is easier, which is more difficult and why.

Problem 1
John had some marbles. He played with a friend and won four marbles. Now he has nine. How many did he have before the game?

Problem 2
Mary had nine sweets. She gave four to her sister. How many does she have now?

Problem 3
Paul had nine buttons in his pocket. His pocket had a hole and some fell out. Now he has four buttons. How many buttons did he lose?

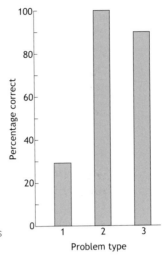

Comment

Look at Figure 7 and check whether your predictions were correct.

As you can see from Figure 7, the problem involving a relation between addition and subtraction (1) was the most difficult to solve. This shows the importance of understanding the relation between addition and subtraction in order to solve some addition and subtraction problems.

Figure 7 Percentage of first graders who solved problems 1 to 3 correctly (data from Riley *et al.*, 1983).

In view of the strong connection between addition and subtraction, it is now considered more appropriate to discuss the development of additive reasoning as a whole rather than the development of each of its parts (addition and subtraction) in isolation. Much research has been carried out comparing the difficulties that children face in solving addition and subtraction problems (Carpenter and Moser, 1982; Riley *et al.*, 1983). This research shows that children may know how to solve a particular numerical computation – that is, they may know, for example, that $9 - 4 = 5$, but may still not be able to solve problems that require just that computation. The understanding of addition and subtraction does not depend only on knowledge of number facts but also on the children's ability to analyse the situations (Brown, 1981; Vergnaud, 1982).

The simplest additive reasoning situations are related to questions in which elements are added to or taken away from groups or 'sets' (referred to as *transformations*). A related and similarly easy type of problem has to do with *joining* or *separating* two sets and asking about the results of this union/separation, for example 'In a family there are three girls and two boys. How many children are there altogether?' Problems that involve the *comparison* of two sets, like 'Mary has five books; Tom has three books; how many more books does Mary have than Tom?' are rather more difficult.

The analysis of the situation described in the problem is not sufficient to characterize its level of difficulty. The information that is unknown is also important. For example, a transformation problem is very easy when the information to be calculated is the result of the transformation (e.g. in Problem 2 of Activity 5, the calculation is '$9 - 4 = ?$'). In this case, the action in the story and the operation to solve the problem are directly related: a transformation that *increases* the number will be solved by *addition*, and one that *decreases* the number will be solved by *subtraction*.

In contrast, when the initial situation is unknown and must be calculated on the basis of information about the transformation and its end result (for example, in

Problem 1 in Activity 5, the calculation is '? + 4 = 9'), the relationship between the action and the operation is inverse: if the action in the problem *increases* the quantity, the operation needed to solve it is a *subtraction*. Inverse problems are significantly more difficult than direct problems.

Representation of inversion problems

Bryant *et al.* (1999) have shown that children's understanding of the inverse relation between addition and subtraction should not be treated as an all-or-nothing phenomenon. That is, the situations in which questions are presented to children have an important effect on whether the children succeed in using the principle of inversion to solve the problem. If the situation allows the child to draw on other and easier logical principles, the problem becomes easier. If the situation requires that the child use the principle of inversion together with another difficult logical principle, the problem becomes more difficult.

In one group of problems, Bryant *et al.* (1999) asked the children questions such as 'What is nine plus seven minus seven?' As the problem was presented, the experimenter acted out the operations by adding seven blocks to a row of nine blocks, and then removing the *same* seven blocks from the row. The set of nine blocks was covered with a cloth, to prevent the children from simply counting the total number of blocks in front of them. The rate of immediate success (that is, answering without delay, which indicates that they were not counting) was 80 per cent for 5 year olds and 90 per cent for 6 year olds. Thus these trials, which were termed by Bryant *et al.* 'inversion with identity', were quite simple. In contrast, when the same question was presented in the absence of support from identity – for example, by adding the blocks to one side of the row and subtracting them from the other side – the rate of success decreased significantly.

Showing understanding through counting strategies

Children can also be observed showing an implicit awareness of principles of addition in their choice of counting strategies. For example, when young children solve problems, they often model the relationships in the problem with concrete objects, like their own fingers. For example, they may solve the problem 'Mary had four sweets; she was given three more by her Granny; how many does she have now?' by lifting up four fingers, then lifting up three fingers, and then *counting them all*. This procedure, although correct, is inefficient. The children could simply lift up three fingers and *count on* from five (that is, from the first number after four). Groen and Resnick (1977) have shown that children do not have to be taught how to count on in order to improve their efficiency. They can discover this improvement by themselves in the course of solving a large number of addition problems.

Groen and Resnick worked with five pre-school children (average age 4 years and 10 months) and started out by teaching them to solve addition problems by representing each number to be added with a set of blocks and then counting all the blocks together. The children were then asked to solve a large number of problems and their procedures were observed. Children not only invented the new procedure of counting on, instead of counting all, but also produced a more efficient procedure, which the researchers termed *'counting on from larger'*. In this latter case, if the first addend happened to be smaller than the second, instead of representing the first number and counting on, children represented the second and then counted on, changing the problem (for example, 2 + 6 was solved as if it read 6 + 2).

As they used this more efficient solution, the children implicitly relied on the property of *commutativity* of addition. This states that the order of the values to be totalled does not alter the sum (i.e. 2 + 6 = 6 + 2). This does not mean that the children could necessarily explain the property of commutativity but they showed awareness of it in their reasoning. Vergnaud (1982) has termed such use of mathematical properties 'theorems in action'. The analysis of children's theorems in action as they solve problems can clearly enrich our understanding of their mathematical knowledge.

2.4 Cultural practices: oral versus written arithmetic

The use of blocks, strokes on paper, or fingers (termed 'manipulatives') to solve computation problems is not part of Western cultural practices today, although it is part of culturally transmitted calculation procedures in countries where the abacus is used.

Western cultures tend to transmit two other arithmetic practices, oral and written arithmetic, with different degrees of emphasis on the transmission of oral arithmetic. Oral arithmetic is often observed in connection with the manipulation of money. When people count money, they are actually carrying out additions that correspond to the values of the notes and coins. Change in shops is often checked by counting up from the value spent, as the coins and notes are placed into the hand of the buyer.

Nunes *et al.* (1993) studied the uses of oral and written arithmetic practices in Brazil. Oral arithmetic is more frequent in everyday settings, outside school, where people are unlikely to turn to paper and pencil or even calculators. For people engaged in the informal economy in settings like street markets, oral arithmetic is the rule rather than the exception. Written arithmetic, in contrast, is the preferred form of problem solving and calculation for school purposes. It is preferred because it offers a formal representation of the problem and because it leaves a trace so that the teacher can see later on how the problem was solved. These two *cultural practices,* oral and written arithmetic, may be more or less known by anyone. They have been described in countries as diverse as the United States and the Ivory Coast (Ginsburg *et al.,* 1981), Liberia (Reed and Lave, 1981), and Brazil (Nunes *et al.,* 1993).

Carraher *et al.* (1985) obtained oral protocols (verbalizations of how they solved problems) from young street vendors in Brazil. The five youngsters who participated in this study were interviewed in two situations: (1) in the streets, where they worked as street vendors, and (2) in a school-like situation, where they answered questions about story problems and arithmetic computations. In the streets they relied exclusively on oral arithmetic. They were very successful and answered correctly 98 per cent of the problems. In the school-like situation they relied mostly on written procedures, which proved much less efficient: their rate of correct responses was 74 per cent to word problems and 37 per cent to computation exercises.

The comparison between their successful performance in the streets and their rather high rate of failure when solving computation exercises suggests that symbolic systems are not merely accessories to people's reasoning. They *mediate* complex reasoning. In other words they are part of the reasoning process and as such change the nature of the activity by their use (Luria, 1979). In a later study, Nunes *et al.* (1993) analysed the influence of symbolic systems not only on the rates of correct and incorrect responses but also on the size of the errors made by children when using either oral or written arithmetic. Three different error bands were defined for this comparison: errors that fell within 10 per cent of the value of the correct answer (for example, between 18 and 22 if the correct response to the problem was 20); errors that were larger than 10 per cent but did not differ by more than 20 per cent from the correct answer; and errors that differed from the correct answer by more than 20 per cent. The percentages of correct responses and errors in each error band for oral and written addition and subtraction are presented in Figure 8. The figure clearly shows that written arithmetic led to larger errors, a tendency that was supported by a statistical analysis of the association between type of strategy used in solving the problem (oral versus written) and error band.

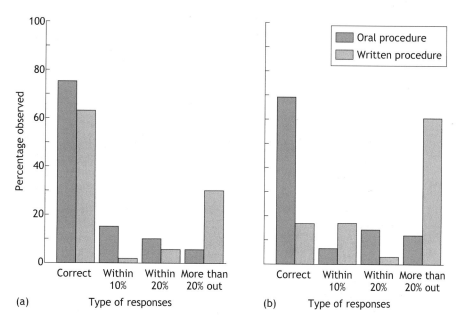

Figure 8   The percentage of correct responses and errors for oral and written addition and subtraction (data from Nunes *et al.*, 1993, p. 47). (a) Percentage of correct responses and of errors within each error band in addition problems. (b) Percentage of correct responses and of errors within each error band in subtraction problems.

Qualitative analyses of oral and written arithmetic also indicated another important difference between these two cultural practices. In oral arithmetic, the children seemed to keep the meaning of the problem in mind. For example, in the division problem below, the boy clearly keeps in mind the fact that he is trying to figure out how many marbles each of the five children will get:

Child: F. Condition: Word problem. Computation: 75 ÷ 5.

F: If you give ten marbles to each (child), that's fifty. There are twenty-five left over. To distribute to five boys, twenty-five, that's hard *(Experimenter: That's a hard one.)* That's five more for each. Fifteen each.

(from Nunes *et al.*, 1993, p. 43)

The references to marbles and children are clear throughout the problem solving procedure. In contrast, in written arithmetic, references to the problem and even to the relative values of digits are set aside. For example, when solving in written arithmetic the same computation, 75 divided by 5, the *digit* '7' is spoken of as 'seven', not seventy, which would take into account its relative value. This loss of meaning in written arithmetic is probably one of the reasons for children's acceptance of responses to computations that would seem, under other circumstances, unacceptable, as illustrated by this example:

Child: Ev. Condition: Computation exercise. Computation: 100 ÷ 4.

[After attempting unsuccessfully to solve the exercise on paper, Ev. claimed that it was impossible. She first attempted to divide 1 by 4, which she decided was not possible, then to divide 0 by 4, and finally gave up. The examiner asked for a justification.]

Ev: See, in my head I can do it. One hundred divided by four is twenty-five. Divide by two, that's fifty. Then divide again by two, that's twenty-five. *(She proceeded here by factoring; two successive divisions by 2 replace the given division by 4.)*

(from Nunes *et al.*, 1993, p. 43)

Such examples illustrate the relative difficulty of written arithmetic for these children. This is further illustrated by a study conducted by Nunes (1993) described in Research summary 1.

RESEARCH SUMMARY I

Brazilian children's oral and written problem solving

This study by Nunes (1993) aimed to look at the influence of the mode of representation used, either oral or written, on the rate of correct responses in solving problems with negative numbers. The problems were about a farmer's profits and losses with his crops during a season. Three pieces of information were involved:

(a) his situation at the beginning of the season, when he could either have some savings or be in debt;

(b) the results of his dealings in each of two crops, which could be a profit or a loss; and

(c) his situation at the end of the season.

The participants in the study were distributed randomly to either an oral or a written condition of solution – that is, either they were not given paper and a pencil and had to solve the problem in their heads or they were asked to write the information down first and then solve the problem.

Oral practices resulted in significantly higher percentages of correct responses. Especially informative was the performance of some children who had been assigned to the written condition. They often made mistakes when solving the problem but then, when attempting to explain their answer orally, realized their mistake and clearly demonstrated their competence in understanding the cancellation of profits and debts. One such example is presented below. It seems that the boy was limited by a poorly learned written practice but, given the opportunity to think without having to manipulate the written symbols, he was well able to make the appropriate inferences about positive and negative numbers.

Problem: Seu Pedro (the farmer's name) started the season with a debt of 10 cruzados (Brazilian currency at the time). He planted manioc and beans. He gained 10 on the manioc and 20 on the beans. What was his situation at the end of the season?

JC: (*19 years old, sixth-grader, assigned to the written condition*) wrote line 1 without indicating whether the number was positive or negative, and line 3 without a sign. Added all the numbers, obtaining 40, which was written on line 4.

Interviewer (I): Was that a profit or a debt?

JC: Profit. No, it's not that. I can't do it on paper.

I: Why?

JC: He had a profit of 10, paid the 10 he owed. Then he still has his profit from the beans, he has 20.

(adapted from Nunes, 1993, p. 69)

Activity 6   *Comparing oral and written arithmetic*

Allow about
5 minutes

This activity will encourage you to reflect on the key differences between oral and written arithmetic for these children, and thereby identify what kinds of factors might increase the ease or the difficulty of learning mathematics in school.

Consider the examples of oral and written arithmetic above and the account given in Research summary 1. Why do you think that the children find oral arithmetic easier than written arithmetic?

Comment

One reason why oral arithmetic practices appear to be more successful for children than written forms of mathematical problem solving may be because this form of reasoning appears to retain the 'human sense' of the problem. The problem retains its everyday, practical meaning and is thought about with reference to quantities. However, by presenting the problem on paper, its human sense is lost. Moreover, the process of translating the elements of the problem into correct mathematical notation also presents the children with an additional step in which errors and confusions can be introduced.

2.5 Different types of number

The preceding discussion points to a difficulty in coping with symbolic ways of representing mathematical concepts and problems, as is the case when children are presented with mathematical notation. While it would seem true that children do experience difficulties in becoming competent at laying out and solving mathematical problems in this way, other more concrete forms of representation are not necessarily unproblematic. This point is well illustrated by one area of mathematical understanding that children find especially difficult to grasp: that of fractions.

The step from understanding integers (whole numbers) to understanding fractions has been described as a major conceptual shift by mathematics educators (Behr *et al.*, 1983; Kieren, 1988) and psychologists alike (Inhelder and Piaget, 1958; Gelman and Meck, 1992). Integers are a much more common part of everyday experience than fractions are. Dealing with money, time and measurement, for example, necessarily involves the use of integers. Typically, fractions are avoided: with the exception of a half and a quarter, fractions are unusual in everyday life. A penny is a fraction of a pound but 15 p is not usually thought of as 15 hundredths of a pound. Pence are thought of as whole numbers and 100 pence are thought of as forming another whole number, a pound. The properties of operations with fractions tend to elude many adults and, not surprisingly, are also difficult for children.

One solution to this apparent difficulty might be to represent the concepts in a concrete way, by showing slices of pizza or cake, for example. However, studies show that this simple representational device, like all forms of representation, affects the children's understanding of the concept. Piaget *et al.* (1960) cut two equal pretend cakes (cardboard rectangles) into halves, cutting one along the height (resulting in two smaller rectangles) and the other along the diagonal (resulting in two triangles). They ensured that the children realized that the two parts of each cake were of the same size. They then asked the children: if one child ate one of the rectangular parts and another child ate one of the triangular parts, would they be eating the same amount of cake?

If the children understood the idea of half as the result of an exact division into two, they should conclude that halves of two equal wholes indicate the same amount irrespective of their appearance. However, children appeared to judge the parts on their appearance and did not rely on the underlying logic of 'dividing the whole'. In a recent study (Nunes *et al.*, 2002), we confirmed Piaget's results using a paper-and-pencil task: 45 per cent of the Year 4 children (aged about 8 years) and 20 per cent of the Year 5 children (aged about 9 years) did not recognize that the two different looking halves were equivalent amounts of cake. For concrete representations to be successful, there must be visual similarity across each of the 'portions' of the whole.

Representing fractions through conventional notation does not appear to make the task any easier. Children have a great deal of difficulty realizing that $\frac{1}{8}$ is a smaller number than $\frac{1}{6}$. Ordering fractions in this way is much more difficult for them than ordering whole numbers. By the age of 8 or 9, children have no difficulty at all in ordering numbers up to 100 or 1,000 by their size or indicating the place of a whole number in a number line. In contrast, Kerslake (1986) found that only one of fifteen youngsters in the age range 12–14 could correctly place $\frac{2}{3}$ on a number line. Kerslake's study was carried out with a small sample, but the results are in line with other research. Mack (1993) reports that the vast majority of her sample of 12 year olds in the United States indicated that $\frac{1}{6}$ was a smaller fraction than $\frac{1}{8}$ because 6 is smaller than 8. However, Mack reports that this was a difficulty observed only when the youngsters were presented with the problems symbolically. If asked to imagine that a pizza was divided into six pieces and an identical pizza was divided into eight pieces, and then to indicate which pieces would be larger, those obtained from the first or the second pizza, the youngsters had no difficulty in giving the correct answer.

Our recent investigations bring support to these results. We presented 142 youngsters in the age range 8 to 10 years with two comparable problems about fractions. In one problem, the youngsters were told that two boys would share fairly one pie and three girls would share fairly an identical pie. Most of the youngsters correctly indicated that each boy would receive more pie than each girl, with rates of correct response varying from 89–96 per cent between the 8 and the 10 year olds. When the youngsters were asked to compare the fractions $\frac{1}{2}$ and , the rate of correct responses dropped to 11 per cent, 31 per cent and 59 per cent, respectively, for the 8, 9 and 10 year olds. These results suggest that the way in which number problems are represented is another powerful influence on the solutions that children will arrive at.

Summary of Section 2

- Piaget's theory proposed that mathematical understanding develops through children's thinking about their actions and experiences. He focused on the logical principles involved in a problem and did not consider how other factors might influence thinking. Further developments have complemented Piagetian theory by considering these factors.
- Building on Piaget's theory, Vergnaud produced a theory of conceptual development that analysed children's understanding of the logical aspects of a concept, as well as their understanding of the situations in which these concepts are used and the symbolic representations that they use during problem solving.
- Strategies used in solving additive reasoning problems can rely on different ways of representing the problem (with blocks or fingers, with oral numbers, with written numbers); these representations affect children's success with additive problems because they mediate children's understanding of the problem to be solved.
- The step from understanding integers to understanding fractions is a major one in the development of mathematical knowledge. Children's ability to understand the equivalence of fractions, to order fractions by magnitude, and to operate with fractions is achieved much later than the same abilities in the domain of whole numbers, and can be facilitated by presenting problems in meaningful situations even if these are only imagined.

3 The development of scientific reasoning

So far you have seen how the study of children's mathematical development has demonstrated that (1) the *logical aspects* of a concept (2) the *situations* that give meaning to a concept and (3) the way that a problem is *represented* mediate children's understanding of mathematics and consequently affect their success. These three aspects of concepts are also major determinants in children's asquisition of scientific concepts. However, there is an important difference in children's understanding of mathematics and science. Children's everyday experiences with mathematical concepts and representations set them on the right track to understanding concepts in mathematics. In contrast, children's everyday experiences in their environment often conflict with their learned knowledge of scientific concepts. This section discusses obstacles that children face when their everyday conception of the world conflicts with their scientific ideas.

3.1 Living in the physical world and understanding physics

Our actions in everyday life require that the nature of the physical world is taken into account. In order to balance on a bicycle or to throw a dart at a particular spot, physical forces must in some sense be understood and overcome. However, how much do we accomplish without understanding? Try Activity 7.

Activity 7   *Assumptions about the physical world*

Allow about   *This activity illustrates that it may be possible to show an implicit appreciation of principles relating to*
5 minutes   *physics, without being able to demonstrate an explicit awareness of them.*

Find a room or other open space and place a box or bin in the centre. Make a paper ball or find a similar object. Now move quickly past the box and drop the ball into it as you pass by. Can you do it?

Now, *imagine* you are running across a room and want to drop (not throw) the ball into the box. Where should you be when you drop the ball in order for it to go into the box? Look at Figure 9 and choose which picture correctly represents where you should be when you drop the ball.

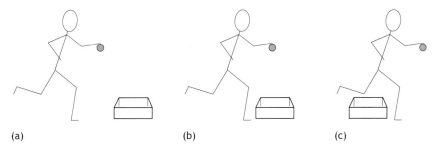

Figure 9   Where should you drop the ball if you want it to fall into the box?

(a)   (b)   (c)

Comment

You should find that the physical task is quite easy. However, it is likely that you have a wrong idea of where you needed to be to get the ball in the box. The correct answer is to release the ball *before* you get to the box (picture a). Although you may have found the question difficult to answer because it demands an explicit awareness of the physical forces acting on the ball, intuitively you knew when to release the ball when you were required to do so for real.

The task you tried in Activity 7 was studied by McClosky *et al.* (1980), who asked college students in physics and other students to say where they should drop the ball from if they were running across a room and wanted to make sure it landed in the box. The students were asked to answer by choosing the correct picture from a set of three similar to the ones in Figure 9.

Physics students were significantly more accurate in answering this question although, as McClosky and his colleagues suggested, they were unlikely to be more successful in actually dropping the ball into the basket. Whereas 73 per cent of the physics students chose the picture in which the stick figure dropped the ball before reaching the target, only 13 per cent of the non-physics students made this correct choice. Among the physics students, the answers were divided between the correct choice and the picture where the ball was dropped directly above the box (27 per cent of the physics students chose this alternative). In contrast, 80 per cent of the non-physics students chose the picture of the stick figure dropping the ball directly over the target and there were also choices in which the ball was dropped after the figure had already run past the box (7 per cent). These results seem to indicate that physics students were thinking about the action differently from the non-physics students with respect to force and motion. The physics students took into account the fact that the ball was already in motion when carried across the room by the running stick figure and thought of its path as it was dropped as the result of this initial force and direction plus the effect of gravity, whereas the non-physics students disregarded the motion of the ball while it was in the stick figure's hand, and thought only about gravity.

This illustrates a key point about understanding scientific concepts: while people can operate successfully within the physical world, they often do so without a genuine understanding of the physical principles that underpin it. Scientific learning is often a challenge to everyday understanding of cause and effect.

3.2 Learning science in the classroom

There are many difficulties involved in learning scientific concepts and making them into ways of thinking about the world. One of the difficulties in learning science is in making distinctions that would not ordinarily be made in everyday life, such as the distinction between temperature and heat. Although the temperature of two ice cubes is the same, even if one ice cube is twice the size of the other, the effect that they have in cooling a drink is different. Many students think that the larger ice cube is actually colder than the smaller one, perhaps as a consequence of the fact that they have different effects in cooling a drink (Erickson and Tiberghien, 1985). Similarly, the temperature of boiling water is the same regardless of the amount of water but different amounts of water will transfer different amounts of heat to the surroundings, and will cool at different rates. Perhaps as a result of this experience, pupils tend to think that if there is more boiling water, the temperature of the water will be higher. Thus they do not distinguish between heat and temperature, even though this distinction is important in physics.

A second difficulty in learning scientific concepts is that they often require reasoning about non-perceptible aspects of the physical world, and this may be another source of difficulty for students. It has been argued by di Sessa (1993) that children's first ideas about the physical world are based on what they perceive in their everyday experiences with physical objects. The difficulties caused by this reliance on immediate perceptual experience are most easily exemplified by the studies on pupils' ideas about the particulate nature of matter. People deal in everyday life with a world that is continuous, in which objects are solid and undivided. Yet, to understand many of the changes they observe in the world, it is necessary to develop a way of thinking that describes solid objects as bundles of 'particles', 'molecules', or 'atoms' – that is, discontinuous elements that are somehow kept together.

Piaget and Inhelder (1974) were pioneers in the investigation of children's understanding of the particulate nature of matter. They set out a pattern of investigation by pointing out that it is when children have to understand change that they come to 'invent' an atomic theory about the world. Piaget and Inhelder asked children to explain what happened to sugar when it was put into water and then stirred. Whereas the younger children seemed to believe that the sugar somehow disappeared, those at the ages of 11–13 were aware of the fact that if the taste of sugar remained in the water, then the sugar itself must still be present in some form. This permanence of a property of sugar – its taste – contradicted the apparent disappearance of sugar from the viewpoint of the older children. In order to eliminate the contradiction between the disappearance of sugar and the preservation of one of its properties – the sweet taste – the older children 'invented' an atomic theory about physical quantities.

Many studies have refined Piaget's original ideas about children's understanding of the particulate nature of matter. Driver *et al.* (1985) and Hesse and Anderson (1992), for example, studied other chemical transformations such as combustion (what happens when wood is burned?) and oxidation (rusting and cleaning bits of iron) and also investigated pupils' conceptions when they observed other changes of state, such as evaporation. An example of the type of responses observed by Driver *et al.* (1985) is presented in Figure 10, where one child is shown attempting to illustrate what happens to particles in each of the three states of matter: solid, liquid and gas. The figure illustrates the difficulty of moving from a world of observables to a conceptual world of non-observed entities. It also illustrates children's own conceptions of changes of state rather than taught solutions.

A third type of difficulty lies in the everyday world view of things as stable, with properties that are part of the very matter of which they are made. As discussed earlier, Piaget and his colleagues hypothesized that children develop a theory about the particulate nature of matter in their attempt to explain the sweetness of the water after the disappearance of sugar: if a property of sugar, sweetness,

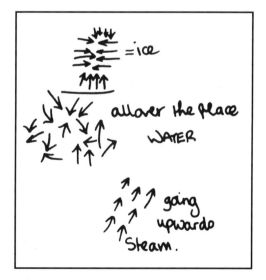

Figure 10 A drawing of an 11 year old's representation of the three states of matter: solid, liquid and gas (Driver et al., 1985, p. 145).

still exists in water, then the sugar must still be there. A conception of the world that only deals in terms of matter and its properties leaves a range of phenomena, such as light, heat and electrical current, unexplained. Chi and her colleagues (Chi and Slotta, 1993; Chi, 1997) pointed out that not all scientific ideas are based on the notion of matter: many important scientific ideas are based on the notion of processes. These researchers suggest that the main obstacle to children's understanding of these scientific ideas is that they need to switch categories, from matter to processes.

Examples of this kind of difficulty are easy to find (Reiner *et al.*, 2000). For example, children may have a natural tendency to treat heat and temperature as substances with the essential property of hotness. Certainly young children find it hard to think of heat and cold as existing independently of objects and thus treat temperature as a property of objects. Similarly, Clement (1982) has provided evidence that young children treat forces as properties of objects. In the case of inanimate objects, children see forces as acquired properties that cause movement; and think that objects stop when this acquired property dissipates in the environment (Vosniadou *et al.*, 2001).

A fourth obstacle to the development of scientific thinking is the fact that many scientific concepts represent *intensive* rather than *extensive* quantities. Extensive quantities, such as height and weight, are measured through the simple application of a unit of measurement that is repeated until the number of units completely describes the quantity. For example, when length is measured in centimetres, the value that is obtained by this measurement is equivalent to the number of times 1 cm – that is the unit – can be fitted onto the object measured. In contrast, intensive quantities, which include density, speed and force, are measured through a ratio between two other measures. So, density is measured as a ratio of mass to volume. Similarly, speed involves a relation between distance and time, and force involves a relation between mass and acceleration.

An everyday intensive quantity is taste. For example, how sweet a glass of lemon juice will taste depends on how much sugar you add to the lemon juice and how much lemon juice there is in the glass. There is a direct relation between the amount of sugar and the sweetness: the more sugar you add, the sweeter the lemon juice will taste. There is also an inverse relation between the amount of lemon juice and sweetness: the more lemon juice there is in the glass, the less sweet it will taste. The results of the investigation reported in Research summary 2 illustrate the difficulty of inverse relations for children.

Intensive quantities

Nunes *et al.* (2002) conducted an investigation of children's understanding of inverse relations. The children (142 in total) were shown pictures of glasses of lemon juice, as those presented in Figure 11.

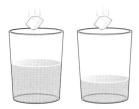

Figure 11   The lemon juice puzzle.

The children were asked first whether they thought that the lemon juice would taste the same in the two glasses. Those children who thought that the taste would be different were then asked to say which would taste sweeter. The percentages of correct responses in Table 1 refer to the total number of children by age for both questions.

Table 1   Percentage of children who correctly responded to the questions about the relative sweetness of the two glasses of juice

	Age in years		
	7	8	9
Will the lemon juice in the two glasses taste the same or different?	44%	70%	60%
If the child said different: which one will taste sweeter?	44%	40%	51%

Source: adapted from Nunes et al., 2002.

Two results should be pointed out from the data in Table 1. First, there were no significant differences between the age groups; so the small improvement in percentages with age could be due to chance. Thus the problem is difficult even for children at age 9. Second, quite a few 8 year olds realized that the taste would be different in the two glasses but made the mistake of thinking that the more juice, the sweeter it would taste. Rather than thinking of an inverse relation, they assumed that the amount of juice and the amount of sweetness would be directly related. In fact, when children are asked to respond to situations where all that matters is the variable that is directly related to the intensive quantity, their performance is perfect. When we asked them to say which lemon juice would taste sweeter when the two glasses had the same amount of juice and different amounts of sugar, the rate of correct responses was close to 100 per cent. These results were replicated in an earlier study by Desli (unpublished).

The intensive quantities that occur in science are usually more complex than those encountered in everyday life because, as we showed earlier, they require distinctions that people do not make in everyday life. It is likely that science teaching involving intensive quantities could profit from the use of analogies with simpler intensive quantities used in everyday life, in the same way that mathematics teaching seems to profit from the use of everyday situations as models for teaching about mathematical concepts and operations. This is a reasonable hypothesis, but further research is needed to test it.

3.3 Scientific principles: parsimony and consistency

By the time that students begin to learn about science in school they already have a great deal of knowledge about the world. However, this knowledge often differs in important respects from the way of understanding the world that teachers aim to convey. Everyday concepts developed about the world and scientific concepts also have different formal characteristics. Whereas scientists strive to explain the largest number of phenomena with the smallest possible set of assumptions, a principle known as *parsimony*, in everyday life people do not think according to this principle.

This is illustrated by the following example. In everyday life you may have one set of explanations that account for why two different objects of the same volume have two different weights. You may have another explanation for the observation that one of them floats and the other one sinks when placed in water. You do not necessarily seek to reduce these two observations to a common principle. In science both observations will be reduced to the same concept, that of density.

> ### Comment
>
> Vygotsky (1978) attempted to explain this difference between everyday and scientific concepts by suggesting that people learn scientific concepts by going from the general to the particular (from rules, to specific instances of that rule), but that everyday concepts are learned by going from the particular (specific instances of an event) to the general (generating the rule). Thus in school children begin learning about density with the rule that in order to compare the density of two materials they must keep their volume the same; then they learn the rule that objects with a mass that is greater than that of an equivalent volume of water will be of greater density and thus will sink. In contrast people do not start from rules in everyday life: they attempt to make generalizations on the basis of sets of observations. Such generalizations will be limited by their experiences, which may not provide the basis for the most parsimonious rule.

A second formal difference is that scientists strive for *consistency* and are (or should be) willing to reject their explanations if they are inconsistent with available evidence or with other valid theories. In everyday life people may not be so ready to use consistency as a criterion for validating their knowledge. For example, Hatano (1993) has observed that young children can respond correctly to some questions about heat, but give different answers to other problems which are inconsistent with their earlier responses. If asked what they would do in order to cool the water in a bath, even young children will say that they would add cold water to it and thereby treat the resulting temperature in the bath as being somewhere between that of the hot and the cold water. However, when asked what is the temperature of the water in a container into which one litre of water at the temperature of 60 degrees and one litre of water at the temperature of 20 degrees were poured, the most frequent answer given by young pupils is '80 degrees'. Whereas in the first problem about the temperature of the water in the bath the resulting temperature is intermediate between hot and cold, in the science classroom problem the resulting temperature is viewed as the sum of the temperature in the two volumes of water. On the basis of a different set of examples, di Sessa (1993) also argued that children's conceptions lack the coherence of scientific theories. However, there is disagreement on this issue. Some researchers suggest that children's theories are coherent even though they are less powerful than adults' theories (Posner *et al.*, 1982).

Summary of Section 3

- The physicist's conception of the world differs from that of the child.
- Some of the difficulties involved in applying learned scientific concepts to everyday ways of thinking about the world result from having to make distinctions that people would not ordinarily need to make. Other hurdles come from the fact that scientific concepts often require reasoning about non-perceptible aspects of the physical world.
- Children may experience difficulty in learning about scientific concepts because the knowledge and conceptions they already have conflict with the concepts being introduced by the teacher. One of the generic differences between naive conceptions and scientific views is that children often explain events in everyday life by referring to properties of objects, related to their matter, whereas the scientific view treats the same phenomenon as a process.
- Many scientific concepts represent *intensive*, rather than *extensive*, quantities. Intensive quantities are measured through a ratio between two other measures, whereas extensive quantities are measured directly, through the repeated application of a unit to the dimension that is being measured. Intensive quantities have different properties from extensive quantities and involve reasoning about inverse relations.
- Scientists operate on the principle of *parsimony*, that is explaining the largest number of phenomena with the smallest set of assumptions. Vygotsky suggests that reasoning can be more parsimonious when concepts are acquired from the general to the particular than when they are acquired from the particular to the general. Scientists also strive for *consistency*. This is not necessary in everyday life.

4 Cognitive development and the acquisition of mathematical and scientific principles

So far we have discussed some of the features of children's mathematical and scientific understanding. This discussion has highlighted in particular the way in which their understanding is mediated by their experiences and everyday notions of mathematical and scientific principles. This frequently conflicts with the more formal ways of understanding and representing the concepts that children encounter in school.

In this section we will consider two practical questions that stem from these observations and from Piaget's theory of cognitive development. The first of these is to do with whether children who have achieved formal operations are more successful at learning scientific and mathematical concepts than those who have not. A second question of importance is 'What factors enable younger children to change their way of thinking?' These questions are significant as they are relevant to how teachers might attempt to teach children to acquire mathematical and scientific understanding successfully.

4.1 Formal operations and scientific understanding

Inhelder and Piaget (1958), once again, were the pioneers in the investigation of children's ability to reason in a scientific way, and suggested that the understanding of scientific methods only develops in adolescence as part of the formal operational stage of development. Two different questions can be asked about the development of formal operations and the acquisition of scientific concepts. One is whether it is necessary or advantageous for adolescents to understand scientific reasoning in order to master the scientific and mathematical concepts taught in school. The second is whether, once scientific reasoning has developed, young people will be able as a result to understand better the scientific concepts taught in school.

Inhelder and Piaget argued that secondary school students need to develop the appropriate cognitive structures before they can master scientific concepts, such as density, or mathematical concepts, such as inverse relations (Inhelder and Piaget, 1958). They also made the interesting claim that youngsters could actually discover many scientific concepts on their own after the appropriate cognitive structures had developed. They expected the 'power of reasoning' to generalize to all contexts, once it had developed.

Relatively little research has been done to test these predictions but the limited evidence available so far seems to support the first part of their assumptions but not the second. A recent study by Piburn (1990) correlated students' success in their science courses with their performance in a test of *propositional reasoning* (that is, a test of their ability to reason about if–then propositions). A significant correlation was found between students' performance in the task of propositional reasoning and their grade in science. An item analysis indicated that this correlation relied on those items which related to reasoning that Inhelder and Piaget expected to develop only at the level of formal operations, whereas those that can be solved at the concrete operational level were not related to success in science.

Activity 8   Understanding correlations

Allow about 5 minutes

This activity will help you to understand the importance of reflecting on the nature of the evidence that theoretical claims are based on.

What problems can you see in interpreting Piburn's results?

SG

Comment

Piburn's results cannot be used on their own to infer that propositional reasoning ability contributed to the students' attainment in science. This is because their grades and their propositional reasoning ability were obtained at the same point in time. While there may be a relationship it is not possible to identify the direction of that relationship: it could equally be the case that the students' science grades contributed to their propositional reasoning ability. To determine the direction of any relationships a longitudinal study is required, in which the science learners are tested for their propositional reasoning *before* they start the science course.

The second prediction from Inhelder and Piaget's theory is about the generalization of formal operational reasoning across contexts. The formal operational stage was conceived by Piaget (Piaget and Garcia, 1971) as a stage in which the operations of thought (such as propositional reasoning) become abstract and therefore independent of their content. This means, according to Piaget, that thinking can now function in a formal way, which makes it possible for children to learn about any scientific domain without the development of new operations of reasoning. This prediction about the generalization of the structures of thought has met a growing degree of scepticism.

Specifically with respect to propositional reasoning, much work has been carried out that indicates its susceptibility to influences from the content of the proposition. For example, Cheng and Holyoak (1985) and Girotto *et al.* (1988) looked at young people's reasoning about several types of if–then propositions. They have suggested that people reason about these propositions not in a formal, content-free way, as originally suggested by Piaget and his colleagues, but rather they rely on pragmatic schemas that involve both formal and content specific elements. For example, when the if–then proposition is a prohibition people are likely to make inferences that differ from those made when the proposition is a promise. Thus the content of a proposition has a clear influence on the inferences that are made even if the propositions have the same form. Activity 9 presents an example of the contrast between prohibitions and promises.

Activity 9

Allow about
5 minutes

Does the content of a proposition affect reasoning?

This activity will help you to see how the content of a proposition can affect the way that people reason about it, as they often rely on their everyday experiences to guide them to an appropriate conclusion.

Here are two types of if–then propositions: promises and prohibition/permissions.

1   If you mow the lawn, I will give you £5. You didn't mow the lawn. Do I give you £5?

2   If you drive a lorry, you must not drive through the city centre. You drive a car. Can you drive through the city centre?

In (1) what do you conclude?

In (2) what do you conclude?

Are there differences? Why?

Comment

In the first proposition, you probably concluded that you were not given £5 because you did not mow the lawn. Although this conclusion seems 'logical' based on your everyday experiences of promises like this one, in fact it is not the logical conclusion. Just because you did not do the task, it does not follow (in strict logical terms) that you will not be given £5. In fact, the proposition does not specify what will happen in this circumstance, only what will happen when you *do* mow the lawn. Similarly, in the second, prohibitive statement, you cannot 'logically' conclude that you can drive through the city centre. The proposition simply states that you cannot drive through the city centre if you are driving a lorry. Although your common sense tells you that you can *imply* that you are permitted because you are not explicitly prohibited ('they would have mentioned it if I was not!'), in fact you cannot come to that conclusion on the basis of the proposition alone. From these examples you can see that when reasoning about promises or prohibitions, people rely on their cultural knowledge to draw their conclusions, rather than on strict logical deduction.

4.2 Conceptual change in individuals

As you have seen, learning mathematics and science is not so much learning facts as learning ways of thinking. Conceptual definitions often sound like 'statements of facts' but they remain meaningless if the concepts do not become part of a way of thinking. It has also been emphasized that in order to learn science people often have to change the way they think in everyday life. For example, in order to understand even simple concepts such as heat and temperature, ways of thinking of temperature as a measure of heat must be abandoned and a distinction between 'temperature' and 'heat' must be learned. These changes in ways of thinking are referred to as *conceptual changes*. But how do conceptual changes happen? How do young people change their ways of thinking as they develop and as they learn in school?

Traditional instruction based on telling students how modern scientists think does not seem to be very successful. Students may learn the definitions, the formulae, the terminology, and yet still maintain their previous conceptions. This difficulty has been illustrated many times, for example, when instructed students are interviewed about heat and temperature or forces, as discussed earlier. It is often identified by teachers as a difficulty in applying the concepts learned in the classroom; students may be able to repeat a formula but fail to use the concept represented by the formula when they explain observed events.

Piaget suggested an interesting hypothesis relating to the process of cognitive change. Cognitive change was expected to result from the pupils' own intellectual activity. When confronted with a result that challenges their thinking – that is when faced with conflict – pupils realize that they need to think again about their own ways of solving problems, regardless of whether the problem is one in mathematics or in science. Conflict was hypothesized to bring about disequilibrium and would result in the setting off of *equilibration* processes that would ultimately produce cognitive change. For this reason, according to Piaget and his colleagues, in order for pupils to progress in their thinking they need to be actively engaged in solving problems that will challenge their current mode of reasoning.

SG

However, Piaget also pointed out that young children do not always discard their ideas in the face of contradictory evidence. They may actually discard the evidence and keep their theory. Activity 10 describes a science lesson where children aged about 6 were asked to observe whether objects floated or sank in water and later in the afternoon were interviewed about what they had learned in their science lesson.

Activity 10   *Do heavy things sink and light ones float?*

Allow about 10 minutes

This activity will encourage you to reflect on the problematic nature of supporting conceptual change in children.

Read the transcript below and note how Billy integrates the evidence that he collects (his observation of the floating carton) with his existing 'theory' that heavy things sink.

The first of the interactions was recorded during a science lesson in which children were asked to make predictions about whether some things would float or sink when put in a basin full of water. The second is an excerpt of an interview carried out with one of the pupils after the lesson.

TEACHER: You have to tell us what you've chosen (*to place in the water*).

BILLY: I've got a milk.

T: You've chosen a carton of a milk.

B: And it's a bit heavy.

T: Yeah!

B: And you can drink out of it and eh ...

T: What's it made from?

LOUISA: It's a carton.

T: It's a carton. What's a carton made from? ... Do you know what cartons are made from? Louisa?

(*Teacher addresses question to group before asking Louisa.*)

L: Cardboard.

T: What's going to happen to your milk?

B: Sinks.

(*Billy puts the carton in the water.*)

T: Oh! What's happened to it?

B: It floats.

T: It's bobbing about on the water. Isn't it? ...

Interview with Billy after lesson one:

INTERVIEWER: What can you remember about what you have just done? Can you tell me a little about what you have been doing?

BILLY: These are all the things that floated and these are all the things that sunk (*referring to chart composed during the lesson*).

I: Tell me a bit about them.

B: The carton floated.

I: Why did it float?

B: It was a bit light ... it's light ... because it's little and light.

Comment

What do you think of Billy's conclusion after the lesson: did he discard his explanation for why some things float and others sink? What does this imply about children's reaction to conflicting evidence? It would seem that Billy's theory that 'heavy things sink' remained intact, despite the 'heavy' milk carton floating. To account for this, he simply re-categorized the carton as 'light' in his explanation. In this way, Billy's theory remained unchanged – but his view of the evidence was altered.

4.3 Conceptual change as a social process

Piaget's hypothesis about how cognitive change progresses was later translated into a teaching approach now termed *discovery learning*. Discovery learning initially took what is now considered the 'lone learner' route. The teacher played the role of the selector of situations that challenged the pupils' reasoning; the pupils' peers had no real role in this process. However, subsequent research has revealed that interpersonal conflict, especially with peers, might play an important role in promoting cognitive change. This hypothesis, originally advanced by Perret-Clermont (1980) and Doise and Mugny (1984), has been investigated in many recent studies of science teaching and learning.

SG

Christine Howe and her colleagues, for example, have compared children's progress in understanding several types of science concepts when they are given the opportunity to observe relevant events either on their own or with peers. In one study, Howe *et al.* (1992) compared 8–12-year-old children's progress in understanding what influences motion down a slope. In order to ascertain the role of conflict in group work, they created two kinds of groups: one in which the children had dissimilar views according to a pre-test (the conflict group) and a second in which the children had similar views. They found support for the idea that children in the groups with dissimilar views progressed more after their training sessions than those who had been placed in groups with similar views. However, they found no evidence to support the idea that the children worked out their new conceptions during their group discussions, because progress was not actually observed in a post-test immediately after the sessions of group work but rather in a delayed post-test (that is, a second test of how the children understood motion down a slope which was given around 4 weeks after the group work).

In another study, Howe *et al.* (1991) set out to investigate whether the progress obtained through group work could be a function of the exchange of ideas during the group sessions. They investigated the progress made by 12–15-year-old pupils in understanding the path of falling objects, a topic that clearly involves conceptual difficulties, as seen earlier. In order to create groups with varying levels of dissimilarity in their initial conceptions, the pupils' predictions and explanations of the path of falling objects were assessed before they were engaged in group work. The group work sessions involved solving computer-presented problems, again about predicting and explaining the paths of falling objects. A post-test, given individually, assessed the progress made by pupils in their conceptions of what influenced the path of falling objects. It was expected that pairs of pupils who had more dissimilar conceptions would engage in more discussion, refer more to their explanations during their discussions, and subsequently show greater progress.

The results supported the idea that intellectual conflict and discussion play a role in cognitive change. Significant correlations were found between the level of dissimilarity between the children in the pair before the collaborative work and the number of references to explanatory factors during discussion, and also between the level of initial dissimilarity and later progress in explanations. In short, the results support the hypothesis that conflict and discussion with peers is related to progress in understanding concepts in science.

Comment

Although the work on peer collaboration can be seen as initially stemming from the Piagetian ideas about the processes of conflict and equilibration, much of the interest that currently surrounds peer collaboration in problem solving is motivated by other views of conceptual development. Within these other perspectives, motivated by researchers such as Vygotsky, Luria and Bruner, conceptual change is viewed as resulting not solely from the child's own activity but also from the child's interactions in a *social* world.

A new concept was developed by Vygotsky in order to address the social nature of cognitive change: the concept of the *zone of proximal development*. The zone of proximal development is the difference between what a child can accomplish in solving a problem working independently and what can be accomplished by the same child with adult help.

> More generally, the concept refers to an interactive system within which people work on a problem which at least one of them could not, alone, work on effectively. Cognitive change takes place within this zone, where the zone is considered *both in terms of an individual's developmental history and in terms of the support structure created by the other people and cultural tools in the setting.*
>
> (Newman *et al.*, 1989, p. 61, our italics)

The concept of the zone of proximal development originates within Vygotsky's theory which assumes that all higher psychological functions have socio-cultural origins. This theory is different from Piaget's. Piaget's concept of assimilation is replaced in Vygotsky's theory by 'appropriation'. This term refers to the taking on and use of 'cultural tools'. A cultural tool may be a physical resource, such as a computer, or a psychological one, such as language. These resources are referred to as 'cultural' tools, because their characteristics or physical properties tell us little about how they might be used. It is our culture, our social history, that 'explains' how to use them. Vygotsky suggested that children are also exposed to socially constructed systems of knowledge, which they begin to use without fully understanding them. However, it is by using them that children gain a better understanding of them. In this way, Vygotsky sees culture and society as providing children with the tools for learning and the knowledge to be learned about. Similarly, Vgyotsky sees learning as an interpersonal affair. Teachers have to guide children through the zone of proximal development by devising ways in which they and the children can function with two very different understandings of the task: the teacher's own, and the children's.

An example of such interactions is described by Newman *et al.* (1989). It consists of a lesson they devised with a teacher about different types of chemicals. The teacher initially told the pupils how certain types of chemicals turn different colours when mixed with an acid or a base. Children were then paired up to do the work and each pair received two chemicals and two indicators (acid or base). They were asked to mix the chemicals and the indicators and to record the four chemical reactions on a worksheet. However, young children have difficulty in being systematic about mixing chemicals and might have mixed the same ones twice, thereby losing important information. In order to prevent this, the teacher gave each child in a pair only one chemical to mix with the two indicators. Thus, although the children worked in pairs and recorded the four results, each child was only responsible for two mixtures.

The teacher and the children had different views of the lesson. The children had no knowledge of the sequence of the lesson: they became involved and interested in the chemical reactions. The teacher had a particular goal within the sequence of her teaching: the recording of the chemical reactions to be carried out by the children. She thus structured the activity so that the children could mix the chemicals, compare results, and discuss what they had seen without being unduly pressured by the planning of the mixing of chemicals. The planning of the experiment was 'off-loaded' by the teacher's assignment of chemicals (one to each child) so that they could (as a pair) effectively generate a full table of mixes and use the results to come to conclusions. This example illustrates how pupils were allowed to use some aspects of a system of knowledge without its full appreciation. Thus although the design of the experiment may have been beyond their level of cognitive development, they were still able to participate in a research activity, recording observations, comparing results, and trying to come to conclusions that would be relevant to the learning of chemical mixtures.

Activity 11   *How do children figure out what science is?*

Allow about
10 minutes

This activity will show you that children and adults have different ideas about what science is about, and encourage you to consider how these differences might be resolved.

Read the transcript below and consider the difference between a teacher's and some students' views of what science is. See if you can think of a way of introducing these students to the teacher's idea of what science is.

CAIN: What's science?

TEACHER: Oh, go on ... you said 'what's science?'

CAIN: What's science?

TEACHER: What's science? Does anybody have any ideas what science is? ... Marcia.

MARCIA: It's when ... you sit down and do your work.

TEACHER: Yeah! What sort of work is science? Daniel.

DANIEL: When you stay in your place.

TEACHER: When you stay in your place. Sarah.

SARAH: Number work.

TEACHER: Number work, is it? Something to do with numbers? Billy.

BILLY: Like when you work with the sand.

TEACHER: Like when you work with the sand. What sort of ... What sort of sand work is science work, because sometimes I get you to work with the sand for number, don't I?

BILLY: Em ...

TEACHER: What sort of things do I ask you to do of ... say ... if it was science and I asked you to go and work with the sand? What sort of things would you be doing?

CAIN: Measuring work.

TEACHER: Em ...

CAIN: I know.

TEACHER: Sh ... we have hands, don't we? *(Shushing Cain, who started the whole thing.)* Paul.

PAUL: Measuring how much sand.

TEACHER: That's more a number job, isn't it? Excuse me, Sarah. ... Jodie.

JODIE: Like when you put heavy things.

TEACHER: Em. Tara.

TARA: Adds up.

TEACHER: Adds up. Richard.

RICHARD: If you could see whether a thing was sinking or floating in the water.

TEACHER: Em, that's science, isn't it?

CAIN: Being quiet.

TEACHER: Tara.

TARA: Pushing the chairs in.

TEACHER: Science is sort of what we call investigating. When we're seeing what's happening ... you were going to say that were you, I thought you might be about to say that. When you think ... I wonder if such and such happens? I wonder what will happen if? Those are the sorts of science questions. I wonder ...

Comment

Working in the zone of proximal development means developing some common ground for understanding science as children gain experience under the teacher's guidance. The transcript is an illustration of just how difficult it is for children to gain an understanding of what science is. They participate in concrete activities that are not direct illustrations of what science is. The teacher's view of science is about asking questions and testing ideas in a systematic way. The children only understand science as a label that describes activities that they do in school. The teacher could orientate the children to her viewpoint by setting up a session such that the children have to generate some 'I wonder' questions for themselves which the teacher could guide them through answering.

Summary of Section 4

- There is some support for the idea that, as children's reasoning becomes more sophisticated, they may become better learners in science.
- There is little support, however, for the idea that young people reach a stage of formal operations where sophisticated forms of reasoning, such as propositional reasoning, are easily applied to any content.
- The search for what promotes cognitive changes in the development of mathematical and scientific concepts has generated at least three main hypotheses that are alternatives to the traditional way of teaching: *discovery learning*, in which children are active but work mostly on their own; *collaborative learning*, in which peers work together to solve problems; and the model of *learning as appropriation*, in which a system of knowledge is progressively mastered as the learner uses it effectively, although initially without a full appreciation of what the system does for him or her.

5 Conclusion

Mathematical and scientific conceptual development does not seem to be simply a question of learning facts or procedures. Both involve the achievement of new ways of thinking and reasoning in generative ways. But it is not enough to analyse the structures of reasoning, as Piaget originally proposed, in order to understand children's progress in mathematics and science. Children do not interact only with the physical environment and do not discover only by themselves the properties of actions and of objects. Societies have developed systems of representation and knowledge to which children are exposed both in school and out of school. Through their participation in social situations, where people use these knowledge systems, the children come to use this knowledge, even if they do not (at least initially) grasp it in the same way that adults do. Whilst exploring their ideas with peers or participating with adults in situations (such as experiments) which they themselves could not create, children become engaged in mathematical and scientific thinking. In this way they may be able to restructure their ways of reasoning and make progress.

However, theorists currently acknowledge that many reasoning problems make specific intellectual demands irrespective of any general level of reasoning ability. Fractions, for example, pose specific difficulties to children and adults alike, which no general theory of mathematical development deals with adequately. The distinction between properties and processes, like heat and light, is another case in point. It causes extraordinary and quite particular problems for children and many adults and, as for fractions, the distinction needs specific research and probably specific educational methods as well.

Current theories about mathematical and scientific development recognize that there are general ways in which children's intellects change as they grow older, but they also take into account the specific problems that arise when children have to add particular techniques or forms of knowledge to their repertoire. This new breed of theories also recognizes that children's ways of thinking about the world may change in particular ways as a result of finally mastering these new and quite difficult forms of knowledge (Vygotsky, 1978).

So while psychologists can recognize that children do move towards a general ability to represent their environment in increasingly abstract and organized ways by inferring rules based on their experiences of the world, often these initial hypotheses are problematic exactly because they are limited by the experiences that the children may have.

Further reading

Nunes, T., Schliemann, A. D. and Carraher, D. W. (1993) *Street Mathematics and School Mathematics,* Cambridge, Cambridge University Press.

Nunes, T. and Bryant, P. (1996) *Children Doing Mathematics,* Oxford, Blackwell.

Stavy, R. and Tirosh, D. (2000) *How Students (Mis-)Understand Science and Mathematics. Intuitive Rules,* New York, Teachers College Press.

References

Behr, M., Lesh, R. Post, T. R. and Silver, E. A. (1983) 'Rational number concepts', in Lesh, R. and Landau, M. (eds) *Acquisition of Mathematical Concepts and Processes,* pp. 91–126, New York, Academic Press.

Brown, M. (1981) 'Number operations', in Hart, K. M. (ed.) *Children's Understanding of Mathematics: 11–16,* pp. 23–46, London, John Murray.

Bryant, P., Christie, C. and Rendu, A. (1999) 'Children's understanding of the relation between addition and subtraction: inversion, identity and decomposition', *Journal of Experimental Child Psychology,* vol. 74, pp. 194–212.

Carpenter, T. P. and Moser, J. M. (1982) 'The development of addition and subtraction problem-solving skills', in Carpenter, T. P., Moser, J. M. and Romberg, T. A. (eds) *Addition and Subtraction: a cognitive perspective,* pp. 9–24, Hillsdale, NJ, Lawrence Erlbaum Associates.

Carraher, T. N., Carraher, D. W. and Schliemann, A. D. (1985) 'Mathematics in the streets and in schools', *British Journal of Developmental Psychology,* vol. 3, pp. 21–9.

Cheng, P. W. and Holyoak, K. J. (1985) 'Pragmatic reasoning schemas', *Cognitive Psychology,* vol. 18, pp. 293–328.

Chi, M. T. H. (1997) 'Creativity: shifting across ontological categories flexibly', in Ward, T. B., Smith, S. M. and Vaid, J. (eds) *Creative Thought: an investigation of conceptual structures and processes,* pp. 209–34, Washington, DC, American Psychological Association.

Chi, M. T. H. and Slotta, J. D. (1993) 'The ontological coherence of intuitive physics', *Cognition and Instruction,* vol. 10, pp. 249–60.

Clement, J. (1982) 'Students' preconceptions in introductory mechanics', *American Journal of Physics,* vol. 50, pp. 66–71.

Desli, D. (1999, unpublished) 'Children's understanding of intensive quantities', PhD thesis, Institute of Education, University of London.

di Sessa, A. (1993) 'Toward an epistemology of physics', *Cognition and Instruction,* vol. 10, pp. 105–225.

Doise, W. and Mugny, G. (1984) *The Social Development of the Intellect,* Oxford, Pergamon.

Driver, R., Guesne, E. and Tiberghien, A. (1985) 'Children's ideas and the learning of science', in Driver, R., Guesne, E. and Tiberghien, A. (eds) *Children's Ideas in Science,* pp. 145–69, Milton Keynes, Open University Press.

Erickson, G. and Tiberghien, A. (1985) 'Heat and temperature', in Driver, R., Guesne, E. and Tiberghien, A. (eds) *Children's Ideas in Science, pp.* pp. 52–84, Milton Keynes, Open University Press.

Gelman, R. and Meck, B. (1992) 'Early principles aid initial but not later conceptions of number', in Bideaud, J., Meljac, C. and Fishcher, J.-P. (eds) *Pathways to Number: children's developing numerical abilities,* pp. 171–89, Hillsdale, NJ, Lawrence Erlbaum Associates.

Ginsburg, H. P., Posner, J. K. and Russel, R. L. (1981) 'The development of mental addition as a function of schooling and culture', *Journal of Cross-cultural Psychology,* vol. 12, pp. 163–79.

Girotto, V., Light, P. H. and Colbourn, C. J. (1988) 'Pragmatic schemas and conditional reasoning in children', *Quarterly Journal of Experimental Psychology,* vol. 40, pp. 469–82.

Groen, G. J. and Resnick, L. B. (1977) 'Can pre-school children invent addition algorithms?', *Journal of Educational Psychology,* vol. 69, pp. 645–52.

Hatano, G. (1993) 'Children's concepts of heat and temperature', paper presented at SRCD Biennial Meeting, New Orleans, March 1993.

Hesse, J. J. and Anderson, C. W. (1992) 'Students' conceptions of chemical change', *Journal of Research in Science Teaching,* vol. 29, pp. 277–99.

Howe, C., Tolmie, A. and Anderson, A. (1991) 'Information technology and group work in physics', *Journal of Computer Assisted Learning,* vol. 7, pp. 133–43.

Howe, C., Tolmie, A. and Rodgers, C. (1992) 'The acquisition of conceptual knowledge in science by primary school children: group interaction and the understanding of motion down an incline', *British Journal of Developmental Psychology,* vol. 10, pp. 113–30.

Inhelder, B. and Piaget, J. (1958) *The Growth of Logical Thinking from Childhood to Adolescence,* London, Routledge.

Kerslake, D. (1986) *Fractions: Children's Strategies and Errors: a report of the strategies and errors in secondary mathematics project,* Windsor, NFER-Nelson.

Kieren, T. (1988) 'Personal knowledge of rational numbers: its intuitive and formal development', in Hiebert, J. and Behr, M. (eds) *Number Concepts and Operations in the Middle-grades,* pp. 53–92, Reston, VA, National Council of Teachers of Mathematics.

Lave, J. (1988) *Cognition in Practice: mind, mathematics and culture in everyday life,* Cambridge, Cambridge University Press.

Luria, A. (1979) *Curso de Psicologia Geral,* Rio de Janeiro, Civilização Brasileira.

Mack, N. K. (1993) 'Learning rational numbers with understanding: the case of informal knowledge', in Carpenter, T., Fennema, E. and Romberg, T. A. (eds) *Rational Numbers: an integration of research*, pp. 85–106, Hillsdale, NJ, Lawrence Erlbaum Associates.

McClosky, M., Carmazza, A. and Green, B. (1980) 'Curvilinear motion in the absence of external forces: naive beliefs about motion of objects', *Science*, vol. 210, pp. 1139–41.

Newman, D., Griffin, P. and Cole, M. (1989) *The Construction Zone: working for cognitive change in school,* Cambridge, Cambridge University Press.

Nunes, T. (1993) 'Learning mathematics: perspectives from everyday life', in Davis, R. B. and Maher, C. A. (eds) *Schools, Mathematics, and the World of Reality*, pp. 61–78, Needham Heights, MA, Allyn and Bacon.

Nunes, T., Schliemann, A. D. and Carraher, D. W. (1993) *Street Mathematics and School Mathematics,* New York, Cambridge University Press.

Nunes, T., Bryant, P., Pretzlik, U. and Hurry, J. (2002) 'Children's understanding of intensive quantities', paper presented at the British Educational Research Association, Exeter, September, 2002.

Nussbaum, J. (1985) 'The earth as a cosmic body', in Driver, R., Guesne, E. and Tinberghein, A. (eds) *Children's Ideas in Science*, pp. 124–44, Milton Keynes, Open University Press.

Nussbaum, J. and Novak, J. D. (1976) 'An assessment of children's concepts of the earth utlizing structured interview', *Science Education*, vol. 60, pp. 535–50.

Perret-Clermont, A. N. (1980) *Social Interaction and Cognitive Development,* London, Academic Press.

Piaget, J. and Garcia, R. (1971) *Les Explications Causales,* Paris, Presses Universitaires de France.

Piaget, J. and Inhelder, B. (1974) *The Child's Construction of Quantities,* London, Routledge and Kegan Paul.

Piaget, J. and Szeminska, A. (1952) *The Child's Conception of Number,* London, Routledge and Kegan Paul.

Piaget, J., Inhelder, B., Szesminska, A. (1960) *The Child's Conception of Geometry,* London, Routledge and Kegan Paul.

Piaget, J., Grize, J. B., Szeminska, A., and Bang, V. (1968) *Epistemologie et Psychologie de la Fonction,* Paris, Presses Universitaries de France.

Piburn, M. D. (1990) 'Reasoning about logical propositions and success in science', *Journal of Research in Science Teaching,* vol. 27, pp. 887–900.

Posner, G. J., Strike, K. A., Hewson, P. W. and Gertzog, W. A. (1982) 'Accommodation of a scientific conception: toward a theory of conceptual change', *Science Education*, vol. 66, pp. 211–27.

Reed, J. J. and Lave, J. (1981) 'Arithmetic as a tool for investigating relations between culture and cognition', in Casson, R. W. (ed.) *Language, Culture, and Cognition: anthropological perspectives,* pp. 437–55, New York, Macmillan.

Reiner, M., Slota, J. D., Chi, M. and Resnick, L. B. (2000) 'Naive physics reasoning: a commitment to substance-based components', *Cognition and Instruction,* vol. 18, pp. 1–34.

Riley, M. S., Greeno, J. G. and Heller, J. I. (1983) 'Development of children's problem-solving ability in arithmetic', in Ginsburg, H. P. (ed.) *The Development of Mathematical Thinking,* pp. 153–200, New York, Academic Press.

Vergnaud, G. (1982) 'A classification of cognitive tasks and operations of thought involved in addition and subtraction problems', in Carpenter, T. P., Moser, J. M. and Romberg, T. A. (eds) *Addition and Subtraction: a cognitive perspective,* Hillsdale, pp. 39–59, NJ, Lawrence Erlbaum Associates.

Vergnaud, G. (1985) 'Concepts et schemes dans une théorie opératoire de la représentation', *Psychologie Française,* vol. 30, pp. 245–52.

Vosniadou, S., Ioannides, C., Dimitrakopoulou, A. and Papademetriou, E. (2001) 'Designing learning environments to promote conceptual change in science', *Learning and Instruction,* vol. 11, pp. 381–419.

Vygotsky, L. S. (1978) *Mind in Society: the development of higher psychological processes,* Cambridge, MA, Harvard University Press.

Chapter 8
A socio-cognitive perspective on learning and cognitive development

Anne-Nelly Perret-Clermont, Felice Carugati and John Oates

Contents

Learning outcomes

After you have studied this chapter you should be able to:

1 describe Piaget's views on the significance of authority, peer collaboration and individual activity for cognitive development;
2 describe Vygotsky's position on the role of social interactions in cognitive development;
3 describe Mead's theory of symbolic interactionism;
4 explain how these theorists' socio-historical contexts may have influenced their thinking;
5 define the concept of 'socio-cognitive conflict' and describe its role in fostering cognitive growth;
6 explain why intersubjectivity is significant in understanding teaching;
7 define 'didactic contract' and explain its significance;
8 discuss how Doise's four levels of analysis offer ways into the study of learning and development.

1 Introduction

In this chapter, we start by reviewing three theoretical positions on cognitive development that have been prominent in research on learning and have had major influences on educational practice. We then explore the importance of recognizing the ways in which children's learning is embedded in and formed by social relationships and practices, and the implications that these have for theory. This leads to a new way of thinking about the processes that are active when learning takes place. It also gives a broader perspective on the factors that may need to be considered when seeking to improve the effectiveness of learning situations, when trying to understand how, why and when children learn.

The ideas covered in this final chapter also offer a new set of perspectives from which to view the ideas and findings presented earlier in the book. In particular, this chapter broadens the frame within which cognitive development can be viewed. It suggests, in a number of ways, that development does not just 'happen' within the individual child, but that it occurs in a context of social customs, understandings and relationships that play an important role in either facilitating or hindering the individual's progress towards more advanced modes of thinking. Further, we argue that this context is an integral part of learning, which defines the meanings that children and teachers give to their joint activities. Learning is embedded in particular social practices, with specific expectations and values, especially, but not only, in school situations.

Our aim in this chapter is to offer a critical analysis of the basic assumptions and orientations of three main theories in developmental psychology, those of Jean Piaget, Lev Vygotsky and George Herbert Mead. We locate their ideas within the dominant cultural ideologies of Europe, Soviet Russia and the United States and consider some of their implications for the ways in which education and learning are conceived and structured. We then bring in new ways of thinking about learning and teaching situations, illustrated and supported with research evidence, to build a richer understanding of the social and psychological processes involved. A particular focus throughout the chapter is on the mutual understandings that participants in such situations hold about the nature of the social relationships supporting teaching and learning interactions; what we describe as the 'didactic contract'.

2 Three theoretical positions

2.1 Jean Piaget and constructivism

Jean Piaget (1896–1980) always firmly believed that learning and development proceed from *within* the child; that the child constructs their own knowledge as an individual, independent activity. According to Piaget, the transmission of knowledge from one generation to the next was not of prime importance for the child's cognitive development. He was convinced that children are the authors of their own thinking, and his theory was based on this perspective; it lies at the heart of the Piagetian conceptual framework. He promoted this point at a time when it was not an accepted notion, except within the developing movements for 'progressive' education in Europe. Although, as you will see, this position generates many problems, Piaget's firm beliefs represented a major step forward in the mid-twentieth century; a time when behaviourism was a dominant model for psychological development.

According to the behaviourist perspective, children are basically passive learners. Children's learning is seen to arise from the rewards and contingencies provided by the environment around them, and development is simply a gradual accumulation of these acquired habits and associations. These ideas originated primarily in the United States at the beginning of the twentieth century and were consonant with the country's dominant ideology at that time. It can be seen, for example, how the underlying behaviourist images of the child as a 'blank slate' with unrestricted potential are linked to the socio-historical context of the United States. At the time when Piaget's views came into prominence in relation to educational policies and practice, behaviourism was being extensively used as a theoretical rationale for the promotion of somewhat traditional, teacher-led forms of teaching. It was also a basis for the introduction of highly structured machine-based instructional methods, in Europe as well as in the United States. For example, behaviourist ideas lay behind the introduction of 'teaching machines', the forerunners of computer-based teaching, and the use of multiple choice answers in instructional materials that were broken up into small 'learning units'.

Piaget's seminal contribution to theories of learning was that he provided strong arguments against reducing the complex process of learning to a simple behaviourist view, arguing instead for the importance of the child's own activity in the construction of knowledge. Educational policy was, to some extent, inspired by the Piagetian position. One important development was that 'discovery learning' became a fashionable approach, in which children were offered richly resourced learning environments, and the role of the teacher was reworked as a 'facilitator' of children's own constructive endeavours, rather than purely being a 'transmitter of knowledge'.

However, despite the 'progressive' label attached to such approaches, and the marshalling of Piagetian ideas as a counter to the behaviourist theory of learning, the individualistic constructivist perspective throws up some serious issues that are also open to critical analysis. Perhaps the most damaging of these is the potential that Piaget's theories offer for ethnocentric interpretations of delays in children's development in different socio-economic and cultural circumstances. For example, it is often the case that children in socially disadvantaged groups, or from countries where there is much poverty and hardship, are found to be delayed in their development relative to their more advantaged peers with better standards of living. Given such findings, the view that development is essentially endogenous (i.e. springing from within the child) inevitably leads to the suggestion that such differences are due to inherent deficits in these cultural groups. Highlighting this problem raises the issue of how the relation between culture and the development of thinking can be reconciled with the Piagetian tradition.

Piaget recognized this issue, but he gave little direct attention to the problem, and neither have those who have built on his theory in orthodox ways. However, as we will show during the course of this chapter, the question is closely aligned with a related issue that Piaget did consider to be of great importance; the relation between the development of the individual and what we will call in this chapter 'authority'. By this we mean the influence of those who can exert power and direction over learners in various ways, by their control of resources, communication, time and routine, by virtue of their greater age or greater knowledge, or by holding positions of respect, such as teacher, lecturer or school head. Perret-Clermont (1996) has suggested that the socio-historical context of the first half of the twentieth century and Piaget's own personal biography were sources of the ethical beliefs he came to adopt. These in turn had a major influence on the role he attached to 'authority' in his theory and the image he had of rational thought and what it could achieve.

Piaget lived in Europe through the blind violence of the First and Second World Wars, which he blamed on the prevailing religious and cultural traditions and their autocratic use of authority over people. Perhaps in reaction to this experience, he rejected the notion of 'authority' and placed his faith in rationality and the autonomy of the individual in non-hierarchical social relationships with peers. In line with this way of thinking, he focused his efforts on identifying the conditions that could lead a child towards developing autonomous, critical and rational thought. As a crucial foundation for this, he placed importance on a capacity to reflect on one's own actions and to apply logical reasoning to one's own behaviour as well as to problems in the world. Piaget doubted whether the external, authoritative influences of education and other social institutions could ever do more than just load children with cultural constraints. This 'baggage' he saw as only giving pre-formed answers to questions that children had neither formulated for themselves, nor attempted to answer in the course of individually developing their own ways of thinking. At the heart of this problem, Piaget believed, lies the asymmetry of status between adult and child, which he saw as constraining children from developing the capacity for autonomous, reflective thought.

This line of thinking is often seen as demoting culture to just a collection of beliefs, social rules and constraints rather than seeing it as providing a legacy of meanings, understandings, narratives and social structures transmitted from one generation to the next. This creates a major problem for seeing how formal teaching can play any kind of role in fostering cognitive development, especially when taken in combination with Piaget's stance that authority inhibits the development of independent thought and reflection. Indeed, Piaget saw formal teaching as an obstacle and a hindrance to cognitive development; for him, interaction between peers was much more important. Piaget's positive view of peer interaction as a fundamental facilitator of cognitive development is an important point, but one that is rarely noted by commentators, who have tended to portray social processes as insignificant in Piagetian theory. And when Piaget himself stressed the importance of peer interactions, he seems to have been unaware that these commonly occur in social settings organized by adults.

Under the banner of 'active learning', some teachers have taken on these three strands of Piaget's thinking (i.e. negative towards authority and positive towards peer collaboration and individual activity) and have concluded that, apart from providing a rich environment, they need to leave children to learn entirely on their own. In contrast to the educational ideology that children learn best by imitating 'correct' models, teachers who wish to be 'Piagetian' seem to feel that they have to stay 'backstage'. Although teachers' direct experience is likely to tell them that an educational environment needs to be carefully structured if it is going to engage children's interest, the received Piagetian view is that organization must come from the children. From this perspective, the teacher must stay in the background, so that their authority and knowledge do not hold back the child. This creates a tension, for example when children might justifiably ask 'If the teacher knows the right answer, why not give it to us rather than expecting us to discover it for ourselves?'.

This approach can be contrasted with more traditional teaching situations, where teachers are likely to seem omnipresent. In such contexts, teachers often start sentences which students are meant to complete (e.g. 'The name of the largest lake in Switzerland is ...?'), and students are then rewarded if they give the 'correct' response. This is a method which is thought to encourage students' participation, but in fact the ultimate aim is for the child to give a response that matches that of the adult. Yet a common theme in both traditional and progressive approaches is that the final aim is for the child to achieve the adult's answer. Is this expectation a type of cultural ethnocentrism, or simply a lack of awareness of cultural constructions?

2.2 Lev Vygotsky and social constructivism

As these difficulties and weaknesses in the Piagetian position have become apparent, various theorists have proposed ways of overcoming them. A contemporary of Piaget, Lev Vygotsky (1896–1934), developed a theory that has also inspired a great deal of original and innovative research and has offered some very useful and practical orientations towards ways of teaching. In contrast to Piaget, Vygotsky's theory placed child–adult interactions at centre stage in development, as the prime channel for the transmission of tools essential for the development of thinking from one generation to the next. His theory thus proposed expert–novice interactions as a key factor in fostering cognitive growth. In this framework, culture plays a vital role, first, in the form of a 'teacher' who takes a tutorial role (using the term 'teacher' in a broad sense, to include parents and older, more able children as well as formal educators) and second, through language and other cultural tools that shape action and thinking. This role involves bridging the gap between the teacher's and the child's levels of competence by connecting with the child's modes of thought and working jointly in what Vygotsky termed the 'zone of proximal development' (see Chapter 7). This is seen as guiding the child towards more advanced forms of thought (i.e. the adult's understanding) by providing him or her with 'tools for thinking' that they can appropriate, one step at a time. By stimulating their students' mental processes, teachers guide students to their way of thinking, by giving them a set of symbolic tools to use in the same ways as teachers do. Then, the students will in turn become able to do this by themselves and it will become their way of thinking.

However, this theory also runs the risk of supporting a form of ethnocentrism. Teachers following this theory could be viewed as placing themselves in an unquestioned position of superior knowledge. For example, the argument against teachers following Vygotsky could be that they, as teachers who possess the cultural tools, make themselves the focus of their students' attention and present these cultural tools as unquestionable.

From a psychological point of view, this image does have some validity. It suggests that learning can be seen as a form of teaching where *passing on knowledge* is the primary process. However, although it offers a partial theory of learning, it is not an adequate theory of development, since all that it explains is how a student comes to resemble a teacher. As can be seen from the way in which Piagetian theory has been used to justify particular educational methods, it is important to distinguish between the basic tenets of the theory concerned and the ways in which it is interpreted and applied by teachers. It is not necessarily that the *theory itself* is flawed or problematic, but rather *how it is applied* in the context of schooling.

Just as Piaget's theory can be better understood as being related to his own, specific historical context and his personal reactions to this, so Vygotsky's theory can be linked to the dominant ideology within which he was located. First, Marxist thinking was the state-sanctioned and preferred mode of explaining many aspects of human life in Soviet Russia, and Vygotsky's theory must be seen in relation to this. It is important to note, for example, that Vygotsky focused on how individual development was located within, even subservient to, broader socio-cultural development. Second, he also emphasized the role of technology, through his continued reference to tools (in a broad sense, he was referring to what we can call cultural 'tools of thinking' as well as physical artefacts). Third, he saw mental development as springing from the use of tools embedded in social activities. His position was broadly aligned with the Marxist view that the development of thought is the outcome of both material conditions and people's activities and struggles.

However, despite these broad differences between the two theorists, there is a parallel with Piaget's reaction to the context in which he was located. Vygotsky also stressed the individual, constructive aspects of development. He did not see the child as simply a passive recipient of culture's transmission of tools, but also as a creative builder of their own thinking. This was not consonant with the prevailing ideology of Soviet Russia, and Vygotsky's work was not widely published for many years, so it is for this reason that Vygotsky's work is often seen as following Piaget, although in fact the two theorists were to some extent independently developing their ideas at much the same time. Another point of agreement between the two lies in their recognition that biological maturation also plays a role, albeit a secondary one, in making certain developments possible on the cognitive plane.

On balance, Piaget saw the control of development as being essentially inside the child, while Vygotsky saw the child's development as being the internalization of outside influences or social co-ordinations. In his theory, Piaget justified his position by seeing the logical progression of development as arising from children's reflections on their own actions, culminating in the achievement of formal operational thought, that is, fully abstract and hypothetico-deductive reasoning. For Vygotsky, however, this achievement was the result of a social, rather than an individual process.

2.3 George Herbert Mead and symbolic interactionism

A third line of theoretical development is relevant to the theme of this chapter, and, like the two theories discussed above, can also be considered critically in the light of its specific socio-historical context and related ideological background. In the first half of the twentieth century, the dominant culture of the United States was committed to the ideals of personal freedom and opportunity. A dominant motif was the individual striving to achieve, while at the same time developing the qualities of concern for others, citizenship and patriotic allegiance. In this context, George Herbert Mead (1863–1931) developed his theory of the social origins of thinking. He argued that shared, social activity, and specifically the process of communication, was the way in which objects and actions came to have meaning, or, in his terms, 'symbolic significance' (Mead, 1934). According to Mead's 'symbolic interactionism' theory, the 'signs' that at first accompany actions then lift the child's understandings to new, symbolic levesl (by 'signs' he meant verbal and non-verbal gestures that come to represent what is happening). Thus, for example, a child does not understand what a tool is just by virtue of its shape, but rather through its incorporation into meaningful tool use. That is to say, a hammer is not a tool simply in and of itself, but becomes a tool through its use in appropriate ways by 'significant others". For the child, seeing a hammer used in specific ways by another person and hence in a social context, imbues the object with social significance. Through such repeated experiences whereby objects, actions and language come to acquire social meanings, the child also begins to form simultaneously a representation of the self and of what Mead called the 'generalized other'. This means that the child becomes able to see themselves and their actions from the perspective of another person, and as a result, begins to *internalize* meanings and values. According to Mead, it is this process of internalization that allows children's thinking to advance from the level of immediate experience to a level of self-reflection. Mead believed that this is an important part of children forming a conscious concept of self, and he believed that the play of young children, in which role-playing other people and their activities tends to be common, was a primary vehicle for this development. This stands in contrast to Piaget's view of the role of other people. According to Piaget, play is at first solitary, and then later (as two or more children play together) becomes 'parallel play', where the players merely co-ordinate their behaviour, but do not truly co-operate. Only in Piaget's final stage of development do they properly take account of other people's real or potential perspectives.

The reason why these different interpretations of the role of play are important is that play can be seen as an excellent example of a form of social activity that is not bound by external authority structures, nor by imposed power relations. Although at times one child or another inevitably 'sets the agenda' for where the play is going, in general, play is an activity that children engage in for its own sake, not for its purpose in relation to some defined outcome. The significance of such reciprocal peer relations for development will be explored in more detail as this chapter progresses.

Summary of Section 2

- Piaget, Vygotsky and Mead are three influential theorists of the development of children's cognition.
- The positions adopted by each of these theorists bear some relation to the socio-historical contexts in which they worked.
- Piaget saw cognitive development as a quest for knowledge and essentially a solitary pursuit with the child constructing their own mental processes. This is called an *endogenous* (internal) process.
- Vygotsky saw the child as acquiring cultural tools through social interaction in the 'zone of proximal development', created with a more able partner.
- Mead saw interactions with significant others as providing the child with new meanings, not only for action, but also for reflection, via social signs.
- Both Vygotsky and Mead stressed *exogenous* (external) sources of development.

3 Social interactions and the development of thought

These three theorists' positions on the development of thought and its relation to social processes became widely disseminated throughout the academic communities of Europe and the United States. This led to a recognition of parallels and disagreements among the theories, which formed the background to the emergence of a new genre of research in the 1970s. This was strongly empirically based, and set out to address the new questions posed by the theoretical debates about the extent to which cognitive development is influenced by social factors. In particular, interest focused on how children negotiate and make use of situations involving conflicts of ideas to make progress in their development. This new line of enquiry took a scientific approach, using standardized tasks and situations, often in laboratory settings, to explore how children resolved the intellectual and social problems posed by conflict. This recognition that an intellectual conflict requires both an intellectual solution and a social solution is central to the ideas explored in this chapter. If someone disagrees with you, and you each want to do more than simply register the difference of opinion (i.e. seek some kind of resolution) you need to do the intellectual work of analyzing the nature of the dispute and do the creative work of coming up with something that can satisfy both parties. But, and this is a crucial point, you also have to do equivalent work towards resolving the *social disjunction* that occurs in conflict situations.

Since the 1970s, the issue of the role of socio-cognitive conflict as a stimulus for development has inspired an impressive body of research. Findings from this research have shown clearly how children, adolescents and adults have a capacity to benefit, in terms of developing their modes of thought, from situations in which the joint resolution of cognitive challenges is required (Perret-Clermont, 1979, 1996; Doise and Mugny, 1981; Perret-Clermont and Nicolet, 1986, 2002; Gilly, 1989; Howe *et al.*, 1990, 1995; Azmitia, 1996; Carugati and Selleri, 1996; Carugati, 1997; Littleton and Light, 1999; Schwarz *et al.*, 2000).

The first important finding was that if children work together to solve a problem, they are often able, by co-ordinating their actions, to arrive at cognitive solutions that neither of them are able to reach alone. This shows the limitations of looking solely at what children can achieve by working on their own, and how such an approach can lead to an underestimation of children's levels of cognitive ability. This issue is especially important when children's abilities are being assessed on the basis of their performance in an educational context. It is also worth noting that the asymmetry of power relations that exists in teacher–student interactions is not present in this sort of peer collaboration. We will return to this point in Section 6.

The second important finding was that when children work together in particular ways on tasks that they cannot initially solve alone, they can, even in the short term, become able to tackle tasks of a similar level of difficulty on their own. In this way, cognitive tools that are first constructed jointly to solve problems in a social situation, then become part of a person's own repertoire of tools that they can use for themselves.

A good example of this is the strategy of only changing one variable at a time if the combined effects of a number of different variables are being explored. This can be a very useful, general-purpose thinking tool, and children are quite likely to begin to formulate such an approach when working together on a problem. They might, for example, find that this offers a way of making the task easier to talk about. Such cognitive tools, although they may initially be used with given materials and in a specific social situation, have a certain degree of stability that often allows them to then be used successfully in other situations and with other materials. In this way, children may be able to generalize their thinking beyond the specific task context in some circumstances.

3.1 Socio-cognitive conflict

The fruitful line of research that we discussed above is guided by the hypothesis that one of the mechanisms by which social interactions can lead to cognitive development is the communication conflicts that arise between partners. The term 'socio-cognitive conflict' has been coined to label this dynamic process that leads to joint cognitive constructions as different (initially incompatible) points of view come into the field of discussion. This hypothesis highlights the crucial functions of conflicting viewpoints and interpersonal communication between partners as they work towards a shared, single response to a problem; to do this they have to 'decentre' from their own, individual perspectives. Of course, the fact that the partners differ in their viewpoints does not necessarily lead to this sort of productive adaptation, since the difference may cause dispute and argument instead. In this case, differences in opinion become much more concerned with the interpersonal relationship than with the task in hand. This is an important point since it stresses that underlying interpersonal relationships are important for a dynamic that in favourable circumstances can lead to productive change and development.

In general, it has become clear that if tasks are solved by simple amicable agreement or by one partner conforming to the other's preferred approach (both of which are solutions to the *social relationship issue* rather than the *task issue*) then neither partner makes progress. Smedslund (1966) hypothesized that it is the shared elaboration of cognitive solutions to communication conflicts that leads to constructive change. It is now clear that such change depends on people agreeing to communicate with each other about the cognitive conflict that happens at the social level as a result of their disagreement.

3.2 Social marking

As a result of studying the effects of changes in the ways in which tasks are presented, a further significant finding has emerged which has identified a process that has been called 'social marking' (Doise, 1986; Rijsman, 1988, 2001; Nicolet, 1995; Carugati and Selleri, 1996). This has helped to show that it is not just the logical structure of a problem that influences success. The match or mismatch of the problem structure with the social rules associated with it is also important, as is the social structure of the partners' interaction. For example, in the classic Piagetian conservation of liquid task, a child is first asked to confirm that the amounts of liquid in two identical containers are, indeed, the same. Then the liquid from one container is poured into another container with different proportions and the child is asked whether the two amounts of liquid are the same. Children find it much easier to solve this problem correctly if the task is presented as a 'fair shares' reward of a drink to each child for their participation in the experiment. Here, the task of judging whether the two containers hold the same amount is supported by the notions of fairness and equity. This particular social marking is therefore based on the concept of 'distributed justice'. But, of course, social marking is itself subject to meaning construction and how it operates in a particular situation will depend on how the children make sense of the social rules that the adult intends to appeal to. For example, evoking the concept of distributed justice is more effective if children are placed in a co-operative situation than if they are expected to compete with each other. Research that has made use of rules to do with the 'right' to have equal quantities of objects or drink have confirmed this phenomenon.

In this section, then, we have shown two broad patterns of findings regarding the social context of experimental conditions. The first contextual effect that we have found is that the cognitive demands that a task makes of a child, and the child's chances of reaching a solution, do not simply reside in the task itself. They are made harder or easier by the social context of the child, the task and other people. A degree of social conflict around possible routes to solving the task can make the finding of a correct solution easier. Once such a joint solution has been found, through the resolution of the socio-cognitive conflict, it can then be available for the child to apply to new tasks with similar demands when working independently. In this way the child's cognitive development has been fostered. The second important contextual effect that we have highlighted concerns the 'match' of the social context to the rules that have to be applied to the task in hand. For example, as we illustrated in respect of the Piagetian conservation task, a match between task and social context also helps children to come to a successful solution. In the favourable circumstances outlined above, then, children can perform at higher levels than those predicted by theoretical positions that only offer individualistic interpretations of cognitive development, such as those of Piaget.

Summary of Section 3

- 'Socio-cognitive conflict', that arises when two children work together to solve a task, can be an important source of development.
- Children working together can often solve problems that they could not solve on their own.
- Tasks are made easier if there is appropriate 'social marking', where the task maps onto a social rule such as 'fair shares'.

4   Meeting of minds: adult–child intersubjectivity

As suggested in the previous section, the ways in which participants in a social interaction make sense of what is going on between them are important for what they achieve together. They can only collaborate and discuss if to some degree they have a shared understanding of the task. Similarly, they need to be able to attend jointly to the same aspects of the task. This 'intersubjectivity', an area of shared experience, may not always be present at the start of interaction; it may take some time to arrive at shared objects of discourse and thinking.

4.1 The relational context

Several studies have shown that the competence that a person can demonstrate is affected by the form of relationship context that they are in (e.g. Labov, 1972). In addition, the implicit understandings held about a relationship and its rules , the 'communication contract', have been shown to structure the conversation and responses of people being tested (Rommetveit, 1978, 1992). A general question that has interested researchers in this area is how best to describe the tools and socio-cognitive patterns within which abstract thinking is constructed. What is it, in a specific situation, that enables two people to draw out a common understanding of a problem and the same view of what might count as a 'solution'? How do they come to engage jointly with the problem, consider the same aspects, apply the same reasoning and carry this through to a solution?

Research by Schubauer-Leoni (1986b) and Grossen (1988) has helped to clarify how these shared understandings come about when a psychologist and a child, or a teacher and a student, interact in situations that involve a child's ability being assessed or a student engaging in learning. As we will show in the next section, these researchers have devised experimental situations that bring out the particular ways in which adults talk and behave to enable children to show their abilities (for example, in showing a mastery of Piagetian-type thought). They also illustrate the ways in which children construct understandings of what is being talked about by the other person and what is in turn being expected of them, and how they should talk about the topic that is at issue between them.

4.2 Children testing children

To show in concrete terms how this intersubjectivity is constructed between a child and an experimenter, Grossen (1988) set up situations in which one child, who had already succeeded on a particular task, was asked to administer the same task to another child. She used tasks such as the Piagetian conservation of liquids task described in Section 3.2. She noticed that many children who seemed to have constructed an idiosyncratic understanding of the psychologist's role, thought that they should warn their partner that there was a trap, for example by saying 'Now watch carefully. I am going to do something with the liquid. But watch and think about this carefully', or by saying 'Now pay attention, because there is a trick!'. Other children started the test, but then turned to the researcher, asking 'Now, should I tell her that there is a trick or not?'. Further, Grossen observed that children who were non-conservers (i.e. they believed that moving a quantity of liquid from one container to another of different proportions changed the amount of liquid) tended to produce correspondingly non-conserving responses from the children that they were testing. Conserving children, on the other hand, tended to elicit conserving responses from their partners.

4.3 Psychologists testing children

When psychologists were observed carrying out the same sorts of tests it was also noted that some types of responses were under-valued while other types were over-valued (Perret-Clermont *et al.*, 1992). For example, a psychologist might seem to be trying to 'extract' from a child not simply a statement that the notion of conservation is understood but rather a specific sort of statement that conforms to their expectations of what counts as a 'proper' conserving response. A failure to produce a response of this more restricted type might then be taken as 'non-conserving', even though the 'difficulty' does not actually lie in the child's failure to understand conservation, but rather in their failure to conform with the tester's implicit rules of how language is used to express understanding. Thus, a simple response of 'Yes' to the question 'And do they have the same amount in?' is likely to be less acceptable to the tester than a spontaneous answer such as 'They have got the same amount in because nothing's been added'. Moreover, sometimes a tester will unconsciously give hints as to the expected answer, for example by praising a 'yes' and then waiting for further elaboration, or sometimes giving no hints at all. Or it may be that the person being tested has such rigid, preconceived ideas about the nature of the testing that they will fail to appreciate any hints that they are given and hence fail to converge with the tester's expectations. This points up how the assessment of a person's competence in a particular, narrow domain can be easily confounded by how competent they are in the much broader domain of shared linguistic understanding, in a context where meanings and social rules are being negotiated (Smedslund, 1977; Hundeide, 1985, 1988; Elbers, 1991; Baucal *et al.*, 2002).

In one study, Bell *et al.* (1991), tested students in a number of ways, in particular by asking them to make a 'sutemi' (a nonsense word). They gave each child a raisin, some toothpicks and some paper, and said 'Now make a sutemi for me', but not a single child asked them what on earth they were talking about or said that they did not know what the word 'sutemi' meant. The children seemed able to construct at least some sort of sense from this question, as if it were simply not possible that an adult would ask a nonsense question; if a question is asked, one must attempt an answer! One has to make the best of what is available. This clearly shows how the implicit understandings of the social rules can have a major effect on how tasks are approached. In the situation just described, it seems clear that children hold a strong, implicit belief that one of these rules is that they must attempt to answer an adult's question, however odd it seems.

Summary of Section 4

- The concept of 'intersubjectivity' refers to mutual understandings of what a task is about and the sharing of attention to the same aspects of the task.
- A child's level of performance on a test task, or in a teaching/learning situation, is partly dependant on the expectations that they have about what behaviour is expected and what is appropriate in the specific situation.

5   The 'didactic contract'

In the 1980s, research looking into the links between context, teachers, students and subject area introduced the concept of a 'didactic contract', a special case of Rommetveit's 'communication contract', to refer to the ways of behaving that teachers and students adopt and the rules that they follow (Brousseau, 1980; Chevallard, 1985). There are two sides to this contract. On the student's side there are expectations of what it is to be a learner, and on the teacher's side there are expectations of what it is to be an effective teacher. This implicit contract reflects the knowledge and understandings of what one has to comply with in educational processes in everyday school life.

5.1   The student's view of 'being a student'

Along with the concepts of intersubjectivity and constructions of social rules that we have already introduced, Schubauer-Leoni (1986a, and b, 1996) took up this idea of a 'didactic contract' to examine how a student manages to learn about a topic while maintaining a relationship with their teacher. She described how a student's answers to a teacher's questions can be seen as an outcome of a particular relation with the adult, not just as a response relating to the subject matter. In a classical teaching situation, the roles tend to be clear; there is a teacher who knows things and can ask questions, and there are students who have to respond in 'correct' ways. To explore this relationship, Schubauer-Leoni carried out some elegant experiments which aimed to clarify how children view 'being a student' and 'being a teacher'. Children in the first and second year of primary schooling had to construct problems which they then put to their classmates or younger children to solve. These 'novice teachers' considered that a good problem is one that cannot be solved without mistakes being made. In other words, if students do not get things wrong, then one cannot be sure that one is a good teacher! This means that the child's notion of 'being a teacher' carries the implicit expectation of occupying a superior position.

In some ways adopting this position may make it more difficult for teachers to play a facilitating role in working out joint solutions with children. Schubauer-

Leoni (1990) has also shown how younger children are more successful at solving problems when the tester is a psychologist who is making a game out of a problem-solving situation than if the tester is a teacher. In contrast, children who have had more experience of school are more likely to succeed if the task is presented as a 'school' task and not as a game.

5.2 Task difficulty and context effects

From Schubauer-Leoni's research, it seems that the child's understanding of the rules and expectations of the social context affects the ease or difficulty that they experience in working towards solutions. It is thought that this is because the task is given meaning by the context in which it is located. This has been shown in several other studies (e.g. Rommetveit, 1978; Hundeide, 1985, 1988, 1992; Light and Perret-Clermont, 1989; Säljö, 2000). However, one study in particular shows this effect very clearly. Säljö and Wyndhamn (1993) gave a task, in a mathematics classroom setting, to competent mathematics students aged 15–16 years that involved finding the postal rates for packages of different weights and sizes. Although the students were given a post office tariff chart, which could be easily used to find the answers to the problem directly, they seemed to be unable to use this simple solution but focused instead, inappropriately, on the proportions of the packages. For them, the didactic contract inherent to the classroom setting carried with it the expectation that that they had to be shown how to apply some newly acquired knowledge, not to use ready-made solutions that were close at hand. So it seems that the students were defining the task as different and more difficult than it needed to be because of the way they had constructed the demands of the task's social context.

5.3 How children interpret adults' questions

Another aspect of the significance of children's interpretations of the didactic contract is how children make sense of adults' questions in teaching and testing situations. In situations like this, a child will interpret questions at two levels: first, at the explicit level of what the question actually asks and second, at the level of what the social rules of the situation define as an acceptable answer. The child is not only trying to work out what the meaning of the task is, but also trying to work out the demands of the social relations in which the task is embedded. A key part of this process is the child trying to guess what answer the adult expects, and what response will please them most (Donaldson, 1978). These two aspects may not necessarily align with each other because the logically correct answer may not seem to be the same answer as the one that fits the social demands of the context. A good example of this is provided by the effects of an adult repeating a question. This has been studied in experiments based on the classic Piagetian conservation tasks referred to in Section 3.2. In the Piagetian version of these tasks, when the child's reasoning is tested, the same question is usually asked twice. First, the child is asked, before any changes are made, the question of whether two amounts (of liquid, lengths of string, balls of plasticine etc.) are the same. Then, the adult transforms the shape of one of the amounts (pouring one amount of liquid into a different container, straightening one length of string, rolling out one ball of plasticine etc.), before asking the child a second time the same question 'Are the amounts the same?'.

But it was found that if this question is *not* asked twice, but only asked once, after the transformation, then children are more likely to give conserving responses, asserting that the quantities have not changed. If both questions are asked, before as well as after the transformation, they are more likely to give non-conserving responses. Why might this be? The idea of the didactic contract helps us to come up with an explanation. In this situation, the child is trying to make sense of the adult's intention, and it is not immediately obvious to the child why the same question is being asked for a second time. People do not usually ask a question if it has already been answered once, and when a *teacher* asks a question twice, it can be taken to mean that they have not been pleased by the first answer, and want a different response. Since the only thing that has changed since the question was first asked is something to do with the materials, a plausible guess is that the tester wants the child to say that the amounts are different!

What this example shows is that, for the child, the implicit social rules of the situation are as much of a problem to be solved as the explicit problem that is being posed. To fail to meet the social expectations, defined by the underlying rules as the child interprets them, would be as much of a failure as a lack of success in solving the explicit problem. In fact, in some situations, getting the socially appropriate response right might be a much more salient issue for the child than getting the explicit answer right.

Although a tester may be genuinely interested in assessing a child's cognitive level, for the child the cognitive demands may be set aside if it is more important for them to be a 'good student', as they see it. The child's sense of what is going on – that they are expected to give responses that meet the adult's expectations – is tied up with their wish to do what they can to maintain the flow of conversation. As a result they are likely to be hesitant at giving responses that are at variance with this sense (Lévy and Grossen, 1991; Perret-Clermont *et al.*, 1992).

The idea of the didactic contract offers a critical reinterpretation of the basis on which children perform in the sorts of tasks that Piaget developed. For him, the ability to conserve was one important marker of a major transition in thinking that signalled the child's progression from one stage of development to the next. His intention in developing all of his ingenious 'tests' was to provide situations that could index clearly the level of cognitive development that a child had reached. Recognizing the significance of the social dimension of this kind of testing throws the feasibility of this aim into question.

Summary of Section 5

- The 'didactic contract' is a term coined to describe the sets of mutual understandings that teachers and students have about the roles of student and teacher.
- Some types of understandings of didactic contracts by children or teachers may have the effect of leading children to perform at levels lower than they might be capable of under different conditions.
- An important aspect of the didactic contract is how it leads to children interpreting teachers' questions in specific ways.

6 The psychology of everyday school life

In the preceding sections, we have referred to several research findings that have highlighted how the social contexts of learning and testing, and how children interpret these contexts, can affect the levels of performance that children show. We have also suggested that this affects the opportunities that they have to advance the levels of their thinking. However, within a conception of cognitive development that stresses the individual origins of cognitive ability, the impact of such studies may be considered limited. They may be viewed, for example, as showing that there are additional variables that affect development, but may not be considered as significant in terms of further implications for theory. However, if social dynamics are considered to be at the centre of the construction of cognitive capacities, this suggests that cognitive development is a much more complex phenomenon. It suggests that these issues of communication, interpretation and negotiation are crucial to the meaning construction that goes on in teaching and learning situations. From this perspective, it seems clear that it is not enough to just study these processes in abstracted, research laboratory situations, but that it is important to study concrete learning contexts in the everyday life of schools, students and teachers.

6.1 How classroom conversation constructs meaning

Classrooms are rather special places. They are a particular type of setting in which there are always specific sets of expectations about social interaction, communication and learning that underpin the exchanges between teachers and students. Almost without exception, classroom conversations are defined by particular types of asymmetric relations. These are a consequence of the understandings that the participants hold, their respective statuses and the institutional powers of the teacher, especially as shown in the time management, social control and assessment practices that they impose. Teacher–student conversations, as a result, are structured in very different ways from most other situations in everyday life.

The implicit assumption that guides most classroom activity is that the teacher poses the questions and knows the right answers. On this basis, a teacher evaluates the student's responses and then uses this information to judge the student's level of competence. Where a group of children show that they understand and accept this basic, underlying social rule, the flow of communication in their classroom is then well regulated on the basis of this consensus. This is generally seen as best fitted to meeting the mutual expectations for good teaching. Edwards and Mercer (1987) and Mercer (1995) have shown how, in classes of 8–10-year-old students, classroom activity and the teacher's language use build shared understandings about these basic social rules which students then use to attribute meaning to their interactions. The teacher uses language to point up and mark these implicit understandings, so that the way talk is organized and used in the classroom by the teacher develops a shared vocabulary which fixes the respective roles of teacher and student. This sets up the particular perspective in which the teacher is expected to lead the student along a path to the acquisition of new concepts and the reorganization and extension of knowledge.

6.2 Classroom discourse and cognitive development

The way in which teachers use language is clearly important for how children acquire knowledge in schools, so it is necessary to consider how the special forms of communication that characterize 'teacher talk' affect children's cognitive development. One of the prime objectives of schooling, after all, is to engage students in forms of learning that bring about changes in their ways of thinking and help them to integrate new knowledge with that which they already possess. Here we might usefully refer to Vygotsky's (1934, 1962) concept of working in the zone of proximal development, that highlights the developmental importance of the difference between what a child can achieve alone and what they can achieve with the help of a more able person.

In the classroom, language is the primary medium through which this asymmetric interaction between teacher and student proceeds and it is also language that supports the interactions that integrate and enrich children's thinking. This position that children's discourse is not just a mirror of their thinking but also the means by which their thinking develops, has guided many studies of classroom discourse in recent years. In real classroom life, many interaction situations, especially those in which the teacher intervenes, cannot truly be described as real debates. Even if they have the superficial appearance of a debate, the underlying social expectations are very likely to be that students should give responses that conform to the teacher's verbally or non-verbally expressed expectations. For example, if a child's response to a question is greeted by silence from the teacher, the child will probably take this silence as a criticism that can only be dealt with by changing the response. A different response is then based not just on a reflective analysis of the answer but also on the child's perception that they need to give a different, more 'correct' response.

A specific type of classroom dialogue that has attracted the interest of researchers is where groups of children seem to be able to develop new understandings through 'externalized reasoning' where they all participate in more of a true debate. In this sort of situation, the teacher's interventions take on a different meaning. Their role can be to get closer to understanding the students' modes of thought, rather than encouraging the student to better understand the teacher's thought processes. Rather than guide them along a preconceived path, the teacher may facilitate the students' discourse and cognitive processes to support the development of new understandings (Mercer, 1995).

These insights have led to a major shift in perspective that now puts at centre stage the relationship between student–teacher debate and the development of thinking (Pontecorvo, *et al.*, 1991; Pontecorvo, 1993; DeGroot and Schwarz, 2003; Schwarz *et al.*, 2003). Seeing the classroom situation as a context in which characteristic types of conversational events take place, where the development of modes of thought are either facilitated or hindered, points up the reciprocal relation between the social milieu and the knowledge of the child (Barth, 1994). The shared cultural practices of school life, the objects that they involve and the communication patterns within them all contribute to a 'referential framework' (Resnick, 1991) for the teaching and learning process.

6.3 Does knowledge transfer out of the classroom?

Schooling is commonly accepted as being a means of equipping children with knowledge that is of value to them outside and after their school-based experiences. The question then arises as to how children make use, in other situations, of knowledge first gained within a didactic contract. In a range of studies, simple arithmetic problems (addition and subtraction) were given to primary school students, sometimes in the classroom and sometimes outside in a nearby room (Schubauer-Leoni and Perret-Clermont, 1997). Young primary school children can easily solve the following problem: 'I make a bunch of five flowers, then I put in another three, then I meet a friend and give him two of my flowers. How many flowers do I have left?'. When they are asked in the classroom, students give brief but adequate 'arithmetic' responses. However, when asked outside the class, on their own with an adult who is not a teacher, they are much more likely to make detailed drawings and give elaborated narratives, for example: 'How did I do it? I put them together, I made a pretty bunch. I found my friend and gave him the blue flowers ...', thus transforming the bunch of flowers into a narrative problem rather than a problem of arithmetic. This has led to an exploration of the implicit understandings of these 'situated problems'. What is it that makes the same problem, presented in the same way but in different situations, produce such very different solutions? Researchers have been puzzled at the findings that, outside the classroom, neither children nor adults tend to use the knowledge gained in school and, in particular, they rarely use arithmetic approaches even when these have been studied and learned in the school setting.

As we saw in Chapter 7, research on this theme was carried out in Recife in Northern Brazil by Nunes *et al.* (1993) who studied the mathematical abilities of street children. At ages of 6 or 7, the researchers found that these children are already surviving independently by re-selling oranges, or doing small jobs, and some of them quickly become highly accurate in working out monetary transactions and giving the correct change. Yet these same children systematically fail in mathematics in their first year of schooling and tend to be rapidly rejected by the educational system. Why is it that they are unable to transfer the knowledge acquired from their street life to school tasks? On the streets, children learn highly complex algorithms to deal efficiently with the buying and selling situations that they encounter, situations that demand accurate calculation. In the school situation, the teacher does not know that the students already possess these practical techniques and when they spontaneously use them in class the teacher tends to treat their strategies as clumsy or incorrect. This then contradicts the children's experiences and does not allow them to reflect on the strengths and limitations of these strategies (in large part oral) that they use in their commercial transactions.

The question thrown up by this research is the nature and extent to which there is a link between the context in which one acquires knowledge and the context in which it is used or transferred, since the desired transfer of knowledge and skills often fails to occur. There can be many reasons for this; perhaps the teacher fails to understand the significance of this aspect, or fails to clarify it, or perhaps the students themselves fail to grasp the relations between the knowledge they have gained in one situation and that required in another. It may also be the case, at times, that knowledge is context-bound without any of the participants being aware of this. Thus we have to consider further the three-way relations in the triangle of teacher, student and knowledge.

6.4   The developmental triangle

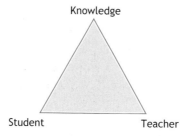

Figure I   The developmental triangle.

In respect of the three points of this triangle shown in Figure 1, developmental psychology has tended just to focus on one point, the student. Research has been primarily concerned with how the student thinks, the stages that he or she goes through, his or her developing modes of thought and what it means to behave well as a student. We have shown so far in this chapter how the development of the individual's knowledge cannot be easily isolated from the other two points, the teacher and the object of knowledge itself, since all of these are situated within an institutional and cultural context. We have also tried to show how much there is to be gained in enriching understandings of cognitive development by considering all three points together. Generally, trainee teachers see knowledge as being their focus, so, for example, in mathematics they may concentrate on how to design a series of lessons, how to demonstrate a formula or how to choose examples to be worked through. We would argue that this is a narrow view of teaching and that to study this aspect unquestioningly, without also considering the other points of the triangle and their relations, is too limited and reductionist.

As far as the teacher is concerned, theoretical and research interest has mainly tended to focus on the socio-emotional aspects of the teacher–student relationship rather than on the ways in which the teacher represents the child's points of view. It has also tended to see teaching in relation to the evaluation of student abilities. It is only very recently that studies have been conducted on how teachers think about intelligence, learning and development, and their mental models of students (for an exposition of the dynamics of causal attributions see Monteil, 1989; with respect to the educational implications of social representations, see Mugny and Carugati, 1985; Selleri *et al.*, 1994; Carugati and Selleri, 1996). However, little is known about the reasons why teachers find it difficult to decentre from their own points of view.

The study of this teacher–student–knowledge triangle in teaching situations is becoming increasingly important. How do teacher-trainers, teachers themselves and psychologists studying 'the triangle' see it functioning? The implicit didactic contract seems to be that the teacher sets tasks that correspond with what he or she wishes the students to know. Because students come to understand what they are expected to know, they then expect to be given exercises that will lead to success in the task. One can talk of a genuine 'micro-culture', with slogans such as 'You have to do this, because it is how you learn properly'; 'If you do it in this way, you get a good mark'; 'If you do this, it means that you have understood'. In other words, students' responses and the roles that they take on are not spontaneous constructions, but are the product of particular teaching practices.

So how can these issues around the meanings of learning situations and the corresponding expected behaviour(s) be addressed? A crucial theme here is the modes of constructing shared understandings between teacher and students that support or do not support students in discovering the knowledge that the teacher wishes to transmit. In what circumstances do children genuinely learn what one is seeking to teach them? The school system and the life of the classroom are usually sufficiently based on well-oiled daily routines to allow students to respond correctly without having properly understood. Students do not often see the aim of schoolwork as being to gain *understanding*, but rather to pass tests successfully. For students, essential achievements are to gain a satisfactory mark for homework, to meet the teacher's expectations and to show that they know what they ought to know. To understand is an optional bonus! This is often what happens if, when a teacher says 'try to understand', the student hears this as 'try to understand how you have to answer, so that I believe that you have understood'! Some students even gain good qualifications without ever having properly experienced the satisfaction of having truly understood something. We believe that to understand is an autonomous act, internal and free, which does not depend on hierarchical structures, nor can it be prescribed or demanded. So there is a risk that this level of deep comprehension, if it has not been experienced, may end up playing no part in the students' field of experience, or even in their expectations.

Summary of Section 6

- In real-life classrooms, implicit didactic contracts are established and maintained, and they constrain meaning, discourse and thinking.
- 'Classroom knowledge' tends to be marked out as involving specific forms of discourse.
- Some forms of discourse (exploratory talk, debate and the resolution of disagreements) are more likely to foster the development of thinking.
- Classroom knowledge does not necessarily always transfer well to other contexts, not vice versa.

7 The socio-cognitive perspective

The methods and scientific culture of modern social psychology aim to focus attention on and develop understanding of the ways in which the individual and the collective are connected. Willem Doise, a social psychologist who has been concerned with this chapter's topic of interest, has differentiated four levels of analysis which can serve as points of entry for studying these connections (Doise, 1982). In this section we make use of these four levels to organize what we have already covered in this chapter, and to see what insights they can offer into the learning process.

  We hope that our preceding arguments have shown convincingly that cognitive development is not just the result of a simple maturation of an innate potential nor is it a simple behaviourist stimulus-response process. It does not result solely from social transmission, pouring knowledge into empty vessels. The recent research that we have discussed in this chapter is beginning to reveal the complexity of the processes that support the development of modes of thinking. That one person can appropriate the knowledge of another, that each generation can build on the experience of the previous one, that cultural life can shape and transform thinking (Bruner 1990, 1991) and that it is possible for new, creative thoughts and ideas to emerge ... these are phenomena that seem miraculous when examined in detail.

7.1 Levels of analysis for socio-cognitive research

Level one — the individual

This first level of analysis is located in the individual student in search of greater understanding. At this level, a student is focused on as a person with a cognitive and an emotional life and a need to establish their identity, and as always engaged in the crucial business of seeking meanings. As well as *acquiring knowledge*, the individual also *makes use of knowledge* to interpret and give meaning to the social contexts in which they find themselves. As well as negotiating the complexities of new forms of thinking and new areas of knowledge, they are equally concerned with negotiating all the social challenges that come their way in handling relationships with peers and more powerful adults.

Level two — interpersonal interaction

The individual person's quest for knowledge, development and meaning described at level one does not take place in a vacuum, but instead, it is situated in relations with other people. At this second level of analysis, attention is focused on interpersonal relations. This level includes all the aspects of interactional dynamics, both the verbal and non-verbal communications through which questions and responses, conflicts and solutions, and interpretations and expectations are formulated and resolved at the collective level. In particular we can observe how intersubjectivity is built out of sharing roles and communication (or didactic contracts), sharing concrete experiences of specific situations and their tasks, and resolving conflicts between differing points of view. This leads to the establishment of shared frames of reference.

Level three — roles and statuses

At this level the dynamics of the development of intersubjective understandings are constructed by intergroup relationships, institutional practices and social rules that govern both the forms and the contents of people's interactions, their expectations and prejudices, and their social attributions of successes and failures. Positions of control, such as those of teacher, give some individuals a special status in defining what counts and what does not count as appropriate behaviour in particular settings. In turn, there are certain expected behaviours associated with the role of student. However, from a psychological point of view, these positions are not just 'givens'. They are themselves learned and negotiated in social situations by individuals with their own personal agendas.

Level four — social representations

The focus at this level is on implicit expectations, traditions and established narratives about what count as teaching, learning and cognitive development. It includes a concern with values, cultural expectations of individuals and collective forms of action. It also includes such social representations as 'what it is to be a teacher', 'what counts as intelligence' or 'what is established knowledge' (Gilly, 1980; Emiliani and Molinari, 1989). Thus the notion of adults acting in professional teaching capacities, with formally given responsibilities for the education of young people is also in itself a social representation, which affects the activities at the lower levels of this analysis. In turn, the experiences of individuals, dyads, classes, schools and experiments may transform existing social representations.

Summary of Section 7

- Doise has proposed that the social nature of cognition can be analysed at four different levels. These four levels focus on different objects of concern.
- Level 1 is the level of the individual engaged in constructing their modes of thought and their knowledge, trying to make sense of their experience.
- Level 2 is the level of actual relationships, interaction and discourse, for example, student–teacher or peer–peer expectations. It focuses on, for instance, the construction of intersubjectivity and mutual expectations.
- Level 3 refers to roles and statuses that frame and constrain the sorts of behaviour that are considered 'proper' for teaching and learning in different contexts.
- Level 4 is the level of national policies and ideologies, systems of social representations, that define situations (such as schools) in specific ways. These may often be dictated by professional training and traditions, and by government policies that define situations in specific ways. But these are always reinterpreted by the participants, for example by teachers and students in specific schools and situations.
- These levels are not independent: one level can affect or transform another.

8 Conclusion

In this chapter we have set out to show how communication contracts and didactic contracts, both of which are largely implicit, govern the transmission of understandings and the conditions of learning. Learning lies at the heart of specific ways of relating which are closely interlinked with the rest of the daily life of the class. Learning is also linked more generally with the ways in which the school operates so as to organize understandings and the dynamics of teacher–student interaction. We have also explained the importance of the ways in which teachers and students construct their own meanings for these practices and traditions. The transmission of experience and knowledge from one generation to the next is seen as something that can be appropriated and interpreted. It can become both a personal and also a collective acquisition, and is thus not a 'miracle' in the sense of magic wand-waving, but instead is a 'technical miracle' of human communication. More precisely, it is a form of social engineering and complex didactics which creates 'spaces for thinking'. These function as transitional zones, bringing about a restructuring of cognitive understanding arising from mutuality, the experience of 'otherness' and the realities of social interaction (Perret-Clermont, 2000; Perret and Perret-Clemont, 2001; Perret-Clemont and Zittoun, 2002).

Seen from a social psychological point of view, learning, in the double sense of 'gaining knowledge from another' and 'developing new competencies' (new for self and also, at times, collectively new) shows itself to be an eminently cultural activity that only takes place if it is socially organized and personally significant. If you, the reader, have accepted the arguments put forward here, you have seen that the understanding of learning processes that we have presented here (which does not exhaust its complexity!) is not the fruit of a series of deductions derived from a set of prior theoretical beliefs, but rather the result of work carried out by researchers seeking to find commonalities in their empirical findings (natural observations, investigations and experiments, analyses of teaching approaches and students' difficulties etc.) and discussing their interpretations of these. As yet, no single theoretical model has been able to account for the complexity of this reality. In this debate among researchers, models are being tested, brought into question and replaced by others in order to, step by step, develop an elaborated understanding of this field of study.

Acknowledgement

This chapter is an updated and modified version of the chapter published in Italian (Carugati, F., and Perret-Clermont, A. -N. (1999) 'La prospettiva psico-sociale: intersoggettività e contratto didattico', in Pontecorvo, C. (ed.) *Manuale di Psicologia dell'educazione,* pp. 41–66, Bologna: Il Mulino.) and an abridged version of the original paper is in press in French.

References

Azmitia, M. (1996) 'Peer interactive minds: developmental, theoretical, and methodological issues', in Baltes P. B. and Staudiner, U. M. (eds) *Interactive Minds: life-span perspectives on the social foundations of cognition,* pp. 133–61, Cambridge, Cambridge University Press.

Barth, B. M. (1994) *Le Savoir en Construction: former à une pédagogie de la compréhension,* Paris, Retz.

Baucal, A., Muller, N., Perret-Clermont, A.-N. and Marro, P. (2002) 'Nice designed experiment goes to the local community', paper presented at the Fifth Congress of the International Society for Cultural Research and Activity Theory, Amsterdam, June 2002.

Bell, N., Schubauer-Leoni, M. L., Grossen, M. and Perret-Clermont, A.-N. (1991) 'Transgressing the communicative contract', paper presented at the Conference of the Society for Research in Child Development, Seattle, Washington, April 1991.

Brousseau, G. (1980) 'Les échecs électifs en mathématiques dans l'enseignement élémentaire', *Revue de Laryngologie-othologie-rhinologie*, vol. 101, pp. 107–31.

Bruner, J. S. (1990) *Acts of Meaning*, Cambridge, MA, Harvard University Press.

Bruner, J. S. (1991) *Car la Culture Donne Forme à l'Esprit: de la révolution cognitive à la psychologie culturelle*, Paris, Eshel.

Carugati, F. (1997) 'Piaget, Vygotski e la questione del «sociale» : un triangolo virtuoso per la psicologia dello sviluppo?', *Eta evolutiva,* vol. 58, pp. 105–15.

Carugati, F. and Selleri, P. (1996) *Psicologia Sociale dell'educazione*, Bologna, Mulino.

Chevallard, Y. (1985) *La Transposition Didactique: du savoir savant au savoir enseigné*, Grenoble, La Pensée Sauvage.

DeGroot, R. and Schwarz, B. B. (2003) *Pe'iluyot Ti'un bakita* (in Hebrew) (*Argumentation in School*), Jerusalem, The Hebrew University.

Doise, W. (1982) *L'Explication en Psychologie Sociale*, Paris, PUF.

Doise, W. (1986) 'Pourquoi le marquage social?', in Perret-Clermont A.-N. and Nicolet, M. D. (eds) *Interagir et Connaître*, pp. 103–5, Cousset, Delval.

Doise, W. and Mugny, G. (1981) *Le Développement Social de l'Intelligence*, Paris, Interedition.

Donaldson, M. (1978) *Children's Minds*, London, Fontana.

Edwards, D. and Mercer, N. (1987) *Common Knowledge: the development of understanding in the classroom*, London, Methuen.

Elbers, E. (1991) 'The development of competence and its social context', *Educational Psychology Review*, vol. 3, pp. 73–94.

Emiliani, F. and Molinari, L. (1989) 'Mothers' social representations of their children's learning and development', *International Journal of Educational Research*, vol. 13, pp. 657–70.

Gilly, M. (1980) *Maître-élève: roles et representations sociales*, Paris, Presses Universitaires de France.

Gilly, M. (1989) 'A propos de la théorie du conflit socio-cognitif et des mécanismes psycho-sociaux des constructions cognitives: perspectives actuelles et modèles explicatifs', in Bednarz, N. and Garnier, C. (eds) *Construction des Savoirs: obstacles et conflits*, pp. 162–83, Montreal, Agence d'ARC.

Grossen, M. (1988) *La Construction de l'Intersubjectivité en Situation de Test*, Cousset, Delval.

Howe, C., Tolmie, A. and Rodgers, C. (1990) 'Physics in the primary school: peer interaction and the understanding of floating and sinking', *European Journal of Psychology of Education,* vol. 4, pp. 459–75.

Howe, C., Tolmie, A., Greer, K. and Mackenzie, M. (1995) 'Peer collaboration and conceptual growth in physics: task influence on children's understanding of heating and cooling', *Cognition and Instruction*, vol. 13, pp. 483–503.

Hundeide, K. (1985) 'The tacit background of children's judgements', in Wertsch, J. V. (ed.) *Culture, Communication and Cognition: Vygotskian perspectives*, pp. 306–22, Cambridge, Cambridge University Press.

Hundeide, K. (1988) 'Metacontracts for situational definitions and for presentation of cognitive skills', *Quarterly Newsletter of the Laboratory of Comparative Human Cognition*, vol. 10, pp. 85–91.

Hundeide, K. (1992) 'The message structure of some Piagetian experiments', in Wold, A. H. (ed.) *The Dialogical Alternative: towards a theory of language and mind*, pp. 139–56, Oslo, Scandinavian University Press.

Labov, W. (1972) 'The study of language in its social context' in Giglioli, P. P. (ed.) *Language and Social Context*, pp. 283–307, Harmondsworth, Penguin Education.

Lévy, M. and Grossen, M. (1991) 'Contrat experimental et acte de questionnement: deux illustrations empiriques de l'articulation entre processus et activité cognitive de l'enfant dans une situation de test piagetienne', *Bulletin de Psychologie*, vol. 44, pp. 229–38.

Light, P. and Perret-Clermont, A.-N. (1989) 'Social context effects in learning and testing', in Sloboda, J. A. (ed.) *Cognition and Social Worlds*, pp. 99–112, Oxford, (Oxford Science Publications), Oxford University Press.

Littleton, K. and Light, P. (eds) (1999) *Learning with Computers: analyzing productive interaction*, London, Routledge.

Mead, G. H. (1934) *Mind, Self and Society*, Chicago, Chicago University Press.

Mercer, N. (1995) *The Guided Construction of Knowledge: talk amongst teachers and learner*, Clevedon, Multilingual Matters.

Monteil, J. M. (1989) *Eduquer et Former*, Grenoble, Presses Universitaires de Grenoble.

Mugny, G. and Carugati, F. (1985) *l'Intelligence au Pluriel*, Cousset, Delval.

Nicolet, M. (1995) *Dynamiques Relationnelles et Processus Cognitifs*, Lausanne, Delachaux et Niestlé.

Nunes, T., Schliemann, A. D. and Carraher, D. W. (1993) *Street Mathematics and School Mathematics*, Cambridge, Cambridge University Press.

Perret, J. F. and Perret-Clermont, A.-N. (2001) *Apprendre un Metier dans un Contexte de Mutations Technologiques*, Fribourg, Editions Universitaires Fribourg.

Perret-Clermont, A.-N. (1979) *La Construction de l'Intelligence dans l'Interaction Sociale*, Berne, Peter Lang.

Perret-Clermont, A.-N. (1996) *La Construction de l'Intelligence dans l'Interaction Sociale* (4th edn), Peter Lang, Berne.

Perret-Clermont, A.-N. (2000) 'Apprendre et enseigner avec efficience à l'école', in Trier, U. P. (ed.) *Efficacitié de la Formation entre Recherche et Politique*, pp. 111–34, Zurich, Ruegger.

Perret-Clermont, A.-N. (2001) 'Psychologie sociale de la construction de l'espace de pensée', in Ducret, J. J. (ed.), *Actes du Colloque. Constructivisme: usages et perspectives en education*, vol. 1, pp. 65–82, Genève, Département de l'Instruction Publique, Service de la Recherche en Éducation.

Perret Clermont A.-N. and Zittoun, T. (2002) 'Esquisse d'une psychologie de la transition', *Education Permanente*, vol. 1, pp. 12–14.

Perret-Clermont, A.-N. and Nicolet, M. (eds) (1986, 2002) *Interagir et Connaître*, Cousset, Delval.

Perret-Clermont, A.-N., Schubauer-Leoni, M. L. and Trognon, A. (1992) 'L'extorsion des réponses en situation asymétrique', *Verbum*, vols 1–2, pp. 3–32.

Pontecorvo, C. (ed.) (1993) 'Discourse and shared reasoning', special issue of *Cognition and Instruction*, vol. 11.

Pontecorvo, C., Ajello, A. M. and Zucchermaglio, C. (1991) *Discutendo si Impara*, Rome, La Nuovo Italia.

Resnick, L. B. (1991) 'Shared cognition: thinking as social practice', in Resnick, L. B., Levine, J. M. and Beherend, S. D. (eds) *Perspectives on Socially Shared Cognition*, pp. 1–22, Washington, DC, American Psychological Association.

Rijsman, J. (1988, 2001) 'Partages et normes d'équité: recherches sur le développement social de l'intelligence', in Perret-Clermont, A.-N. and Nicolet, M. (eds) *Interagir et Connaître: enjeux et régulations sociales dans le développement cognitif*, pp. 123–37, Paris, L'Harmattan.

Rommetveit, R. (1978) 'On Piagetian cognitive operations, semantic competence and message structure in adult–child communication', in Markova, I. (ed.) *The Social Context of Language*, pp. 113–50, Chichester, Wiley.

Rommetveit, R. (1992) 'Outlines of a dialogically based social-cognitive approach to human cognition and communication', in Wold, A. H. (ed.), *The Dialogical Alternative: towards a theory of language and mind*, pp. 19–44, Oslo, Scandinavian University Press.

Säljö, R. (2000) 'Concepts, learning and the constitution of objects and events in discursive practices', *Cahiers de Psychologie*, no. 46, Université de Neuchâtel, pp. 35–46.

Säljö, R. and Wyndhamn, J. (1993) 'Solving everyday problems in the formal setting: an empirical study of the school as context for thought', in Chaiklin, S. and Lave, J. (eds) *Understanding Practice: perspectives on activity and context*, pp. 327–42, Cambridge, Cambridge University Press.

Schubauer-Leoni, M. L. (1986a) 'Le contrat didactique: un cadre interprétatif pour comprendre les savoirs manifestés par les élèves en mathématiques', *European Journal of Psychology of Education*, vol. 1, pp. 139–53.

Schubauer-Leoni, M. L. (1986b, unpublished) *Maître-élève-savoir: analyse psychosociale du jeu et des enjeux de relation didactique*, PhD thesis, Faculté de Psychologie et des Sciences de l'Education, Université de Genève.

Schubauer-Leoni, M. L. (1990) 'Ecritures additives en classe ou en dehors de la classe: une affaire de contexte', *Résonances*, vol. 6, pp. 16–18.

Schubauer-Leoni, M. L. (1996) 'Etude du contrat didactique pour des élèves en difficulté en mathématiques', in Raisky, C. and Caillot, M. (eds) *Au-delà des Didactiques, le Didactique,* pp. 160–89, Bruxelles, De Boeck Université.

Schubauer-Leoni, M. L. and Perret-Clermont, A.-N. (1997) 'Social interactions and mathematics learning', in Bryant, P. and Nunes, T. (eds) *Learning and Teaching Mathematics: an international perspective*, pp. 265–83, Hove, Psychology Press.

Schwarz, B. B., Neuman, Y. and Biezuner, S. (2000) 'Two wrongs may make a right ... if they argue together!' *Cognition and Instruction*, vol. 18, pp. 461–94.

Schwarz, B. B., Neuman, Y., Gil, J., and Ilya, M. (2003, in press) 'Construction of collective and individual knowledge in argumentative activity: an empirical study', *The Journal of the Learning Sciences*, vol. 12.

Selleri, P., Carugati, F. and Bison, I. (1994) 'Compagni intelligenti e compagni bravi a scuola', *Rassegna di Psicologia*, vol. 6, pp. 29–52.

Smedslund, J. (1966) 'Les origines sociales de la décentration', in Bresson, F. and de Montmollin, M. (eds) *Psychologie et Épistémologie Génétique: thèmes piagétiens,* pp. 159–67, Paris, Dunod.

Smedslund, J. B. (1977) 'Piaget's psychology in practice', *British Journal of Educational Psychology,* vol. 47, pp.1–6.

Vygotsky, L. S. (1934) *Myslenie i rec'. Psichologiceskie issledovanija,* Moskva-Leningrad, Gosudarstvennoe Social'no-Ekonomiceskoe Izdatel'stvo.

Vygotsky, L. S. (1962) *Thought and Language*, Cambridge, MA, MIT Press.

Acknowledgements

Grateful acknowledgement is made to the following sources for permission to reproduce material within this book. Every effort has been made to contact copyright holders. If any have been inadvertently overlooked the publishers will be pleased to make the necessary arrangements at the first opportunity.

Chapter 1

Table

Table 1: Younger, B. and Gotlieb, S. (1988) 'Development of categorization skills: changes in the nature or structure of infant form categories?', *Developmental Psychology*, (24), pp. 611–19, The American Psychological Association, Inc.

Figures

Figure 1: Harold Taylor/Oxford Scientific Films; *Figure 3:* Younger, B. and Gotlieb, S. (1988) 'Development of categorization skills: changes in the nature or structure of infant form categories?, *Developmental Psychology*, (24), pp. 611–19, The American Psychological Association, Inc.

Chapter 2

Text

Reading A: Christophe, A. and Morton, J. (1998) 'Is Dutch native English? Linguistic analysis by 2-month-olds', *Developmental Science*, vol. 1 (2), pp. 215–19, Blackwell Publishers Ltd; *Reading B:* Harris, M. and Chasin, J. (1999) 'Developments in early lexical comprehension: a comparison of parental report and controlled testing', *Journal of Child Language*, 26, pp. 453–60, Cambridge University Press.

Figures

Figure 2: Johnson, E. K. and Jusczyk, P. W. (2001) 'Word segmentation by 8-month-olds: when speech cues count more than statistics', *Journal of Memory and Language*, vol. 44, p. 555, Academic Press; *Figure 3:* Johnson, E. K. and Jusczyk, P. W. (2001) 'Word Segmentation by 8-month-olds: when speech cues count more than statistics', *Journal of Memory and Language*, vol. 44, p. 557, Academic Press; *Figure 5 and Figure 9:* Fenson, L., Dale, P., Reznick, S., Bates, E., Thal, D. and Pethick, S. J. (1994) 'Variability in early communicative development', *Monographs of the Society for Research in Child Development*, vol. 59 (5), p. 42, The Society for Research in Child Development, Inc., University of Michigan; *Figure 6:* Elman, J., Bates, E., Johnson, M., Karmiloff-Smith, A., Parisi, D. and Plunkett, K. (1996) *'Rethinking Innateness: a connectionist perspective on development'*, MIT Press; *Figure 7:* Jones, S. *et al.* (1992) 'Human speech and language', *The Cambridge Encyclopedia of Human Evolution*, Cambridge University Press; *Figure 8 and Figure 10*: Fenson, L., Dale, P., Reznick, S., Bates,

E., Thal, D. and Pethick, S. J. (1994) 'Variability in early communicative development', *Monographs of The Society for Research in Child Development*, vol. 59 (5), p. 73, The Society for Research in Child Development, Inc., University of Michigan.

Chapter 3

Text

Reading A: Mehler, J. and Dupoux, E. (1994) 'The organ of language', *What Infants Know: the new cognitive science of early development*, pp. 146–50, Blackwell Publishers Ltd; *Reading B:* Karmiloff-Smith, A. (1992) *Beyond Modularity: a developmental perspective on cognitive science*, MIT Press.

Figures

Figure 4: Reprinted by permission of the publisher from *The Postnatal Development of the Human Cerebral Cortex vols I-VIII* by Jesse LeRoy Conel, Cambridge, MA.: Harvard University Press, Copyright ©, 1939, 1975 by the President and Fellows of Harvard College; *Figure 5:* Photo courtesy of Leslie Tucker, Centre for Brain and Cognitive Development, Birkbeck College; *Figure 6:* Scott Camazine/Science Photo Library; *Figures 7 and 8:* Neville, H. J. *et al.* (1998) 'Cerebral organisation for language in deaf and hearing subjects: biological constraints and effects of experience', *Proceedings of The National Academy of Science, U.S.A.,* vol. 95, © Copyright 2002, The National Academy of Sciences, U.S.A.; *Figure 9:* Reprinted from *Brain and Language*, vol. 61, p. 351, Reilly, J. S. *et al.,* 'Narrative discourse in children with early focal brain injury', Copyright (1998), with permission from Elsevier.

Chapter 4

Text

Reading A: Aitchison, J. (1998, 4th edn), 'A blueprint in the brain', *The Articulate Mammal: an introduction to psycholinguistics*, Routledge/Taylor & Francis.

Chapter 6

Figures

Figure 1: Frith, U. (1989) 'Figure 3: The false belief paradigm', *Autism: explaining the Enigma*, Blackwell Publishers Ltd; *Figure 3:* Whiten, A. (1991) *Natural Theories of Mind: evolution, development and simulation of everyday mindreading*, Blackwell Publishers Ltd; *Figure 4:* Meltzoff, A. N. (1995) 'Understanding the intentions of others: re-enactment of intended acts by 18-month-old children, *Developmental Psychology*, vol. 31, (5) Copyright © 1995 by the American Psychological Association. Reprinted with permission.

Chapter 7

Text

The observations in Activities 10 and 11 were collected by S. Allen in a small-scale study for an Open University course and are reprinted with permission.

Figure

Figure 10: Driver, R. (1985) 'Beyond Appearances: the conservation of matter under physical and chemical transformations', in Driver, R., Guesne, E. and Tiberghien, A. (eds) *Children's Ideas in Science*, Open University Press.

Name index

Subject index